The Hybrid Media System

Oxford Studies in Digital Politics

Series Editor: Andrew Chadwick, Royal Holloway, University of London

The Hybrid Media System

POLITICS AND POWER

ANDREW CHADWICK

Oxford University Press is a department of the University of Oxford.
It furthers the University's objective of excellence in research, scholarship,
and education by publishing worldwide.

Oxford   New York
Auckland   Cape Town   Dar es Salaam   Hong Kong   Karachi
Kuala Lumpur   Madrid   Melbourne   Mexico City   Nairobi
New Delhi   Shanghai   Taipei   Toronto

With offices in
Argentina   Austria   Brazil   Chile   Czech Republic   France   Greece
Guatemala   Hungary   Italy   Japan   Poland   Portugal   Singapore
South Korea   Switzerland   Thailand   Turkey   Ukraine   Vietnam

Oxford is a registered trademark of Oxford University Press
in the UK and certain other countries.

Published in the United States of America by
Oxford University Press
198 Madison Avenue, New York, NY 10016

Library of Congress Cataloging-in-Publication data
Chadwick, Andrew,
The hybrid media system : politics and power / Andrew Chadwick.
pages cm. – (Oxford studies in digital politics)
Includes bibliographical references and index.
ISBN 978–0–19–975947–7 (hardback) – ISBN 978–0–19–975948–4 (paperback)
1. Communication in politics.   2. Mass media–Political aspects.   3. Internet in political
campaigns.   I. Title.
JA85.C435 2013
320.01'4–dc23
2012051580

For Sam and Katie

Contents

Acknowledgments

The idea for this book goes back a long way, possibly all the way back to 1993, when I was a masters student on Margaret Scammell and Tom Nossiter's course on political communication at the London School of Economics and Political Science (LSE). More recently my thinking was shaped by participating in a seminar on "The Internet and the Death of Television?" held at Royal Holloway, University of London in February 2008. The lively exchanges between the panelists and the audience that night convinced me of the need to break out of our silos and study how the interactions between older and newer media logics shape political life.

I would like to express my gratitude to the following, who have, with their valuable criticisms, suggestions, and encouragement supported this book in a variety of ways during its development: C. W. Anderson, Nick Anstead, Emily Bell, Charlie Beckett, Yochai Benkler, Lance Bennett, Bruce Bimber, Bob Boynton, Robin Brown, Erik Bucy, Andrea Calderaro, Craig Calhoun, Bart Cammaerts, Manuel Castells, Sarah Childs, Lilie Chouliaraki, Christian Christensen, Simon Collister, Nick Couldry, Aeron Davis, Michael X. Delli Carpini, James Dennis, Bill Dutton, Jocelyn Evans, Steven Fielding, Deen Freelon, R. Kelly Garrett, Myria Georgiou, Rachel Gibson, John Gregson, Oliver Heath, Richard Heffernan, Matthew Hindman, Sarah Hobolt, Philip N. Howard, Oliver James, Mary Jacobus, Michael J. Jensen, Andreas Jungherr, David Karpf, Anastasia Kavada, Daniel Kreiss, Rasmus Kleis Nielsen, Steven Livingston, Robin Mansell, Helen Margetts, Alister Miskimmon, Karine Nahon, Sarah Oates, Ben O'Loughlin, Zizi Papacharissi, Barbara Pfetsch, Eaon Pritchard, Terhi Rantanen, Alexa Robertson, Laura Roselle, Chris Rumford, Alexandra Segerberg, James Stanyer, Damian Tambini, Cristian Vaccari, Karin Wahl-Jorgensen, Silvio Waisbord, Nathan Widder, and Andy Williamson.

I am especially indebted to Ben O'Loughlin, who was kind enough to read and comment with penetrating intelligence and good humor upon almost the entire draft manuscript. I would also like to thank Bruce Bimber, Angela Chnapko, and Philip N. Howard for their comments on the initial book proposal and C. W. Anderson, Lance Bennett, David Karpf, Daniel Kreiss, and Rasmus Kleis Nielsen for their detailed comments on earlier drafts of some of the material. The diverse network of scholars and practitioners with whom I interact on Twitter has been a constant source of inspiration and insight. It goes without saying that this book's errors or shortcomings are entirely my own.

I am deeply grateful to those working in British media and politics who allowed me to interview them for this book. Not only did these individuals agree to meet me, they also gave very generously of their time, despite working in fields where punishing schedules and tight deadlines are the norm. I hasten to add that the individuals and the organizations specifically mentioned herein bear no responsibility whatsoever for my interpretations or conclusions, nor do any opinions expressed herein constitute the official policy or opinion of any organization or organizations mentioned.

My department at Royal Holloway, University of London, has been generous in providing the time required to complete this book. Research leave that came after my period as head of department proved to be helpful during the project's formative stages. For the financial assistance that made possible some of the fieldwork for this book I thank Royal Holloway, University of London's Research Strategy Fund, and the Department of Politics and International Relations. Thanks should also go to the Garden House Day Nursery, without whom this book would literally not have been written: clear personal evidence of the importance of time as a social resource, which is one of the sub-themes of my argument. I also thank staff at the following institutions: the Bedford and Founders Libraries at Royal Holloway, University of London; the British Library of Political and Economic Science at the London School of Economics; the University of London Library at Senate House in Bloomsbury; and the British Library.

Many of the ideas in this book were previously aired at conferences, workshops, and symposia. These include, in chronological order: the American Political Science Association's Annual Meeting at Boston in August 2010, the Royal Holloway Department of Politics and International Relations research seminar in February 2011, the University of Westminster Communication and Media Research Institute's research seminar in February 2011, the European Consortium for Political Research Conference at Reykjavik, Iceland in August 2011, the British Economic and Social Research Council/Hansard Society/Manchester University Roundtable on Social Media and Campaigning held at the British Parliament in November 2011, and the London School of Economics Department of Media and Communications Research Dialogues Seminar in November 2011. Last but certainly not least, it was an unforgettable honor to present an overview of this book to the Holberg International Memorial Prize Symposium, at Bergen, Norway, in June 2012, alongside esteemed prize winner Manuel Castells and symposium participants Bill Dutton, Helen Margetts, Terhi Rantanen, Annabelle Sreberny, and Göran Therborn.

I am continually impressed by the dedication and professionalism of the excellent team at Oxford University Press in New York. As everyone who has worked with Angela Chnapko knows, there is no finer commissioning editor. Angela's enthusiasm, hard work, tact, sound judgment, and knowledge of her field are second to none. My thanks also go to the anonymous peer reviewers: that they improved the original proposal and the book is unquestionable. I owe a special debt of gratitude to a particularly important reviewer who undertook a detailed developmental review of the entire manuscript.

Some of the material presented in chapter 4 appears in Andrew Chadwick (2011) "The Political Information Cycle in a Hybrid News System: The British Prime

Minister and the 'Bullygate' Affair," *International Journal of Press/Politics* 16 (1), 3–29, and Andrew Chadwick (2011) "Britain's First Live Televised Party Leaders' Debate: From the News Cycle to the Political Information Cycle," *Parliamentary Affairs* 64 (1), 24–44.

Finally, I dedicate this book to my wife Sam and our daughter Katie. Katie often seems to worry that my books do not contain many pictures. She was born just as the momentous events that form the subject of chapters 6 and 7—the campaign to elect Barack Obama president of the United States—reached their historic climax.

The Hybrid Media System

Introduction

"You Might as Well Go Home and Watch it on Sky News"

London, Saturday May 8, 2010. In the fallout from the inconclusive outcome to the British general election two days ago—the first "hung" Parliament in thirty-six years—senior politicians of all parties descend upon Westminster. The Conservatives and the Liberal Democrats seek a deal to form a coalition government. As the behind-closed-doors coalition talks begin, television reporters swarm around the grand entrances to Westminster's government buildings, empowered by an election in which their medium has renewed its dominance during the staging of Britain's first ever live televised prime ministerial debates.

The elite media feeding frenzy intensifies. With talk in the air of a deal on a fairer voting system as a condition of the Liberal Democrats agreeing to a coalition, a group of around a thousand people, many of them wearing purple, from a range of political campaign and activist groups—Take Back Parliament, Power2010, and 38 Degrees—somehow manage to identify the location of the secret party talks. The protestors march from Trafalgar Square to Transport House in Smith Square, where Liberal Democrat leader Nick Clegg is discussing strategy with senior colleagues in advance of a meeting scheduled later that day with Conservative leader David Cameron.

As the purple march enters Smith Square, David Babbs, the director of activist network 38 Degrees, receives a phone call. Sky News, one of Britain's 24-hour television news channels, would like him to appear in a live interview with their on-scene presenter, Kay Burley. Babbs agrees and makes his way around the corner, to where the nation's most important broadcast news reporters are camped on the green overlooking the Palace of Westminster and close to a gathering crowd of noisy protestors. Babbs composes himself for the interview, but before he and Burley go live to camera, Burley asks, "Can you tell these people to shut up?" "No, that's not how it works," Babbs replies (Interview 15 May 2010).[1] The interview begins, and within a few seconds Burley is hostile. As Babbs tries to explain that he and the 38 Degrees members want to make their arguments about a more democratic voting system known to the British public, Burley repeatedly interrupts him with verbal jabs about the futility of the demonstration: "it's not going to make any difference..." "what are you protesting for?..." "why do you need to protest?...." And then comes Burley's killer line: "You might as well go home and watch it on Sky News...."

*   *   *

Against the backdrop of high political drama in Westminster, this encounter crystallizes in one brief episode significant aspects of political communication as we hurtle through the second decade of the twenty-first century.

Consider the mediated experience of these events. I was not watching Sky News on television at the time of this live interview. In common with the vast majority of the hundreds of thousands of people who were transfixed by Kay Burley's extraordinary and unreasonable treatment of David Babbs, I watched the exchange later that day, on YouTube, or, to be precise, on the YouTube app on my iPhone. But what exactly did I and the hundreds of thousands of others watch, as the interview video clip flowed across television, websites, Twitter, Facebook, blogs, personal computers, smartphones, tablet devices, Xboxes, Nintendo Wiis, and web-enabled Blu Ray disc players, to name just a few of the ways you can now "watch" the internet.

What I watched on the YouTube app on my iPhone was, in fact, a web video of a phone video of a television broadcast video: a video of a video of a video. A person who goes by the YouTube moniker "lanerobertlane" had been sitting at home watching the interview live on television. Possibly sensing from the interview's first few moments that this might be an unusual encounter, lanerobertlane hurriedly pulled out his smartphone, switched on its video camera, pointed it at his television, and turned up the television using his remote control. Just as you manage to focus on the jerky images you are jolted by the sound of the remote being plonked down onto a coffee table. Lanerobertlane, who remains out of shot throughout, then uploaded the video file to YouTube. Within an hour or so, tens of thousands had viewed it, an online flash campaign had erupted on Twitter and Facebook, and protestors had congregated in real space around the Sky News stage in Westminster to try to disrupt Burley's subsequent interviews by holding up placards within camera shot and shouting "Sack Kay Burley." The Burley moment entered the YouTube hall of fame as one of the most excruciatingly bad examples of political interviewing in recent history. As I write today, lanerobertlane's video of a video of a video has been viewed 383,783 times on YouTube and has generated 2098 comments (lanerobertlane, 2010).

On that day, and when I interviewed him as part of the research for this book nineteen days later, David Babbs handled the episode calmly and with dignity. What seems to have most angered YouTube's lanerobertlane and the broader networks of protestors was Burley's suggestion that Babbs "go home and watch it on Sky News." 38 Degrees is part of a new generation of political organizations, like America's MoveOn, Australia's GetUp!, and the transnational movement, Avaaz, that shrewdly combine the logics of newer media, older media, and real-space events to mobilize activists, often in real time, as a means of applying pressure on political elites for a wide range of progressive causes. In 38 Degrees' case, this has ranged from political reform to the environment, media regulation to poverty, and from fighting cuts in Britain's publicly funded National Health Service to opposing the privatization of the nation's public forests. The last thing 38 Degrees members wanted to hear from Kay Burley was that they should go home, sit on the sofa, and watch the post-election drama on television. And yet, 38 Degrees' leader was appearing live on Sky News *precisely because* he recognized the power and immediacy of television as a medium. And if sympathizer lanerobertlane had not been sitting on his sofa *watching* television, there would have been no YouTube video to upload and circulate, little awareness of the unfairness of the Babbs interview, and less attention in the mainstream media to whether the Liberal Democrat party was about to betray its long-held pledge to electoral reform.

At the same time, Kay Burley is a well-established broadcast journalist working for BSkyB, which is partly owned by Rupert Murdoch's News Corporation empire, a global media conglomerate that has placed television and newspapers at the core of its strategy for more than thirty years. Probably the last thing Burley wanted to hear was that Babbs was representative of a movement of several hundred thousand people, most of whom explicitly reject the television-era, passive spectatorship logic of political communication the Sky News broadcaster both personified and, on this occasion, explicitly advocated. And yet, Babbs and his noisy comrades provided an obvious sense of drama and authentic liveness to this occasion, a sense that the election was an issue being discussed and argued about across the land—as, indeed, it was. Visible manifestations of unfolding drama are precious resources for all professional broadcasters. Burley was no exception here, and clearly saw how the protests fitted with television media logic.

This was, perhaps, a clash of ideologies, between the progressive center-left and a right-wing media empire. The fortunes of News Corporation have since declined, as Rupert Murdoch was forced to react to allegations of widespread phone-hacking at one of his British newspapers, the *News of the World*, by closing the paper down. Murdoch's son, James, was forced to stand down as chairman of BSkyB. 38 Degrees has since expanded its membership to over one million and has led successful mobilizations against a number of key policies of Britain's Conservative-led coalition government.

But viewed more broadly, the Burley interview, the protests that surrounded it, and the mediation of both, involved a confluence of older and newer logics in the organization and communication of political expression. At stake here was not only what was being said, but also how and by whom it ought to be said. This moment condenses key questions of who has power in the mediation of politics. It is but one episode among many in the ongoing construction of the hybrid media system.

The Hybrid Media System

The rapid diffusion of new communication technologies creates a pressing need to rethink the complex and multifaceted forces that are reshaping the political communication environments of the western democracies. At stake is whether we are living through a time of fundamental change in the nature of political life as a result of the disruptive influence of digital communication. Who is emerging as powerful in this new context? This book seeks to provide an empirically informed interpretive account of key aspects of systemic change in the political communication environments of Britain and the United States. It attempts to do this by employing a new type of focus on the classic concerns of political communication scholarship: the interactions among political actors, media, and publics. I argue that Britain and the United States have what are now best characterized as hybrid media systems.

In this book I start from the premise that in our analyses we should try as far as possible to integrate the roles played by older and newer media in political life. We require a holistic approach to the role of information and communication in politics, one that avoids exclusively focusing either on supposedly "new" or supposedly "old" media, but instead maps where the distinctions between *newer* and *older* media matter, and where those distinctions might be dissolving. Older and newer are relative terms. We need to understand how *newer* media practices in the interpenetrated fields of media and politics adapt and integrate the logics of older media practices in those fields. We also need to understand how *older* media practices in the interpenetrated fields of media and politics adapt and integrate the logics of newer media practices. This requires a perspective that discusses the systemic characteristics of political communication, but such a perspective must, I believe, be firmly rooted not in abstract structural prejudgments but in empirical evidence and specific illustrations of these forces *in flow*. This task is all the more important because it is clear that media systems in Britain, the United States, and around the world are in the middle of a chaotic transition period induced by the rise of digital media.

The key to understanding the hybrid media system is a conceptual understanding of power, but one that can be illustrated empirically. The hybrid media system is built upon interactions among older and newer media logics—where logics are defined as technologies, genres, norms, behaviors, and organizational forms—in the reflexively connected fields of media and politics. Actors in this system are articulated by complex and ever-evolving relationships based upon adaptation and interdependence and simultaneous concentrations and diffusions of power. Actors create, tap, or steer information flows in ways that suit their goals and in ways that modify, enable, or disable others' agency, across and between a range of older and newer media settings. The book examines a range of examples of this systemic hybridity in flow, through the analysis of political communication contexts ranging from news making in all of its contemporary "professional" and "amateur" forms, to parties and election campaigns, to activist movements, and government communication. I argue that hybridity offers a powerful mode of thinking about media and politics because it foregrounds complexity, interdependence, and transition. Hybrid thinking rejects simple dichotomies, nudging us away from "either/or" patterns of thought and toward "not only, but also" patterns of thought. It draws attention to flux, in-betweenness, the interstitial, and the liminal. It reveals how older and newer media logics in the fields of media and politics blend, overlap, intermesh, and coevolve. Hybrid thinking thus provides a useful disposition for studying how political actors, publics, and media of all kinds interact.

In his influential book from the early 1990s, *Media Performance*, Denis McQuail fleetingly but revealingly referred to a media system as "simply all relevant media" (McQuail, 1992: 96). McQuail was writing in a different era, one future generations will perhaps look back on as the zenith of the twentieth-century period of "mass communication." But while the context has shifted dramatically, we would do well to adopt McQuail's parsimonious formulation as our guide for understanding political communication today. In its own way, *The Hybrid Media System* tries to go beyond some of the limitations of existing treatments both of newer media and politics and of older media and politics. Too often the scholars in these two camps have talked past each other. Worse still, they have sometimes completely ignored each other's central themes and contributions. This is a broad generalization, of course, but it is only in the last few years that digital media and the internet have started to be recognized as genuinely important by those working in what we might term the "historic mainstream" of political communication scholarship (Chadwick & Howard, 2009). And on the other side, much of the work on the internet and politics has been problematic. It has often been blind to non-internet media forms and too often dominated by assumptions about "revolutionary" change or by a too narrowly drawn frame of "politics as usual." By neglecting the interrelationships between older and newer media logics, I believe research in this field is missing some important developments in the evolution of political communication. This book demonstrates one way—but by no means the only way—to explore these developments.

Outline of the Book

In this book, my overall goal is to blend theoretical and conceptual discussion with detailed analysis of the hybrid media system in flow. The book unfolds as follows.

In chapter 1, I outline what I term an ontology of hybridity; a way of approaching the study of the social world that moves us away from "either/or" thinking toward "not only but also" thinking. I show how this ontology of hybridity develops out of diverse and multidisciplinary strands in the social sciences and how the themes and dispositions of this body of research may, with appropriate theoretical and empirical development, generate new ways of exploring some of the classic concerns of political communication. Hybrid thinking also serves as a platform for my understanding of the three other central conceptual themes of this book: power, the idea of a system, and media logics, all of which are discussed in this chapter.

Chapter 2 explores what hybridity has meant in practice throughout the history of media. This story goes back a long, long way, but this chapter focuses on some key developments since the fifteenth century. I present these neglected histories of media hybridity not only because previous interactions between older and newer media are interesting in their own right, but more importantly because history provides some important conceptual pointers that then to go on to inform the contemporary studies that make up the rest of the book. Chapter 2 is not designed to be an all-encompassing traditional narrative history but serves as a revisionist account of intriguing episodes in hybrid media. It shows how the technologies, genres, norms, behaviors, and organizational forms of older and newer media have often been deeply intertwined, and how periods of important change have been shaped by continuities with the past. The social and technological dynamics these histories reveal are instructive for understanding the hybrid media system of the present era, to which I turn in chapter 3.

Chapter 3 builds upon the themes of chapter 2 but goes beyond it to establish the contemporary context for the analyses of political communication that follow in chapters 4 to 9. This chapter sets the scene for these more detailed illustrations of the hybrid media system by focusing on the changing nature of audiences, shifting patterns of media use, the salient structural characteristics of broadcasting, newspaper, and online media, and the emergence of new hybrid forms of mediality.

Following chapter 3, the emphasis shifts toward deeper exploration of key events and processes that reveal the hybrid media system in flow. Chapter 4 proposes a new approach to political news making based on what I term the political information cycle. The chapter examines the mediation of two extraordinary news events of the 2010 British general election campaign: the Bullygate scandal and Britain's first ever live televised prime ministerial debate. I show how political information cycles are built on news-making assemblages that combine older and newer media logics. They are composed of multiple, loosely coupled individuals, groups, sites, and temporal instances of interaction involving diverse yet highly interdependent news creators that plug and unplug themselves from the news-making process, often in real time. Using original data gathered during two intensive periods of live qualitative research, I show how the hybrid mediation of politics now presents new opportunities for non-elite actors to mobilize and enter news production through timely interventions and sometimes direct, one-to-one, micro-level interactions with professional journalists. I also show how these new power relations must be set within the context of professional politicians' and professional journalists' ongoing status, prestige, access, expertise, and influence.

Chapter 5 builds on several of the themes of chapter 4's account of news making. Here, however, I take a different tack by examining the extraordinary rise to prominence of WikiLeaks in the late 2000s and early 2010s. This chapter tells the story of the symbiotic relationship that emerged between WikiLeaks, its network of supporters, and those professional journalists who were so crucial to the success of the 2010 war logs and embassy cables "megaleaks." But this chapter goes beyond WikiLeaks' role in news making to consider the strengths and weaknesses of its sociotechnical model and its norms of operation for political organization, mobilization, and influencing the news agenda more generally. I show how the effective resources for taking action in the hybrid media system in this case emerged from the relational power and interdependence among WikiLeaks, the newspaper and broadcast media, and the distributed online networks of activists that mobilized in support of both WikiLeaks and the professional journalists during the U.S. government's unprecedented attempts to censor the internet during late 2010 and early 2011.

Chapters 6 and 7 expand further upon the theme of political organization by considering recent developments in the field of American election campaigning. In chapter 6, I provide a detailed reinterpretation of the fabled 2008 Obama for America campaign and show how this became a decisive period in the ongoing construction of the hybrid media system in American media and politics. I argue that the Obama campaign's significance in building a new model for successful presidential campaigning lay not in its use of the internet *per se*, but in how it so ruthlessly integrated online and offline communication, grassroots activism and elite control, and older and newer media logics. Obama for America displayed a keen and hitherto neglected awareness of the continuing power of older media logic in election campaigns.

Chapter 7 continues the revisionist approach of Chapter 6, but paints the 2008 U.S. presidential campaign on a broader canvas. Through a detailed analysis of key episodes in the mediation of the campaign, I show how the real-space spectacles of candidate appearances continued to generate the important television, radio, and newspaper coverage that remains so crucial for projecting the power of a candidate and conveying enthusiasm, movement, authenticity, and common purpose to both activists and nonactivists alike. I discuss how these television-fuelled spectacles now also integrate with newer media logics of data-gathering, online fundraising, tracking, monitoring, and managed volunteerism. A major theme running through this chapter is the growing systemic integration of the internet and television in presidential campaigns. Indeed, although traditional newspaper organizations still play an important role, as revealed in my revisionist interpretation of the framing of Republican vice presidential candidate Sarah Palin, it is the tension-riddled but increasingly integrated duopoly of television and online video that is the most significant development in this field. Chapter 7 also shows how the hybrid media system can shape electoral outcomes by providing new power resources for campaigns that can create and master the system's modalities—and severe penalties for those who cannot. But this same system also provides resources for journalists who seek to challenge campaigns and hold them to account, and for citizen activists who are occasionally empowered by newer media to intervene on their own terms, away from formal political and media structures, and through spreading forms of expression inspired by the field of entertainment but also professional investigative journalism.

In chapters 8 and 9 I examine the book's main themes from another perspective, when I employ an ethnographic approach to explore in more detail the hybrid media system's evolving norms. Here the context switches back to Britain and I draw upon evidence I gathered from insider interviews in 2010, 2011, and 2012 with those working in a sample of organizations at the heart of Britain's media-politics nexus in London. Chapter 8 examines the fields of news and journalism; Chapter 9 political activism, election campaigning, and government communications. During this fieldwork I met party communication staff; journalists; program-makers and editors working in radio, television, newspaper, magazine, and news agency organizations; independent bloggers; the director of a prominent public relations company; senior regulatory staff at the Office of Communications (OFCOM) and the Press Complaints Commission (PCC); communications staff working inside government departments and in the Prime Minister's Office in Number 10 Downing Street; and members of the renowned million-strong progressive political activist network, 38 Degrees. This ethnography revealed much boundary-drawing, boundary-blurring, and boundary-crossing, as the logics of older and newer media interact, compete, and coevolve. I show how this boundary work is creating compelling new hybrid norms for the conduct of news making among professional journalists and "amateur" bloggers, and for the conduct of political activism, election campaigning, and government communications. I reveal how integrated divisions of labor between older and newer media practices are emerging in the daily work of actors in these fields, and how the different types of integration are sometimes bolstering and sometimes weakening the power of those whose dominance rests upon older broadcasting and print media practices.

Finally, in the Conclusion to the book I draw together the book's main arguments about hybridity, power, systems, and media logics.

1

An Ontology of Hybridity

Hybridity offers a powerful way of thinking about politics and society, a means of seeing the world that highlights complexity, interdependence, and transition. It captures heterogeneity and those things that are irreducible to simple, unified essences. It eschews simple dichotomies and it alerts us to the unusual things that often happen when the new has continuities with the old. The original Greek sense of the hybrid as something that questions conventional understandings and the accepted order suggests how the metaphor usefully unsettles some of our fixed conceptions. Hybridity is inevitably associated with flux, in-betweenness, the interstitial, and the liminal. It is about being out of sync with a familiar past and a half-grasped future. It provides a useful disposition for studying political communication.

Hybridity's Origins

According to the *Oxford English Dictionary* the word hybrid has its origins in Latin and in ancient Rome. From the very beginning, the term has held connotations of the unusual or exotic. During the late nineteenth century the *Encyclopedia Britannica* referred to its Greek usage for "an outrage on nature" (Warren, 1884). Latinized versions of hybrid began to work their way into English texts during the early seventeenth century, and the first recorded usage emerged in the 1601 translation of the *Natural History*, first published in A.D. 79 by Roman statesman and philosopher Pliny the Elder. Pliny's thirty-seven-volume work includes a series of bizarre animal and part-human creatures drawn from far-flung corners of the globe, descriptions of which he had gathered during his traveling conversations with storytellers. Pliny's imagining of the hybrid as the unusual continued to exert an influence through to the late medieval period. Traces of this connotation survive to this day.

During the seventeenth century, hybridity acquired a racial meaning as a label for mixed racial inheritance. More importantly, however, during this period the term's meaning was "transferred," and it began to be used in a figurative sense to describe any entity derived from "heterogeneous or incongruous sources" or with "a mixed character." The formal codification of the word and the acquisition of its modern scientific meaning began in 1775, when John Ash's English dictionary included the definition "begotten between animals of different species, produced from plants of different kinds." The same sense was used in 1801 by U.S. president Thomas Jefferson, and in 1828 a botanical definition was included in Noah Webster's famous *American Dictionary of the English Language*.

This usage of hybrid spread during the mid-nineteenth century and found its way into the writings of several scientists, including most notably Charles Darwin, as it gradually acquired a more neutral inflection associated with the expanding science of genetics.

These two broad sets of usages—the specialist one common in scientific discourse, especially genetics, and the figurative one characteristic of literary, artistic, and everyday discourse—continued throughout the twentieth century and into the contemporary period. Specialized associated meanings include, for example "hybrid computer," used in the 1950s to describe machines that combined emerging digital technologies with the features of older analog computers based on hydraulics, mechanics, or simple electronics.

There are limits to etymology. But this brief sketch hints at several useful preliminary aspects of hybridity as a metaphor for thinking about politics and society. It is intriguing that the figurative meaning of the term emerged early in its English usage. This points to the attraction of the metaphor as a tool for capturing heterogeneity. Hybridity alerts us to the unusual things that happen when distinct entities come together to create something new that nevertheless has continuities with the old.

Hybridity in the Social Sciences

In recent decades, hybridity has diffused across a diverse array of social science disciplines and fields, as well as broader categories of social and political thought; it is one of the few genuinely interdisciplinary trends. The idea is now endowed with a loose but identifiable set of themes about the workings of the social world. In other words, thinking in terms of hybridity amounts to something like an ontology, where ontology is understood as a theoretical disposition that enables us to ask and answer some new and different questions about the nature of contemporary society. A central appeal of this ontology of hybridity is its means of capturing and explaining the significance of processes that might be obscured by dichotomous, essentialist, or simply less flexible orientations.

I use ontology here in a very basic sense. A philosophical term, originally from metaphysics, it refers, in the words of Daniel Chandler and Rod Munday, to "assertions or assumptions about the nature of being and reality: about what 'the real world' is…." Ontologies often contain "hierarchical relations" as "certain entities may be assigned prior existence, higher modality, or some other privileged status" (Chandler & Munday, 2011). Ontologies are necessary because, as John Scott and Gordon Marshall argue, "Any way of understanding the world, or some part of it, must make assumptions (which may be implicit or explicit) about what kinds of things do or can exist in that domain, and what might be their conditions of existence, relations of dependency, and so on." (J. Scott & Marshall, 2009: 531).

In political science, comparativists have recently turned to the concept of "hybrid regimes" as a means of quelling growing frustration with the steadily expanding range of cases that display messy mixtures of democracy and authoritarianism. For example, Larry Diamond (2002) argues that many countries now have regimes that are best seen as "pseudodemocratic." There has been a proliferation of "adjectival" regime types, such as "competitive authoritarianism." In Steven Levitsky and Lucan Way's extensive study, this captures the integrated coexistence of what appear to be formal democratic rules, such as free and fair elections, with religious or military elite coercion, excessive patronage, and the flouting of the rule of law by those in power (Levitsky & Way, 2010). A key theme here is transition. Many African, Asian, and Latin American countries have embarked on what, during the early phases, appeared to be journeys toward liberal democracy. But for a variety of reasons some regimes have become frozen in a pseudodemocratic stasis that those living in the West may find counterintuitive and normatively objectionable, even though these regimes are stable and broadly legitimate (Karl, 1995). As Richard Sklar (1987: 714) has argued, democracy is "an increasingly complex form of political organization. From that perspective, every country's democracy is, at best, a composite fragment. Everywhere, democracy is under construction." Political scientists have therefore started to question teleological assumptions about the inevitability of democratic transition. Increasingly, the focus is on hybridity as a "new and resilient" type of regime (Brownlee, 2009: 517; see also Ekman, 2009).

This literature contains several important assumptions that have broader relevance for the study of media and politics. The static and universalizing analytical frameworks for the categorization of regimes and systems that were dominant during the Cold War era have now been jettisoned in favor of more complex, differentiated approaches. Hybrid regime theory reveals how democratic and authoritarian political practices intermesh and simultaneously coevolve. An important part of this shift is a renewed emphasis on understanding how regimes transition from one to another, how old and new institutional forms and behaviors blend and overlap, and how messy those transitions are when judged against fixed and abstract criteria. The notion of a hybrid system draws attention to change and flux, the passing of an older set of cultural and institutional norms, and the gradual emergence of new norms. But hybridity is not always and everywhere a state of obvious transition. In the case of systems that began to democratize but then froze at some point along the way, hybrid status has become the norm because it offers a lasting settlement enjoying broad legitimacy, or it concretizes the balance of power among societal groups. Alternatively, hybridity may be based on the creation and continuance of what are termed "reserved domains." These are areas where elites have the capacity to retain strategic control over pockets of resources essential to their ongoing power and influence, and they exist alongside domains in which elites tactically cede control (Valenzuela, 1992). As we shall see throughout this book, attempts to create reserved domains are an important part of the struggle for preeminence among those associated with older and newer media logics.

Nonlinearity is an important principle here. According to some scholars of comparative politics, the paths to a hybrid regime are several and depend in part upon the characteristics of preceding arrangements. Simple authoritarian regimes may gradually grant minor concessions as a result of internal pressures, crises or international stimuli, as has been the case in sub-Saharan Africa, for example. New electoral regimes may emerge rapidly out of the old authoritarian settlement but may also have strong vestiges of the past, such as over-mighty executives, as is the case with Russia and several other post-communist systems. And democracies may sometimes "regress" toward authoritarianism, by retaining democratic elements like elections while executive power is gradually extended, as is the case in some Latin American countries.

Approaches in which regimes are the unit of analysis have been accompanied by new directions in a cognate field: the social science of governance and regulation. Scholars in this field emphasize complexity, diversity, and the simultaneous coevolution of seemingly contradictory social, cultural, economic, and political practices. Ash Amin, an economic geographer, has written of new "micro worlds" of regulation, in which informational flows and networks constitute "an unfolding regime of heterarchical order that is topological, hybrid, decentered, and coalitional in its workings" (Amin, 2004: 217; see also Bulkeley, 2005). Henry Farrell, an international relations scholar, traces the emergence of "'hybrid' forms of governance ... in which states seek—individually or in concord—to set general rules or principles under which transnational private actors implement policy and adjudicate disputes" (Farrell, 2003: 278). Karin Bäckstrand argues that there has been a general shift toward "hybrid, bifurcated, pluri-lateral, multi-level, and complex modes" of governance based on multistakeholder dialogues and partnership agreements (Bäckstrand, 2006: 468; see also Risse, 2004). Marc Allen Eisner portrays U.S. environmental governance as a "hybrid of traditional command-and-control regulation, government-supervised self-regulation, and corporate voluntarism, reinforced by the market and procurement" (Eisner, 2004: 161; see also Lockwood & Davidson, 2010). Meanwhile, political theorist Terry McDonald sketches out a model of democratic regulatory governance that derives its legitimacy from a hybrid blend of principles associated with state and non-state institutions, the assumption being that neither sector has the capacity to provide an integrated system (see also P. S. Berman, 2007; Macdonald, 2008). Finally, the work of Nobel-prize winning political scientist Elinor Ostrom suggests a hybrid approach to the governance of scarce common-pool resources, one that blends centralized enforcement of community rules and privatized competition. Ostrom's work thus highlights the complexities of contextually specific, hybrid incentive structures in shaping power relations among actors (Ostrom, 1990; Sandler, 2010).

Hybridity has also proved influential in an area that overlaps with governance and regulation: the study of organizations. This encompasses interpretations of the shifting nature of life *inside* organizations but also the increasingly fluid interactions *between* organizations. This is an interdisciplinary trend, as scholars from fields as diverse as management, sociology, political science, information science, and communication have become increasingly preoccupied with explaining the dialectical co-presence or the integration of a huge range of variables, such as: hierarchical and networked modes of coordination (Fimreite & Lægreid, 2009); elite control and individual autonomy (Clegg & Courpasson, 2004; Courpasson & Dany, 2003; Hodgson, 2004); centralization and decentralization (Ashcraft, 2001); technological artifacts and organizational norms and routines (Bloomfield & Hayes, 2009); voluntarism and directive planning (Langlois & Garzarelli, 2008; Shah, 2006); bureaucratic and market-based interorganizational and intraorganizational relationships (Foss, 2003); formal and informal divisions of labor (Ashcraft, 2006); expertise and lay knowledge (Bjørkan & Qvenild, 2010; D. Scott & Barnett, 2009); rationality and affect (Ashcraft, 2001); online and offline mobilization repertoires (Chadwick, 2007; Goss & Heaney, 2010); "entrepreneurial" and "institutional" modes of engagement (Bimber, et al., 2009); "protest" and "civic" forms of collective action (Sampson, et al., 2005); "alternative" and commercial models of news production (Kim & Hamilton, 2006); advertising-funded and state-regulated broadcasting (Born, 2003); institutional isomorphism and individuation (Pedersen & Dobbin, 2006); and "Americanized" election campaigning styles and nationally specific approaches (de la Torre & Conaghan, 2009; Nord, 2006; Plasser & Plasser, 2002). This diverse and impressive body of research is informed by hybrid thinking.

Media and cultural shifts have of course played important roles in the constitution of these new hybrid domains, creating new relations of complex interdependence in the local-translocal and national-transnational spheres. It should therefore come as no surprise that the field of cultural studies has been inscribed with conceptual disputes about hybridity. Central concerns have included the production, transmission, and contested reception of media texts (Gilroy, 1993), and, more recently, digital technologies of transnational communication. Hybridity has emerged in postcolonial studies as a critical response to the dominance of "cultural imperialism" (Holton, 1998: 161–185). While cultural imperialism suggests the relatively effortless exporting of western cultural values to non-western contexts, hybridity scholars argue that the reality is in fact messier (Kraidy, 2005). Central to this usage of hybridity is cultural resistance through ironic subversion—the idea that historically "subaltern" cultural movements have selectively engaged in the integration and adaptation of aspects of dominant cultural genres in order to blunt the latter's potential hegemony (Bhabha, 1994; Said, 1994). Some scholars have explored the construction of racial and ethnic identities through mediated communication in postcolonial settings such as diaspora communities (Arnold & Schneider, 2007; Gillespie, 1995; Shome, 2006) and there is now a growing body of work examining hybrid media genres such as world music, the Latin American telenovela, the Bollywood film industry, and the subtle but significant changes that are made to "localized" television format shows that now form an important sector of the global entertainment industry, such as *The X-Factor* and *Who Wants to be a Millionaire*, to name just two.

These cultural treatments of hybridity have often drawn attention to fundamental questions of ideology and power. The construction of hybridity is often portrayed as a heavily politicized and competitive process of interaction at critical historical junctures, as groups engage in struggle to assert their power and autonomy. Studies of cultural hybridity also reveal that the flow of cultural power is rarely unidirectional (Glynn & Tyson, 2007; Shim, 2006; Wang & Yeh, 2005). Some processes of hybridization are best seen as constructing "strategic inauthenticity," whereby cultural creators deliberately incorporate non-indigenous genres as a means of challenging dominant or stereotypical expectations in their respective cultural fields (Luvaas, 2009; Taylor, 1997: 125–146). More broadly, the turn toward hybridity in cultural studies presents a challenge to analyses based on the oppositional interaction of static social phenomena. My aim here is not to argue for the importance of these specific examples, nor for the particular importance of cultural explanation per se, but rather to establish a general orientation toward power and change in the underlying dynamics of a system. It strikes me that these insights on power, appropriation, and counter-appropriation offer some useful conceptual resources for studying a system of political communication in which there are ongoing struggles between older and newer media logics.

Linked in part to this literature on hybridity in cultural change is a broader concern with the ever-evolving nature of media genres. For example, attention is now shifting to the increasingly porous boundaries between "hard" news and "entertainment" genres in political communication (Williams & Delli Carpini, 2011). Emblematic of this shift is of course the popularity of political comedy talk shows like *The Daily Show* in the United States (Baym, 2005: 262). Talk shows, especially those featuring audience participation, have always hybridized and integrated news and entertainment genres (Livingstone & Lunt, 1994; see also Wadensjö, 2008). But *The Daily Show* takes this to extremes, combining humor with serious discussion of politics, media bias, and political hypocrisy, all through a highly entertaining satirical lens. As Geoffrey Baym writes, "Discourses of news, politics, entertainment, and marketing have grown deeply inseparable; the languages and practices of each have lost their distinctiveness and are being melded into previously unimagined combinations" (2005: 262; see also D. G. Young, 2011). Documentary, long considered a "serious" media form for politics, has undergone a transformation over the last decade, with the rise of hybrid genres such as fictional or semi-fictional "mockumentaries," "docu-soaps," "game-docs," and "biopics" (Kilborn, 2003; Mast, 2009). Very recent political events are now routinely adapted by television dramatists, a good example being the BBC show *On Expenses*, which aired in 2010, within less than a year of the 2009 MPs' expenses scandal, one of the biggest crises in the history of the British parliament. At the same time, fictional shows, like HBO's *Veep* and the BBC's *The Thick of It* increasingly integrate highly detailed plot lines and contextual information from real or half-real contemporary political events, in what Kay Richardson, Katy Parry, and John Corner term "secondary performance" of the political (Richardson, et al., 2012: 19). Meanwhile, genres such as cookery shows are putting the "info" back into infotainment, as public health campaigns and political mobilization occur in the older-media-meets-newer-media networked spaces facilitated, but by no means dominated by, high-profile "celebrity chefs" like Jamie Oliver.

The internet and digital media are, of course, especially powerful in these processes. The internet and digital media hybridize and integrate a wide range of "ancestral" (C. R. Miller & Shepherd, 2004) genres in the process of creating new genres (Chadwick, 2006: 4–9; Crowston & Williams, 2000). They also encourage users and audiences to engage in what Clay Spinuzzi terms "subversive interactions": the injection of familiar genres and routines into new and unfamiliar information environments (2003: 3). Journalists now routinely appropriate the genres of social media sites and hybridize these with their preexisting routinized, professional practice. But newer media are not uniquely powerful here. Older media have been steadily reinventing themselves. Television is now a prolific hybridizer of genres, especially since the emergence of so-called "reality" formats in the 1990s (Wood, 2004). And televisual style is now shot through with digital style. Various concepts have been proposed to capture these trends, from the "multimodality" approach that first emerged in the field of sociolinguistics (Kress, 2010) and which has been taken in new and fruitful directions by Manuel Castells with his concept of "mass self-communication" (Castells, 2009), to "remediation" (Bolter & Grusin, 1999), "interdiscursivity" (Fairclough, 1992), "interpractice" (Erjavec, 2004), and "convergence culture" (Jenkins, 2006).

Finally, the sociology of science and technology has given rise to what is probably the most radical understanding of hybridity: actor–network theory. Most often associated with the philosopher Bruno Latour, actor–network theory's central claim is that modernity has been based upon a seemingly "natural" but actually artificial ontology that distinguishes between "nature" and "society," or between the human and "nonhuman" domains. Actor–network theory posits that the world is based upon "hybrid networks" of human and nonhuman hybrid subject-objects. In this perspective, nonhuman "actants" have a form of agency that emerges, not from the intrinsic capacity of nonhuman "things" to act alone, but rather from these things' interdependent interactions with other resources—both technological and human—in a given sociotechnical system. These hybrid networks must be analyzed holistically in order to understand the interplay of technologies and social actants (Latour, 1993: 10–11; see also Latour, 2005).

Actor–network theory is heavily dependent upon the idea of hybridity. By freeing us from modes of either/or thinking, and by creating a generalized principle of "symmetry" between people and "things," it enables us to identify sociotechnical systems whose functioning depends upon the intermingled agencies of the social and the technological. Indeed, Latour's assumption is that the very terms "social" and "technological" are merely labels of convenience that do not hold any substantive meaning. As he vividly puts it "…when we find ourselves invaded by frozen embryos, expert systems, digital machines, sensor-equipped robots, hybrid corn, data banks, psychotropic drugs, whales outfitted with radar sounding devices, gene synthesizers, audience analyzers, and so on, when our daily newspapers display all these monsters on page after page, and when none of these chimera can be properly on the object side or on the subject side, or even in between, something has to be done" (Latour, 1993: 49–50).

Actor–network theory's relational theory of agency and power is controversial primarily due to this understanding of hybridity, but the approach has radiated out from its origins in the sociology of science and is now starting to influence many different fields of inquiry, including anthropology, political theory, the sociology of organizations, social psychology, communication, and cultural studies (Saldhana, 2003). Its influence has been particularly strong in human geography (Lulka, 2009; Thompson & Cupples, 2008; Whatmore, 2002) and is now growing in information systems research (Heeks & Stanforth, 2007; Ranerup, 2007). More recently, some scholars have integrated some of the themes of actor–network theory with broader philosophical ideas in poststructuralism and empirical developments in political communication. Most important here is the idea of the assemblage, which I discuss in chapter 4. Originally introduced by Gilles Deleuze and Félix Guattari (Deleuze & Guattari, 2004), the idea of the assemblage has recently been stripped down to its essentials and used as a means of capturing the heterogeneous social and technological aspects of collective action in news making and political campaigning (Chadwick, 2011a, 2011b; Kreiss, 2012; R. K. Nielsen, 2012). Situating power and agency in the context of integrated but still conflict-ridden systems comprising people and technologies offers a creative orientation for the study of media and politics.

Hybridity's Analytical Challenges

Despite offering these rich theoretical resources, an ontology of hybridity also presents challenges. To what extent can hybrids be understood as something analytically unique "in themselves," and as something new? Is the whole notion of hybridity logically dependent upon prior and coherent fixed categories? Does it always entail the ultimate resolution of contradictions? One way of addressing these problems is to distinguish between two basic modes of hybridity. In one sense, hybrids may be seen as "diluted" versions of their antecedents. A more suggestive approach, however, is "particulate" hybridity, which sees antecedents' characteristics as always in the process of being selectively recombined in new ways (Wade, 2005: 609). Particulate hybrids are recognizable from their lineages but they are also genuinely new. Newness derives from the particulate recombination of prior elements. Though I did not use the terms diluted and particulate, I have previously argued for the importance of both of these forms of hybridity as outcomes of the influence of the internet on political organizations. Older organizational forms—political parties and interest groups—now blend together their own preexisting campaigning styles with mobilization repertoires typically associated with social movement organizations. Particulate hybrid organizations, such as MoveOn, the American political movement, selectively recombine mobilization repertoires typically associated with political parties, interest groups, and social movements (Chadwick, 2007).

This particulate idea of hybridity is similar to cultural theorist Edward Said's notion of the "contrapuntal," which he borrowed from musicology. As Said put it, "in the counterpoint of western classical music, various themes play off one another, with only a provisional privilege being given to any particular one; yet in the resulting polyphony there is concert and order, an organized interplay that derives from the themes, not from a rigorous melodic or formal principle outside the work" (Said, 1994: 59–60). Counterpoint is an intriguing musical technique, found most vividly perhaps in Bach's well-known work, *The Goldberg Variations*. It relies not upon strict harmony—compatible notes played simultaneously—but the weaving together of quite distinct melodic lines that may occasionally intersect at certain points to create a harmony that is substantial but often only temporary. As Marwan Kraidy has convincingly argued, this contrapuntal thinking is "well suited for understanding the relational aspects of hybridity because it stresses the formative role of exchanges between participating entities" (Kraidy, 2005: 13).

Hybridization is therefore a process of simultaneous integration and fragmentation. Competing and contradictory elements may constitute a meaningful whole, but their meaning is never reducible to, nor ever fully resolved by, the whole. Particulate hybridity is the outcome of power struggles and competition for preeminence during periods of unusual transition, contingency, and negotiability. Over time, these hybrid practices start to fix and freeze; they become sedimentary, and what was once considered unusual and transitional comes to be seen as part of a new settlement, but that new settlement is never entirely fixed.

The social sciences have arguably been riddled with what Jan Nederveen Pieterse has termed "boundary fetishism" (2001: 220). The ontology of hybridity constitutes an important and suggestive critique of that thinking. I believe this ontology provides a fruitful approach to understanding the interactions between older and newer media logics in contemporary politics and society and it can help shed new light on the relative power of actors in a media system. Attempts to control, police, and redraw boundaries, and the power struggles that criss-cross domains are important defining features of contemporary political communication. For every example of a boundary between older and newer media in the communication of politics, there are examples of that boundary being transgressed. Throughout this book I show how this ontology may illuminate important aspects of the evolving media systems of Britain and the United States.

Power and System

I now turn to discuss how this ontology of hybridity informs three further core themes of this book. First, the power relations among political actors, media actors, and publics associated with older and newer media. Second, the idea of a system. And third, the idea of media logics.

The concept of power and the concept of a social system have each been central to the social sciences and this is not the place to rehearse these long-running debates. But working on the basis that evidence and theoretical hunches coevolve interdependently as one moves forward with any research, it is important that I sketch out the theoretical assumptions that I have found useful when writing this book. Throughout and in the concluding chapter I revisit these ideas as I reflect on the cases and examples.

As I argued in the previous chapter, a useful starting point for studying media and politics is Denis McQuail's deceptively simple definition of a media system as "simply all relevant media" (McQuail, 1992: 96). I say "deceptively simple" because, while McQuail's definition may have been reasonably self-evident during the late period of mass communication toward the end of the twentieth century, "simply all relevant media" has a more challenging edge to it in the highly diverse media system in which we now find ourselves.

Any understanding of power must involve an examination of the relationships between social actors, but less obviously it must also encompass the relationships between social actors and technologies, because technologies enable and constrain agency in the hybrid networks and sociotechnical systems identified by actor–network theory, as I discussed above. As the Weberian tradition in the social sciences has maintained, the exercise of power must always involve an interactive social relationship of some sort. However, as Steven Lukes has argued, these interactions may be understood very broadly as the social relations that create the cultural and ideational contexts in which the essential precondition of power—the construction of meaning—takes place (Lukes, 2004). But only by exploring concrete interactions and exchanges among social actors, and how media are used in and come to shape those interactions and exchanges, can we get inside the power relations that prevail in a given setting (Blumler & Gurevitch, 2005). The many and diverse interactions among social actors may aggregate to constitute systems, as David Easton's influential approach in political science has maintained (Easton, 1957, 1965).

There is nothing rigid or mechanical about seeing social life as based upon systems. It is not necessary to suggest, along with functionalist sociologists such as Talcott Parsons, that there is a single, overarching social system that integrates all social functions to produce a stable order (1951). Nor is it necessary to assume that there is a single "system level" to which all aspects of social life are said to conform. Indeed, unlike a related concept common in the social sciences, "regime," system may often connote flexibility, adaptability, and evolutionary change emerging from the sum of social interactions. Regime, on the other hand, connotes hierarchy, fixity, and asymmetries of power in social relations. Systems will often exhibit these features, but they may also exhibit horizontality, fluidity, and equality. And, as Manuel Castells has argued, institutionalized power relations frequently meet with "counter-power," as the social movements that are increasingly built upon networked communication come to challenge state and corporate institutions (Castells, 2007).

We may extend this analysis further. Following Brian McNair, I assume that all systems are characterized by varying degrees of inherent complexity, instability, and messiness. Systems contain many nonlinear elements and often undergo long, unpredictable, and chaotic periods of change. As McNair says, systems "exhibit structure, but of an irregular kind. Communication systems are never in exactly the same place twice" (McNair, 2006: xiv). Systems are based on competition, conflicts over resources, and desires for preeminence, but systems analysis also carries an assumption that a great deal of interdependence exists among the salient actors. Actors compete and some gain the upper hand, creating what Robert Keohane and Joseph Nye have termed relations of "asymmetrical interdependence" (Keohane & Nye, 1989). But even the most powerful in any system must cooperate with those who are less powerful, in the pursuit of collective goals. Cooperation of some sort is required for the maintenance of a system, for the production of useful social goods and the authoritative allocation of resources, however broadly those resources may be defined (Easton, 1957: 386–387). This sometimes gives those with fewer obvious resources the power to act in ways that force adaptation among those who seemingly had greater resources before specific interactions began. And as the pluralist approach of Robert Dahl and many others has maintained, those who are powerful in one social field may not necessarily be powerful across all social fields (Dahl, 1961).

A recent twist on these ideas of emergence and interdependence is David Singh Grewal's theory of "network power." Power, Grewal argues, may be based on simple sovereignty in the Weberian mould, which is understood as the power of an individual or group to compel others to do something they would rather not do. This power is often but not always backed by legitimized forms of collective decision-making. On the other hand, power may also be based upon what Grewal terms "relations of sociability," which are defined as "the accumulation of decentralized, individual decisions that, taken together, nonetheless conduce to a circumstance that affects the entire group" (Grewal, 2008: 9). These relations of sociability increasingly exist in network form, but these networks are not entirely chaotic and spontaneous. Over time, networks come to rely on emergent standards, which are shared norms and practices that facilitate cooperation. If we assume that in any given social field the value of a network is directly related to its size (because larger networks grant access to greater amounts of resources like money, communication, audiences, social support, or whatever the relevant resource happens to be) we may also generalize that social actors will want to belong to those larger networks. (The relevant networks in a given social field may be comparatively large or comparatively small—size is not an absolute but a relative concept.) It is the social value of the norms and practices in the larger network that make individuals want to join it. By joining, one gains access to the resources, or the "network power" that resides in the cooperative relationships facilitated by those different norms and practices. This is why individuals constantly adapt their norms and practices to join networks that will provide them with advantages of varying kinds. There are many examples of this process in action in this book. Actors constantly mobilize but also constantly traverse the logics of older and newer media to advance their values and interests.

Conceiving of power as relational, as evolving from a series of interactive exchanges among those who are articulated by chains of dependence and interdependence allows us to move away from abstract, structural prejudgments and generalizations about the specific categories of people who are supposedly powerful or the specific roles that people must supposedly always perform if they are to be powerful. It also enables us to move beyond abstract statistical approaches to media systems. Instead, it suggests a focus on the diversity of mechanisms and behaviors that enable power to be exercised in discrete contexts (Reese, 1991). In this sense, the idea of a system as I use it in this book also involves the idea of "practice" as it has recently been elucidated by media scholar Nick Couldry. As Couldry argues, "A practice approach starts not with media texts or media institutions but from media-related practice in all its looseness and openness. It asks quite simply: *what are people* (individuals, groups, institutions) *doing in relation to media* across a whole range of situations and contexts? How is people's media-related practice related, in turn, to their wider agency?" (2012: 37, emphasis in original). Power in a media system might be understood, then, in a non-reductive and multifaceted sense, as the use of resources, of varying kinds, that in any given context of dependence and interdependence enable individuals or collectivities to pursue their values and interests, both *with* and *within* different but interrelated media.

Systems are based upon social differentiation; divisions of labor emerge among actors and there is a recognition that the pursuit of goals, especially in important large-scale societal projects like politics, media, or business, for example, cannot be undertaken without some embedded, regular structures for managing cooperation and conflict over time. These structures that make up a system may take the form of organizations, but now, in an era of digital media that are best understood as forms of communication *and* organization, these structures for cooperation may be relatively loose, spontaneous, and supple, and continually adapted and readapted according to the goals being pursued (Bennett, 2003; Bennett & Segerberg, 2012; Chadwick, 2007, 2012).

Embedding norms and acting with regularity are important parts of exercising power in any system. But so, too, is acting with timeliness, which is to be distinguished from acting with regularity. Timeliness and the mastery of temporal rhythms are important but surprisingly neglected social forces (but see Adam, 1990; Gershuny, 2000; Goodin, et al., 2008; Rifkin, 1987). Yet attention and the ability to create and to act on information in a timely manner are both key to successful communication. Actors try to master time by shaping its social understandings according to their own values and interests. Actors often flout regularity in order to cause shock and surprise and get ahead of the game. These aspects of temporality and how they are enabled and constrained by different media are on show at many points in this book.

A further key aspect of systems is their continual recreation. Systems must be constructed, enacted, and continuously reenacted, often with incremental modifications, by social actors. With the passing of time, the modifications that emerge from the interactions among actors may amount to the decisive reshaping of a system. As Michael Mann's macro-historical account of social power has argued, the reshaping of power relations may emerge from direct challenges to existing institutional forms, or it may emerge "interstitially," from new practices that cannot be fully integrated into the existing institutionalization settlement, but which grow at the edges of existing institutions and in the boundary spaces between those institutions (Mann, 1986: 15).

Systems, then, are always in the process of becoming, as actors simultaneously create and adapt. As Couldry argues, drawing upon the social theory of Pierre Bourdieu, a system "generates the conditions under which the practice is itself possible" (2012: 39). Only through analysis of discrete practices and moments of interaction are we able to identify these conditions. They cannot be generated in the abstract or by statistical snapshots but must be illustrated through specific examples of things in flow. In this book, this means analyzing how the technologies, genres, norms, behaviors, and organizational forms associated with older and newer media shape politics.

From Media Logic to Hybrid Media Logics

Identifying how older and newer media shape politics must also involve some basic assumptions about how the practices of media interact with the practices of other social fields. A fruitful concept here is "media logic." First introduced by sociologists David Altheide and Robert Snow (1979), the concept of media logic was originally developed to identify how the assumptions, norms, and visible artifacts of media, such as templates, formats, genres, narratives, and tropes have come to penetrate other areas of social, economic, cultural, and political life. Peter Dahlgren has usefully condensed the idea of media logic as "the imperatives that shape the particular attributes and ways of doing things within given media and even within specific genres." This, he argues "pertains to the procedures of selection, form, tempo, informational density, aesthetics, contents, modes of address, and production schedules" (Dahlgren, 2009: 52).

In the media logic perspective, media logic comes to shape the practices of those working outside the media field, and over time the boundaries between media and non-media fields become highly porous. Here I use "field" in the sense articulated by Pierre Bourdieu, to refer to a social category with its own norms and practices that provide the resources (or forms of "capital")—be they cultural, professional, bureaucratic, emotional, or aesthetic—for exercising power, often in small-scale, everyday contexts (Bourdieu, 1984). Fields are permeable and the logic of media frequently intervenes in other fields. Media treatments of sport, religion, politics, and terrorism, for example, have over time shaped the practices of actors in these respective fields, transforming key aspects of how they behave, blurring the boundaries between media and non-media. In politics, for example, Altheide and Snow have argued that practices derived from entertainment formats have increasingly become "folded" into the production of political news, hence the hybrid formulation "infotainment" (Altheide & Snow, 1992: 466). Lance Bennett has drawn attention to the growth of dramatic soundtracks and "action movie editing" in television's reporting of war (Bennett, 2005: 175). Over time, those working in other fields become dependent upon media logic and must conform to it in order to access the resource media offer: the ability to communicate with mass publics. As Altheide and Snow pithily explain, "today all social institutions are media institutions" (1991: ix).

Media logic provides a useful approach to understanding the power of media and the power relations within media. It moves us away from accounts that begin from the perspective that media systems and political systems are somehow separate and that the former are largely explained by the characteristics of the latter (though for a greatly nuanced approach see Hallin & Mancini, 2004; Siebert, et al., 1956). Media logic points us toward a different approach, one focused on studying how the discrete interactions between media elites, political elites, and publics create shared understandings and expectations about what constitutes publicly valued information and communication. The who, when, how, and why questions that inform the daily practice of political and media actors evolve over time to create a shared media culture based upon an underlying media logic (Altheide, 2004: 294). This media culture shapes the public's expectations of what "politics" is. In the long run, it means that those seeking to influence public discourse must adapt their communication strategies to fit the dominant formats required by media logic.

Media logic can explain why political actors and publics often seem to behave in ways that indicate that they have "internalized" the expectations and norms of the media field. The staging of pseudo events designed with favorable media coverage in mind is a classic example of media logic (Boorstin, 1964), but so too are the perpetually evolving yet commonly shared understandings of what constitutes a "good story" or "exciting visuals," what is "too long" for television or "won't work on the internet," and so on. Media logic theory suggests that "effective" political communication comes to be seen as that which taps into embedded social expectations of what makes for "appealing" media coverage in a context of hypercompetition among media. And all of this takes place within a commercial media environment that serves as the primary context within which information about politics is produced and communicated. Media logic theory therefore suggests that we try to understand the processes of sense making that emerge in the daily practices of those in the fields of media and politics; the ongoing decisions about "what goes where" in the construction of mediated political discourse. These are the decisions that shape the emergence and subsequent evolution of media logic.

Despite its obvious strengths, however, the media logic approach has some limitations. It was developed in the era of mass communication, when the dominance of electronic broadcast media was more firmly entrenched than it is today. It also attributed great power to formal media institutions. And while Altheide and Snow observed differences between how print and broadcast media shaped non-media fields, they had in mind a singular media logic that was said to pervade social and political life.

Today, the media environment is far more diverse, fragmented, and polycentric, and new practices have developed out of the rise of digital communication. Lance Bennett has put this in stark terms: the theoretical challenge begins with "the core question of just what we mean by 'media' these days" (Bennett, 2003a: 18). This calls for a reappraisal of the idea of media logic and its disaggregation into different competing yet interdependent *logics*. Writing about news, for example, Mark Deuze has argued that a new logic of "multimedia journalism" emerged in the early 2000s (Deuze, 2004). A further point is that while those in "non-media" fields like politics may have been shaped by media logic, they have in turn acted back on the media field as part of a continual process of mutual adaptation and interdependence. Altheide and Snow maintained that media and culture are reflexive (1992: 466), but these processes of mutual adaptation are arguably neglected in media logic accounts. Thus, while media logic has had an influence on the conduct of politics (as the related literature on "mediatization" has demonstrated (Mazzoleni & Schultz, 1999)) this logic is best seen, not as a force that emanates from media and then acts upon politics, but rather as a force that is *co-created* by media, political actors, and publics.

A convincing and refreshing perspective on all of this has recently been outlined by Sam Popkin. Popkin argues that political actors compete to best respond to media change, while media actors compete to best respond to political change. But he goes a step further. The practices of media and political actors become so interpenetrated, and the alliances between them so strong, that the disruptions caused by the emergence of newer media affect the status and power of both media *and* political elites. In other words, it is not that newer media technologies simply become new and different tools that existing media elites can use to more effectively hold politicians to account, nor is it the case that newer media technologies simply provide existing political elites with new opportunities to outsmart media (Popkin, 2006: 336). Instead, existing media and political elites both have much to lose from the emergence of newer media. Both must (and generally do) adapt, or see their power decline, and occasionally newer media technologies may create new elites.

This book therefore begins from a more expansive idea of media logic. It seeks to understand the interactions that determine the construction of media content but also how these interactions take place across and between different older and newer media. Competing media logics can emerge that disrupt the dominant media logics that were previously established. Today, does media logic still derive from the mass broadcast media that so decisively shaped political communication during the second half of the twentieth century? Altheide and Snow argued that over time publics become familiar with media logic and expect to see its characteristic formats applied across all content, including politics. But in the early twenty-first century the media system is a much more fluid and contested place. The range of sources of information has expanded in ways that were unimaginable in the era of broadcast dominance. Audience familiarity is still an important aspect of media logic, but disruptive media logics may now come from online networks that seek to shape representations of political life according to their own interests and values, using digital communication tools that previous generations could not access. This creates alternative and competing sources of authenticity and audience familiarity, outside of those that were dominant in the era of mass broadcasting.

Given the panoply of newer ways in which politics can now be communicated, it therefore makes sense to move away from Altheide and Snow's idea of an all-encompassing, hegemonic media logic driven by the values of commercialism and entertainment. Instead, today we can conceive of politics and society as being shaped by more complex interactions between competing and overlapping media logics, some of which may have little or no basis in, or are antagonistic toward, commercialism. Indeed, given the long-standing traditions of public service provision in the United States and Britain, which commit broadcasters to the creation of public affairs content, together with what we are now discovering about how audiences learn about politics from "nonpolitical" entertainment formats, perhaps the original media logic approach was overstated, even during the heyday of broadcast media.

It also makes sense to move away from the idea of a relatively passive mass audience whose frames and perceptions are heavily shaped by a dominant media logic, and toward a model that foregrounds not only the increasingly diverse sources of audience frames and perceptions, but also the growing ability of some, though not all, activist "audience" members to play direct and concrete instrumental roles in the production of media content through their occasionally decisive interventions. It makes better sense, then, to use the plural, media *logics*; or what Dahlgren terms "an ensemble of simultaneously operative media logics" (Dahlgren, 2009: 54).

As this book shows, in politics, older and newer media have what we might term, borrowing from the hybrid regime theories I discussed earlier in this chapter, their own "internal" reserved domains of practice that actors seek to defend and protect. At the same time, however, the boundaries between older and newer media are always porous, as the disruptions caused by the emergence of newer media are gradually working their way through the institutions of the previously dominant print and broadcast media system. Importantly, the hybrid media system constantly requires judgments and interventions about which medium is most appropriate for communicating a political event or process. How political and media actors shape and are shaped by older and newer media logics, and the extent to which they mobilize, traverse, and integrate these logics to exercise power, is what this book is about.

The Hybrid Media System as an Analytical Approach

A final word about the design of this study. In this book, I situate the analysis in the context of Britain and the United States. Not only is this for pragmatic reasons—these are the countries which I find most compelling to study and which have provided the main focus of my previous research—it is also because these are historically important liberal democracies. As such, the trends and patterns in these countries ought to be of interest and significance for those concerned with political communication more generally. However, in this book I do not seek to make any claims about the media systems of countries other than Britain and the United States.

In addition, I have chosen not to organize this research according to the traditional model of cross-country comparison. That there are important differences between how political communication has been and continues to be conducted in Britain and the United States is undeniable and there are many valuable ways these differences may be studied. For this book, however, I considered it more important to begin from the inevitably contested but defensible premise that Britain and the United States share sufficient basic similarities, such that it is possible and desirable to develop ideas that speak to some enduring concerns of readers in both countries.

My aim with this book, then, is to present the hybrid media system as a general *analytical approach*, and to do so in a way that remains rooted in empirical examples drawn from the two countries upon which I focus. None of this is to say that the idea of the hybrid media system will not travel. It might be used to explore other liberal democratic systems as well as authoritarian or semi-authoritarian systems. Indeed, any context in which it is important to try to make sense of political communication by exploring the interactions between older and newer media logics will hopefully benefit from the approach.

2

All Media Systems Have Been Hybrid

New technologies is a historically relative term.
—Carolyn Marvin[1]

Mediation without remediation seems to be impossible.
—Jay David Bolter and Richard Grusin[2]

The "content" of any medium is always another medium.
—Marshall McLuhan[3]

All older media were once newer and all newer media eventually get older. But older media of any consequence are rarely entirely displaced by newer media. Even telegraph messages and cassette tapes, for example, haunt the present, sharing with newer media the affordances of representation and transmission, though their performance of these roles is no longer socially sanctioned except by small groups of hobbyists. Things are complicated by the continuing evolution of newer media, as once new forms will continue to accrete and hybridize newer affordances, a good example being the extraordinary metamorphosis of the mobile phone into a multifunction computing device during the first decade of the twenty-first century.

As a successful newer medium starts to age, its physical characteristics as well as the social norms that surround it start to become less visible. What was once awkward and contested becomes habitual and settled. The focus begins to shift away from the physical apparatus—the "technology"—and the initial generation of social conventions around a medium's use. In time, the febrile attention to the "work" performed by a medium gives way to more leisurely attention to the events undergoing representation and we tend to lose sight of what makes a medium so significant. And yet the technological facets and initially-established social norms of a medium never entirely fade but continue to shape patterns of use and the sense of what a specific medium is and of how it differs from other media.

As Carolyn Marvin has argued, the history of newer media is "less the evolution of technical efficiencies in communication than a series of arenas for negotiating issues crucial to the conduct of social life; among them, who is inside and outside, who may speak, who may not, and who has authority and may be believed" (1988: 4). To revisit the ideas of Bruno Latour, whom I discussed in the previous chapter, this process involves hybrid networks consisting of social and technological entities whose constant interactions are generative of power and agency. Lisa Gitelman's historically-informed definition of media is also particularly instructive here. In her view, media are best seen as "socially realized structures of communication, where structures include both technological forms and their associated protocols, and where communication is a cultural practice, a ritualized collocation of different people on the same mental map, sharing or engaged with popular ontologies of representation." Throughout history, then, a medium has tended to be "a vast clutter of normative rules and default conditions, which gather and adhere like a nebulous array around a technological nucleus" (2006: 7). Newer media technologies accrete newer media publics, but those publics are best seen as the hybrid, partly amalgamated combinations of groups, organizations, and social norms and practices that were previously associated with older media. Groups come to see certain media both as tools and as domains in which they expect to exercise their power, through mechanisms such as professional expertise, control over resources, and mastery over media genres and organizational routines. Newer media partially reconfigure social, economic, political, spatial, and temporal relationships among existing media elites, political elites, and publics. They do this by providing different normative contexts and terms of engagement for the interactions among these groups.

This book begins from the perspective that any medium is best understood in terms of its position in a system of interdependent relationships with other media. All media systems are, to greater or lesser extents, and for greater or lesser periods, hybrid media systems, but this hybridity is too often overlooked. I therefore take inspiration from Asa Briggs and Peter Burke, who, in their classic history of media argue that "it is necessary to look at the media as a whole, to view all the different means of communication as interdependent, treating them as a package, a repertoire, a system ... To think in terms of a media system means emphasizing the division of labour between the different means of communication available...." (Briggs & Burke, 2009: 19). A fruitful way to identify who exercises power in political communication involves focusing on the evolving interrelationships among older and newer media logics.

Media and "Newness"

Newer media have always been presented as improvements upon their predecessors, in terms of their ability to convey what media theorists Jay David Bolter and Richard Grusin have termed "immediacy": the sense of presenting a transparent window on the "real." For example, early printers, most notably Gutenberg, made use of the conventions of the handwritten manuscript, but improved the handling of ink to enhance the legibility of texts. Early photographers were inspired to improve on the perspective-drawing functions of the *camera lucida*. Photographs were seen as more immediate than paintings, television more immediate than cinema.

But each new medium's claim to superiority constantly brings it into competition and conflict with older media, with the result that how newer media differ from older media becomes much more obvious and visible. Bolter and Grusin argue that this creates a second important aspect of media emergence, which they term "hypermediacy." Hypermediacy refers to how newer media are often less about transparency and immediacy than they are about the "remediation" and hybridization of other media forms. Examples from history are as diverse as photomontage, ornate baroque cabinets, medieval manuscripts, and eighteenth-century iconotext prints featuring characters communicating through comic-style speech bubbles. But the internet and digital media, with their multiplicity of visual genres and interfaces, and their simultaneous recombinations of text, image, audio, and video, are extreme forms of hypermediacy in action.

The "newness" of a newer medium comes, then, not from technological novelty in itself, but from the ways in which newer media "refashion older media and the ways in which older media refashion themselves to answer the challenges of new media" (Bolter & Grusin, 1999: 15). If we look at media this way, we start to notice that the blurred boundaries between media and their uses are just as important as the neat distinctions that supposedly separate them. There are continuous, strategic, and often surprising processes of hybridization at play. Lady Eastlake, wife of Sir Charles Lock Eastlake, the first president of the Royal Photographic Society, captured the significance of photography in suitably hybrid terms in the mid-nineteenth century. It was, she said, neither "the province of art nor description, but...a new form of communication between man and man—neither letter, message, nor picture—which now happily fills the space between them" (quoted in Briggs & Burke, 2009: 162). Early radio systems of the 1920s were often described as "radio telephones." Charles Jenkins called his first mechanical television of the late 1920s "radiovision" (Wu, 2010: 38, 142). Early cinema drew heavily upon photography, the novel, the theater, and even the genres of circus and magic trick shows. Music halls and fairgrounds were where films were first displayed; jugglers and acrobats appeared on the bill at Louis Lumière's 1896 film exhibition at the Empire Music Hall in London's Leicester Square. George Méliès, another influential early filmmaker, started out as an illusionist (Briggs & Burke, 2009: 164). Only later, in the 1910s, did dedicated cinemas emerge. But the traces of theater lingered into the middle of the century, as live pianists and organists continued to appear on the bill in the new "dream palace" cinemas. Early television was used exclusively for live transmission and it drew upon the traditions of late-nineteenth-century electric light shows, vaudeville theater, and radio serials (which likewise drew upon nineteenth century novels, which likewise were serialized in periodicals) (Briggs & Burke, 2009: 2). As British cinema, radio, and television flourished from the 1920s to the 1960s, so too, unexpectedly, did print, due to the growth and improvement of mass education and the reduced costs of producing and distributing printed paper. In 1920, around half of British adults read a daily paper. By 1947, that figure had reached 83 percent (Briggs & Burke, 2009: 223). Even in the United States, where television had reached 90 percent of homes by 1959, it was not until the early 1970s that television began to overtake newspapers as the public's main source of news (Williams & Delli Carpini, 2011: 61). Television's undoubted dominance as a medium came surprisingly late.

What count as new media at any given time are therefore best seen as hybrids of newer and older media. Roger Fidler, who predicted the emergence of tablet computing when working as an adviser to news organization Knight-Ridder in the early 1990s, termed this "mediamorphosis": "a continuum of transformations and adaptations...brought about by the complex interplay of perceived needs, competitive and political pressures, and social and technological innovations" (Fidler, 1997: 16, 23). As media emerge, they simply throw the ongoing hybridization of older and newer into sharper relief. While the evolution of media has most often been presented as a linear history in which one medium replaces another, only to be replaced by another, and then another that better jells with societal demand (see for example Levinson, 1998), this linearity does not adequately capture the messiness, complexity, and long duration of the transitions. Older media practices can renew themselves in response to the new. Technologies may possess socially useful affordances that enable their persistence. It is often noted that as television diffused in the United States during the 1950s, cinema attendance declined massively, halving in less than a decade (Briggs & Burke, 2009: 212). But despite the threat from television, radio, with the help of the new electronic transistor, underwent a significant period of adaptation and expansion. Stations proliferated and advertising revenues increased, with the result that the U.S. Federal Communications Commission (FCC) decided to restrict the granting of fresh radio licenses in 1962 (Briggs & Burke, 2009: 209). It became apparent that radio's affordances were different from those of television, cinema, and newspapers. Like television, radio was a monitorial, real-time medium, but listening to radio was a more intimate and individual experience than viewing, and it was cheaper to produce content for the radio than for television. It helped that American commercial radio interests lobbied the FCC in the 1940s in order to defend their medium's position, but there was also widespread skepticism about television's superiority over radio when it came to reaching a mass audience. More recently, and as I show in greater detail in subsequent chapters, in response to the development of digital media practices, broadcast media and newspapers have undergone decisive periods of adaptation and coevolution in order to maintain their legitimacy and preeminence in representing and shaping publics.

Power and the Negotiated Emergence of Newer Media

If media are best seen throughout history as bundles of cultural, social, economic, and political practices, these practices are shaped by competitive yet interdependent processes of hybridization involving multiple actors operating in and across diverse settings. At stake during the emergence of media are negotiated relationships of power, authority, and prestige among groups of actors associated with particular media forms. This book explores these processes at work in recent years, but although hybridization in media systems occurs in different ways, at different paces, and at different times, it is not a new phenomenon. There are precedents, and these provide some interesting pointers for understanding the present.

ORAL-PRINT MEDIA

During the fifteenth and sixteenth centuries, scribes attacked the printing press on the grounds that this newer technology threatened their existence. Church leaders also feared the loss of control that would arise once ordinary individuals could read religious texts for themselves. From the mid-fifteenth century onward, oral culture persisted, adapted, and renewed itself over the course of three centuries, as the practices of orality were integrated into an evolving print culture (Briggs & Burke, 2009: 15, 25–26; Zaret, 2000). The period of the English Civil War is rightly depicted as the time of a spectacular outpouring of independent news-sheets, pamphlets, and petitions, but it was also punctuated by significant physical gatherings, such as the Putney Debates of 1647. Oral culture assumed renewed significance following the Restoration of the English monarchy in 1660 and the repression of the nascent free press and its replacement by a state-censored *Gazette*. Oral traditions were further rejuvenated in the old and new spaces of face-to-face exchange, such as pubs, clubs, learned societies, coffeehouses, bookstores, and churches (Zaret, 2000). By the early eighteenth century, London contained around three thousand coffeehouses, such as Button's, Lloyd's, Slaughter's, and Garraway's. These, and Parisian cafés like Le Procope, acted as the physical engine rooms of the Enlightenment, but they were also hybrid spaces in which printed newspapers, pamphlets, and books were read aloud and discussed in public. As Jürgen Habermas puts it, these were spaces in which "literature had to legitimate itself" (Habermas, 1989: 33).

Public rituals, performances, games, festivals, and exhibitions of varying kinds were important parts of the hybrid media systems of early modern Europe. Religious and political street processions combined music, images, text, and the spoken word in dialogic flows of communication that bound together rulers and ruled through mutual gestures of goodwill. These rituals were also used to orchestrate critiques of the established order. During the late sixteenth century, organized public theater started to integrate these different media forms and give them an entertainment inflection, and theater later went on to play a role in the pre-revolutionary ferment in late eighteenth-century France, alongside a wide range of media forms and genres such as pornography, comedies, and utopias (Briggs & Burke, 2009: 36, 83; Darnton, 1995).

The emergence of printed books and pamphlets was a major cause of the Protestant Reformation, but oral culture and visual media also played important roles here, too. Martin Luther's vernacular translation of the Bible was undoubtedly instrumental, but so were his hymns and the many paintings and iconic woodcut prints depicting religious scenes and images of Luther and his wife. Following the wave of Calvinist-led iconoclasm that spread across Europe during the early sixteenth century, the Catholic church, initially reluctant to popularize visual representations of religious stories out of fear that to do so would empower worshippers to challenge the authority of the religious elite (Grabe & Bucy, 2010: 31), nevertheless responded with a renewed emphasis on grand sacred icons that specifically sought to counter the Protestant critique (Briggs & Burke, 2009: 68). The Reformation was therefore in part a power struggle about the perceived appropriateness of competing media forms to adequately represent the sacred.

The character of these spaces of oral culture also influenced the genres of the emergent pamphlet, newspaper, and journal press of the time, helping to forge new practical norms of legitimacy and consent in political communication. The pages of the *Spectator*, published 1711–1712, contained a virtual "club" modeled on the real thing in London. It featured individuals drawn from diverse social groups, including a merchant, a country squire, a priest, and a "rake." The first significant popular news journal, the *Athenian Mercury*, which ran from 1691 to 1697, fielded around six thousand questions from readers. Priests would arrange for their favorite sermons to be printed and they, in turn, would come under the influence of the sermons of others, as well as religious guidebooks, which emerged during the early fifteenth century. Performers would resell printed books after reciting from them in streets and market squares. Printed lyric sheets for popular folk ballads, some of them critical of Catholic orthodoxies during the Protestant Reformation, were frequently displayed in English and German taverns, to encourage public singing. During England's Glorious Revolution of 1688, these developments also intersected with the repertoires of street processions, as well as the growth of symbolic goods such as playing cards, medals, plates, and teapots (Briggs & Burke, 2009: 39–79). Print media were of huge significance during the French Revolution of 1789: around 250 new newspapers were founded in that year alone and published political writing flourished. But widespread illiteracy in French society also fueled the continued importance of face-to-face meetings in political clubs, in addition to the older traditions of iconoclasm, festivals, and processions. Sites of oral and physical interaction therefore became enmeshed with an emergent print culture, and print culture itself acted back upon oral culture and shaped it partly in its image.

Print culture therefore took several centuries to fully deal with the vestiges of its pre-print past. Handwritten manuscripts continued to be used for the circulation of public documents until well into the eighteenth century. Some writers deliberately eschewed printed books and preferred to restrict the supply of their work to friends and networks of cultural and political elites, as a means of building communities around ideas or of escaping religious and political censorship. This was especially important in countries such as Russia, where most printing presses were based in monasteries, but it was also widespread in eighteenth-century Paris, where there was an organized industry of scribes churning out hundreds of underground texts critical of Louis XIV (Briggs & Burke, 2009: 37–38). Handwritten newsletters continued to circulate even after the rise of printed news-sheets, not least because they could be personalized according to their wealthy readers' interests.

The continuing importance of visual imagery also points to a further theme in the history of media hybridity: the integration of information and entertainment. The history of the press is often portrayed as the victory of reason and informed debate and what would in the twentieth century become known as "hard" news. But the reality is more complex. The press systems of Britain and the United States have always featured a hybrid blend of entertainment and information. As Bruce Williams and Michael Delli Carpini have argued, early American newspapers like the *American Aurora* (Williams & Delli Carpini, 2011: 22–23) contained a bizarre mixture of political debate, sexual scandal, and satire. In the late eighteenth century there was no coherent understanding of what would, in the late nineteenth and early twentieth centuries, emerge as the policed boundaries between news and entertainment, and between producers and consumers. New York's *Sun*, which ran from 1833 to 1950, featured entertainment alongside politics and public affairs, including a series of richly-illustrated hoax stories in 1835 supposedly revealing life on the moon. London's *Bell's Weekly Messenger*, which ran from 1796 to 1896, carried cartoons as well as sensational content and information related to horse racing, health, and court reports. *Reynolds's News*, founded in 1850 by former Chartist G. W. M. Reynolds, combined news, radical liberal opinion pieces, short stories, and illustrations. Britain's *Daily Mail*, founded in 1896 and very much a creature of the turn toward more overtly commercial models of journalism that occurred in the late nineteenth century, was the first daily paper to have a "women's page" (Briggs & Burke, 2009: 181–195).

As the nineteenth century progressed, conversational styles of journalism that borrowed from oral traditions continued to encourage lively and pluralistic representations of public opinion in the American press. These were based on multiple genres, including fictional storytelling and sensationalism, and were given new impetus in the 1880s with the growth of printing methods that enabled photographs and illustrations to be more faithfully reproduced. It was not until the American Progressive Era of the early twentieth century, which saw the professionalization and institutionalization of journalism, that these vestigial influences of oral and early print culture started to fade, as an informational model of "objectivity" in reporting began to edge out the older "storytelling" model. In the process, modern "scientific" understandings of the proper role of American news media emerged.

Most influential here were the ideas of Walter Lippmann, who argued that a combination of expert media and political elites operating in the context of a citizenry with only limited capacities for political engagement was the best set of operating principles for a mass democracy. The social responsibility theory of the media cemented these ideas in the mid-twentieth century, as the separation of news and entertainment, fact and opinion, and producers and audiences—principles first developed for print during an era of increasing concentration of ownership—also came to characterize the bedrock of an even more concentrated power structure: American broadcasting (Williams & Delli Carpini, 2011: 25, 32, 40–49, 57–60).

Principles similar to those of Lippmann animated Britain's BBC, founded in 1922 as the British Broadcasting Company but transformed in 1927 into the devoutly noncommercial British Broadcasting Corporation. Its first director general, Lord Reith, argued that to hand over broadcasting solely to entertainment interests would amount to "prostitution" and he famously described the BBC's mission as being to "inform, educate, and entertain." His patrician public service vision of due impartiality in broadcast media heavily shaped the content of radio and television in Britain, guaranteeing the BBC a widely-admired, publicly-funded monopoly over broadcasting, until the foundation, in 1955, of a still heavily-regulated commercial alternative: the Independent Television Authority. In the United States, even though radio and television developed along more commercial and entertainment-driven lines and the idea of a fully-fledged publicly-funded broadcasting monopoly was rejected, the FCC, founded in 1934, exercised limited though still significant regulatory functions through its power as license holder. The "fairness doctrine" was introduced in 1949, and, though it was eventually repealed in 1987, acted as a means of guaranteeing news coverage of public affairs and the impartial treatment of opposing views. The introduction of the Public Broadcasting System (PBS) in 1967 gave information and education programming a more prominent, if still highly precarious role alongside entertainment in the American media system.

PRINT-AURAL MEDIA

The emergence of recorded sound in the late nineteenth century—the first genuinely mass medium not to be based on print—provides a particularly intriguing illustration of the power struggles that shape the hybridity of a newer medium (Gitelman, 2006: 25–86). Edison's tinfoil phonograph first emerged during 1878 and was presented as a means of storing and reproducing speech, as the machine was paraded in a series of exhibitions at educational lyceums. Clockwork music boxes were very familiar to the nineteenth-century public and the first exhibitions of the transmission of sounds using telephones took place as early as 1876 and 1877. Early uses of the phonograph were rarely about music and performance, but were instead focused upon the social practices of public speech and the enunciation of printed texts. Exhibitors and their audiences would record their own sounds, including recitals of Shakespeare and popular poetry, but also everyday bodily noises like coughs and sneezes. These shows were genuinely interactive occasions. The hybridity of this newer media form was signaled literally by the inscribed surfaces of the scraps of indented tin foil that attendees would take home as "printed" mementos of their "recordings." Until they were replaced by superior, non-removable wax cylinders, tinfoil souvenirs became an essential part of the shared rituals of Edison's "talking machine" exhibitions, and helped to construct a nascent public around this emerging technological form.

These talking machines were marketed as devices for businesses and Edison himself predicted that the phonograph would mark the end of printed books. During the late 1880s and early 1890s, however, in attempts to popularize the device, battery-powered motorized phonographs containing pre-recorded music on wax cylinders began to be installed in public spaces such as hotels, bars, and purpose-made public rooms, on a pay-for-play basis. Their educational uses were downgraded and these public installations offered no facility for self-recording. Still, the poor sound quality of the early models meant that users had to listen individually, using headphones or "hearing tubes." Rooms often contained up to sixteen sets of headphones connected to a single machine. These pay-per-play public phonographs were based in part on older practices of public print culture. Not only were recorded announcements inserted into the beginning of each musical recording, cards containing promotional descriptions of what was to be heard were also placed above the machines; listeners would read these as the machine played the sounds. Individuals listened "together alone," in hybrid public-private spaces that were portents of later media, particularly the cinema, but also radio, television, and the internet. Recorded sound was therefore first perceived as a "public" (or semipublic) rather than a private or domestic medium, and the phonograph's design and its social practices were heavily influenced by the public cultures of print and performance in the late Victorian period.

When phonograph companies began selling recordings to local stores, this contributed still further to the construction of a public whose identity was based upon listening to a shared repertoire of music. But by the turn of the twentieth century, things started to shift. Berliner's rival gramophone device became more popular and cultural and economic changes combined to literally "domesticate" recorded sound, as it was increasingly designated entertainment to be consumed privately in the home. The result was the emergence of sound recordings as a newer mass medium. It represented a rupture with print, but the practices of print media still helped shape it during its first few decades.

A recurring pattern in the history of the emergence of newer media is one that reverberates strongly in the present era of digital media. In the early stages, newer media, both technologically and in terms of their associated elites and publics, are very much up for grabs. The boundaries between producers and consumers blur as the medium is negotiated and defined through a series of technological innovations, competitive interventions, and boundary-drawing among early users (Gitelman, 2006: 15). It was certainly the case with the phonograph's transition from tinfoil sheets to wax cylinders to gramophone recordings. A technology that began life as a means of capturing dictated speech in offices steadily accreted a range of public, semipublic, and private social practices. Middle-class women were key shapers of the early recording industry, as were emerging conceptions of idealized domesticity reflected in the rise of consumer culture, with its popular monthly magazines, mail order catalogs, and department stores as sites for the marketing of new recordings to the public. The commercial model of the early recording industry, based as it was upon the collection, storage, display, and repetitive playback of categorized individual records (mostly excerpted versions of public performances) bore traces of print culture's established practices around books. The social status associated with having certain types of music in the home was accompanied by the democratization of the rituals associated with collecting and curating cultural objects. But the read-write, user-shaped characteristics of the early phase of the medium faded as it spread to homes, and recorded sound evolved into an essential component of all mass broadcast media.

"ELECTRIC" MEDIA

The late nineteenth and early twentieth centuries also witnessed the invention and contested negotiation of other important newer communication media: the telephone, wireless transmission, and, most curiously, electric light (Marvin, 1988). Again, hybrid recombinations of older and newer media are much in evidence.

The social embedding of these newer media was sparked by the broader public's access to electrical power, but the process was also driven by new technical and professional elites: scientists, inventors, engineers, and businessmen who were eager to define the newer media and legitimate their enhanced status and prestige with and within them. Like several of the phenomena I discuss in the rest of this book, these newer "electric" media were assemblages. They consisted of technologies, such as generators, wires, switches, batteries, and handsets; hierarchical divisions of labor between the technical and creative elites and the associated workers required to run the new communications infrastructure, such as telephone operators and maintenance staff; and older media-empowered groups, such as press proprietors, journalists, theatrical entertainers, and politicians, who sought to adapt and exploit the newer media for their own advantage.

The emergence of electric media gave rise to a panoply of new cultural anxieties, social ambitions, modes of social control, and futuristic utopias, as many aspects of the older media rituals of nineteenth-century society became layered with newer affordances. Ithiel de Sola Pool's extraordinary research of the early 1980s, published in his book *Forecasting the Telephone*, catalogs more than 180 distinct predictions about how the phone would change American (and global) culture, society, and politics (Pool, 1983a). There were particularly strong concerns over the telephone's disinhibiting effects and the new ease with which social connections could be made using the technology. Among wealthy households, this was often expressed as distaste for the potential for untrammeled communication with those of lower social status. There was a public and political aspect to this. For example, Chauncey Depew, a U.S. senator between 1899 and 1911, was harassed by telephone "maniacs" eager to speak to him about his latest newspaper article. In 1889, a man was imprisoned on the grounds of lunacy after he insisted that a long-distance phone office in Syracuse connect him directly to the New York City home of the famous millionaire, Mrs. Vanderbilt. Doctors and other professionals complained of being constantly hounded by patients eager to be given detailed advice over the phone (Marvin, 1988: 67, 86–88).

There was also much anxiety about the telephone's capacity to erode the privacy and social stability of the middle-class home. Newspapers and periodicals contained panicked reports of servant couples eloping following long-distance romances, and of fraudsters using phones to target wealthy families. Phone company workers, such as maintenance staff and operators—the "all-night telephone girls"—were able to listen in on private conversations. Party lines, which were often shared among ten or more households, meant that inadvertent eavesdropping of neighbors' conversations was inevitable. Domestic robberies were often reported as being the outcome of thieves listening in on party lines. Many hotels and stores kept a shared phone for use by customers, either for a small fee or as part of their service. The first successful prosecution under nascent wiretapping laws in the United States was an 1891 case involving betting fraud based on intercepting calls relaying horse racing results (Marvin, 1988: 69).

Government and the law fought back using the same technologies. Boston's police stations had phones as early as 1878. By the late 1880s, London police had their own separate phone system with special lines connecting senior police with Parliament, the War Office, and the Fire Brigade. The British government, eager to maintain control of its imperial periphery, was a prodigious user of electric media and at first resisted the democratization of the phone on the grounds that it ought to be their reserved domain; opening it up would compromise the quality of the official government service (Marvin, 1988: 98–101). Yet at the same time, journalism and scientific commentary was teeming with speculation about the educational and "civilizing" effects of using the phone to connect disparate societies around the globe, in a reference back to print culture. These were discourses of the potential for the disembodied pursuit of self-discovery through learning about the riches of other cultures, as the phone was presented as an ideal way to hear eloquent speeches by public figures and to learn about literature, museums, and picture galleries (Marvin, 1988: 204). The parallels with the reception of the internet in the 1990s and 2000s are striking.

These social hopes and fears turned upon the idea that the phone's newness as a medium was subverting established understandings of community, family, social hierarchy, and politics by blurring personal and professional boundaries and disturbing preexisting relations of power and influence. The phone reconfigured the rules of communication and social protocols around secrecy, publicity, and access.

Later broadcasting practices also owe their origins to early experiments with using the telephone system to transmit live events. Though they were the preserve of the wealthy, in 1880s London and Paris, plays, concerts, opera, and even religious services were transmitted live from theaters and churches to remote dedicated rooms containing multiple phone headsets (Briggs & Burke, 2009: 145; Marvin, 1988: 209). Over the next three decades, the "theaterphone" practice of "broadcasting" theater, music, and sports spread across several major U.S. cities, including New York, Boston, Philadelphia, and Chicago. Interactive applause would scratch its way back across the party lines.

Political campaigns were given the theaterphone treatment. During the elections of the 1890s the telephone was featured as a means of connecting politicians with journalists and the public. Real-space rallies and speeches were broadcast live to houses; people would pass around the headset and comments from the listeners would be relayed back to the candidates and the rally crowd. During the 1892 election, the telegraph started to be pushed aside, as the phone emerged as the medium of choice among journalists eager to send election results back to their editors in the shortest possible time. The phone was also a better means of informing the elite clientele of the clubs and hotels in the major U.S. cities. During this period, the American Bell Telephone company often combined the roles of reporter, editor, and broadcaster. Bell organized printed cards of previous election results for those who subscribed to its service, it edited the reports that it received from local papers, the police, and local officials, and it regularly sent fresh packages of results down the line to eager audiences. This organizational innovation was improved upon during the 1896 election by AT&T in New York, when more than a hundred staff managed a network of reporters, hotels, clubs, local exchanges, and subscriber lines allowing listeners to hear the results as they arrived and were read aloud by phone operators. And for those unable to connect by phone, the results were remediated in real time, projected onto cityscapes with huge electric lamps.

While the phone and recorded sound were the major developments in electric media during the late nineteenth-century, this period also saw an explosion of announcements, news, and advertising mediated by electric light (Marvin, 1988: 152–190). This was a prototypical form of mass broadcasting, but it was based upon audiences viewing information en masse, together in the cityscape, not in private, but in public. In 1892, giant searchlights installed at New York's Madison Square Garden and the roof of Joseph Pulitzer's World Building were used to broadcast the incoming presidential election returns using color-coded streams of light projected onto clouds and nearby buildings (Marvin, 1988: 186). In an excellent historical example of the media hybridity I discuss later in this book, the color codes were publicized days in advance by the major New York newspapers, so that the public would be able to decode the signals in real time on the night of the election.

During the early years of the twentieth century these prototypical broadcast news-making assemblages were increasingly professionalized, as demand increased for the immediacy offered by the phone and technological improvements made the telecommunications system more reliable. Yet, in their party lines, amateurs also had their own arenas for hearing and spreading news. These early examples almost always revolved around the live transmission of events, but it was not long before the idea of scheduled programming of a variety of entertainment and news content (some of it provided in-house, some of it aggregated from newspapers and magazines) was evident in telephone "broadcasting" "channels" such as Budapest's Telefon Hirmondó and its American imitator, New Jersey's *Telephone Herald* (Marvin, 1988: 218–218). Despite the diffusion of public telephone booths during the early twentieth century, these adventures in phone-mediated broadcasting were undoubtedly the preserve of a wealthy minority. And yet their significance is manifold. They were hybrids of visual and oral culture, newspapers and the telephone, and they offered glimpses of what would come later with the rise of radio and television, as the classic one-to-many scheduled broadcasting model would become entrenched, even though phone broadcasting had provided for one-to-one and many-to-many interaction in public and semipublic settings.

ASSIMILATION AND PARASITISM

Media hybridity also arises when newer media are assimilated into, or are parasitical upon, institutions once established for older media.

For example, in its early years, the British telegraph was shaped by the signaling techniques developed by the rail networks. Railroad companies were among the early investors in telegraphy, and they, along with other private companies were bought up and placed under the control of the Post Office under the terms of the 1868 Telegraph Act (Briggs & Burke, 2009: 133). This Act, which laid the foundations for what would become known as "telecommunications policy," introduced a new understanding of telegraphic messages, one based upon previous conceptions of the postal service. From then on, twenty-word telegrams were to be subject to a uniform charge, a development that pleased the press, who were increasingly reliant upon the wires for communicating news. The British telephone system developed in a similar fashion. In 1880 the Post Office took over the phone network and ran it on a license and royalty basis until 1912, when full public control was established. And in 1904, the Wireless Telegraphy Act positioned the Post Office as the license-granting body at the center of a regulatory system for emerging wireless radio.

Telegraph and railroad companies were also closely aligned in the United States. Western Union capitalized on its links with railroad interests and by the 1890s it was carrying 80 percent of America's telegrams. Though there were calls for the U.S. Post Office to take over the company, the defenders of private monopoly successfully argued that a large, integrated system run by the private sector would be better for consumers and for future research and development. A similar approach was adopted with telephony. AT&T, established in 1885, grew quickly and in 1909 absorbed Western Union telegraphy. AT&T was exempted from the anti-trust Graham Act of 1921, and by the end of the 1930s, 83 percent of all U.S. telephones were under AT&T's control (Briggs & Burke, 2009: 145–146). When it came to wireless radio, the U.S. Postal Service did not assume the power enjoyed by its British counterpart, but the pattern of emergence from existing institutions was similar in some respects. For example, during the American radio mania of the early 1920s, many of the stations grew out of newspapers, universities, cities, and even local stores.

Similarly, the development of American national television networks was initially dependent upon long-distance telephone infrastructure. Before the emergence of cable and satellites, AT&T's lines and microwave towers were the only reliable means of distributing programming across a vast territory. Part of the revolutionary nature of cable television when it arrived later in the twentieth century was its ability to bypass this infrastructure. It was a hybrid assemblage of satellites, receiving antennae, wired cable distribution, and local and national content production that enabled commercial pioneers like CNN-founder Ted Turner to emerge as a powerful player alongside the national free-to-air television networks during the late 1970s. Turner's first "superstation," WTCG, took content first beamed to the Atlanta area and distributed it via satellite across the entire United States at the flick of a switch in 1976. And, though the principle of packet-switching that was so essential to the development of internet communications was initially rejected by AT&T in the 1960s (Wu, 2010: 174), before the break-up of the Bell system in the early 1980s, the ARPANET was hugely dependent upon AT&T's telephone network.

It is also often forgotten that from the 1960s to the 1990s the fate of home computing, and the idea of information-based computer networks more generally, was dependent upon developments in television. From its very beginnings, but especially after the FCC's 1969 ruling that American cable companies should provide local programming, cable television was often portrayed as a medium for the provision of a wide range of interactive information services. Firmly established in more than half of American homes by the mid-1980s, cable was the original "converged" medium for a "wired nation," as journalist Ralph Lee Smith dubbed the United States in a 1970 essay for the *Nation*, later published as a book (R. L. Smith, 1972). The values of the early cable television industry bore many similarities to the do-it-yourself and hacker values that played such an important role in the development of the internet from the 1970s onward.

Activist broadcasters such as Fred Friendly, who would later play a major role in the founding of PBS, pushed for public access cable television in New York during the late 1960s and hoped for cable channels that would be dedicated to political reporting and public debate (Wu, 2010: 183). Interactive television slowly stuttered into life during the 1970s, with the launch of local cable systems like QUBE in Columbus, Ohio, which featured interactive opinion polls. Across the advanced industrial economies, several so-called "viewdata" services were also launched, such as teletext or videotex. Designed for the display of text and very simple graphics on a television screen, viewdata services were delivered either by telephone line, cable, or wireless broadcasting. The British Post Office established Prestel (from the hybrid term "press telephone") in 1979, and several newspapers opted to become information providers on the Prestel network, though tellingly the majority were antagonistic. The French Minitel system was more successful, and persisted until 2012.

The interrelationship between television, telecommunications, and computing did not end there. Early home computers like the Commodore PET and the Sinclair Spectrum were designed to be viewed on a television. Their popularity was driven by games loaded into digital memory in suitably hybrid fashion via audio cassette players, but it was also due to their easy interface with what was already a familiar part of the domestic interior. And television interests soon weighed in on this new environment. The BBC, for example, launched its BBC Micro computer in 1981. And yet the sector could also be selective in its embrace of the television as a medium for digital communication. In the late 1980s, the BBC resisted the British government's plans to approve the expansion of cable television, just as the U.S. networks had done through a number of legal challenges targeted at cable companies from the late 1950s to the 1970s.

In many respects, therefore, television acted as the midwife of home computers and digital newer media. Competition, conflict, and interdependency among media and their publics—the characteristics of the hybrid media system—were in evidence once again, just as they were going all the way back to the emergence of print.

RESERVED DOMAINS

By now, it should be clear that throughout history the emergence of a newer medium is never a simple matter of the bursting into life of a revolutionary new technology that effortlessly finds a market and reconfigures culture, society, and politics. But nor is it about the simple and inevitable betrayal of the revolutionary change envisaged by a newer technology's founders and early adopters. It is a combination of these two processes. Even the most obviously superior media can become sidelined for years or even decades, as powerful interests seek to defuse their impact. There is contingency, competition, and rivalry; subterfuge and naked self-interest; delay and blockage. There are attempts by those in positions of power derived from associations with older media to create reserved domains in which that power can be maintained, at least until they have attempted to shape newer media in their own image (for the discussion of reserved domains see chapter 1). These forces can often have perverse effects, further contributing to systemic hybridity. The surprisingly slow development of American television and the utterly tortuous development of its frequency modulation (FM) radio (Wu, 2010: 125–135, 136–156) provide some of the best examples of older media's lingering power and the creation of reserved domains.

First trialed in public by the idealist inventor, Edwin Armstrong, FM radio was a major advance on the amplitude modulation (AM) technology that had fueled the extraordinary growth of the U.S. radio industry during the 1920s. FM had a much higher signal to noise ratio and better sound quality. Unlike AM, FM required low power transmitters and was more efficient and cheaper to run. In the early 1930s, FM had the potential to create a second wave of radio innovation, but it was not to be. Edwin Armstrong was hired in the 1920s by his old friend and fellow amateur radio enthusiast, David Sarnoff. By the end of the decade, Sarnoff had become the legendary president of the Radio Corporation of America (RCA) and director of the U.S. National Broadcasting Company (NBC). By 1934, Armstrong's FM technology had been perfected, but Sarnoff and the RCA, backed by industry body the Radio Trust, deliberately stalled its further development for fear of undermining the business model they had established with AM. Sarnoff broke up Armstrong's lab in the Empire State Building and spent the next twenty years employing a variety of methods to stall the replacement of AM by what was clearly a superior technology.

By the 1930s, the American radio industry had established a large, government-sanctioned business based on advertising across its AM networks. Sarnoff and the Radio Trust conducted a public campaign to cast doubt on FM as a replacement for AM. These arguments jelled with others calling for a focus on television as the promising new medium of the era and they were given forceful backing by the RCA-NBC broadcasting duopoly that emerged in the 1930s. The AM radio industry successfully pushed the FCC to effectively ban the granting of commercial FM station licenses between 1934 and 1940, and RCA refused to switch to manufacturing FM radio sets. When the regulatory thaw came after World War II, the new structure crippled FM. The FCC placed strict power limits on FM transmitters, a move that required FM stations to buy new machinery and instantly condemned four hundred thousand consumer radio sets to obsolescence. Almost twenty years after its inception, FM was dealt a huge blow from which it would not recover until the 1970s. AM remained alive and well, and would continue to dominate the U.S. radio landscape for decades.

Similar forces shaped the early years of American television. By the end of the 1920s, mechanical television was a proven if fragile technology. A nascent independent industry was, however, beginning to form. In its early phase, it was characterized by competition among different inventors, such as John Baird, Charles Jenkins, and Philo Farnsworth. But powerful radio interests, most obviously David Sarnoff (again) of RCA and NBC, wished to mold television in the image of commercial radio. Sarnoff wanted to see the new medium develop according to the advertising and mass entertainment model that he had perfected with AM. More than that, following what he perceived would be a simple translation of radio programming into the new medium of television, Sarnoff wanted established radio industry players to run television in a similar regulatory environment of FCC-sanctioned oligopoly. As he did with radio, Sarnoff successfully lobbied the FCC, who were already receptive due to their desire to see such a valuable national resource led by what they saw as responsible and experienced industrial leaders. Sarnoff convinced the FCC that television was an immature technology that ought to be delayed because it was not ready for marketing to the public. As a consequence, the FCC restricted its licensing program to strictly experimental operators and refused to countenance commercial television for more than a decade. In the meantime, Sarnoff brazenly stole Philo Farnsworth's electronic television technology and went on to gain a decisive advantage with the launch of RCA's television system at the 1939 World's Fair in New York. Not surprisingly, RCA television was a lot like commercial AM radio— with pictures.

The creation and protection of reserved domains also shaped the development of American cable television. The cable pioneers of the 1940s established primitive but effective systems for retransmitting free-to-air television across physical wires to those areas where the signals were weak. As the technologies of retransmission improved and cable operators began to bring in content from other areas, the free-to-air networks began to see them as a threat to the dependable audiences that provided their advertising revenues. Legal challenges to the cable industry followed, based upon arguments that cable was infringing intellectual property rights through retransmitting content without permission. These resulted in a landmark Supreme Court decision in 1968, which found that the cable operators were not liable, but they also led to an FCC ruling banning cable companies from the hundred largest urban areas in the United States, as part of an attempt to boost the development of ultra-high frequency (UHF) television—a move that severely hindered the development of cable until a series of rulings undid the restrictions and brought the industry within the pale of existing copyright law in the late 1970s (Wu, 2010: 180–181). By that stage, cable was being transformed by entrepreneurs like Ted Turner, the founder of CNN, into either a commercial subscription model or one based upon entertainment and niche advertising. And yet traces of the medium's origins in the interactive and data services model continued in the form of local public access networks and C-SPAN and can be seen today in the role that cable companies have played in promoting broadband internet infrastructure. Nobody would pretend that cable television has been an unqualified boost to American democracy, but by eventually loosening the grip of CBS, NBC, and ABC, it changed the face of American broadcast media and it served to embed many of the values that went on to inform the popularization of the internet: individual control, niche content, information services, customization, and diversity, albeit within limits.

Digital Newer Media

How do digital newer media and the internet fit into this brief history of media hybridity?

In common with previous newer media, digital media have borrowed heavily from print traditions. The basic and familiar "page" organizes a vast array of online material and it is still difficult to imagine the internet without this metaphor. Since the early human–computer interfaces of the 1950s, the physical spaces and objects for organizing printed materials in the modern organization—desktops, files, folders, and so on—have also become synonymous with digital interfaces of various kinds. Bibliographic metaphors, and the practices associated with libraries and books as social institutions, were important in shaping the prototype internet of the 1950s and they remain so: in 2012, Google's search still refers to all of its web objects as "documents." The classic visionary texts of early computing, Vannevar Bush's *As We May Think* (1945) and Joseph Licklider's *Libraries of the Future* (1965) sought to create systems that would free societies from the rigid and bureaucratic capture of information, but these texts were full of references to the print culture into which the internet was born. Records, files, cabinets, desktops, shelves, cards, microfilm, and paper all played important roles in the sketches of what would later become the ARPANET (Gitelman, 2006: 98–121).

Licklider's approach was shaped by the international scientific community's concerns about the growth of published information during the post-1945 research boom. The document, broken down into its bibliographically-defined constituent parts, was seen as the canonical unit, and its efficient storage and retrieval the answer to the growing mountains of paper generated by government and corporations. Information increasingly came to be seen as a disembodied commodity consisting of sources of data that were capable of being processed and measured in identifiable quantities. Information was perceived as self-evidently growing, a resource to be exploited. The idea of the "information society" also originates in the early 1960s, as Fritz Machlup's economic analysis of the "production and distribution of knowledge" in the United States came to displace an older view of information as a shifting but finite resource innate in social relationships and passed down and exchanged between individuals in discrete social contexts (Crawford, 1983).

Yet if digital newer media have been influenced by print, they have also been influenced by—and have coevolved with—a surprising array of other media. In Lev Manovich's convincing account (2001) today's digital media are best seen as products of the co-development of visual media and computerization. The point of origin here goes all the way back to the 1830s, when modern photography arrived in the shape of the daguerreotype. Photography then went on to influence broadcast media's affordances for recording, manipulating, and displaying sound and images. But the 1830s also saw the birth (of sorts) of modern computing, with Charles Babbage's Analytical Engine, a prototype mechanical "computer" theoretically capable of mathematical calculations. Computerization, a twentieth-century development whose pace quickened after the Second World War, introduced the principle of digitizing analog media artifacts so that they could be manipulated as data. In this interpretation, the development of digital new media is actually the outcome of the coevolution of "media machines" and "computing machines." After all, during the 1890s, when photography was being turned into moving images by Edison and the Lumière brothers, the U.S. census was also being transformed by Hollerith's electric punch-card tabulating machines. In 1936, when Konrad Zuse built the first operational digital computer, the medium on which he recorded binary instructions was, of all things, second-hand 35mm cinema film (Manovich, 2001: 25).

It might seem surprising, but digital media and the internet owe a lot to film and cinema (Manovich, 2001: 78). Digitization rests upon the sampling of points in time so that those moments may later be manipulated. Film recording, editing, and projection all rely on the same principles, and have done since the emergence of prototype projection devices such as Eadweard Muybridge's now-famous Zoopraxiscope (1879), which conveyed movement by rotating still photographs that had first been captured from different perspectives. Digital media interfaces routinely combine moving images with audio and text, but text-based intertitles and musical sequences have also been staples of cinema since its very beginnings in the late nineteenth century. Cinema relies upon frame, screen, and window metaphors; so do almost all computing devices. Cinematic visual techniques such as zooming, tracking, and point-of-view are to be found in many online interfaces. Computer games are obvious examples that rely upon cinematic (and novelistic) genres to achieve their realism and fantasy effects, but at the same time games rely on "augmented reality" applications for displaying ambient information about a player's environment. Video sharing sites such as YouTube and Vimeo can be seen as descendants of the early twentieth-century "cinema of the attractions" (simple films depicting events such as fast-moving trains) that preceded the emergence of narrative cinema (Rizzo, 2008). Digital media are often considered to be "new" due to their affordance for interactivity and engagement, but as Erik Bucy convincingly argues, the concept of interactivity is far from straightforward: it may be a product of a technology, a communication context, or individually-held perceptions (2004: 376). For example, post-1920s "modern" cinematic style has been dominated by techniques consciously designed to heighten cognitive engagement among the audience and to visually represent human thought, such as montage and fast cutaway editing. Interactivity is not exclusively the product of a physical encounter with a media object, such as clicking a hyperlink.

The hybrid development of digital newer media was also influenced by a radically different medium, one that also influenced television: radar. During the 1930s and 1940s, radar embedded the idea of a screen that could be updated in real time according to the data being monitored. This was a significant departure from photography and film, which were based on the capture and storage of events that would then be played back in a predictable sequence and without further intervention from the audience. Digital media environments have steadily integrated the affordances of photography and film, but they have also made extensive use of radar's "real-time screen" as an interface whose elements are manipulated in order to allow us to act upon information. This concept of a display-of-the-present that enables user intervention was an important break with older media (Manovich, 2001: 99–103). It quickened the processes of mediation and it enabled acting in real time over great distances (Manovich, 2001: 169). In James Beniger's (1986) account of technological evolution, such monitorial technologies reveal a growing "systemness," as communication and information flows of all kinds become more central to the controlled and functional integration of modern societies.

Building upon these aspects of digital media, the internet has been based upon the continuous assembly, disassembly, and reassembly of modular data. Its read-write environment is based on an assortment of text, still images, audio, and video, some originally analog, some digitally native, pulled in from scattered databases and acted upon in real time by human and software agents. As David Weinberger has argued, the internet contributes to a new "order of order" where the systems for categorizing and organizing information now transcend the limitations of the pre-digital realm (Weinberger, 2007). The internet's assorted hardware, such as graphics and sound processors, monitors, and telecommunication networks, also contribute to its deep hybridity as a medium. During the early period of its expansion in the 1990s, web pages were relatively simple, but since then the internet has increasingly come to rely upon dynamically-generated applications and other objects created in real time according to pre-programmed scripts and routines, not to mention a huge and diverse array of real-time human interventions. It has become almost nonsensical to imagine such a thing as an unmodified web "page." Static web sites, like the Geocities home pages that once flourished in the 1990s, are now the subject of nostalgic parody. We can put this another way by borrowing terms from systems theory. The internet is less "autopoietic" than it is "allopoietic." Autopoietic systems are closed, boundaried, and self-reproduce through the interactions of their internal practices. This concept has recently found favor among those seeking to argue, on the basis of the work of Niklas Luhmann, for the distinctiveness of a new online media culture (Deuze, 2006, 2007). Allopoietic systems, in contrast, are open, receive a variety of inputs and produce a variety of outputs, and are created by combinations of forces and resources external to those systems (Kickert, 1993). This seems to better capture the hybrid nature of the internet.

Yet there is a paradox here. Immense speed and transience—the flow of real-time communication and the simultaneous multitasking facilitated by the interfaces of computerized media devices—is now everywhere accompanied by immense archival permanence, very much in the spirit of Licklider's and Bush's original ideas from the 1940s and 1950s. Like early television and radio's relative lack of scheduling and prerecording, the internet encourages what Philip Auslander has termed "liveness," (2008: 11–24) and this is not only based upon real-time mediation but also interactivity. The nature of liveness in today's hybridized real-time flows of communication is a theme that recurs throughout this book. But for every example of liveness or even temporal indeterminacy (like web pages without dates or the incessant flows of Twitter and Facebook updates) there are also examples of what we might call "time-stamp culture." Real-time flows of information are more prevalent than ever, but online, in what is an important break with broadcasting, there has also been a backlash against flow and transience and a strong promotion of the archival. The shift toward the adoption of global standards on metadata means that many digital objects, from web pages to digital photographs to digital video files, have their provenance embedded, making tracking and tracing much easier. Marking updates with correct time stamps has become a source of pride among bloggers and some professional journalists. The internet is becoming the archive par excellence. And because the manipulation of discrete digital artifacts such as audio, video, images, and text stored in databases has now become the norm in the production of *all* media content—from newspapers to broadcasting—reusable pieces of information flow across media in the form of ready-made resources from which journalists, politicians, and sometimes citizens can quickly construct and publish new narratives. Even the most ephemeral and locationally-specific of media, like street art, have been given a new permanence and solidity by the internet, as artists like Banksy and Shepard Fairey will attest after finding that their work has reached massive audiences through online circulation. Being able to access and repurpose existing media artifacts is dependent upon the existence of networked databases that allow content to flow and be sifted, sorted, tagged, and continuously augmented. Digital production encourages disaggregation and disassembly, but also reaggregation and reassembly. The rise of these modular representational dissections of events has also gone hand in hand with the proliferation of online video as well as consumer technologies such as the hard-disk-based digital video recorder, which further contribute to the democratization of the archival.

3

The Contemporary Contexts of Hybridity

In this chapter I move from the past to the present and establish the broad contours of media system hybridity in contemporary Britain and the United States. My aim here is to lay some contextual foundations for the more detailed analyses of the hybrid media system in flow, which comprise chapters 4 to 9. In this chapter I focus on four overarching themes: the nature of audiences, shifting patterns of media use, the structure of broadcasting, newspaper, and online media, and the rise of new hybrid forms of mediality. Though the sources of evidence are somewhat different, the chapter is, in many respects the latest installment of the ongoing history of media hybridity I traced in chapter 2.

I turn first to Britain, which is the context of my analysis of news making in chapter 4 and the discussion of sense making in media and political fields in chapters 8 and 9. Britain also forms an important part of the context of my interpretation of WikiLeaks in chapter 7.

Britain

By the late 2000s, multi-channel digital television had reached more than 80 percent of British households and in several areas of the country, such as Scotland and the northwest of England, penetration rates were much higher[1] (U.K. Office for National Statistics, 2009: 4). Television news channels continue to grow in number, and a panoply of different news forms now exists in the broadcasting environment, from short bulletins and soft news content on the entertainment channels, to relatively detailed "serious" coverage on BBC Radio Four, to round-the-clock treatments on channels such as Sky News, the BBC News Channel, Euronews, and even the BBC Parliament channel. There is no shortage of political news in contemporary Britain but audiences are increasingly fragmented across the channels, the schedules, and the quasi-scheduled time-shifting environments of digital video recorders, the BBC's multiplatform iPlayer, and mobile video applications. As part of an evolving process of adaptation and renewal, broadcasting has become ever more concerned with offering audiences customizable, personally tailored modes of consumption and interaction.

By any standards, the British public's use of the internet has grown at a remarkable rate over the past two decades. About 73 percent of households now have access, up from 58 percent in 2003 (Oxford Internet Survey, 2011). Just as significantly, 96 percent of all households that have the internet use a broadband connection (Oxford Internet Survey, 2009: 4). The diversity of means by which individuals can access information online has also increased. The internet is no longer a computer-based medium. Mobile access has grown in popularity and is continuing to grow: by 2009, 20 percent of internet users owned a mobile smartphone (such as an Apple iPhone) or a mobile broadband device that they plug into their laptop computer (Oxford Internet Survey, 2009: 9). Mobile phone adoption more generally has reached extraordinary levels in Britain: in 2008, there were 74 million mobile phone accounts for a population of 60 million (U.K. Office of Communications, 2008).

This new diversity of opportunities for internet access plays an important role in creating multi-tasking lifestyles in multi-connection households. Around a quarter of those with satellite or cable television use it to access the internet. About a third (32 percent) use a mobile device to access the internet while in the home—a figure that trebled between 2005 and 2009, reflecting the popularity of wireless handheld devices with built-in web browsers, e-mail, messaging software, and applications provided by the major online social network providers. Hybrid consumption patterns are strongly emerging among some sections of the public. By the late 2000s, 71 percent of internet users reported "doing more than one activity while online, such as listening to music, watching TV, or using the telephone" (Oxford Internet Survey, 2009: 12, 36). The very recent shift toward tablet computing, with Apple's iPad having sold 55 million units since its 2009 launch, has intensified these trends (Associated Press, 2012).

The most startling change since the mid-2000s comes in the form of mass participation in the creation of online content, as British media and the public alike have not escaped the global wave of web 2.0 and social media. It is easy to forget just how quickly this shift has come about. It has been fueled by the enormous growth of blogs, online social network sites such as Facebook and Twitter, collaborative production sites such as Wikipedia, and news aggregators and discussion sites such as Digg, Reddit, Yahoo Buzz, and the BBC's Have Your Say, to name but a few examples (Chadwick, 2009). By the late 2000s, almost half (49 percent) of British internet users maintained a profile on an online social network site, more than a fifth (22 percent) regularly updated a blog, and more than a quarter (27 percent) participated in online discussion. Older online communication forms such as instant messaging (64 percent of users) and e-mail (97 percent) are now quite simply ubiquitous in British society (Oxford Internet Survey, 2009: 21).

There are some signs that internet use is displacing time previously spent by the British public on other media, though typically the patterns are unclear and television news is retaining its dominance in key respects. In 2009, non-internet users spent an average of twenty-five hours per week watching terrestrial television, but internet users spent only fifteen hours per week. Equally significant are the different usage patterns that appear to be opening up between the internet and television. Thirty percent of those who use the internet perceive it to be their most important source of information—ahead of television (11 percent), newspapers (seven percent), and radio (six percent) (Oxford Internet Survey, 2009: 33). According to the Oxford Internet Survey of 2007, among internet users, levels of trust in the internet as a source of information were higher than for television and newspapers (Oxford Internet Survey, 2007). And yet the flagship British television news shows remain remarkably powerful. Following a period of decline in the 1990s, between 2004 and 2009 the scheduled news bulletins on the major terrestrial channels—BBC1, ITV, Channel 4, and Channel Five—lost only 200,000 viewers. Younger people are much less likely to watch television news, raising the question of whether these age groups will eventually adopt the habits of their parents, but overall there has been no dramatic systemic decline in the audiences for British television news since the early 2000s (U.K. Office of Communications, 2010). Television has adapted. We also need to unpick those data from 2007 about levels of trust in the internet as a source of information, because in Britain the highly trusted public service media organization, the BBC, has, over the last fifteen years built its own gigantic online presence.

It does seem clear, however, that television's traditional monopoly on news is loosening, not only because online news sites are more prepared to take risks by publishing stories without the standards of verification usually required of professional journalists, but also because the horizontal nature of social media communication now means it is much more likely that news will spread across interpersonal networks before official press releases are issued. Some big political news stories now break first online and are picked up by television and print journalists who obsessively follow their e-mail, Twitter, Facebook, and blog feeds in the hunt for new leads. I cover these dynamics in much greater detail later in this book.

At the same time, however, major British television and newspaper journalists like the BBC's Political Editor Nick Robinson and ITV's Business Editor Laura Kuennsberg have adapted and now often "scoop" themselves by releasing their own stories online long before they officially file their reports or go into the newsroom to record a broadcast package for the evening news. And it must also be noted that the large, dedicated news organizations, particularly the BBC, share vast amounts of content internally across their web and television divisions. This provides them with an ongoing structural advantage when it comes to breaking news. While British newspapers and commercial broadcasters are certainly under pressure, BBC broadcasting is in a stronger position, largely as a result of the publicly funded license fee. Despite complaints of unfair competition, the BBC continues to build a sophisticated web presence which, by 2011, was attracting more than forty million monthly unique visitors (Shearman, 2011). It has adopted many of the features used by other news organizations, such as stories with comments, message boards, and chat rooms, and it also integrates citizen-generated video into its news narratives, especially during exceptional events: good examples include the London underground bombings of 2005 and the G20 protests of 2009. The BBC also has the hugely successful iPlayer, which runs on computers, mobile phones, and tablet devices, but is increasingly integrated into new televisions, satellite and cable television set-top boxes, gaming devices such as Microsoft's XBox and Nintendo's Wii, not to mention a whole host of devices like the Slingbox or Apple TV that enable users to send streamed video wirelessly from their computers or smartphones to their television screens.

Television therefore shows signs of resilience and of the successful creation of reserved domains of power. The story is more complex for British print media. Nowhere have the pressures of the changing media system been more strongly felt than in the British newspaper industry. Declining print edition circulations, increasing online readerships, competition from free papers and online news providers and blogs, shrinking and more thinly spread advertising revenues, and the economic recession of the late

2000s have all taken their toll on traditional British newspapers. And yet, even here there is an important story of adaptation and continuing power.

Like their American counterparts, for whom the pressures are eerily similar, British print media are in the middle of a painful transition toward new models of organization, production, and distribution. Part of this story is now familiar. Readership of print editions across all newspaper sectors has been in decline for several decades due to competition from television. But the internet accelerated this trend and introduced new forces. As in America, British newspapers' initial reaction to the internet in the 1990s was to ignore it in the hope that it might prove to be a fad. This was soon followed by a strategy of placing the content of the printed version of a paper onto a website in the hope of attracting sufficient "eyeballs" to generate advertising revenue. Some papers, such as the *Financial Times*, experimented early on with subscription models, only to scale these back due to a lack of subscribers and the lure of the advertising model when times were good during the economic boom of the mid-2000s. When times got hard during the advertising recession of the late 2000s, they tried again with the pay-per-view model. Many local and regional papers either lacked the resources to develop their own websites or stayed out of the game entirely for fear that they would cannibalize their print editions. The circulations of British local and regional printed newspapers fell by almost 40 percent between 1989 and 2009 (U.K. Office of Fair Trading, 2009: 12).

It now seems clear that the pay-per-view model can be made to work online where an outlet has a distinctive niche, as is the case with the *Financial Times* and the *Wall Street Journal*. By April 2012, almost half (47 percent) of the *Financial Times*'s paying readers subscribed to its digital editions (Financial Times, 2012). It remains to be seen whether more general news outlets can also make this model work. In June 2010, two of Rupert Murdoch's News Corporation's online news sites, the *Times* and the *Sunday Times*, were placed behind a "paywall." By January 2012, the *Times* had 119,255 digital subscribers, of whom roughly half were iPad users, and a print circulation of 405,113. However, print circulation of the paper has also declined steeply since the digital subscription model began. For example, it fell by 24,441, or 5.7 percent, during just a five-month period from September 2011 to January 2012 (O'Carroll, 2012). The other national newspapers have experimented with paid models, but none has chosen to follow the Murdoch press. Even the *Daily Mail*, whose online offerings have soared in popularity both in Britain and abroad over the last few years to reach more than fifty million monthly visitors by 2012, remains wedded to its print edition and its website advertising-and-eyeballs model, not least because the web edition only generates 2.6 percent of the *Mail*'s total revenue (Economist, 2012).

Google now dominates the online advertising market, but online the revenue per reader is substantially smaller than for traditional printed classified advertising. Ceding in-house control over advertising mechanisms to an external company (Google) with a near-monopoly in its market is also unattractive for newspaper owners and editors. At the regional and local levels, where 80 percent of papers' income derives from advertising, the press have long relied upon classified ads to sustain themselves, but revenues from these have almost halved since the late-1990s, due to competition from online outlets such as eBay and Craigslist (U.K. Office of Fair Trading, 2009: 10).

There are signs, however, that advertising-and-eyeballs may soon start to pay off. By the mid-2000s, spending on internet advertising as a whole had eclipsed spending on print advertising. By 2011 it had also eclipsed spending on television advertising (Sweney, 2011). News consumption habits among the British are also shifting. In 2007, the number of internet users who reported that they read a "newspaper or news service" online stood at 30 percent. In the space of just two years, this number almost doubled, to reach 58 percent (Oxford Internet Survey, 2009: 32). More generally, by 2009 75 percent of internet users reported reading news online, though this included non-newspaper sources such as blogs (Oxford Internet Survey, 2009: 20). Most strikingly, the growth in newspapers' online editions contrasts starkly with the decline of their printed editions. According to data from the UK Office of Fair Trading, from 1987 to 2007, annual sales of national newspapers declined by roughly a third. Between 1998 and 2007 sales fell quite sharply for the print editions of all the national papers except the *Daily Star* and the *Daily Mail* (U.K. Office of Fair Trading 2008). Yet during the 2000s the websites of all of the national newspapers saw massive growth, with the *Mail* and the *Telegraph* more than doubling their monthly unique users in just a two-year period between 2008 and 2010 and the *Guardian* showing strong growth in its online readership (Chadwick & Stanyer, 2010). Now, about one-fifth of the *Guardian's* revenue comes from its online news and two-thirds of its approximately thirty-two million monthly visitors are from outside Britain, with one-third living in America. Many newspapers are adapting and are now beginning to consolidate their roles as some of the most powerful players in online news (Economist, 2012).

An example of the enduring power of the traditional newspapers but also of how this power is refracted through the prism of the hybrid media system is the furor over British MPs' expenses in 2009—arguably the Westminster Parliament's most serious crisis since the emergence of British democracy. Huge quantities of data on MPs' expenses claims were leaked from Parliament in digitized form on optical discs. The *Daily Telegraph* took the initiative, with its decision to purchase the discs for £150,000 and to run, in print and online, an extended series of revelations about MPs' fraudulent expenses claims, spanning almost three weeks in May 2009 (BBC News Online, 2012). The newspaper employed a team of researchers who took a total of ten days to sift through the data and extract the most damaging documents. The paper also carefully staged each day's new releases to cause the maximum impact on other media. Frequent television appearances and blog posts by the paper's political columnist, Benedict Brogan, were a key part of this. Broadcast news and political blogs engaged in a sustained feeding frenzy as day after day MPs' expenses were the top story across all news outlets. This was an example of "old-fashioned" and well-resourced investigative journalism, but with a difference: the hybrid media system accelerated and amplified the news and distributed the information across all platforms. As the *Telegraph* released information online and in printed form, other news organizations were able to pick up the new revelations and run their own stories. And, in a final twist, some weeks later, when Parliament officially released what amounted to 458,000 pages of data, the *Guardian* symbolically thumbed its nose at the *Telegraph* by starting its own "crowdsourcing" campaign to publish yet more revelations. In a response to Parliament's censoring of the files, the *Guardian* published the entire database on its website and invited ordinary readers to identify, log, and discuss the MPs' expenses claims. By November 2009, its readers had reviewed 225,000 pages (Guardian, 2009). So in addition to revealing the ongoing influence of older media logics, this episode also revealed the growing importance of the internet, not just as a channel for the communication of information, but also as a mechanism of organization and networked collective action in the creation of news. This is one of the key aspects of media system hybridity I explore throughout the rest of this book.

The older British news organizations have also responded to the threat of blogs and social media by appropriating internet genres as a way of generating audience loyalty. A key development is online social interaction. Despite early resistance during the 1990s and 2000s, during the last half decade interactive commenting spaces have flourished in online news. Space for reader participation is now less tightly restricted and reader's views are much more visible across all online news platforms. All of the major British news sites now have well-established interactive features, such as op-ed columns with open commenting, message boards, and blogs. The major newspapers' and the BBC's message boards receive hundreds of thousands of comments per month. Readers are also now encouraged, and sometimes paid, to submit video footage and other user-generated material to news sites. Twitter, Facebook, and Flickr are important trawling grounds for professional journalists looking to source pictures and video. National news organizations are also attempting to position themselves as online social networking hubs, where, in addition to reporting and debating political developments, a reader can post pictures, socialize, or even set up a date. In 2010, the websites of the *Daily Express*, the *Star*, and the *Daily Telegraph* began allowing their readers to set up their own blogs. The adaptation of news organizations to the digital media environment is creating new opportunities for citizens to engage in political debate and express their opinions in new environments like blogs, Facebook, and Twitter, but these spaces are also now occupied by and in some cases directly provided by older media actors.

This is not to say that alternative online news sites do not attract significant audiences or exercise meaningful power. Some high profile British blogs attract a relatively large readership. For example, Paul Staines's Guido Fawkes blog attracts around 350,000 unique visitors per month and regularly averages 100,000 daily page views. In 2008, Staines had a 2.3 percent share of overall blog visits in Britain and another Conservative blogger, Iain Dale, had a 1.9 percent share. Though these are small audiences when compared with those for blogs at the BBC and the *Guardian*, which had a combined 33 percent share over the same period, things are surprisingly finely balanced. If we set aside the BBC and *Guardian* blogs, alternative online news looks remarkably competitive, because Dale and Guido Fawkes have never been too far behind the mainstream newspaper blogs of the *Times* and the *Telegraph* (Goad, 2008).

A further factor here is that cost-cutting has contributed to the undermining of the authority of professional broadcast and newspaper journalism. Creating timely, relevant, and challenging news is an expensive business, especially if a story involves an investigative element. However, the revenues to support this kind of activity have been falling for several years. Almost all commercial news organizations and the BBC have seen deep cuts and radical restructuring of staff and budgets (Davies, 2008). Writers and editors in what were once powerhouses of in-depth reporting and commentary, such as the *Observer* and the *Sunday Times*, now sit side-by-side with upstart individual or group blogs, most of which have a keen awareness of niche interests and very short news cycles. The top political bloggers in Britain regularly produce articles that are indistinguishable from those published in the op-ed sections of newspapers. Bloggers have low overheads and some have large readerships, solid advertising revenues, and other sources of income that they derive from their role in the hybrid media system, such as appearance and speaking fees. Freed from the bureaucracy of the professional newsroom, some bloggers are also able to conduct background investigations and move among political and media elites, as we shall see at various points throughout this book. One example is Paul Staines, whose long-running series of exposés about former Labour government minister Peter Hain in 2008 culminated in damaging revelations about the origins of donations to Hain's campaign fund for the deputy leadership of the Labour Party. These were partly instrumental in Hain's decision to resign his ministerial post and this was widely reported as the first victory of the British "blogosphere."

There are limitations, however, to interpreting episodes like this solely as the result of the heroic power of online media. During the spring of 2009, the leak to Staines of an e-mail exchange between Gordon Brown's special advisor Damian McBride and former Blair adviser turned Labour blogger Derek Draper shed an unflattering light on Downing Street's approach to media management. "Smeargate," as it became known, revealed a plan by McBride to establish a supposedly independent website called Red Rag that would contain personalized attacks on leading Conservative politicians and their families. The story was shaped by the interaction of older and newer media logics. It involved a right-wing blogger, (Staines) whose website, Guido Fawkes, emulates classic British tabloid journalism, with its mix of innuendo, gossip, and rumor. But Staines's "scoop" was dependent upon the support of two traditional British newspapers, for Staines did not publish the contents of the Draper–McBride e-mails on his blog but instead handed them to journalists at the *Daily Telegraph* and the *Sunday Times*, who duly broke the stories and shared the credit.

An often-rehearsed criticism of bloggers is that they are "amateurs" who lack the professionalism and ethical standards of trained journalists (see for example Keen, 2007). Bloggers have been accused of being less discerning in what they publish and as likely to disseminate unsubstantiated political gossip as much as genuine political news. However, some of the popular British bloggers have now moved toward hybrid, semi-professional models of organization along the lines pioneered by the *Huffington Post* in the United States (discussed below), or they have been co-opted in the service of professional journalism. In 2011, successful Conservative blogger Iain Dale set up a "current affairs mega blog" which has a group of almost seventy writers. And in 2012, Paul Staines started writing columns for the print edition of the established newspaper, the *Daily Star*.

Despite all of these developments online, older news media organizations continue to play the pivotal roles in British politics. The media professionals at the heart of these organizations have their reserved domains of power. As we shall see in chapters 8 and 9, they remain deeply embedded in the routines and insider networks of Westminster, Whitehall, and the major metropolitan centers. They interact with politicians and senior civil servants on a daily basis in the Westminster lobby system, which, by its very nature has an exclusive membership—one that does not include bloggers. Politicians still largely stage their media interventions to coincide with the rhythms of the broadcasting and newspaper newsrooms, which remain important routes to large audiences and maximum publicity. Older media organizations have the collective financial and organizational resources to outscoop exclusively online upstarts, and to leapfrog newer media outlets with the launch of expensive new initiatives such as online television delivery platforms like the iPlayer and ever more elaborate web environments that *combine* editorial authority *and* popular participation. As chapters 8 and 9 will reveal more fully, the patterns of sense making among political staff, journalists, and activists suggest that in this hybrid system older media logics increasingly operate in relations of interdependence with newer media logics: professional news organizations increasingly capitalize on newer media as a resource, tapping into the viral circulation of online content and weaving it into their news genres and production techniques, while also regularly engaging and interacting with newer media actors.

The United States

Similar hybrid forces now shape the media system of the contemporary United States, which forms the context of my interpretation of election campaigning in chapters 5 and 6, and of my discussion of WikiLeaks and news making in chapter 7.

To get things underway, consider Bruce Williams and Michael Delli Carpini's powerfully concise summary of the current situation in America, which they gleaned from data from the U.S. Census Bureau, Media Dynamics Inc., and the Pew Research Center Internet and American Life Project. It is worth quoting at length:

> To list the developments in communications that have occurred over the past twenty-five years is to be reminded of how radically different the media environment of the early twenty-first century is from what preceded it. For example, in 1982, as Shanto Iyengar and Donald Kinder were doing the research for their seminal work on the agenda-setting power of television news, *News That Matters*, fewer than 2 million personal computers were sold in the United States; the average home received approximately ten television channels; only 21 percent of American homes had a VCR; and the internet and mobile phones were, for all intents and purposes, nonexistent. By the late 2000s, annual U.S. computer sales had grown to 250 million, more than three-quarters of U.S. households had at least one personal computer, the average number of channels received had increased to more than 130, greater than 90 percent of homes had VCRs and/or DVD players, more than three-quarters of U.S. households had an internet connection (and more than 50 percent had high-speed connections), the number of websites increased from about 100 (in 1993) to more than 160 million, more than three-quarters of adult Americans had a cell phone or PDA (Personal Digital Assistant), and nearly one-third of households had a digital video recorder (DVR) such as TiVo.
>
> On any given day in December 2009, more than seven of every ten adult Americans went online. And what do people do when they go online?.... [Consider] the extensive and diverse range of activities engaged in by sizable percentages of people who use the internet, ranging from sending or reading e-mail (90 percent), to seeking directions (86 percent), looking for medical information (80 percent), buying a product (75 percent), seeking news (72 percent), visiting a government website (66 percent), watching a video (62 percent), seeking out political information (60 percent), social networking (47 percent), reading a blog (39 percent), playing online games

(35 percent), and donating to a charitable cause (19 percent).... [Consider] the generally still small but collectively revealing percentages of "wired" adults who act as information producers by sending e-mails (90 percent), sending instant messages (39 percent), uploading photos (37 percent), sending text messages (35 percent), rating a product (31 percent), tagging online content (28 percent), sharing files (27 percent), posting comments to a newsgroup or blog (22 percent), participating in a chat-room discussion (22 percent), sharing something online that they created (21 percent), creating content specifically for the internet (19 percent), creating their own web pages (14 percent), working on someone else's webpage (13 percent), creating their own blogs (12 percent), remixing existing online material (11 percent), and/or creating an online avatar (6 percent) (Williams & Delli Carpini, 2011: 77, 84–85).

These developments have both shaped and are shaped by shifting patterns of media use. American television audiences have fragmented over the last three decades. Contrast broadcast television's heyday—the mid-1960s era of 6.8 stations per household and duplicate programming (Prior, 2007)—with the early twenty-first century, when 85 percent of American households face a bewildering yet empowering choice of several hundred cable television channels, and when about 78 percent of the public can access vast swathes of online content (International Telecommunication Union, 2011). Americans are continuing their love affair with television, but they are increasingly switching their attention from just a few general channels to a broad range of channels and platforms that cater to niche interests. Advertisers and program makers have responded to this by creating ever more differentiated content. In 2009, the average number of television channels watched per week in the United States was 16, with just 2.2 hours per viewer devoted to each channel. From the early 1980s to the early 2000s the big three broadcast networks—ABC, CBS, and NBC—lost around a third of their audience share. When it comes to television news, cable national news audiences overtook nightly network news in the mid-2000s. Local television news is also under threat as a result of the recent declines in advertising income. Network news retains its dominance during important events such as elections and recent disasters like the 9/11 attacks and Hurricane Katrina, though even here the growth of cable has been very strong: the cable audience for election night in November 2008 was 27.2 million, close to the 32.9 million for the networks. News programming has changed over the last decade, too, as greater competition and cost-cutting have diminished the amount of investigative and basic journalism while increasing the quantity of talk shows driven by opinionated "celebrity" news anchors. At the same time, there has been an insurgence of alternative sources of news, such as late-night comedy, reality shows, socially engaged television drama, cinema, and music, which blur the boundaries between news and entertainment and often engage and educate viewers in politically relevant ways. All of these trends are stronger among younger segments of the population, but as the young age, they carry these habits forward through the life course (Williams & Delli Carpini, 2011: 78–79, 82).

At the same time, however, we need to exercise some balance when interpreting these trends. Audiences may be more fragmented and the range of media much greater, but television is still hugely dominant for the American public. In fact, while Americans are now consuming more media than ever before, they are also watching more television than at any point in the nation's history. Measuring these things can be like walking through a minefield, but according to respected industry research company Nielsen, in 2011 television was still six times more popular than the internet. By then, around 289 million Americans were watching an average of 159 hours per month of television, compared with a total of 191 million who were using the internet on a computer for an average of 26 hours per month (Nielsen, 2011a).

There are, however, interesting trends in the area of video. By 2011, around 142 million Americans were watching video on the internet for an average of five hours per month, while 29 million were watching video on a mobile phone for an average of four hours per month (Nielsen, 2011a). These figures may be small when compared with those for traditional television, but they are still significant, and they grew substantially during the late 2000s: between 2008 and 2011 time spent watching video on the internet using a computer grew by 80 percent, while time spent watching video on a mobile phone grew by 20 percent. Growth in television time-shifting through the use of DVRs like TiVo was also significant for the American public during the late 2000s: between 2008 and 2011 this practice increased by 66 percent (Nielsen, 2011b). As early as 2009 Nielsen found that each month around 60 percent of television viewers were also using the internet while watching television (Nielsen, 2010). As in Britain (and elsewhere), there are also newer set-top box technologies that hybridize television, film, music, gaming, and internet video, such as the Apple TV and the Boxee Box. There is also some evidence that streaming television online is beginning to have a negative impact on cable television subscriptions (Nielsen, 2012). As we shall see in chapters 6 and 7, online video is changing some of the power structures of U.S. presidential campaigns, but in ways that are far from obvious, not least because online video now often works interdependently with television.

A sense of balance is also required when we consider patterns of political news use, particularly during U.S. presidential campaigns. By the presidential election of 2008, there had been significant shifts in this field. That year, 56 percent of citizens reported that they had received some campaign news online—an increase of 15 percent on 2004, and 26 percent on 2000. There were also steep rises in the numbers of people reporting the internet as their "main source of campaign news" in 2008. Back in 2000, this stood at just 11 percent. In 2004, it had risen to 21 percent. By 2008, it had reached 36 percent (this was higher than for newspapers, which in 2008 stood at 33 percent). If we break these numbers down by age, the results are even more startling. Among the under-30s, 58 percent stated in 2008 that the internet was their main source of campaign news, compared with 60 percent who named television. In other words, among the young, the internet was just as important as television for following the 2008 campaign (Pew Research Center, 2008a).

These trends are undoubtedly significant and some scholars, including Philip N. Howard and I, have discussed the rise of digital distribution and the growing group of political "omnivores" who consume news across a wide range of platforms (Howard & Chadwick, 2009). The growing importance of a range of secondary media for political information has been an established trend since the late 1990s (Massanari & Howard, 2011). But let us unpack these U.S. data a little, as a means of exploring the complex interactions between older and newer media logics.

When faced with findings that reveal a "rise" in the consumption of campaign news "online" and a "decline" in the consumption of campaign news in "print," we need to consider just how much online campaign information actually originates with newspaper sources. By 2008 all significant American newspapers and, indeed, broadcasting companies, had ceased to rely solely upon print and broadcast distribution and had moved into a variety of online distribution models. Campaign news that originates with "newspaper," "radio," and "television" companies now also spreads across the internet via at least four principal mechanisms: the organizations' own websites; their formal presences on Facebook, Twitter, Flickr, and other social media sites; the news syndication sections of the major websites, such as Google News, MSN, and Yahoo; and the gigantic video and audio content hub that is YouTube. Given the adaptation to the internet among newspapers and broadcasters and the amount of print and broadcast news that is now repurposed for online consumption, it is very difficult to identify the true significance of these declines in audience numbers for "newspapers" and "television." The 2008 Pew surveys do nevertheless provide some interesting clues.

As Table 3.1 reveals, the websites of America's traditionally important broadcast and print news organizations like CNN, Fox, the *New York Times*, and the *Washington Post* feature prominently among the top websites for campaign news. These sources are joined in the table by newer media players—the semi-professional blogs such as the *Drudge Report* and the *Huffington Post* had established large audiences by 2008, just like their British counterparts I discussed above. And yet, chief among the newer media are Yahoo, MSN, Microsoft, and AOL. These are portals and news aggregators that mostly repurpose the content of the big news brands (like CNN and the *New York Times*) whose own websites already feature among the most popular sources of news. In other words, television and newspapers, and their audiences, are now well and truly online, and in a variety of forms. This should caution against simple narratives about the decline of older news media.

The rise of the internet as a source of campaign information is genuinely significant; nobody could deny that. But just as significant is the fact that television has not declined: it is still the most important campaign medium for two-thirds of American voters. Even 60 percent of the under-30s still cited it as their main source of news in the 2008 campaign. And, while those citing television as their main source of campaign news fell overall from 76 percent in 2004 to 68 percent in 2008, this is best seen as fluctuation around a solid base, because in 1996 the number for television was 72 percent and in 2000 it was 70 percent. A similar trend can also be observed for radio (Pew Research Center, 2008a).

Of course, we also need to consider the relative importance of different media during campaigns. The pattern here is somewhat clearer, with television emerging as relatively strong and printed news as relatively weak. While, as I have argued, we need to bear in mind that many newspapers have maintained their power by remediating print content for online distribution, in 2008 purely print media continued their long-running decline, and this was particularly the case among younger voters. Television and the internet were the most important media overall for gaining information about the campaign. Because Pew often ask respondents to list their two main sources of campaign information, they captured this new duopoly. Television and the internet are prospering, but the outlook for newsprint is bleaker.

Television's remarkable endurance is also reinforced by emerging patterns of online news consumption. Among online media, reading blogs and visiting candidate websites

Table 3.1 **Top Websites for U.S. Presidential Campaign News in 2008 (percentages)**

CNN	27
Yahoo	17
MSNBC/NBC	13
Candidate websites	13
Fox	11
MSN/Microsoft	9
Google	7
New York Times	6
Local newspaper/TV/Radio	5
AOL	5
Other conservative blogs/sites	5
Political parties/organizations	4
Drudge Report	4
Polling sites and aggregators	3
Washington Post	3
YouTube	2
Huffington Post	2
Other liberal blogs/sites	2
BBC	2
ABC	2
Other blogs	2
Politico	2

Notes: responses from those voters who stated that they got campaign news online. Respondents could list up to three responses.

Source: (Pew Research Center, 2008a).

were quite popular in the 2008 campaign. Roughly a quarter of the electorate consumed campaign information in this way. But watching videos was by far the most popular form of online activity: 39 percent of voters reported having watched a campaign-related online video. The age divisions were again pronounced: 65 percent of voters under thirty years old watched online video but this dropped to 38 percent for voters aged between thirty and sixty-four, though 38 percent of voters in this age group is still a huge number of people. Furthermore, using Pew data, Jeff Gulati reports that 28 percent of all voters viewed a candidate's speech online, 27 percent watched an interview, 23 percent saw at least one candidate debate, and 21 percent viewed at least one advertisement (Gulati, 2010). While there was plenty of content from speeches, interviews, debates, and advertisements that appeared only online in 2008, most of these important campaign events were first mediated by television, before being remediated by online media.

In other words, the basic context of the contemporary American presidential campaign is that publics voraciously consume online video, but a large amount of that video does not actually originate online. So here we see two trends that are very similar to what we saw in the British context: first, older media in general have adapted and are now powerful players in online news; and second, American citizens increasingly use digital media to engage with campaign content that has originated in some way with television. As new internet video platforms like Hulu and the iTunes Store continue to expand, these trends are likely to continue. And, as chapters 6 and 7 reveal, if we switch the analytical focus away from opinion surveys and toward a consideration of the actual interactions among campaigns, media, and publics, things look even more hybridized.

Since the turn of the century, the growth of blogging and user-generated content of all kinds, spanning activities such as social movement activism, election campaigning, and governance has been even more remarkable in America than it has in Britain. But again, as in Britain, matters are often more complex than they first appear. U.S. broadcast and newspaper media are working through a period of adaptation and change as they capitalize on the internet for their own purposes in sourcing, assembling, and distributing news. Richard Davis's case studies of the interactions among professional journalists, campaign staff, and elite bloggers illuminate the opportunities but also the constraints experienced by all of these groups (R. Davis, 2009). Marcus Messner and Marcia DiStaso's (2008) analysis of the content of the *New York Times*, the *Washington Post*, and the 120 most popular U.S. blogs finds evidence of "intermedia agenda setting": in other words, bloggers source from newspapers and journalists source from bloggers. The celebrated cases of blogger power in the United States, such as, for example, the exposure of Senator Trent Lott's controversial remarks at a political dinner in 2003 that prevented him from becoming Senate Majority Leader, are best interpreted as the outcome of conflict, competition, and interdependence among bloggers and elite broadcast and newspaper journalists (Drezner & Farrell, 2008).

It is also the case that the U.S. blogosphere has changed in important ways since the first waves of excitement during the mid-2000s. While blogging continues to be very popular, a great deal of online content production that in the mid-2000s would have found expression in blogging now appears on social networking sites, particularly Facebook, which at the time of writing in mid-2012 is used by more than 155 million Americans, or 50 percent of the entire U.S. population (Socialbakers, 2012).

At the same time, some of the successful U.S. bloggers have become semi-professionalized. They act as consultants to campaigns, interest groups, government agencies, and traditional media. The blog and other interactive internet genres are no longer the radical departure they once were; they have been appropriated by all elite sectors of public communication in the United States, from politicians and agency officials to professional journalists to television and radio presenters. Moving in the direction of something like a model of a professional news organization, there are group blogs like the *Huffington Post*. Founded in 2005 by Arianna Huffington, a former columnist, California gubernatorial candidate, and wife of a U.S. Congressman, the *Post* soon attracted venture capital funding and evolved into a hybrid of group blog and professional news organization (for Huffington's vision see Huffington, 2007). It combined articles from well-known public figures with commentary pieces by academics and even investigative pieces. It enjoyed the low overheads that derive from online-only publication, not to mention an army of several hundred unpaid volunteer writers. By the time it was acquired by AOL in 2011 for $315 million, the *Post*, with more monthly visitors than the *New York Times* website (Economist, 2012), was a world away from the cliché of the plucky independent blog running on a shoestring budget.

New digital network repertoires of collective action have also now proliferated across the American political landscape. The Wisconsin labor protests and Occupy sit-ins of 2011 and 2012 were the latest important manifestations of the networked activism that began in earnest during the late 1990s (Bennett, 2003; Bimber, 2003; Castells, 2004; Chadwick, 2006: 114–143; 2007). Lance Bennett and Alexandra Segerberg have shown how the Occupy movement scaled from local to national and then to transnational with great speed via the sharing of collective action memes (2012). However, Occupy also sought to reconfigure the power of mediation by professional media. Borrowing from the repertoires of the early 2011 Egyptian pro-democracy rebellion centered on Cairo's Tahrir Square, Occupy activists hybridized real-space physical presence with their own instantaneous social media resources and publishing channels—flows of information that they knew would be monitored and reassembled by professional journalists eager to create authentic representations of their protest camps.

It is also important to note that these digital network repertoires are no longer the preserve of movement activism. They have now also been seized upon by television figures in order to raise profiles and promote both conservative and liberal agendas. This is an area where there are some important differences between the U.S. and Britain, because in Britain the public service broadcasting model constrains editorializing in broadcast news. In America, where the constraints are weaker, there have been some interesting recent interactions between broadcasting and the internet in this field. In August 2010 controversial conservative radio and Fox News host Glenn Beck organized a one-hundred-thousand-person "Restoring Honor" rally on the National Mall in Washington DC. Beck was able to tap into the horizontal online networks established by the libertarian Republican Tea Party movement, whose supporters turned out in large numbers, but the event also revolved around Beck's reputation as a radio and television presenter. A few months later, in response to a suggestion by Joe Laughlin, an ordinary user of the news aggregator site Reddit, Jon Stewart and Stephen Colbert mobilized an estimated two hundred thousand people from among networks of liberal activists to participate in what they jokily termed a "Rally to Restore Sanity and/or Fear," again on the National Mall. The idea of using the rally to raise donations for DonorsChoose, a educational charity website, also came from Joe Laughlin and his Reddit comrades (Adams, 2010). Although largely satirical in its approach, Jon Stewart stated in public on several occasions that his aim was to draw attention to the lack of reasoned debate in the American news media and the influence of partisan extremism on public discourse (Agence France-Press, 2010).

Hybrid Mediality

These processes of hybridization in Britain and the United States stretch beyond the simple availability of greater numbers of devices and media channels. Professional media producers can now more easily manipulate media resources, but citizen "produsers," to use Axel Bruns' formulation (2008), increasingly play their part. And the range of media resources has expanded as political actors and newspaper and broadcast journalists have also adopted media practices associated with the internet. As the internet diffused in the 1990s, its modalities, genres, and interfaces influenced other media. This process was particularly evident in the field of television news, which has come to rely on sophisticated visual techniques that are employed by editors in order to leaven "hard" news for a general audience, such as digital animation, montage, overlay, and data visualization. The broadcasting of all live events now rests upon a whole host of practices that seek to deliberately (and some would say artificially) construct a sense of the real-time (Auslander, 2008: 15–22). These include ever-changing news tickers, split screens with simultaneous film footage and commentary, and the use of live studio audiences, not to mention simultaneous Twitter feeds and Facebook status updates. These techniques are themselves symbolic of the immediacy of television and its power in integrating and representing dispersed real-time events (Bolter & Grusin, 1999: 188) but these older affordances are now increasingly amplified by digital newer media. Customization, searching, filtering, copying, and pasting have become the norm in newsrooms and in political activism and campaigning. At the same time, the internet has been an important part of the transition away from the idea of computers as office machines and the growth of computing devices of many kinds, from notebooks to smartphones to tablet devices, as technologies for consuming and producing all forms of media.

During the 1996 elections in the United States, CNN presented all of the results on their website as they rolled in. This was the first time that broadcasting's immediacy—its status as a real-time medium for informing the American public about their political fate—was contested. CNN's site crashed on several occasions due to the demand, but it was a hint that some form of integration of the television screen and the computer screen might become the experience for future election nights. Fast forward to 2012, when 11 percent of Americans *dual-screened* the first live televised presidential debate. In other words, they watched the debate live on television but simultaneously followed along and in many cases produced real-time social media commentary about the debate (Pew Research Center, 2012).

In its use of computer-style interfaces, television has often provided viewers with little more than an illusory sense of interactivity. But television interactivity has recently evolved a great deal in response to the internet. Television news now frequently displays viewer commentary that has been supplied via e-mail, text message, Twitter, or webcam, as part of a digital montage approach to representation. Television news shows like Al Jazeera's *The Stream* stretch this approach still further, by emulating the interfaces of online communication in a hybrid mix of Skype video calls, Facebook posts, Twitter updates, and traditional broadcast news anchors. So in an important sense, subject still to the influence of editorial gatekeeping, audiences can sometimes mobilize the logics of newer media to exert greater power over the flows of real-time television news, as it happens. Television streamed over the web grants viewers an even more literal sense of control. We may choose to stop the stream, browse to other sites, place our web chat, Facebook, or Twitter feeds alongside the streaming video, and watch these competing but also complementary representations unfold in real time. By contributing commentary online we are both the subject and the object of this hybrid system. If digital new media hybridize media of representation, communication, and monitoring, the contemporary experience of watching a television show while participating in online discussion about the show on Twitter further recombines these associations, encouraging us to make rapid shifts backwards and forwards along a continuum from passive consumption to active production.

Television program makers now seek to create content that will spark such connections across media, with the central aim of fostering online communities and networks that will generate and recirculate resources signifying loyalty and enthusiasm. Even if program makers do not consciously do this, a vast range of amateur online content that connects in one way or another with what happens on television is often only a Google search away. Some entertainment media have pushed this approach beyond branding tie-ins and toward what Henry Jenkins has termed "transmedia storytelling." The Matrix trilogy of Hollywood films is Jenkins' classic early example, with its blend of professionally produced and consciously integrated transmedia narratives distributed across the film, the Blu-ray extras, the web downloads, and the computer games that have all coevolved with online communities' discussions of the film's meaning and appeal. This process transcends earlier approaches which saw the simple duplication of a "base" product like a film character (2006: 95–96).

But does the term "convergence" adequately capture these processes? First popularized during the 1970s as a way of describing the integration of computers, broadcasting, and telecommunications systems as the carriers of images, sound, and text, forty years on the idea of convergence continues to exercise its grip on the media industries and scholars alike, even though the reality has always been much messier than envisaged. The central problem with convergence has been its underlying assumption of a single delivery platform to which all media will inevitably be drawn. In practice, as Jenkins himself has admitted, there have been partial and shifting alliances between different media, as well as competition and resistance to change among older media in response to the new. Turf wars among those involved in the production and distribution of media and information have always diluted convergence. Where it does occur, convergence has been partial and contingent and based in discrete sectors of the media; it has not happened in the holistic sense originally predicted by influential scholars such as Ithiel de Sola Pool (1983b). The democratization of media production that is occurring through the proliferation and distribution of digital technologies requires us to move beyond convergence theory's preoccupation with the production and dissemination of content through a single hierarchically organized delivery channel.

One problem with the "convergence culture" approach is its equation of "online" with "grassroots" activism. The rise of online media elites, the increasing use of the logics of online media by those working in older media together with the ongoing intervention by non-elites in the construction of political news and information brings this dualism into question. When such large numbers of bloggers are now integrated into professionalized or semi-professionalized news production, when citizen activists are integrated into news-making assemblages through their participation as bloggers or Twitter and Facebook users, and when the vast majority of older media organizations have moved into the online environment, it is not always accurate to counterpose an online participatory culture against a centralized, top-down, broadcast media culture.

In addition, transmediality continues to evolve, as new genres associated with the hybridization of television with newer online social media are increasingly brought into play. Nick Anstead and Ben O'Loughlin's pioneering analysis of real-time tweeting during the BBC's famous political discussion show *Question Time* in 2009 reveals the same logic but extends the analysis beyond genre. Anstead and O'Loughlin identify the emergence of politically engaged audiences who "use online publishing platforms and social tools to interpret, publicly comment on, and debate a television broadcast while they are watching it," creating "centripetal dynamics that pull disparate and often-distanced individuals into a mainstream political event" (Anstead & O'Loughlin, 2011: 441, 457). As we shall see at many points throughout this book, these are emerging as important facets of campaign communication and the construction of news. Jenkins argued that the rise of online fan communities means that the main dynamic in television is the "shift from real-time interaction toward asynchronous participation" (Jenkins, 2006: 59), but in fact the reverse seems to be occurring, as ad hoc online communities now routinely form on Twitter and Facebook in response to television shows as they are aired. Little of this was in evidence during the early period of the internet in the 1990s and 2000s. But when the real-time communication affordances of social media suddenly emerged in the mid-2000s, this pushed things in a different direction, and in ways that simultaneously enhance the popularity and legitimacy of both online and broadcast media forms.

Finally, transmediality is now also structured by users in ways that have nothing to do with professional media's attempts to generate "buzz." Take, for example, the group of individuals who use Twitter to assume the identities of the fictional cast of the television political drama, *The West Wing*. Though they have no connection with the show, their linguistic styles are eerily similar to those of the original characters. But their expression goes beyond mere mimicry, as they playfully construct a hybrid political space somewhere between fictional television entertainment and online political activism. In theirs and the worlds of their thousands of followers, the current president of the United States is not Barack Obama, but Matthew Santos, while "former president" Jed Bartlet tweets from a position of highly informed and highly engaged semi-retirement. The key point here is that the commentary of the Twitter *West Wing* cast is almost entirely aimed at current political events. "Bartlet" spends a great deal of time baiting real-life Republicans as well as commenting, often in considerable detail, on the daily machinations of Washington politics (Bartlet, 2011). As the anonymous author behind the account says, "I'd rather they see Jed Bartlet when they read the tweets, and not me." His approach, he says, is to read "a few political pages bookmarked on Twitter ... every morning to sort of get a bearing on what I'm going to tweet about that day and what President Bartlet would have to say about that" (Pappas, 2010). The facade of pure role play occasionally drops when the characters interact with other fans who enthuse about their recent viewings of reruns of the "real" television show. During such fleeting moments, this transmedia remediation of the original show is exposed, before normal business is resumed.

Conclusion

To revisit the phrase I used in the opening to chapter 2, all older media were once newer and all newer media eventually get older. Media and media systems are always in the process of becoming. The power relations within and between media—where media are understood as confluences of technologies, social practices, and publics—change over time, and with important results. But the older and the newer adapt, interact, and coevolve. This is a process characterized by immense flux, competition, and power. Media practices intermingle and compete, but sometimes aspects of media practice may become sealed off from outside influence, following processes of boundary-drawing and the delineation of reserved domains.

As this chapter has shown, the media systems that are the focus of this book—those of Britain and the United States—are now hybrid, contradictory, mixtures of older, newer, and what Andrew Hoskins and Ben O'Loughlin have rightly termed "renewed" media (Hoskins & O'Loughlin, 2010). Older media, primarily television, radio, and newspapers are still, given the size of their audiences and their centrality to public life, rightly referred to as "mainstream," but the very nature of the mainstream is itself changing. While older media organizations are adapting, evolving, and renewing their channels of delivery, working practices and audiences, newer media are achieving popularity and becoming part of a new mainstream. Television retains its primacy in the mediation of politics, though it is now accompanied by a panoply of online media activity, some of it facilitated by broadcasters themselves. Politicians, journalists, and publics are creating these new complexities—and adapting to them. Political communication is in transition. While broadcasting still remains at the heart of public life, the nature of mediated politics is evolving rapidly and is being pushed and pulled in multiple directions by multiple actors. Some of these forces are contradictory, some are integrative; all are generative of systemic hybridity.

The way political elites, media elites, and publics produce and consume political information is changing. As use of the internet and mobile technologies has grown, so these media have become an important space for those creating and consuming political news. Audiences have never had access to so much political information through such a variety of news media. Digital technologies provide new opportunities for audiences to engage in political activities, express their opinions, and contribute public information in historically unprecedented ways. In some respects, the internet is contributing greater fluidity and openness to what social movement scholars would term the political opportunity structure: the constellation of political institutions that enable and constrain collective action and mobilization (Kitschelt, 1986). Increasingly, publics are able to exert influence and hold politicians and media to account through the use of newer media logics. All of the evidence suggests that growth in the numbers taking advantage of these newer media logics is likely to continue, but this growth will occur in the context of the evolution of older media's power and older media logics.

The rest of this book examines in more detail a range of examples of hybridity in flow in the contemporary media systems of Britain and the United States. I begin in the next chapter with an interpretation of some of the momentous events surrounding the British general election of 2010.

4

The Political Information Cycle

> The means of communication which are the signs of the highest
> forms of civilization are the most perfect by aid of electricity
> simply because they are instantaneous. There is no competition
> against instantaneousness.
> —Erastus Wiman, President of the Great Northwestern
> Telegraph Company of Canada, 1899[1]

During the weekend beginning Friday February 19, 2010, just weeks before the start of the 2010 British general election campaign, Labour Party Prime Minister Gordon Brown became the subject of an extraordinary media spectacle. Quickly labeled "bullygate," the crisis was sparked by revelations in a then-unpublished book by Andrew Rawnsley, one of Britain's foremost political journalists (Rawnsley, 2010a). Though some of Rawnsley's book had been leaked to the press three weeks earlier, and leaked once more during the afternoon of Saturday, February 20, extended extracts were printed in the paper edition of the *Observer*, one of Britain's oldest and most respected newspapers, as part of its "relaunch" edition on Sunday, February 21. Coming a week before Rawnsley's book's official publication date, these extracts were timed for maximum impact. They centered on the prime minister's alleged psychological and physical mistreatment of colleagues working inside his office in Number 10, Downing Street.

Bullygate was potentially the most damaging political development of the entire Brown premiership, not only due to its timing—on the verge of a closely fought general election—but also due to its shocking and personalized nature. These were potentially some of the most damaging allegations ever to be made concerning the personal conduct of a sitting British prime minister. The Bullygate affair became a national and international news phenomenon, dominating the headlines in all British news media, as well as those on CNN, Fox, ABC, and CBS news in the U.S., and thousands of outlets across the globe.

But during the course of that weekend beginning February 20, and into the early part of the following week, the Bullygate affair took several momentous twists and turns. New players entered the fray, most notably a body known as the National Bullying Helpline, whose director made the extraordinary claim that her organization had received phone calls from staff inside Number 10 Downing Street. This information created a powerful new frame during the middle of the crisis. As the story evolved, events were decisively shaped by mediated interactions among politicians, nonprofit group leaders, professional journalists, bloggers, and citizen activists organized on Twitter. What were seemingly clear-cut revelations published in a national newspaper became the subject of fierce contestation, involving competition, conflict, and partisanship, but also processes of interdependence, among a wide range of actors and in a wide range of media settings. Over the course of a few days, doubts about the veracity of the bullying revelations resulted in the collapse of the story.

Just a few weeks later, on April 15, 2010, Britain held its first ever live televised prime ministerial debate. Arguably the most important single development in the mediation of British politics since the beginning of television election coverage in 1959, the debate came during one of the most intriguing and closely fought general election campaigns in living memory. The debate—the first of three, though none of the others had its dramatic impact—altered the course of the election, propelling the third-party Liberal Democrat leader Nick Clegg into the media spotlight as his party rose in the opinion polls immediately following his "winning" performance. News and commentary on the three prime ministerial candidates' performances was orchestrated, produced, co-produced, packaged, and consumed across online, newspaper, and broadcast media in real time during the event, but this news and commentary was also integrated into later stages of the media coverage. News frames developed in real-time interactions were mobilized and augmented and eventually became the subject of fierce contestation between the right-wing press and centrist and left-of-center online activists organized on Twitter and Facebook. At the epicenter of this hybrid media storm was a large ad hoc Facebook group established spontaneously by political activists in support of Clegg after the debate performance, and a right-wing newspaper backlash, including a supposed investigative scoop by the Conservative-supporting *Daily Telegraph* which claimed that Clegg had received party donations from three businessmen directly into his personal bank account. The story was denied by Clegg, but more importantly it quickly became the focus of a widespread online flash campaign that eventually forced the *Telegraph's* deputy editor to issue a defense on the paper's blog within a matter of hours of the article being published. Shortly afterward, in a manner similar to the Bullygate story of a few weeks earlier, the story of Clegg's expenses collapsed.

These two episodes—Bullygate and Britain's first prime ministerial debate—provide compelling windows on Britain's hybrid media system. This chapter provides an analysis of how these episodes were mediated. It is based in large part upon what we might term "live ethnography": close, real-time, observation and logging of a wide range of newspaper, broadcast, and online material, including citizen opinion expressed and coordinated through online social network sites (for a discussion of the emerging practice of "live" research see Elmer, 2012). In the case of Bullygate, this observation took place as the story broke, evolved, and faded, over an explosive five-day period in late February 2010. In the case of the prime ministerial debate, the fieldwork covered the processes of mediation before, during, and shortly after the main event itself, but extended through the week that followed—a period dominated by the uncertainty and flux caused by Clegg's instant media breakthrough. Throughout, I provide a detailed narrative reconstruction of the key interactions among politicians, broadcasters, newspapers, and key online media actors.

This chapter provides evidence of the increasingly hybrid nature of political news production today. But it extends the analysis and sources of evidence away from the organizational settings that are so often typically seen as the loci of news making. The chapter identifies subtle but important shifts in the balance of power shaping this field. A crucial arena in which this balance of power now plays out is what I call the "political information cycle." Political information cycles are becoming the systemic norm for the mediation of important political events. They are an essential element of the hybrid media system.

From the News Cycle to the Political Information Cycle

Originally, "news cycle" simply meant the predictable daily period between the latest and the next issue of a newspaper; a time for gathering, writing, editing, compiling, selecting, and presenting new material or new developments related to recent coverage. However, "news cycle" has since become a concept widely used but seldom theorized, despite the fact that much of the influential early work on the sociology of news production in newspaper and broadcasting implicitly or explicitly describes cyclical routines and the importance of time (see for example Galtung & Ruge, 1965; Gans, 1979; Golding & Elliott, 1979; Molotch & Lester, 1974; Roshco, 1975; Schlesinger, 1978; Tuchman, 1978). Philip Schlesinger, writing of how "time concepts are embedded in their production routines," even went so far as to dub the news media a "time-machine" (1977: 336).

These pioneer studies of news production revealed much about immediacy, timeliness, the professionalized mastery of deadlines, and competition between outlets over sources and angles. But none could have foreseen the extent to which journalism was transformed during the 1990s and 2000s. The emergence of "rolling" broadcast coverage and the internet have generated heated discussion of the so-called "24-hour news cycle." New technologies—satellites, e-mail, digital content management systems, for example—have led to the compression of news time, and single daily news cycles are becoming rarer. There has been a growing strategic awareness among politicians that timely intervention during certain stages in the gathering and production of news is more likely to produce favorable outcomes (see, for example Barnett & Gaber, 2001; Sellers, 2010; S. Young, 2009) and the growing interpenetration of political and journalistic elite practice has been driven by the temporal rhythms of radio and television (Barnett & Gaber, 2001: 42–46). But while the news cycle has been the subject of some major critical studies (Davies, 2008; Kovach & Rosenstiel, 1999; Rosenberg & Feldman, 2008), it is more common to see the "24-hour" prefix briefly mentioned only in passing, as a kind of shorthand in normative analyses of the harmful effects of journalists' clamor to be first to the story, the incessant manufacturing of fresh angles to prevent things turning "stale," and the monitoring and "churning" of other outlets' content or PR releases in a process said to lead to "content homogeneity" and poorly sourced stories (A. Bell, 1995; Boczkowski & De Santos, 2007; Davies, 2008; Garcia Aviles, et al., 2004; Jones, 2009; Klinenberg, 2005; Kovach & Rosenstiel, 1999; Patterson, 1998; Redden & Witshge, 2010).

Irrespective of their approach, however, those who have explored the news cycle have hitherto been united by the fundamental assumption that the construction of political news is a tightly controlled game involving the interactions and interventions of a small number of elites: politicians, officials, communications staff, professional news workers, and, in a small minority of recent studies, elite bloggers (Barnett & Gaber, 2001; Callaghan & Schnell, 2001; Davies, 2008; R. Davis, 2009; Gans, 1979: 116–146; Golding & Elliott, 1979; Messner & DiStaso, 2008; Molotch & Lester, 1974; Patterson, 1998; Roshco, 1975; Schlesinger, 1977, 1978; Sellers, 2010; Stanyer, 2001; Tuchman, 1978; S. Young, 2009). While these elite-driven aspects of political communication are still very much in evidence, I want to suggest that recent shifts require a reinterpretation of the importance of time, timeliness, and cyclical processes in the power relations shaping news production. Ultimately, however, this may require a different set of assumptions and observations about how news is now made.

Political information cycles possess certain features that distinguish them from "news cycles." They are complex assemblages in which the logics—the technologies, genres, norms, behaviors, and organizational forms—of supposedly "new" online media are hybridized with those of supposedly "old" broadcast and newspaper media. This hybridization process shapes power relations among actors and ultimately affects the flows and meanings of news. The concept of assemblage, as I use it here, builds upon and extends some of the ways in which it has been employed in recent studies of political campaigning and mobilization. In his ethnographic study of congressional campaigning, Rasmus Kleis Nielsen writes of how the concept of assemblages allows us to see a campaign's "relational character; and to grasp how interdependent, loosely coupled elements develop the capacity to pursue personalized political communication together, all the time retaining their distinct character as they eschew formal organization and fail to solidify into anything one would recognize as a single entity or institution" (R. K. Nielsen, 2012: 28). Similarly, C. W. Anderson's book on the evolution of metropolitan journalism in the United States explores how digital technologies have facilitated assemblages combining long-standing local news organizations and other areas of journalism-like practice, such as neighborhood blogs, citizen media associations, local charitable bodies, and activists (C. W. Anderson, 2013).

The idea of assemblage originates in the social theory of Gilles Delueze and Félix Guattari. Delueze and Guattari argued that assemblages can be understood as the ever-evolving confluential expressions of specific "machinic" forces of many varying kinds, such as, for example, technologies, language, architecture, rituals, flows of information, and even bodily functions (Deleuze & Guattari, 2004). This perspective has also been influential for actor–network theory's idea of hybrid networks, which I discussed in chapter 1. But my thinking here owes more to the sense in which the concept of assemblage has been employed by Manuel DeLanda, who argues for the broad value of the idea for the social sciences. Of key importance is the assumption that there are permeable boundaries between different modular units of any given collective endeavor, and the meaning and force of any individual modular unit—whether it be a technology, a frame, a message, and so on—of that endeavor can only be understood in terms of its relations with other modular units. As DeLanda writes: "We can distinguish ... the properties defining a given entity from its capacities to interact with other entities ... These relations imply, first of all, that a component part of an assemblage may be detached from it and plugged into a different assemblage in which its interactions are different." Assemblages, then, are "wholes characterized by *relations of exteriority*" (DeLanda, 2006: 10; emphasis in original). Deleuze and Guattari provide the example of books, which only function as "books" through their relationship with a whole range of other ideas, technologies, cultural forms, and collectivities of social actors. It is a book's relations of exteriority that defines its function (Deleuze & Guattari, 2004: 4). In a similar vein, William Bogard has written that "assemblages are multiplicities of interfaces" (2009: 17). I understand assemblage to be simultaneously a process and an event. As this chapter shows, assemblages are composed of multiple, loosely coupled individuals, groups, sites, and temporal instances of interaction involving diverse yet highly interdependent news creators and media technologies that plug and unplug themselves from the news-making process, often in real time.

Certain points flow from this conceptualization. Political information cycles may involve greater numbers and a more diverse range of actors and interactions than news cycles as they are traditionally understood. They are not simply about an acceleration of pace nor merely the reduction of time devoted to an issue, though these facets are certainly evident. Rather, they are characterized by more complex temporal structures. They include many non-elite participants, most of whom now interact exclusively online in order to advance or contest specific news frames or even entire stories, sometimes in real-time exchanges but also during subsequent stages of the cycle of news that follows a major political event or the breaking of a story. As I argued in chapter 2 and have previously noted in relation to digital media and mobilization (Chadwick, 2007), the presence of vast searchable online archives of news content means that stories or fragments of stories can lay dormant for weeks or even months before they erupt and are integrated into the cycle. The sources of these pieces of information may be very diverse.

Broadcasters and newspapers now integrate non-elite actions and information from the online realm into their own production practices and routines. Using digital tools, non-elite activists may sometimes successfully contest television and press coverage of politics. The more that professional broadcast and newspaper media actors use digital services like Twitter and Facebook, the more likely it is that broadcast and newspaper media will become open to influence by activists who use those same tools. Yet television and newspaper journalists also seek to be selective in their own coverage, as they try to outperform new media actors in incessant and often real-time power struggles characterized by competition and conflict, but also negotiation and interdependence. In contrast with the older idea of the news cycle, much of this now takes place in public or semi-public online environments.

Political information cycles work on the basis of cross-platform iteration and recursion. This serves to loosen the grip of journalistic and political elites through the creation of fluid opportunity structures with greater scope for timely intervention by online citizen activists. Some of these timely online interventions are at the individual-to-individual level and have often fallen beneath the radar of news studies, in both older and newer media environments. The combination of news professionals' dominance and the integration of non-elite actors in the construction and contestation of news at multiple points in a political information cycle's lifespan are important characteristics of contemporary political communication. The overall aim here is to explore the ongoing interactions between older and newer media logics, how these interactions shape an important news event over the periods of time that come before and after the event itself, and how framings and interpretations are created, and later reinforced or contested, in intra-elite and/or elite-activist news-making assemblages.

#Bullygate

The Bullygate political information cycle effectively began with what is now a familiar dynamic in the political news environment: the publication of leaked content from a "tell-all" book (Rawnsley, 2010a) on the front page of the *Mail on Sunday* on January 31, 2010, three weeks before the *Observer* published its extended extracts on Sunday, February 21, and four weeks before the book's official publication date of March 1[2]. The *Mail*'s article reported that the Rawnsley book contained three specific claims about the prime minister's behavior toward his staff in Number 10. These were that Brown: "Hit a senior aide who got in the way as he rushed to a reception at No 10"; "physically pulled a secretary out of her chair as he dictated a memo to her"; and "hurled foul-mouthed abuse at two aides in his hotel room in America in a state of semi-undress after reports that he had been snubbed by President Obama" (Walters, 2010a). Despite its appearance on the front page of the *Mail*'s paper edition, the story's reception is best described as muted. The main Conservative Party supporting blog, *Conservative Home*, linked to the piece, and Britain's most-read political blog, the right-wing libertarian Guido Fawkes, published a brief post (Fawkes, 2010; Montgomerie, 2010c), but the story effectively lay dormant until Saturday, February 20.

In the build-up to its publication of the Rawnsley extracts on Sunday February 21, the *Observer* was in the process of a widely advertised "relaunch" in a bid to reverse the long-term decline in its readership. This was, therefore, partly a matter of intermedia competition between the paper and its rivals among the Sunday press. The Rawnsley extracts were an opportunity to increase exposure and boost readership for the paper's first relaunched edition. Indeed, this strategy was reflected in the paper's deliberate exclusion of the extracts from its free online edition until two days after they had appeared in the printed edition, though, as we shall see, due to the widespread recycling of the story online across all outlets, this tactic failed.

The British media's regular politics, commentary, and opinion cycle now reaches a crescendo with the weekend newspapers and the Sunday political television shows. Sunday newspapers feature the heavyweight commentary and columnist content in British political news. Yet "the Sundays" are now essentially published well in advance because online editions are released to the web throughout Saturday evenings. As a result, the Sundays now play an increasingly important role in defining the news agenda for the equally influential Sunday morning political television, particularly the BBC's 9:00 a.m. *Andrew Marr* show, but also Adam Boulton's 11:30 a.m. show on Sky News, and the BBC's midday *Politics Show*.

Aware that the bullying revelations were about to be published, in the run-up to the weekend beginning February 19, the Labour government took three steps to preempt what would likely become the dominant news agenda. First, a week earlier, Brown appeared in an extended and highly personalized interview on the popular *Piers Morgan's Life Stories* television chat show on ITV. This appearance was widely regarded as part of a strategy to "humanize" the prime minister in the wake of criticisms that he had kept too much of his private life hidden and lacked a "common touch" among the electorate. Second, Brown granted an exclusive in-depth interview to Brian Brady, the *Independent on Sunday*'s Whitehall Editor and a long-standing reporter on the insider politics of the Labour Party. The interview, which was broadly favorable to the prime minister and timed to coincide with the publication of the *Observer*'s extracts, was used by Brown to deny the allegations that he mistreated his staff. Third, Brown attended a Labour Party rally at the University of Warwick—one of several such pre-election events—at which he gave a headline-grabbing speech in front of professional reporters from both broadcasting and newspapers, as part of the official launch of Labour's election theme: "a future fair for all."

Soon after the Warwick speech had ended (at around midday Saturday) Brown participated in an exclusive recorded interview with the well-known Channel 4 News presenter Krishnan Guru-Murthy, as part of a package for that evening's television news bulletin to be aired at 7:10 p.m. Extraordinarily, Guru-Murthy quizzed the prime minister on whether he "hit" his staff. Brown strongly denied this, saying: "I have never hit anyone in my life" (Channel 4 News, 2010b). As soon as the interview was completed, Oliver King, a program editor for Channel 4 News, posted a message to his Twitter account stating that his channel had secured the "only network TV interview" with the prime minister that day, and that it would be shown on television that evening (King, 2010). The interview was in fact uploaded to the Channel 4 News website at 4:00 p.m., some three hours before the interview was actually broadcast on television (Channel 4 News, 2010d). The video's publication was accompanied by a Twitter update linking to the file from Ed Fraser, another program editor at Channel 4 News (Fraser, 2010a). The story of the prime minister's first public refutation of the bullying allegations therefore actually broke online, three hours before the "exclusive" "broke" on television, and long before the Sunday's *Observer* went to press.

Within twenty minutes of the appearance of the Channel 4 video online on the Saturday afternoon, three essentially identical wire stories emerged on the websites of the *Daily Mirror*, the *Daily Star*, and the *Daily Express*. These repeated the allegations that had been leaked in the *Daily Mail* at the end of January, but added Brown's refutation from the Channel 4 interview from earlier that day (Daily Express, 2010; Daily Mirror, 2010a; Daily Star, 2010c). Thus, by the time Guru-Murthy's exchange with the prime minister was broadcast on Channel 4's early evening news bulletin (Channel 4 News, 2010b), the Bullygate story's momentum had already started to build, and it was spurred on by the fresh angle provided by Brown's decision to address the allegations head-on. The Channel 4 interview with Brown continued to provide fodder for other journalists in the run-up to the publication of the online editions of the Sunday newspapers at midnight (see for example News of the World, 2010).

But long before the Sundays appeared, further important details of the *Observer*'s extracts started to emerge on Twitter and blogs. Ed Fraser of Channel 4 News posted a message at 9:33 p.m. stating that Brown allegedly received an "unprecedented reprimand" for his behavior from the Cabinet Secretary and Head of the Civil Service, Sir Gus O'Donnell (Fraser, 2010b). This information was not yet in the public domain. Fraser had access to a "pre-release" of the *Observer* extracts and had decided to post this new information to Twitter—during a period when it was likely to have the greatest impact, and certainly before the *Observer* was publicly available (Fraser, 2010c). Within ten minutes, Fraser's tweet had been widely recirculated ("retweeted") and had been linked to from the popular *Conservative Home* blog (Montgomerie, 2010a). A further potentially damaging piece of information—that Britain's most senior civil servant had allegedly conducted an internal investigation into Brown's behavior—broke on Twitter and was now driving the story, forcing Downing Street and the Cabinet Office to issue a statement of denial to journalists at 10:27 p.m. (The statement was not published: its precise timing was revealed by the BBC's political editor, Nick Robinson, on BBC television's Ten O'Clock News on Monday February 22, 2010).

At this point, interactions on Twitter began to assume a much greater importance in the flows of information. At 11:14 p.m., Labour's new media spokesperson, the Member of Parliament (MP) for Bristol East, Kerry McCarthy, started to use her Twitter updates to post the hashtag "#rawnsleyrot." Her aim was to popularize the tag as a means of discrediting the bullying allegations before they were published (McCarthy, 2010b). At that stage, McCarthy was one of the most popular MPs on the social network service, with more than 6000 followers (as this goes to press she has 14,500 followers). Despite it being close to midnight on a Saturday evening, the #rawnsleyrot hashtag was quickly circulated among her followers.

As is now the norm among the British press, the broadsheet Sunday newspapers published their full online editions between midnight on Saturday and 3:00 a.m. on Sunday, several hours before the printed editions were widely available across the country. The *Observer* carried a brief "teaser" as the lead item on its website, in the hope that readers wanting more would buy the relaunched paper edition at the newsstands, but there was sufficient detail in these excerpts for the public to be aware of the story's sensational nature. The article contained several key pieces of information. Aside from the by-now public allegation that Cabinet Secretary Sir Gus O'Donnell had allegedly investigated the prime minister's behavior and had warned him to change his approach, the article chronicled a series of other alleged episodes. These included when an aide allegedly feared that Brown was about to "hit him in the face"; when Brown allegedly grabbed Gavin Kelly, his deputy chief of staff, by his jacket and "snarled" into his face; and when Brown allegedly "roughly shoved aside" and swore at Stewart Wood, a senior adviser on foreign affairs (Helm & Asthana, 2010a). The broadly centrist *Independent on Sunday* ran its Brian Brady interview featuring Brown denying the allegations. The Conservative-supporting *Sunday Times* and *Sunday Telegraph* ran articles that had been updated at the last minute to include the details of the alleged mistreatment, Brown's Channel 4 interview from Saturday afternoon (the *Telegraph* simply embedded Channel 4's video), and Downing Street's late-night statement of denial (Oakeshott, 2010; Sunday Telegraph, 2010c).

On Sunday morning a torrent of media coverage appeared, as news outlets scrambled to cover the bullying revelations for fear of missing the weekend's main story. Broadcast news plugged into the emerging news-making assemblage. At 9:41 a.m., in an attempt to shape the news for the remainder of the day, senior government figure Lord Mandelson, then minister for business and innovation and a key architect of the Labour Party's media strategy since the 1980s, appeared on the BBC's *Andrew Marr* show to defend the prime minister and to deny the bullying allegations. Mandelson's argument was that the *Observer's* relaunch and the imminent publication of Rawnsley's book had created perfect publicity opportunities for both author and newspaper, and that the story was essentially an overblown stunt (BBC, 2010a). This appearance had an immediate impact on the political information cycle. Within a couple of hours, the *Sunday Telegraph*, the *Independent on Sunday*, the *Sunday Mirror*, the *Sun*, and the *Sunday Times* had all reported Lord Mandelson's television intervention. Mandelson's defense was in turn reinforced by the appearances of Harriet Harman, then deputy leader of the Labour Party, on Sky News's *Sunday Live with Adam Boulton* at 11:30 a.m., as well as the appearance of the then home secretary, Alan Johnson, alongside Andrew Rawnsley, on the BBC's midday *Politics Show* (BBC, 2010c; Churcher, 2010; Coates, 2010b; Sky News; Sun, 2010; Sunday Telegraph, 2010d). Both Harman and Johnson, as one would expect of cabinet colleagues, made strong statements in support of the prime minister. The dominant frame was therefore shifting away from Brown's personal denials and toward the supportive messages of the cabinet. The BBC's most senior political journalist, political editor Nick Robinson, posted what can best be described as a cautious article to his blog at 12:30 p.m., shortly after Johnson and Rawnsley had left the BBC's television studios. In the absence of new information, Robinson effectively hedged his bets: "what is not in dispute here is the description of how the PM behaves," he wrote, but he also went on to state that "we don't and may never know" if there was an internal investigation into Brown's behavior (Robinson, 2010a). Though things were finely balanced, the government and its supporters were successfully contesting the story. Even though by this stage it was evident that this major political news, *potentially* the biggest for years, was receiving saturation coverage across all platforms, including the 24-hour television stations, BBC News and Sky News, it still pivoted on who was more believable: Rawnsley or Brown and the government. This uncertainty was reflected in the coverage during the Sunday afternoon, as several more newspaper articles reported the allegations and Lord Mandelson's refutations from the early morning *Andrew Marr* show (Barker, 2010; Brogan, 2010). In short, by Sunday afternoon, the story appeared to be fizzling out.

ENTER THE "NATIONAL BULLYING HELPLINE"

It was at this point that the political information cycle took a remarkable twist, as interactions in the online and broadcasting modules of the assemblage drove the news production process.

Following MP Kerry McCarthy's late-night instigation of the #rawnsleyrot hashtag campaign on Twitter, an online community consisting of political activists eager to defend or attack the *Observer*'s revelations had quickly emerged on Twitter. They used a variety of hashtags, including #rawnsleyrot, #bullygate, and #rawnsleyright, among others. Elite bloggers had also joined the fray. For example, Conservative supporters Iain Dale and Tim Montgomerie continued to update their blogs and link to new developments via Twitter throughout the Sunday afternoon (Conservative Home, 2010b). Many professional journalists were also engaged in the Twitter conversation, scanning updates in the hunt for tip-offs in advance of the Sunday evening television news bulletins.

But at 4:52 p.m., Lucy Manning, ITV News' television political correspondent, posted the following to Twitter: "National Bullying Helpline tells ITV News they have had several calls from staff at Downing Street complaining about bullying culture" (Manning, 2010). This was the first time this explosive new information was made public. Though the BBC would later claim that it broke the story on television (BBC News, 2010c), if breaking a story means being the first to make it public, it was actually Manning who broke the National Bullying Helpline story—on Twitter. Fifty-six seconds after Manning's tweet, the first person to retweet her message was none other than the tell-all book's author, Andrew Rawnsley (Rawnsley, 2010b). Within thirty minutes, Manning's tweet had been retweeted by twenty-eight other Twitter users. These included: Conservative Party Chairman Eric Pickles, Conservative MP David Jones, and Conservative blogger Iain Dale. But the remainder were, to judge by their Twitter profiles, a mixture of journalists, local political activists, bloggers, and the politically interested from across Britain, all united by the fact that they followed the journalist Lucy Manning on Twitter (Google Replay Search, 2010b). Within an hour, sixty Twitter users had issued updates referring to the National Bullying Helpline. Although data on the number of followers each of these Twitter users had at the time are unavailable, it is safe to assume that, while bearing in mind that the data are skewed by individuals with large followings (Channel 4 News presenter Krishnan Guru-Murthy then had more than twenty thousand) the number of Twitter users potentially exposed to this information, before it came anywhere near a rolling news television screen, ran into the hundreds of thousands. Moreover, as we shall see, the interactions between professional journalists and these various groups of online "amateurs" went on to have a decisive impact on events.

The National Bullying Helpline information was of crucial importance. No longer was it simply a case of Brown's and the government's word against Rawnsley's. Now, there appeared to be an impeccably independent third party, a charitable trust working for a good cause, which it was presumed had kept a log of telephone calls that could be traced to Number 10. This had all the makings of a sensational development in the story.

The majority of the sixty Twitter users who engaged with ITV journalist Lucy Manning's message during that first hour after she broke the helpline news simply retweeted her message. However, as the conversation developed, several individuals began to add their own information and comments. At 5:27 p.m., Twitter user Sarah Nuttall, who is not a journalist but a copywriter based in Goole, East Yorkshire, commented: "Oh dear & the Patron of the National Bullying Helpline is .... wait for it .... Ann Widdecombe. Be afraid. Be very afraid Mr Brown!" (Nuttall, 2010). Ann Widdecombe was at that time a well-known Conservative MP (she retired her seat in 2010), and a television presenter, author, and former Home Office minister. Sarah Nuttall's message was quickly retweeted by several others, including, at 5:30 p.m., Carole Benson, a mature student of history at Teesside University in the northeast of England. Nine minutes after Benson's message, Krishnan Guru-Murthy, the Channel 4 News television presenter, intervened on Twitter: "been looking into 'National Bullying Helpline' after the Downing Street claim. they have 2 Tory Patrons and Cameron quote on website," he said (Guru-Murthy, 2010).

On the surface, these events appear to be unrelated. What do a copywriter from East Yorkshire, a student from Teesside, and a senior journalist from Channel 4 News have in common? The answer is this: Sarah Nuttall was the first to point out that the National Bullying Helpline seemingly had links with the Conservative Party. Carole Benson retweeted Nuttall's message. Krishnan Guru-Murthy followed Carole Benson on Twitter and read her update (Doesfollow, 2010). A few minutes later, Guru-Murthy sent out a speculative tweet to his twenty thousand followers, pointing out the National Bullying Helpline's Conservative links. Due to the size of Guru-Murthy's following, a Twitter storm ensued, with tweets and retweets of Manning's original tweet about the National Bullying Helpline and Guru-Murthy's tweet about its "Tory patrons." A point that was to later emerge as important—that the National Bullying Helpline may have breached its clients' confidentiality—was also raised by Sacha Zarb, a Labour-supporting events manager based in northern England (Zarb, 2010). New angles and information were therefore quickly introduced into the political information cycle and these were to recur as the National Bullying Helpline news went mainstream over the next few hours and into Monday morning's headlines.

Inside the BBC and ITN newsrooms, journalists had been considering if, when, and how to run with this new National Bullying Helpline information. The chief of the helpline, Christine Pratt, had contacted BBC and ITV news earlier in the day (BBC News, 2010c). But it was not until 5:48 p.m. that the BBC, in an effort to preempt Lucy Manning's scoop that she first aired on Twitter but was now lining up for the BBC's arch rival ITV News's 6:00 p.m. bulletin, posted an online video in which Christine Pratt claimed that employees inside Number 10 had called her organization (BBC News Online, 2010b). Two minutes later, the BBC Politics Twitter account linked to the BBC news website's video of Pratt. At precisely the same moment, BBC television "broke" the National Bullying Helpline story when its news channel, which was at that stage in the middle of running a live special broadcast of film and television stars on the red carpet at the London BAFTA awards, updated its foot-of-screen news ticker with the message: "The BBC understands that staff working in the prime minister's office have called an anti-bullying charity to complain about the way they have been treated" (BBC, 2010b; BBC News, 2010a).

At 6:04 p.m., ITV News on television featured Lucy Manning's Bullygate package as its top story and the studio anchor went live to outside Number 10, where Manning revealed a statement from the National Bullying Helpline chief, Christine Pratt. The statement read: "The calls we have received suggest there is a culture of bullying within Downing Street. Whether Gordon Brown is the perpetrator or not, we cannot say. We know that someone who works at No. 10 has been off sick because of the effect of this on their health" (ITV News, 2010c).

The BBC and ITV were therefore confident enough about the veracity of the National Bullying Helpline's claims to run with this as their main story for the evening news. However, Channel 4 took a different approach. Recall that their presenter, Krishnan Guru-Murthy, had become aware during his engagement with Twitter users that the National Bullying Helpline had the prominent Conservative MP, Ann Widdecombe, as one of its patrons. Channel 4 News ran with Bullygate as its top story and featured an interview with Rawnsley, but at no point was the Helpline mentioned, even though the Channel 4 team was aware of the information (Channel 4 News, 2010c). Clearly, Channel 4 News had access to the details because it and ITV both get their news from parent company ITN, albeit from separate divisions. An editorial decision was therefore taken at Channel 4 News to hold off on the Helpline development due to uncertainty about the source. Although it is impossible to say with absolute certainty that the journalists' interactions on Twitter were the cause of this decision, we can infer that it was an important factor.

Once the Helpline news had appeared on the BBC News Channel's foot-of-screen ticker and ITV's 6:00 p.m. television bulletin, it was immediately picked up by the newspapers. At 6:29 p.m., the Telegraph became the first paper to report the Helpline story on its website (Sunday Telegraph, 2010b). It was not until 7:02 p.m. that the BBC presented a full package including, for the first time, a video interview with National

Bullying Helpline chief Christine Pratt and extended live-to-anchor commentary from the BBC's deputy political editor, James Landale (BBC News, 2010b). Landale's report also included a second denial of Brown's bullying, this time from the Cabinet Office, who stated that the Cabinet Secretary, Sir Gus O'Donnell, did not speak with the prime minister about his behavior. As soon as James Landale's report had ended, his senior colleague, Nick Robinson, posted an update to his BBC blog arguing that Lord Mandelson's defense of the prime minister earlier in the day had "backfired," but once again the blog post made no mention of the National Bullying Helpline (Robinson, 2010b). The frame was shifting, and this was a period of uncertainty. Two minutes later, the *Telegraph* added further material to its story originally published at 6:29 p.m., fleshing out the claims about the Helpline (Sunday Telegraph, 2010a). This was followed by a number of new articles published in quick succession, as the newspapers scrambled to integrate the new information. Over the next four hours, the *Star* (7:19 p.m.), the *Mirror* (7:30 p.m.), the *Mail* (8:31 p.m. and 10:46 p.m.), the *Sun* (9:19 p.m.), the *Financial Times* (10:27 p.m.), and the *Times* (11:18 p.m.) all added the news about Christine Pratt and the Helpline. And yet not one of these online newspaper articles raised the issue of the contested origins and status of the organization (Barker, 2010; Coates, 2010a; Daily Star, 2010b; Sun, 2010; Sunday Mirror, 2010; Walters, 2010b).

But it was doubts about the National Bullying Helpline's status that led Vijay Singh Riyait, not a journalist but an IT engineer and Labour-supporting activist with his own blog (www.sikhgeek.com), to send a Twitter message to Channel 4's Krishnan Guru-Murthy at 9:16 p.m. Riyait pointed to an anonymous blog that had been set up some six months earlier to act as a channel for those with grievances against the National Bullying Helpline. Labeled "The Bullying Helpline: the last thing you need if you're being bullied," the blog raised questions about the organization's working practices, in particular its relationship with a company, HR & Diversity Management, owned by Christine Pratt and her husband (Anonymous, 2010). The link to this hitherto obscure blog was first posted to Twitter earlier that evening by Jo Anne Brown, the head of Dignity Works, a management consultancy and rival to the National Bullying Helpline, specializing in workplace "bullying and harassment" (Brown, 2010). The link had been recirculated in the emerging Twitter storm, which now centered upon the Helpline's alleged Conservative Party links, its charitable status, working practices, and the publicity-seeking behavior of its chief. Vijay Singh Riyait, the IT engineer and amateur blogger, had picked up Jo Anne Brown's link and decided to forward it to Channel 4 News via Guru-Murthy.

Within the space of a few hours, then, the National Bullying Helpline's motives had been called into question. A new set of actors from the charity and management consultancy sector were now plugging into the news-making assemblage. These individuals were seeking to use Bullygate as a means of publicizing their own work and to criticize a rival for its alleged breach of ethics on client confidentiality. Twitter enabled these actors to intervene and shape the flow of news because their expressed skepticism served to heighten awareness of the Helpline's organizational status among journalists and bloggers monitoring their Twitter feeds.

This increasing skepticism soon began to be reflected in the "mainstream." The first hint was a cautious blog post from the BBC's political editor Nick Robinson at 9:35 p.m. on Sunday evening. Robinson reported the doubts about the Helpline, and mentioned that there was a supportive statement from Conservative leader David Cameron on the Helpline's website. He also reported that Downing Street had issued a response to the Helpline's allegations, stating that they had never been contacted by the organization. It was also revealed that the Labour MP Anne Snelgrove had helped publicize the Helpline when it was established but had severed her links when she became aware of complaints that the organization was allegedly referring calls to the private consultancy business run by Christine Pratt's husband. Robinson went on: "Colleagues checked the status of the charity and questioned Ms. Pratt's claims. We can't, of course, verify the truth of her allegations—merely report them and Downing Street's response to them" (Robinson, 2010c).

Shortly after Robinson's blog post, BullyingUK, another anti-bullying charity, intervened. It issued a strongly worded press release on its website criticizing the National Bullying Helpline for breaching confidentiality and it sent a message to Nick Robinson's Twitter account to alert him to the release (BullyingUK, 2010a, 2010b). Meanwhile, the volume of comments had been building on Robinson's blog from readers pointing out the potential problems with the credibility of Christine Pratt as a source.

At this point, however, no professional journalist was willing to publicly question Pratt's testimony. As the evening drew to a close and the next day's newspapers were in the process of being finalized, the Helpline's claims seemed set to dominate the headlines as the political information cycle moved into Monday morning. The frame was finely balanced.

"WHO ARE THE NATIONAL BULLYING HELPLINE?"

Late on Sunday evening, at 11:28 p.m., however, there was yet another decisive shift. A left-of-center amateur blogger, Adam Bienkov, posted an article to his well-known political blog, *Tory Troll*. The post was entitled "Who are the National Bullying Helpline?" Bienkov wrote that the whole story "immediately smelt funny" and he criticized the BBC for failing to check its facts. He had spent the evening researching publicly available online sources such as the Charity Commission's website and the internet's Whois database, which lists the owners of web domain names. These sources showed that a number of senior Conservatives were associated with the Helpline, that it had a number of informal links with the Conservative-controlled Swindon local council, and that it was late in filing its accounts and had "registered just £852 in expenditure since they were established" (Bienkov, 2010). Bienkov then posted a link to the post on Twitter. A few minutes later, Labour MP Kerry McCarthy retweeted Adam Bienkov's blog post to her six thousand followers, and this was in turn retweeted many hundreds of times late into the night (McCarthy, 2010a). Bienkov's blog post assembled in readable form what had, until then, been a dispersed and fragmented set of messages and counter-messages on Twitter.

During the early hours of Monday, February 22, the newspapers' digital editions were uploaded as the political information cycle moved into a decisive final phase. Uncertainty over the National Bullying Helpline angle continued, and was revealed in the lack of consensus in the mainstream newspaper press. The *Independent* and the *Guardian* still made no mention of Christine Pratt's allegations, though they did publish pieces on the Rawnsley book (Anderson, 2010; Ashley, 2010; Guardian, 2010). It was not until 7:00 a.m., when the *Guardian* published a commentary piece by Jonathan

Freedland, that the paper mentioned the Helpline, and even then it was in neutral terms (Freedland, 2010). By now, however, the focus had shifted once again to the broadcast studios. To defend her claims, Pratt appeared on the two major early morning national television shows, GMTV and BBC Breakfast. More significantly, she also appeared alongside Labour MP Anne Snelgrove on BBC Radio Four's highly influential *Today* program. As part of the interview, *Today*'s presenter John Humphrys read out extracts from e-mail messages from disgruntled clients of the Helpline and suggested that Pratt's husband's company had been "angling for business" with people who had called what was supposed to be a charitable organization. These e-mails had been passed to Humphrys by Anne Snelgrove (BBC Radio 4, 2010c). It was clear that the frame was now shifting toward outright skepticism about the National Bullying Helpline.

Christine Pratt's television and radio appearances then fed into new stories for the newspapers. The *Daily Star* and the *Daily Telegraph* simply reported Pratt's appearances (Daily Star, 2010a; Irvine, 2010). In the background, however, things were shifting. At 9:29 a.m., the BBC's political correspondent Laura Kuenssberg posted on Twitter that one of the patrons of the Helpline, Professor Cary Cooper, had resigned from the Helpline's board (Kuenssberg, 2010c). Cooper is a prestigious scholar in the field of management and workplace studies and is well-known for his media appearances. This was a major blow to the entire Bullygate frame.

Perhaps sensing that the power of the story was beginning to recede, the Conservative Party leader, David Cameron, now attempted to seize the initiative. At 10:45 a.m., while speaking at a pre-election conference in east London, Cameron suggested during questions that there ought to be an official inquiry into the bullying allegations inside Downing Street. He recommended that the former Parliamentary Commissioner for Standards, Sir Philip Mawer, conduct the inquiry. Immediately, Tim Montgomerie, editor of the *Conservative Home* website and an attendee at the Cameron conference, broke this information on Twitter. Half an hour later, the BBC's Laura Kuenssberg tweeted the news that Cameron had called for an official inquiry (Kuenssberg, 2010a; Montgomerie, 2010b). Understandably, Cameron's intervention had a huge impact on the news agenda. Within forty minutes the *Times* published an article stating that the paper had been in contact with Pratt the night before, when she had told their reporter that "they [staff in 10 Downing Street] had been in contact by e-mail, by phone and that they [the Helpline] could see the computers used to download their literature" (Coates, 2010c).

The unfolding story was now being mediated almost in real time. Two minutes later, at 11:36 a.m., Laura Kuenssberg tweeted that Labour minister Lord Mandelson had accused the Conservatives of "directing" Christine Pratt. At 11:47 a.m., *Times* journalist Jenny Booth reported that Cameron, and now the opposition Liberal Democrats' leader, Nick Clegg, had both called for an official inquiry. Five minutes later, Laura Kuenssberg, who had clearly been in contact with the Conservatives to ask them to confirm or deny Lord Mandelson's allegations, tweeted that the Conservatives "totally reject idea they had anything to do with charity allegations" (J. Booth, 2010; Kuenssberg, 2010b, 2010e).

Once again, the focus shifted back to broadcasting. BBC Radio Four's influential lunchtime news show *The World at One* led on Lord Mandelson's remarks from mid-morning and reports that the Conservatives had strongly denied the allegation that they had links to Christine Pratt. The show's presenter, Martha Kearney, interviewed Peter Watt, a former general secretary of the Labour Party, who spoke of Brown's occasional bad temper. Kearney also interviewed Professor Cary Cooper, who stated that he had resigned from the National Bullying Helpline on the grounds of its breaches of client confidentiality. Liz Carnell, the head of the rival organization BullyingUK, was also interviewed, and reported that she had asked the U.K. Charity Commission to carry out an investigation into the alleged breaches of confidentiality at Pratt's organization (BBC Radio 4, 2010d).

At 2:04 p.m., Christine Pratt appeared on Sky News, in what was to prove her last live television interview of the Bullygate affair, only around twenty-two hours after her initial intervention. At 3:25 p.m., Downing Street released a third statement of denial and at 4:24 p.m. Laura Kuenssberg tweeted that civil service head Sir Gus O'Donnell had again confirmed that he had never raised any concerns with Brown. At 4:37 p.m., Andrew Rawnsley responded directly to this denial on Twitter: "Sir Gus O'Donnell spoke to the Prime Minister about his behavior. My source for that could not be better," he said. Then, Gordon Brown used an interview with the *Economist* magazine to further deny the allegations (BBC News, 2010c; Economist, 2010; Kuenssberg, 2010d; Rawnsley, 2010c; Sky News, 2010b).

Meanwhile, the National Bullying Helpline was falling apart. Its three remaining patrons announced their resignation from its board: television presenter Sarah Cawood, Conservative councilor Mary O'Connor, and, more importantly, Ann Widdecombe, the Conservative MP whose association with the organization had led to the suspicions regarding its alleged alignment with the Conservatives and which had first sparked the investigations by Twitter users and blogger Adam Bienkov. By early Monday evening, the newspaper websites began reporting the patrons' resignations rather than Pratt's confirmation of the events alleged in Rawnsley's book (Daily Mirror, 2010b).

By the time of Britain's most-watched television news show, the BBC Ten O'Clock News, later that Monday night, the Bullygate story was effectively finished. The BBC led on the story. While it repeated Cameron's and Clegg's calls for an official inquiry, it reported that the U.K. Charity Commission was now investigating the National Bullying Helpline. It sent a reporter, John Kay, to the Helpline's headquarters in Swindon, in order to show that its offices were next-door-but-one to those of the local Conservative Party. Though the BBC did not draw its own conclusions, it reported that this was likely to add to the speculation that Christine Pratt may have been politically motivated. BBC political editor Nick Robinson pointedly stated that the BBC had "broken the story" about the Helpline, when in fact this was not strictly the case. In his final piece to camera, Robinson said: "It is now official. There was no bullying in that building behind me [Number 10], there will be no inquiry, the cabinet secretary gave no warning, at least by the latest statement that he has issued" (BBC News, 2010c). Robinson went on to say that the story raised broader concerns about the prime minister's character, but the fact that he began his report with the official denials is an indication of how far the initial story had evolved over the course of three days.

Finally, on February 25, the U.K. Charity Commission issued a press release stating that it was conducting a formal investigation of 160 complaints about the working practices of the National Bullying Helpline. The helpline suspended its operations (U.K. Charity Commission, 2010).

I now turn to the events of a few weeks later that provide this chapter's second case study: the mediation of Britain's first live televised prime ministerial debate in 2010.

Britain's First Live Televised Prime Ministerial Debate

INTEGRATING AND PREEMPTING

Stage one of the prime ministerial debate's political information cycle began long before the debate itself and was based on the integration and preemption of potential real-time responses through specific decisions about the format and timing of the event. The terms of engagement for the debates emerged during the early part of 2010, after more than seventy individual rules had been hammered out in numerous meetings involving party strategists, journalists, and television producers. These rules were left largely unmentioned during the first debate but were prominently displayed on the integrated ITV debate website (ITV, et al., 2010). The agreed format required that questions were not presented to candidates in advance of the debate, that audience members would not applaud, shout, or heckle, that program producers would not use cutaway shots explicitly focusing on the audience's reactions to statements, and that the debate moderator would not introduce material outside of the scope of the audience's questions. There was even some ambiguity around whether the audience would be allowed to laugh at jokes; they did, though with a reserve that betrayed uncertainty.

It is clear that British broadcasters paid close attention to the format and tone of previous American presidential candidate debates. The studio format was eerily familiar. The three candidates stood side-by-side behind lecterns and faced the presenter and a small, handpicked, studio audience at ITV's Granada television studios in Manchester. The candidates gave tightly scripted one-minute opening and closing statements, then responded to a range of questions from the audience. This was followed by periods of varying length, during which the leaders directly engaged with each other. The first half of each debate was assigned a specific policy theme: home affairs, international affairs, and the economy. These rules became the subject of media coverage, when, the day before the first debate, Conservative leader David Cameron stated in a BBC television interview that he was concerned that the format might prove sterile and that the public might be "short-changed" by the experience. This move was quickly condemned by the other parties on the grounds that the Cameron team had already agreed to the rules, but this episode reveals how much the design of the format was politicized (Stacey & Pickard, 2010). The rules also became the subject of seven hundred complaints to the British broadcasting regulator, OFCOM (Sweney, 2010).

As occurs in the United States, broadcast media and the national newspapers heavily trailed the television debates during the opening stages of the election campaign. There were repeated mentions of the "historic" nature of television's role in informing public opinion. Douglas Alexander, the Labour Party's election campaign manager, had predicted that the debates would cast a long shadow over the election media coverage, possibly absorbing as many as nine campaigning days—three days for each debate (Wintour, 2010). This proved a conservative estimate. The media trailers began many weeks before the official start of the campaign and coverage ratcheted up during the first week of the campaign proper, culminating in two days of preview features on television and in the mainstream newspapers. The entire week following the first debate was heavily shaped by media reaction to those first ninety minutes in Manchester and this established a pattern for the reporting of the two subsequent debates.

These preview features were typically concerned with "learning lessons" from candidates' triumphs and mistakes in the United States. The historic footage of the famous Kennedy-Nixon debate from 1960 was wheeled out time and again, as was Lloyd Bentsen's famous "You're no Jack Kennedy" dismissal of Dan Quayle in the 1988 vice presidential debates, though the inconvenient truth that Quayle ended up on the winning side was usually forgotten. Television's treatment was dominated by commentary from an assortment of "body language experts," "language experts," and opinion polling companies.

The scheduling of the debates had a crucial bearing on their impact, creating the perfect conditions for a powerful integrated cycle of coverage and commentary. All three were given slots on Thursday evenings, in television's hallowed 8:00–10:00 p.m. prime time. This schedule ensured close temporal integration with the rhythms of the British elite media's regular politics, commentary, and opinion cycle, which as I explained above now reaches a crescendo with the weekend newspapers and the Sunday political television shows. BBC and ITV, the major television news players, run their main nightly news shows at 10:00 p.m., so this scheduling meant that they could guarantee immediate post-debate coverage in these regular bulletins and could in turn influence editorial deadlines at newspapers. Thursday evenings have also long been the favored slot for British television's most influential political discussion show, *Question Time*, which was aired as usual on the BBC soon after each debate. Running the debates on Thursdays thus jelled with political broadcasting traditions and was part of a bid by broadcasters to maximize their audiences and their power. The television audience for the first debate was 9.4 million; about 16 percent of the British population and a huge figure for this type of programming (BBC News Online, 2010a).

ORCHESTRATING IN REAL TIME

Stage two of the political information cycle is best characterized as the orchestration of real-time action. It involved the following: instant reaction based on snap, unrepresentative, self-selecting, online polls on ITV's and the main newspapers' websites; small studio panels of citizens operating sentiment dials which generated real-time reaction "worm" charts overlaid on top of the live streaming video on the ITV website; the expression of citizen opinion, primarily through Twitter and Facebook; and minute-by-minute live blogs produced by professional journalists during the event.

ITV's website featured a live video stream of the television coverage, but it also carried a rolling comment facility provided by the Canadian company CoveritLive (CoveritLive, 2010). This allowed members of the public to post messages that appeared underneath the video feed as it happened. The ITV web page also featured a real-time reaction worm laid over the streaming video of the debate. This was a dynamically updated line chart depicting the changing negative and positive responses of a small, selected panel of twenty undecided voters watching the debate on television, armed with dial boxes in rooms in the nearby marginal constituencies of Bolton North West and Bolton East (ITV News, 2010a, 2010b).

The *Times*, the *Telegraph*, the *Guardian*, the BBC, and MSN all carried live blogs, while Sky News, Channel 4 News, the *Times* and the *Mirror* supplemented their sites with text comments provided by an embedded instant message service, again provided by CoveritLive (Belam, 2010; Collins & Blake, 2010; Metcalfe, 2010; Sparrow, 2010; Times, 2010). A Twitter "sentiment tracker" provided by the web company Tweetminster funneled real-time text content analysis of Twitter messages, with hashtags such as #leadersdebate, #ukelection, or #ge2010, into the ITV website. Overall, during the ninety-minute debate, 211,000 individual Twitter messages were produced, as users structured their commentary and conversations using these shared hashtags. The messages were produced at an average rate of thirty-nine per second, as 47,420 individual Twitter users engaged in real-time discussion (O'Loughlin, 2010). This cemented the emergent role played by Twitter and Facebook as backchannels adopted by the politically interested to form ad hoc discursive communities around major live television events.

Some journalists, most notably Nick Robinson, the BBC's political editor, preempted their post-debate appearances on the 10:00 p.m. television news by posting their initial reactions to the debate on their blogs and on Twitter (Robinson, 2010). Channel 4 News's Krishnan Guru-Murthy, eager to intervene despite the absence of a late-night bulletin on Channel 4, joined hundreds of other British journalists in posting real-time commentary on Twitter (Google Replay Search, 2010a).

One issue here is how the Twitter audience compared with the television audience. Twitter's design is asymmetrical and some well-known individuals amass huge armies of followers. Many less well-known but still important individuals, especially those inside or on the margins of the Westminster "village" have follower lists running into the several thousands. These 47,420 active debate tweeters constituted just half a percent of the total television audience of 9.4 million. But the important number here is the combined amount of followers these 47,420 active tweeters had—in other words, the number of people who were potentially exposed to commentary on the debates. Note "potentially": we have no means of verifying actual exposure in this case. Unfortunately, these data on follower counts are impossible to obtain, so consider a hypothetical illustration based on a mixture of conservative assumptions and what we already know from large-scale studies of message propagation on Twitter (Kwak, et al., 2010; Ye & Wu, .2010). At the time of the debate, Labour's Alistair Campbell had 44,000 followers, the comedian Chris Addison had 24,000, and Channel 4 News's Krishnan Guru-Murthy had 27,000. All three were active tweeters during the prime ministerial debate. Granted, these are celebrities, albeit minor ones, and we know that Twitter as a whole has a long tail of users with relatively few followers; in June 2009, the company itself revealed that the average number of followers per user was 126 (Weaver, 2009). There are also important unknowables, particularly the amount of mutual following inside the network of 47,420 active debate tweeters, and the extent to which individuals outside the active network followed multiple individuals inside it. Bearing these caveats in mind, let us somewhat artificially but conservatively assume that each of the 47,420 active debate tweeters had an average of just fifty "unique" followers. This produces a potentially exposed audience of 2.4 million individuals. Then there is further propagation of content, either through Twitter's retweet feature or selective repetition of others' messages, through which the followers-of-followers are also potentially exposed. The basic statistic that "47,420" Twitter users tweeted about the debate therefore only tells part of the story, which is that due to its design Twitter can quickly scale in ways that expose surprisingly large potential audiences to political messages.

It should come as no surprise, then, that the political parties were eager to selectively present their own participants in the Twitter and Facebook social media debate back-channels. This was done to create excitement and engagement through a constructed sense of liveness, but also as an attempt to influence broadcasters' and newspapers' coverage. For example, Labour featured three live Twitter feeds on its home page, from "politicians," "bloggers," and "Labour on Twitter" (The Labour Party, 2010). These were hand-picked and highly sympathetic to Labour. The Conservatives' site featured CoveritLive's real time text commenting facility (Belam, 2010).

ITV News' and Sky News' home page featured a Facebook Connect widget that pulled in comments in real time from Facebook's Democracy UK page (Facebook, 2010). The *Guardian's* website had a live feed, featuring constantly updated messages from its own journalists on Twitter, an online poll, and a crude "sentiment tracker" which relied upon individuals to click plus or minus buttons for each of the three parties as they watched the debate (Sparrow, 2010). At least this had the virtue of transparency, unlike the several Twitter sentiment trackers whose text mining algorithms were left unpublished. This is a development which should signal huge accountability and transparency problems if, as seems certain, such devices are to become a permanent feature of campaign coverage across the advanced democracies. The *Guardian* tracker poll was deeply flawed and it was reportedly manipulated through automated page loading by staff in the Liberal Democrats' central office. Their IP addresses were banned by the *Guardian's* online editor, Janine Gibson, once the activity was discovered during the debate (Gibson, 2010).

Sky News could not resist starting to "analyze" the performances before the debate had actually ended. Having arranged an instant text messaging real-time tracker poll of 1608 viewers, run by Fizzback, a "real-time survey company," Sky used interim "results" to declare the Conservatives' David Cameron the "winner," just a third of the way into the ninety-minute show. Fizzback provided two sets of interim results—at thirty minutes and sixty minutes in. The thirty-minute results page remained on Sky News's main web page until later that night, when the full results emerged and revealed Liberal Democrat leader Nick Clegg as the debate winner by a large margin. Fizzback used instant text message polls of selected samples from what the Sky News website claimed was a panel of ten thousand individuals and it also tracked real-time responses to specific policy issues on a scale from −10 to +10, again by text message (Chung, 2010). Earlier, Sky News' press release had stated that Fizzback's panel would consist of "more than 6000 voters" and that it would be "pre-selected to represent the demographics of the whole of the UK" while "rigorous quota sampling and weighting of the results will be overseen by Futuresight [another market research company] to ensure the results are robust." The precise nature of the sampling and method were not published, though mention was made of what was termed "The unique Fizzback Artificial Intelligence Engine" (Sky News, 2010a).

Broadcasters and the newspapers tried to construct a particular role for digital media. Facebook and smaller, niche organizations such as CoveritLive and Tweetminster were integrated into the production in ways that were perceived to add value to the television viewer's experience. They were there to do the things that television itself was ill-equipped to do: real-time crunching of huge volumes of online social network data, sentiment analysis, and the attention-grabbing visualization of results. This creates a qualitatively different sense of hybrid liveness around an event, one that does not rely upon traditional political broadcasting and newspaper genres, which, in this context—live blogging aside—were staid and familiar. A similar symbolic liveness has previously been observed in interactive "reality" and comedy entertainment formats (Levine, 2008; Ytreberg, 2009). As Nick Couldry argues, liveness is often now a "cross-media construction" (2002: 286). Online media's role in the televisual aspects of the leaders' debate rested upon technological expertise and a willfully "geeky" attention to the flow of vast amounts of data. The ITV web page epitomized this hybrid integration, with its live video feed direct from the television studio situated alongside the various internet widgets tracking data from the social network sites. ITV's presenter Alistair Stewart explicitly drew attention to the website's affordances at the start of the debate, when he asked viewers not only to follow along on television, but to "join in" on the website (ITV News, 2010a).

The problem here, though, is that this broader strategy of integration sometimes blunted digital media's affordances for presenting a wider range of expression in the event's immediate framing. The digital players ended up tailoring their offerings in ways that closely fitted with the broadcasters' and newspaper editors' requirements. There was little transparency around the precise methods involved in real-time sentiment analysis of online text, which is far from an exact science, but these data were too often presented as social facts by the television and newspaper websites, and by the online companies themselves. These real-time digital genres often therefore simply reinforce the older normative problems associated with ritualistic shortcuts to "public opinion" through opinion polls (Herbst, 1993). They provide a sanitized, symbolic presence for the public (Bennett, 1994) in what is essentially an orchestrated, one-to-many broadcasting environment. That they do so in real time compounds the problem, because there is even less scope for journalists to explain key issues such as sample size, method, self-selection bias, and any number of problems associated with the unpublished algorithms used for text mining.

Nevertheless, broadcasters themselves were able to use digital media tools in ways that laid bare some of the techniques that have been the staple of political communication specialists for decades but which are usually hidden from public view. The depiction of backstage processes is a case in point. In the hours and minutes leading up to the debate, several professional journalists, including Laura Kuenssberg, then the BBC's chief political correspondent, posted pictures from their camera phones, capturing something of the character of "spin alley." Here on display was a backstage space set aside for the post-debate huddle involving journalists, politicians, and the parties' press officers, complete with a giant screen and rows of desks covered with laptops, smartphones, and notebooks (Kuenssberg, 2010f). ITV formally held exclusive rights over backstage photographs taken during the debate itself (Rogers, 2010), so depicting spin alley then mostly fell to bloggers, albeit elite ones, such as *Conservative Home*'s Tim Montgomerie, who posted camera phone pictures on Twitter of senior Conservative Jeremy Hunt, former Liberal Democrat leader Paddy Ashdown, and Labour's Peter Mandelson briefing journalists before the debate had actually ended (see for example Montgomerie, 2010). These semi-illicit photos clearly influenced the mainstream coverage. The *Times* election blog managed to sneak out some photographs the following day (Rogers, 2010), and by then television news was running behind-the-scenes material showing the parties' communications teams grouped with numerous journalists. Such coverage became part of the fabric of the remaining two debates and illustrated the ways professional journalists used the logics of digital media to subvert attempts at spin (see for example Kuenssberg, 2010).

Thus, "process" and "meta-coverage" were very much in evidence (Cappella & Jamieson, 1997; Esser, et al., 2001; Patterson, 1993). And yet the implications here are ambiguous. Similar, if less formally organized, spaces in which journalists, politicians, and communications staff come together to establish common understandings of a major event, like the leader's speeches at the annual party conferences, have been a crucial part of the reporting of major political events in Britain for decades (Stanyer, 2001). Yet due to the real-time framing of reaction in the prime ministerial debates, spin alley assumed a new significance. The smuggling out of surreptitiously taken camera phone shots by some journalists and bloggers, as well as Twitter updates condemning party staff and journalists for getting together before the debate had ended, served to expose these machinations to the viewing public. And this was also part of a meta-game: the simultaneously competitive and cooperative interactions between newer and older media logics.

MOBILIZING IN REAL TIME

The third stage of the prime ministerial debate's political information cycle involved journalist commentary, the reporting of a range of further instant opinion polls—this time by established polling companies—and more traditional interviews with representatives of the three main political parties. These took place immediately following the debate. Television journalists ran their post-debate interviews from the backstage newsroom. This conveyed a sense of the urgency and importance of the media's presence, but these episodes were formal, staged, and in a space away from the busiest parts of the room. They provided little genuine sense of the ongoing interactions that were out of shot, in spin alley. And they largely featured senior politicians from each main party, whose judgments predictably divided along party lines.

This stage was dominated by discussion of the orchestrated real-time mechanisms that had framed stage two. A good example was ITV's mobilization of selected excerpts from its twenty-person backstage reaction panel, complete with a rerun of the computer-generated graphic of the worm chart the panel had collectively produced for the ITV website live during the debate (ITV News, 2010b). The BBC featured its own worm poll analysis, provided by Ipsos MORI and based on a sample of thirty-six "undecided voters from the Manchester area" (Ipsos MORI, 2010). As I discussed above, the information generated during stage two was mostly the result of unrepresentative, non-transparent, and in some cases easily manipulated instant polls and sentiment trackers. And editorial decisions about which footage to use must, out of necessity, have been taken before the debate actually drew to a close, during the scramble to assemble video packages by the 10:00 p.m. television news deadline.

Four "traditional" yet instant polls, all using transparent sampling methods, were published within a few minutes of the end of the debate. These were based on a variety of methods. YouGov/the *Sun* used an online survey of its pre-recruited panel of viewers (YouGov, 2010). ComRes/ITV News used automated phone calls to poll a pre-recruited panel of 4032 members of the public (ComRes, 2010). The *Times/* Populus relied on a pre-recruited online panel from which it sampled 1004 individuals (Populus, 2010). Angus Reid used an online panel, whose responses were filtered directly and in real time onto its website—before its poll had actually ended (Angus Reid Public Opinion, 2010). All of these polls showed Nick Clegg to be the clear debate winner. Conservative leader David Cameron came second in all but one. Fifteen minutes after the debate drew to a close, ITV's 10 p.m. news revealed the results of its ComRes post-debate poll. The results gave Clegg 43 percent against Cameron's 26 percent and Gordon Brown's 20 percent (ITV News, 2010b). This poll showed the extent of Clegg's breakthrough and went on to play a crucial role in shaping stage four of the political information cycle.

If the real-time information was opaque or flawed, what can be said of these post-debate polls? All were conducted by reputable polling companies who subscribe to the British Polling Council's code of practice. Yet because they are so influential in determining journalists' interpretive frames—perhaps rightly so when the only alternative sources of immediately available information are post-debate interviews with politically biased personnel from the parties—we need to consider the inevitable compromises that accompany rapid reaction polling. Some of the potential pitfalls are illustrated by the ComRes/ITV poll conducted right after the third debate on April 29. This had Cameron as the debate winner with 36 percent, Clegg with 33 percent, and Brown with 26 percent. But the voting intention profile of this poll's sample was not representative, at least if judged in the context of other polls conducted around the same time: 36 percent of respondents in this poll were Liberal Democrat supporters, 35 percent were Conservative supporters, and just 24 percent preferred Labour (Gibbon, 2010). If we assume that supporters of a particular party are more likely to have favorable attitudes toward their party leader's performance in a televised debate, the profile of a poll sample becomes an important variable in shaping its results. In this case, the results inflated Clegg's rating. Although the internet has enabled polling companies to publish their methods for all to read, in the scramble to present the results, journalists and presenters only rarely highlight these methods.

AUGMENTATION

Stage four of the debate's political information cycle consisted of more detailed post-debate analysis and commentary by broadcasters and the newspapers. First up was the BBC's flagship long-form public affairs show, *Newsnight*. An hour after the debate it featured a blow-by-blow dissection by the news anchor and two journalists, an expert round table including former party communication advisers, and a session with a now-obligatory "body language expert" and the *Times* restaurant and television reviewer, A. A. Gill (BBC2, 2010a). By this point, the major newspaper editors were making decisions about the front pages of the following day's print editions and their websites were updated with analysis of the debate. The overwhelming majority of the next day's papers, including the Conservative-supporting outlets, contained coverage of the Clegg "surge" (Chapman, 2010; Daily Star, 2010d; T. N. Dunn, 2010; Grice, 2010; Lyons & Beattie, 2010; Pierce, 2010; Porter, et al., 2010; Watson & Coates, 2010; Watt & Wintour, 2010; Yelland, 2010).

For broadcasters, the debate's influence on routine news values was immediate. The morning after the debate, as the print editions of the papers were absorbed, the major agenda setters—BBC Radio 4's *Today* program, BBC Five Live, and the ITV and BBC breakfast television shows—were saturated with commentary. The *Today* program's morning prime time slot, just after Radio 4's 8:00 a.m. news bulletin, was devoted to a feature based on Frank Luntz, an American opinion pollster and political consultant long-favored as a BBC pundit (BBC Radio 4, 2010a). The night before, Luntz had run his own thirty-two-person reaction-dial "focus group" for the *Sun* newspaper, complete with its own real-time worm chart. The *Sun* filmed Luntz and the panel at work and prominently displayed an edited *video* clip on their website the next day. Luntz's and his panel's verdicts were unequivocal: Nick Clegg was the winner, by a large margin (Luntz, 2010).

Friday's daytime and evening broadcast news bulletins were accompanied by continuing online discussion on the most popular political blogs—Iain Dale, Guido Fawkes, *Conservative Home*, *Labourlist*, *Left Foot Forward*, and *Liberal Democrat Voice* (Conservative Home, 2010a; Fawkes, 2010; Labourlist, 2010; Left Foot Forward, 2010; Liberal Democrat Voice, 2010). By now, YouTube featured several hundred edited video clips that had been uploaded by the news organizations, the parties, and members of the public (YouTube, 2010). Twitter users continued to label their messages with the #leadersdebate, #ge2010, #ge10, and #ukelection hashtags (Twapperkeeper, 2010b). This continued throughout the remainder of the campaign, and took an interesting twist, as we shall see.

By Friday evening, BBC, ITV, and Channel 4 News all led on a different story—the closure of UK airports caused by a volcanic ash cloud in Iceland. But Nick Clegg's victory came a close second. In-depth reporting on Friday evening included Channel 4 News's *FactCheck* feature, which covered exaggerated claims concerning the wastefulness of local police forces made by David Cameron during the debate. As has become the norm, the *FactCheck* team of reporters used Twitter throughout the day to post "teasers" and interact with potential audience members about the content of their evening bulletin (Channel 4 News, 2010a) (For more on the general significance of *FactCheck* see chapter 8). Friday evening's coverage also saw the first installment of an extraordinary miniseries on Channel 4's 7:00 p.m. news show. Entitled "Britain's Next Boss," this featured a studio audience and three expert guests: "entrepreneur James Caan, comedienne and now leadership consultant Ruby Wax, and business psychologist Dr. Adrian Atkinson." As presenter Krishnan Guru-Murthy explained: "Who's got the personality to lead this country, the character to deal with a crisis? On Britain's Next Boss we'll put the three main party leaders under the microscope... This show is a policy-free zone, because some of the biggest tests of a prime minister are on things never mentioned in manifestos." The expert panel began with commentary on sound- and image-bite excerpts of the previous night's leaders' debate. Broadcast media logic prevailed.

The remainder of stage four stretched across the weekend into Monday and in turn went on to frame the build-up to the second debate which came during the third week of the election campaign. Friday's commentary and analysis fed into the weekend newspaper journalists' copy deadlines and editors' final decisions on the contents and layout of the weekend print editions. The Sunday morning political television shows shoveled up the fallout from Thursday evening's debate and used it as a means of emphasizing the importance of the second debate, which was scheduled for just four days later. Once again, the dominant frame was Clegg's remarkable performance in the televised debate.

CONTESTATION

Following a weekend of remarkably positive broadcast and newspaper coverage from organizations across the entire political spectrum, the Liberal Democrats started the third week of the campaign with a huge boost in the (traditionally conducted) opinion polls. Some polls placed them on an almost equal footing with the Conservatives; in most, Labour were unexpectedly relegated to third place (T. Young, 2010). The *Sun* carried Nick Clegg's victory on its Monday morning front page (T. N. Dunn, 2010). Suddenly, the election had become a genuine three-party contest and this unleashed much soul-searching commentary among the press, especially the pro-Conservative papers such as the *Daily Mail*, the *Times* and the *Daily Telegraph*. Broadcast journalists, too, began to exercise much greater scrutiny over the Liberal Democrats' policy platform. This was palpable in the BBC's major news shows, which were now characterized by a "who is the real Nick Clegg?" frame (see for example BBC Radio 4, 2010b).

It was primarily television that played the predominant role in the Liberal Democrats' surge by raising public awareness of Clegg's approach as leader and of the Liberal Democrats as a party. Yet there were early signs that the internet was also playing an important role. The Liberal Democrats became the first UK party to have a Facebook group—albeit an unofficial one—to recruit a higher number of members than the dues-paying membership of the party itself. The group, "We got Rage Against the Machine to #1, We Can Get the Lib Dems Into Office!" had been founded just two days before the first television debate by a young Liberal Democrat activist, Ben Stockman (We Got Rage Against the Machine to Number 1 …, 2010). Taking its name from the successful online charitable fundraising campaign to prevent the winners of 2009's X-Factor talent show from reaching the number one slot in the music charts, the Facebook group quickly grew to more than 100,000 members within just three days of the first debate. This placed it way ahead of the other parties' Facebook groups and fan pages, official or otherwise, and the group went on to reach 165,000 members by election day three weeks later. While the earlier online campaign against X-Factor had been a matter of newer media logic confronting older media logic (in this case the inauthenticity of television talent shows), the Liberal Democrats "Rage" group was very different. Here it was a case of newer media mobilization coming to the aid of what were seen as broadcast media's authentic representations of Clegg in the television debate.

Some of the post-debate polls seemed to reveal that the Liberal Democrats had picked up significant new support from voters under the age of thirty-five (Helm & Asthana, 2010b). Clegg presented himself as a "fresh" alternative to what he continually described as the "old parties," and this was based upon a narrative of what he termed "real change." The "Rage" Facebook group was evidence of this "outsider" appeal. Weakly aligned voters, especially the young to middle-aged, educated, middle-class citizens that dominate online politics, were looking for something resembling a movement for reform. A hung parliament was the prize, leading to electoral reform as a condition of Clegg entering into a coalition with Labour or the Conservatives.

The increase in support for the Liberal Democrats greatly unsettled the Conservative-supporting newspapers, who were now torn between reflecting the rise of Clegg—clearly a major political story with a popular grassroots frame—or turning their fire on the Liberal Democrats. This tension was soon resolved. Within a couple of days, and once it became clear that "Cleggmania" was not likely to falter in the short term, the right-wing newspapers turned, producing torrents of critical coverage in the run-up to the second debate. For example, the *Daily Mail* ran an extraordinary series of stories on Clegg. One suggested that the Liberal Democrats' leader had uttered a "Nazi slur" on Britain in 2002 when he had suggested that victory in the Second World War had made it more difficult for the British to accept that other European countries were more prosperous (Shipman, 2010). The piece remarked that Clegg had "a Spanish wife, a Dutch mother and a Russian grandparent, [and] began his career as a Brussels bureaucrat and moved to Westminster after a spell as a Euro MP." The "debate" section of the *Mail*'s site was dominated by articles on the Liberal Democrats and Clegg, from "Dirty Tricks of the REAL Nasty Party" (Oborne, 2010) to "How the LibDems Would Release 60,000 Convicts" (Slack, 2010) and "The LibDems are a Party Full of Shadow Lobbyists" (Waghorne, 2010).

Worse was to come for Clegg. The night before the second televised leaders' debate, the *Telegraph* announced on its website that its debate-day front page would feature what it framed as an investigative scoop: a report that Clegg had received party donations from three businessmen directly into his personal bank account (Winnett & Swaine, 2010). The *Telegraph* had trawled through the vast archive of documents it had bought in order to run its months-long series of exposés on MPs' expenses in mid-2009. Clegg was given a chance to respond to the story before the *Telegraph* published. His office issued a holding statement saying that he had used the money to pay for a member of staff and that these donations were reported in the parliamentary register of members' interests. The *Telegraph*'s online article was quickly circulated late that night via the *Conservative Home* website and on Twitter. It was also picked up within minutes by BBC *Newsnight*'s political correspondent, Michael Crick, who, at around 10:35 p.m., and in a taste of what was to follow, hinted that in his view it was an unremarkable revelation (BBC2, 2010b).

But during the following morning—the day of the second televised debate—there unfolded an extraordinary series of events that reveal how newer media logics can intervene in areas where older media logics seem to be supremely powerful. As news of the *Telegraph*'s "scoop" reverberated through media and online networks, it became obvious that some journalists—on both the right and the left—were becoming skeptical of the *Telegraph*'s front-page story. By mid-morning, a satirical online flash campaign had emerged on Twitter, reflecting and further reinforcing this skepticism. Tens of thousands sardonically added the hashtag "#nickcleggsfault" to their status updates. These messages ranged from political observations to ludicrous statements such as "We've run out of houmous #nickcleggsfault," or "Have hairy toes, #nickcleggsfault" (Twapperkeeper, 2010a). By the middle of the day #nickcleggsfault had become the third most popular shared hashtag, not just among the then 7.5 million Twitter users in the UK, but the entirety of Twitter's then 105 million global users.

Suddenly, through a combination of elite and activist skepticism, the *Telegraph* was thrown on the defensive. Sensing that the Clegg donation story was not being as well-received as he had hoped, the paper's deputy editor Benedict Brogan took the unusual step of issuing a defense on the paper's political blog. By that stage, however, the BBC's Radio Four presenter, Evan Davis, had posted on Twitter: "Extraordinary. Twitter parodies undercut media attacks on Clegg (#nickcleggsfault). Telegraph ends up defending itself" (E. Davis, 2010). Later that afternoon, the BBC's digital election correspondent, Rory Cellan-Jones, published a blog post about the #nickcleggsfault meme, adding further fuel to the Twitter campaign (Cellan-Jones, 2010).

Later that evening, just before Clegg walked on stage in Bristol for the second leader's debate, his office produced bank statements proving that there had been no financial wrongdoing. The *Telegraph*'s intervention was over. The publication of Clegg's financial records was the most important direct factor in blunting the story's impact and keeping it off the evening television news, but this came in the context of a growing awareness among elite journalists, spurred in part by the online mobilization among activists earlier in the day, that the *Telegraph*'s story was not all it appeared to be and was driven by excessive partisan bias. The *Telegraph*'s expenses "scoop" thus collapsed as a result of harmonious interventions in older and newer media settings.

As the election campaign progressed, the second and third live televised prime ministerial debates closely followed the pattern established by the first, with real time broadcast and live streaming and real-time online activist and journalist interventions becoming firmly embedded in the hybrid mediation of the events. Within fifteen minutes of the beginning of the second debate, the Liberal Democrats uploaded Clegg's one-minute opening statement to YouTube and posted links to it on Facebook and Twitter (Libdemvoice, 2010; Pack, 2010). Once again, campaign communications staff and journalists could not resist interacting before the debate had ended, but others were willing to use social media backchannels to reveal this. For example, *Daily Mirror* reporter Kevin Maguire reported on Twitter that the Conservatives' press officer Paul Stephenson was "trying to brief hacks in the Bristol centre while [the] debate's on" (Maguire, 2010). Snap polls and sentiment tracking played an even greater role in the second and third debates. Sky News dropped Fizzback after the first debate, for unknown reasons, but immediately after the second and third debates Sky announced the results of its YouGov instant poll, which placed Cameron first, closely followed by Clegg and Brown. Broadcast interviews were once again constantly framed by this instant poll. And by the time of the second debate, the BBC and Sky had joined ITV in foregrounding their own small audience panels with sentiment dials and worm charts.

Britain's first ever live televised prime ministerial debate fundamentally changed the dynamics of the 2010 British election campaign. While the Liberal Democrats' poll surge fell away during the final week of the campaign, "Cleggmania" had three important tangible effects on the outcome of the election. First, the Manchester debate established that precious commodity—campaign momentum—for the Liberal Democrats. The Conservative and Labour leaders were on the back foot until very late in the race. Brown was a consistent loser in the media commentary and the snap polls following all three debates. Cameron was widely perceived to have disappointed during the first two events; he staged a strong recovery during the third, but this came just a few full campaigning days before polling day. Second, because the Liberal Democrats ended the campaign with a 3 or 4 percent increase from where their share of the popular vote had stood in pre-campaign polls, they avoided being wiped out in some seats by the electoral swing to the Conservatives. The Liberal Democrats' total of fifty-seven seats could eas-ily have been substantially lower had they not benefited from the boost provided by the prime ministerial debate. Third, the debate greatly enhanced Clegg's overall credibility with the media and the public, smoothing the Liberal Democrats' historic transition into coalition government with the Conservatives, and Clegg's personal rise, against the odds, to the position of deputy prime minister alongside prime minister David Cameron on May 11.

Conclusion

Britain's first ever live televised prime ministerial debate revealed that competition and conflict, but also interdependence, among broadcasters, the press, and digital media actors—the latter including some online activists organized in informal social network environments—have become real forces in the mediation of political life. The selective real-time coverage of early stages of the political information cycle and the occasional integration of greater numbers of non-elite actors in the construc-tion and contestation of news at multiple points in the cycle's lifespan are emerging systemic norms in the mediation of high-profile political events. The 2010 election debates were an opportunity for British broadcasters to deal a blow to their tradi-tional competitors in the newspaper sector, but they were also widely framed as a means of exposing the deficiencies of digital media, in order to force home television's advantage as the principal medium of political communication for the British public, a status it undoubtedly retains. Previews, analysis, and commentary concerning the debates dominated news coverage across all media for the entire campaign, leading many commentators to label 2010 a "TV election." But the analysis here suggests that this label is only partially correct and ultimately misleading. It fails to capture the real-ity of Britain's hybrid media system.

The analysis of the Bullygate affair reveals the same processes at work. This sensa-tional political news story received cross-media saturation coverage across all outlets for an entire weekend, as the logics of online blogs and social media were hybridized with those of broadcast and print media. There was a book whose contents were leaked to a national newspaper three weeks before it was excerpted in a rival national newspa-per as part of that rival's relaunch strategy. There was a prime minister who tried to pre-empt the revelations by appearing on a television talk show a week earlier, granting an interview to a further rival national newspaper, and using an exclusive interview with a television news program to deny the allegations the day before they were published. There were journalists operating in a hypercompetitive environment, interacting with each other and with ordinary citizens in public and online, breaking stories and new information on the web, on their own blogs, or on Twitter, hours before they appeared in scheduled broadcast news bulletins. Some journalists clearly picked up valuable information in online interactions with ordinary members of the public. A backbench MP orchestrated a Twitter hashtag campaign in order to attack the story's credibility, forcing the book's author to respond directly on Twitter in order to defend himself. An amateur blogger conducted online research encompassing the archives of a seemingly unrelated anonymous blog set up six months earlier in order to reveal the dubious credibility of a source that most mainstream news journalists appeared not to have bothered to research.

These cases reveal how a range of new real-time genres, non-elite interventions and elite-activist interactions are coming to assume a greater role in the shaping of political news. These news-making assemblages are dominated by political and journalistic elites, amateur and semi-professional bloggers, the public relations industry, digital marketing firms, and politically active citizens, but they also involve greater numbers of players and a more diverse range of actors than news cycles ever did.

Broadcasters and newspapers now integrate non-elite actors and information from the online realm. They also use digital marketing techniques and intermediary consultancies, not only to convey to audiences the increasingly important online activity taking place around political events, but also to marshal specialized techniques, such as the appealing presentation of behavioral data in real time, which broadcast media and newspapers are still surprisingly ill-equipped to provide for themselves. Established television and newspaper genres sit cheek-by-jowl with newer digital genres in a hybrid but integrated flux of remediation (Bolter & Grusin, 1999).

In some respects these processes duplicate and amplify aspects of broadcast coverage that have long been considered problematic. Most notable in the case of the prime ministerial debate was the inauthentic expression of public opinion through snap polls whose symbolic value to news media is always likely to prove attractive in a hybrid media system with pressures to create ever greater amounts of "fresh" content for print, the web, and broadcast, all at the same time. The potential for news outlet bias to color the design and reporting of what seem on the surface to be "neutral," technologically driven devices like sentiment analysis for monitoring online expressions of public opinion could become of greater concern in future.

An important outcome of these news-making assemblages are interpretive frames that are strongly determined by how real-time coverage is orchestrated during and immediately after an event. But political information cycles are not simply about single events or the acceleration of news time; the idea of a "24-hour news cycle" does not capture their multiplicity. Political information cycles rest upon a subtle political economy of time. This involves not only the often-rehearsed "speeding up" or "efficiency" of communication but also the importance of continuous attention and the ability to create and to act on information in a timely manner. Those who recognize the importance of time and the circulation of information—when to act quickly, when to delay, when to devote intensive attention to the pursuit of a goal, when to repeat, when to act alone, and when to coordinate—are more likely to be powerful. The logic of newer media enables a more diverse range of actors to shape time in order to pursue their values and interests. In an era when we are surrounded by clichés such as "always-on connectivity" and "24/7 media," and when we are witnessing seemingly contradictory phenomena such as the simultaneous shrinkage and extension of news cycles, the economy of time is a neglected but crucial force in political communication. In the contemporary era, those who have the resources to intervene in the political information cycle are more able to exercise power; those who lack these resources are less able to be powerful in political life.

In an increasingly fragmented media environment, in which growing segments of the audience are turning away from older channels of delivery, political information cycles increase the likelihood that multiple, fragmented audiences will be exposed to political content and they increase opportunities for intervention by citizen activists. They can fashion a form of unifying "publicness" that has been undermined by media fragmentation.

Increasingly, this is how important political news is produced. The hybrid ways in which politics is now mediated presents new opportunities for non-elite actors to enter news production assemblages through timely interventions and sometimes direct, one-to-one, micro-level interactions with professional journalists. Contrary to the skeptics, bloggers and social media users are not always "parasitical" upon the "mainstream" media. Equally, professional journalists do not slavishly chase every last online utterance by bloggers and social media users. As they did in the past, journalists use their considerable power and professional resources to influence news agendas, control the flow of information, outdo their rivals, and undermine the new media upstarts. But at the same time, online activists and news professionals alike are now routinely engaged in loosely coupled assemblages in the pursuit of new information that will propel a news story forward and increase its newsworthiness. Much of this activity is episodic and it occurs in real time as stories unfold. It is therefore easy to miss and can only be reconstructed through detailed qualitative research based on live media ethnography.

Political information cycles contain pockets of intense engagement, but this is not "crowdsourcing" or the "wisdom of crowds" (Howe, 2008; Surowiecki, 2004). Intra-elite competition is a dominant feature of this environment and the non-elite actors in this study were mostly, though not exclusively, motivated and strategically oriented political activists, or those with at least some interest in following politics. Their behavior suggests an awareness that carefully timed interactions with elite politicians and professional journalists will occasionally be able to play a role in shaping the news. Small numbers of individuals made the truly decisive interventions, and we will always need to pay careful attention to deciphering who actually does the powerful work in these environments. At the same time, however, we should not lose sight of the fact that ordinary citizens, using digital technologies that enable them to cross from the outside to the inside of the elite political-media nexus, may now, on occasion, affect the meanings and flows of political information in new ways.

5

Power, Interdependence, and Hybridity in the Construction of Political News: Understanding WikiLeaks

> Assange bedevils the journalists who work with him because he refuses to conform to any of the roles they expect him to play...He's a wily shape-shifter who won't sit still...
> —Alan Rusbridger, editor of the *Guardian*[1]

> If it feels a little bit like we're amateurs, it is because we are... Everyone is an amateur in this business.
> —Julian Assange, WikiLeaks[2]

> If you want us to do something for you, then you've got to do something for us.
> —David Leigh, journalist[3]

WikiLeaks has been described by one of its former leaders as "the most aggressive press organization in the world" (Domscheit-Berg, 2011: Chapter 10, para. 36, Kindle Edition). Alan Rusbridger, the long-standing editor of Britain's *Guardian* newspaper called the U.S. embassy cables stories of 2010–2011 "the biggest leak in the history of the world" (Rusbridger, 2011). Greg Mitchell of the *Nation* described what WikiLeaks does as "the megaleak" (Mitchell, 2011).

But what is WikiLeaks? Is it a website, an e-mail list, or a globally distributed technological infrastructure based on secure encryption standards? Is it a publishing business, a professional investigative online news magazine, or a public relations agency acting on behalf of anonymous clients? Is it an elite-centric lobby group, a netroots social movement pressing for radical transparency in all areas of life, or a secretive group of dedicated activists? Is it a collective of radical poets and artists, a transnational, distributed online network of hackers, or an educational foundation funded by charitable donations? Is it a loosely connected series of conferences and alternative festivals? Is it truly global or embedded in specific national media systems? Or is it just one person: Julian Assange?

WikiLeaks is all of these things and more. Its hybrid media logics reveal important shifts in how political news is created but they also raise issues of broader significance for political organization, mobilization, and communication in the present era.

WikiLeaks' Impact on Political News

From its inception in 2006, WikiLeaks has had a significant impact on political news, across a wide range of issues and in a large number of countries. It is impossible to do justice to the full scope of these interventions here, but consider the following summary.

On America's Thanksgiving Day, November 25, 2009, WikiLeaks published more than half a million confidential pager messages that had been gathered by the U.S. National Security Agency during the September 2001 terrorist attacks on New York and Washington. In July 2010, in alliance with Britain's *Guardian*, America's *New York Times*, and Germany's *Der Spiegel*, WikiLeaks released around seventy-five thousand documents related to U.S. military incidents in the war in Afghanistan. These documents contained detailed reports of all the major events of the conflict, including casualty numbers. Up until that point, the U.S. military had said that statistics on civilian casualties were not recorded (Leigh & Harding, 2011: Ch. 8, para. 10, Kindle Edition). The *Guardian* and *Der Spiegel* published leaked reports mentioning previously unreleased civilian deaths that were caused by experimental long-range weaponry used by a secret military squad named Task Force 373. These stories made it public that Task Force 373 was working on a special two-thousand-person "kill or capture" list of key targets. There were deep divisions among coalition forces over the civilian deaths caused by these tactics. There were also concerns about the extent to which such special forces were subject to political as opposed to merely military control. The documents brought to light how civilian deaths had become a depressingly regular feature of daily military operations in Afghanistan and how difficult it was to obtain clear and timely confirmation from official sources about such deaths: the majority of those detailed in the logs had simply gone unreported by the media. Tensions caused by attempts to undermine the military strategy of containing the Taliban in Afghanistan were also exposed, when it transpired that Pakistan had been launching attacks on Afghan soldiers at the border between the two countries (Leigh & Harding, 2011: Ch. 9, paras. 8–24).

In October 2010, again in alliance with press partners, WikiLeaks released around four hundred thousand confidential Iraq war field reports. These revealed many cases of systematic torture and abuse by the Iraqi army, most of which had been ignored by the U.S. authorities. The reports also made it possible to identify at least 66,081 civilian deaths that had occurred as a result of the war in Iraq between 2004 and 2009. (The logs did not cover the most bloody period of the conflict—the invasion of 2003.) Not only did this leak directly contradict the official view that there were no detailed records of civilian casualties, it also enabled the anti-war think tank and campaign group Iraq Body Count to corroborate its own research. Upon analyzing the field reports Iraq Body Count concluded that they contained records of 109,932 deaths. When they added these deaths to their own numbers, Iraq Body Count were able to say publicly that between 99,383 and 108,501 civilians lost their lives in Iraq between 2003 and the end of 2010 (Leigh & Harding, 2011: Ch. 10, paras. 17–19).

The embassy cables leak of November 2010 saw WikiLeaks hand to five newspapers—the *Guardian*, the *New York Times*, *Der Spiegel*, *Le Monde*, and *El País*—some

251,287 confidential internal U.S. State Department memorandums originating from embassy and consulate staff in no fewer than 180 countries. During the first day of what would turn out to be months of coverage of the cables, the *Guardian's* website attracted 4.1 million unique users—its highest ever daily audience (Leigh & Harding, 2011: Chapter 15, para. 24). The embassy cables revealed that in 2008 and 2009 the U.S. government had circulated to the CIA, the FBI, America's staff at the United Nations (U.N.), and thirty U.S. ambassadors' offices a request that they should start gathering "biographic and biometric information on UN security council permanent representatives." This included iris scans, fingerprints, and DNA samples, as well as personally identifiable data trails such as frequent flyer accounts, passwords, and encryption keys. Details of telecommunication and computer systems inside senior officials' bureaus were also requested. This surveillance program affected large numbers of U.N. staff, including its leadership and secretary general, Ban Ki-moon (R. Booth & Borger, 2010; Mazzetti, 2010). Spying at the U.N. has long been suspected, but here, for the first time, was public, documented proof. This "national human intelligence collection directive," signed by Secretary of State Hillary Clinton, was previously entirely secret.

Further revelations—far too many to mention here—emerged from the embassy cables leak. Here are some of the more prominent from the first few days of newspaper articles. During the 2000s, not only Israel but also King Abdullah of Saudi Arabia had been secretly urging the United States to launch a military attack on Iran as a means of containing the rogue state's growing nuclear program; the Saudi leader suggested that the U.S. "cut off the head of the snake" (Sanger, et al., 2010). The U.S. military had been more heavily involved in Yemen than had been publicly admitted: this was facilitated by a secret pact between the U.S. military and the Yemeni president, Ali Abdullah Saleh, according to which the Yemenis would claim that they were the perpetrators of ongoing attacks on local al-Qaeda branches (Shane & Lehren, 2010). The cables unveiled the reality of the U.S. government's attitudes toward Russia: diplomatic correspondence stretching back over several years had provided Washington with acute analyses of the interpenetration of officialdom and organized crime in Vladimir Putin's regime (Chivers, 2010). Deep divisions between North Korea and China were catalogued, as was China's censorship of Google and the often fragile nature of the "special relationship" between the United States and Britain. Corruption on a grand scale was exposed, such as the alleged export of $9 billion out of Sudan by its president, Omar al-Bashir. The close nature of the linkages between Shell Oil and the Nigerian state were made public (D. Smith, 2010). A leak from a 2009 cable written by the U.S. ambassador to Tunisia, Robert Godec, detailed in highly critical terms the autocratic and corrupt nature of the Tunisian regime led by president Ben Ali, as well as the growing unrest that would eventually erupt into the country's pro-democracy uprising during the Arab Spring of early 2011 (Shane, 2011). The Tunisian dissidents were encouraged by American opinion and the potential international support for their cause that they predicted would flow from the publication of the U.S. ambassador's views. And finally, the cables told of disturbing and sometimes bizarre tensions in the diplomatic relationships between the U.S., Britain, and Libya. Most worryingly, the then Libyan dictator Colonel Qaddafi, offended by his treatment in New York during August 2009 (he had been refused permission to pitch a tent outside the U.N. headquarters) had delayed shipment of thirty-five metric tons of uranium that was to be sent back to Russia as part of an agreement to reduce Libya's nuclear stockpile. The highly radioactive substance sat in unlocked containers at the Tajora nuclear plant for a month, potentially risking an environmental disaster (Leigh, 2010).

The WikiLeaks embassy cables leaks fueled an extraordinary response in the United States. Two Republican congressmen for Michigan, Pete Hoekstra and Mike Rogers, called publicly for WikiLeaks' leader Julian Assange to be tried for treason and issued the death penalty. Former 2008 vice presidential candidate Sarah Palin asked publicly why Assange had not been targeted personally by the U.S. security services, when he was a "terrorist" on a par with al-Qaeda and Taliban leaders. Democratic Senator Joe Lieberman led a successful campaign for the WikiLeaks website and its online payment facilities to be closed down (Arthur, 2010; Slajda, 2010). Meanwhile, back in Europe, Javier Moreno, the editor of Spain's *El País*, said that "measured by its international impact, it's probably the biggest story this newspaper has ever been involved with" (Moreno, 2010). And as this book goes to press in the fall of 2012, the story of WikiLeaks is still evolving, as Julian Assange sits in asylum in London's Ecuador embassy as part of an attempt to resist extradition to Sweden on allegations of sexual misconduct involving two women—allegations that he claims are false and politically motivated but which the Swedish authorities claim are genuine.

In sum, WikiLeaks matters. But what is it, how did it come to play such an important role, and what is its significance for political mobilization and news making?

Leaking, Publishing, Producing, Mobilizing: WikiLeaks as a Hybrid Media Actor

WikiLeaks sits within broader networks of affinity. It is steeped in the traditions of libertarian hacker culture and the free and open source software movement. It is influenced by the technologically enabled transnational leftist movements that were first established during the 1990s by environmentalists, feminists, anarchists, and human rights groups. For all the talk of WikiLeaks being a virtual online network, face-to-face interaction has always been an important aspect of its operation. The hacker-run Chaos Computer Club's (CCC) headquarters in Berlin have provided space for meetings of its activists (Domscheit-Berg, 2011: Ch. 1, para. 17). The CCC's annual Chaos Communication Congress and its numerous workshops and events provided a platform for Julian Assange, Daniel Domscheit-Berg, and others to spread the word and solicit technological expertise and donations. The CCC has also been a key player in developing the structure through which WikiLeaks is funded. WikiLeaks is a nonprofit, but it operates according to a slightly unusual arrangement: its staff are not paid directly but are permitted to claim expenses for running the organization from the Wau-Holland-Stiftung, a German charity (Wau-Holland-Stiftung, 2011). This budget is organized under five headings: "infrastructure, campaigns, travel expenses, legal advice, and remunerations." Infrastructure covers technology costs. Campaign costs include editorial work, verifying and anonymizing data, and media production associated with major leaks. Claims for costs associated with legal advice are restricted to the organization; individuals are not entitled to these funds. Remunerations to "only a few heads of project and activists" are "based on the remuneration scheme of Greenpeace" (Wau-Holland-Stiftung, 2011).

Some of the weaknesses of WikiLeaks' hybrid role as news maker, technology platform provider, and activist movement are illustrated by its constant financial worries. An e-mail sent to previous donors in 2009 mistakenly contained a list of addresses in the cc: field. It was reported to have contained only 58 names. Previous insider Daniel Domscheit-Berg's book mentions a donor list of 106 people (Cryptome, 2011; Singel, 2009) but by August 2009 one of WikiLeaks' several PayPal accounts contained only $35,000 (Domscheit-Berg, 2011: Ch. 6, para. 4). Whether the number of donors was 58 or 106, one thing is clear: until the headline-making leaks of 2010, WikiLeaks struggled to attract significant financial support. Even the increase in donations during the big leaks of 2010 were insufficient to put it on a more permanent and sustainable footing.

Various solutions to the funding problems were proposed. There were ongoing discussions about whether the organization should shift to a more permanent charitable model, a move resisted by Assange (Domscheit-Berg, 2011: Ch. 10, para. 42). Wealthy individual donors were approached, including George Soros, the billionaire financier. In 2009, Domscheit-Berg and Assange submitted a proposal to a program funded by the Knight Foundation, a U.S.-based charitable body, to no avail. The publicity surrounding the 9/11 pager leaks of 2009 and a subsequent keynote appearance by Assange at the Chaos Communication Congress brought in around $200,000 in donations. This enabled Assange to pay some expenses to the core WikiLeaks team and it enabled the WikiLeaks network to renew some of its computer hardware (Domscheit-Berg, 2011: Ch. 10, para. 31). The *Collateral Murder* film release of April 2010, which showed U.S. helicopter gunmen killing twelve people (including two Reuters journalists) in Baghdad provided an opportunity to raise donations in the form of rights payments from television stations eager to broadcast the video on their news bulletins (Domscheit-Berg, 2011: Ch. 13, para. 21). Assange and Domscheit-Berg also offered exclusive interviews in return for donations: the *Washington Post* reported in November 2010 that WikiLeaks had offered the *Wall Street Journal* and CNN access to the embassy cables on the basis of a confidentiality agreement that would see WikiLeaks receive a payment of $100,000 if that agreement was broken (Farhi, 2010).

The press and broadcast coverage of the momentous leaks of 2010 generated an increase in donations and by the end of the year WikiLeaks had received a total of €1.33 million, or about $1.85 million. A fraction over half of these donations were direct bank transfers; the rest were received in the form of 25,755 individual PayPal payments. The average PayPal donation was just $36. The April 2010 *Collateral Murder* film generated a monthly spike in PayPal donors: 6,359 payments contributed to a total of almost $242,000 that month alone. This was enough to enable Assange to start to build a more permanent structure for WikiLeaks, or something like it, complete with salaried positions for staff. November and December 2010 also saw significant sums raised through PayPal—$69,000 and $146,000 respectively—but these need to be set in context alongside bad months like May 2010 ($14,000) and

September 2010 ($5,000) (Wau-Holland-Stiftung, 2011). As 2010 drew to a close and allegations of sexual misconduct were brought by the Swedish prosecutor against Assange and PayPal decided to freeze WikiLeaks' account following pressure from the U.S. government, donations via bank transfer increased substantially. Despite the fact that Assange was forbidden by the Wau-Holland rules from accessing these funds for "individual-related legal advice or legal representation in court proceedings" (Wau-Holland-Stiftung, 2011) over $560,000 was raised through this mechanism in December 2010 alone. Assange's personal projected legal costs were estimated at £400,000 in 2011 (Leigh & Harding, 2011: Ch. 18, para. 17). In a bid to cover these costs, in late December 2010 he negotiated a contract and deals with thirty-eight publishers around the world to produce his autobiography, and he handed the advance over to the legal team who were fighting the Swedish authorities' attempts to extradite him. Assange's book was published in late 2011 and he immediately disowned it and announced publicly that he had attempted to prevent its publication by withdrawing from his publishing contract (Assange, 2011). At the time of this writing (fall 2012), the outcome of the legal appeal process against Assange's extradition is still unknown.

WikiLeaks' financial base has therefore always been extremely precarious and even the increase in donations during 2010 was insufficient to put it on a more permanent and sustainable footing. But to what extent does the funding actually matter?

Internet and mobile communication have been absolutely central to WikiLeaks' routine operation and publishing strategy. Encrypted Jabber IRC chat rooms are key sites of daily decision making, encrypted e-mail provides links between the key organizers, and the website evolved over time into a secure network of servers installed by local volunteers in several countries (Domscheit-Berg, 2011: Ch. 10, para. 10). Skype is used in preference to ordinary telephone lines (Leigh & Harding, 2011: Ch. 4, para. 11). Non-networked encrypted notebook computers are routinely used to transport leaked data. After long periods of rather chaotic instability, this system gradually acquired enough capacity to deal with large amounts of leaked data and the several million web hits per day that have become common during major releases. Web hosting was deliberately placed in the hands of PRQ, a company based in Sweden, where there is a relatively liberal free-speech tradition and a comparatively strong record of resisting internet censorship (Khatchadourian, 2010). Established by Gottfrid Svartholm and Fredrik Neij, two founders of the Pirate Bay BitTorrent directory, PRQ specializes in protecting the identity and security of its users.

This infrastructure for *leaking* is buttressed by technologies that have evolved over the last decade, bolted together to provide anonymity for whistleblowers: SSL, secure FTP, FreeNet secure peer-to-peer networks, numerous prepaid mobile phone SIM cards, satellite pagers, CryptoPhone mobile devices, and Tor, the volunteer-driven secure network protocol (United States Army Counterintelligence Center, 2008). These technologies enshrine in code WikiLeaks' founding credo: the identity of leakers, in all of its digital traces, is to remain entirely hidden, even from WikiLeaks staff (Domscheit-Berg, 2011: Ch. 14, para. 16).

Based upon multiple web servers scattered across a range of legal jurisdictions, as well as distributed peer-to-peer systems like BitTorrent, WikiLeaks' *publishing* infrastructure also has built-in redundancy and can be quickly mobilized by volunteers to counter legal or hacking attacks on the main site (Arthur, 2010; Brian, 2010). The significance of this redundancy was first demonstrated in 2008 when the Julius Bär bank successfully persuaded a California court to order that the wikileaks.org domain should be removed from the domain name system (DNS). The servers hosting the documents remained online, however, and, in an early example of the growing interpenetration of WikiLeaks and the professional media, the *New York Times* and CBS News published the leak site's IP address. This quickly circulated across social media sites and allowed the public to continue to access the site until the domain was reinstated ten days later. During the November 2010 embassy cables leak WikiLeaks' main site was again removed from the DNS by its registration company, EveryDNS, on the grounds, the company said, that the massive distributed denial of service attacks aimed at bringing down the WikiLeaks site were affecting its other customers. A new Swiss mirror domain, wikileaks.ch soon appeared (Arthur, 2010). Within a couple of weeks, the total number of mirrors reached 1,885 (Brian, 2010). Impressive, but also partly irrelevant, for the cables had already been widely distributed via the peer-to-peer BitTorrent network. This publishing infrastructure has also made it easier to quickly release private correspondence and legal threats provoked by WikiLeaks' data leaks. WikiLeaks soon developed an informal rule that it would always seek to publish the particularly aggressive responses to its leaks (Domscheit-Berg, 2011: Ch. 17, para. 43). The belief that it is the duty of WikiLeaks to provoke the subject of a leak to file a lawsuit on the grounds that this will provide more publicity for the leak itself makes for a radically destabilizing approach, one not characteristic of traditional news media.

WikiLeaks is, therefore, a sociotechnical system, whose affordances provide both structure and agency for its principle of anonymity. It rests upon a keen awareness of how the internet has changed the traditional dynamics of source-journalist relations during whistle-blowing. The internal infrastructure is suited to communication at a distance, among small groups, on highly specialized subjects, involving large amounts of digital data that must be quickly moved across international borders. And the desire to be "a neutral submission platform, pure technology" (Domscheit-Berg, 2011: Ch. 17, para. 19) initially marked it out as radically different from a strong current in traditional investigative journalism, where knowing information about a source has been a key part of verifying a leak. A leaked U.S. Army Counterintelligence Center report of 2008 described this leaking and publishing infrastructure as displaying "a high level of technical capability and resourcefulness" (United States Army Counterintelligence Center, 2008).

All this gives the impression of a slick and well-organized entity, but this is far from the truth. The principle of total anonymity through pure technology has been applied only selectively. For example, in May 2009 WikiLeaks volunteers actively solicited information by compiling a public wiki listing their "most wanted leaks" (WikiLeaks, 2009a). *Guardian* journalists David Leigh and Luke Harding report that Adrian Lamo (the hacker whom U.S. soldier Bradley Manning is alleged to have informed of his alleged role in leaking the embassy cables in 2010) claims that Assange "developed a relationship" with Manning and established encrypted FTP channels for him to upload materials (Leigh & Harding, 2011: Ch. 6, paras. 13–15). In other words, the total anonymity-pure technology principle has sometimes been dropped in the interests of the safe delivery of verifiable leaks. WikiLeaks has constantly mutated. It has shifted its mode of operation, selectively applied aspects of its self-created socio-technical system, and even before the leaks of 2010 it sometimes behaved more like a team of traditional investigative journalists on the hunt for whistle-blowers.

WikiLeaks has therefore been polymorphous, chaotic, often reliant upon the personal resources of its key protagonists, and sometimes slow to live up to its own ideals. Constantly beset by technical problems—it went offline completely for a month in the winter of 2009–2010 and its archive remained inaccessible for a further six months—the picture that emerges from the accounts of Assange and Domscheit-Berg is of small groups of volunteers lurching from crisis to crisis. Domscheit-Berg claims that during his involvement, which ended in the autumn of 2010, it was a network of "around eight hundred volunteer experts" but there was no effective way of integrating their efforts, particularly when it came to verifying leaks (Domscheit-Berg, 2011: Ch. 17, para. 14, Ch. 21, para. 13).

Minimal volunteer participation stems from an absence of governance mechanisms suitable for building trust in what are usually decentralized and fleeting online encounters. There is an essential contradiction at the heart of WikiLeaks: how is it possible for a distributed army of volunteers to safeguard secrets? Even the WikiLeaks name itself is partly misleading. The organization began as a traditional wiki and it developed an e-mail distribution list, but open online co-creation has seldom been a meaningful part of its operations due to the need for absolute secrecy and expert judgments on how to edit and distribute leaked materials. The e-mail list members have mostly been inactive (Domscheit-Berg, 2011: Ch. 2, paras. 28–29).

Yet it is equally important not to lose sight of some of the key strengths of this operation. WikiLeaks has exploited digital technologies' capacity for enabling very small groups and even individuals to project substantial organizational power. In their external communication they have referred to personnel in the "tech department" or "legal services," and according to Domscheit-Berg he and Assange established e-mail inboxes under pseudonyms to convey the impression that there was a bigger permanent staff (Domscheit-Berg, 2011: Ch. 2, para. 24). Despite its patched-together and contingent nature, nothing approaching WikiLeaks' infrastructure has existed in the world of mainstream media. This assemblage of secure hardware, encryption software, networks of interdependent sources, activists, and journalists *is* WikiLeaks. Sporadic bursts of volunteer activity and donations aside, this sociotechnical system is effectively what has enabled it to function as a global news-making entity without a central headquarters and staff. By 2010, WikiLeaks had a working policy of verifying leaks, a 350,000-strong e-mail list (Domscheit-Berg, 2011: Ch. 2, para. 43), and it was able to draw upon the network resources of Anonymous, the online hacktivist network. Assange has occasionally been able to mobilize the volunteer labor of hundreds and sometimes thousands of others. For example, the 9/11 pager messages were mirrored across volunteers' servers in 2009 and there was a large-scale distributed effort to redact information from the Afghan war logs via a web-based system that had been custom-built by WikiLeaks technical staff in 2010 (Domscheit-Berg, 2011: Ch. 10, para. 16).

WikiLeaks' organizational structure is therefore best seen as an array of overlapping circles of constantly changing size, in the middle of which is Assange as "editor-in-chief," surrounded by the "core team." Daily operations are managed by a small number of key players. The most important members of the core team have been activists—a mix of anarchists, greens, and libertarian hackers interested in internet and information policy issues—but the personnel has quite frequently changed and has often included trained journalists. Assange is undoubtedly the most powerful individual, but his power is dependent upon assembling networks of expertise. The core team has changed in reaction to events, the task at hand, and the geographical context. During periods when leaks are being prepared the team has led a nomadic existence, shifting from city to city as the job demands it and tapping into pools of resources provided by sympathetic political activists and media workers on the ground in locations around Europe, Scandinavia, the United States, Africa, and Australia.

WikiLeaks has global purview but it has plugged into existing national and local networks of expertise and activism; these are important resources in its ability to shift repertoires from activist group to government lobbyist to quasi-professional news organization. For example, in 2009 it operated as a technical advisor and lobbyist during a period when Germany's parliament was considering a controversial new Access Impediment Law designed to filter online criminal content (Domscheit-Berg, 2011: Ch. 8, paras. 1–32). The Iraq war documents release of 2010 was carried out with the assistance of the activist NGO Iraq Body Count. By the time of the embassy cables leak a couple of months later, Assange had, in addition to the deal brokered with newspapers, built further networks among London media. These included journalists from Al Jazeera, Channel 4 News, and staff at the Bureau of Investigative Journalism at City University. Assange worked with the Bureau's in-house production company to devise two television documentaries that were sold to Channel 4 and Al Jazeera (Leigh & Harding, 2011: Ch. 11, para. 16).

Periods of intense activity involving small dedicated teams working in close proximity have presaged the publication of fresh leaks. Again, this approach capitalizes on the affordances and the logics of digital media. Routine tasks of journalism can now be performed successfully and convincingly on the fly, far from the confines of the newsroom. Video and audio editing, the digital enhancement of images, and subtitling have all been carried out by WikiLeaks to a standard that matches and sometimes exceeds professional broadcast news and documentary.

COLLATERAL MURDER

The creation of the *Collateral Murder* film in early 2010 well illustrates how WikiLeaks has used digital tools to behave like a professional media production company. But the film also reveals WikiLeaks' role as an activist cause group, eager to present its own version of events to try to set the news agenda. After acquiring the leaked video, Assange assembled a small team of colleagues in Iceland, where WikiLeaks had recently become well-known due to its leaking of a list of generous loans made to shareholders of the failed Icelandic banks of 2008. The editing and production tasks were carried out during a month-long house rental in Reykjavik. At this time, with the assistance of legal advisors and Icelandic activists, WikiLeaks was also lobbying the Icelandic legislature, business leaders, and telecommunications providers to support

the establishment of the Modern Media Initiative, a legal settlement for media freedom and technological development on the island (Assange, 2011: 185–198; Leigh &
Harding, 2011: Ch. 5, para. 12).[4]

Those who joined Assange included Birgitta Jónsdóttir, MP for the newly formed
Icelandic Movement Party; Rop Gonggrijp, a Dutch online activist, businessman,
and WikiLeaks donor; Smári McCarthy, a volunteer computer programmer; Kristinn
Hrafnsson and Ingi Ragna Ingason, both television journalists; and Gudmundur
Gudmundsson, an activist and experienced audio editor (Khatchadourian, 2010).
Hrafnsson and Ragna Ingason traveled to Baghdad using their own money to inter-
view eyewitnesses and conduct background research for the press package that
accompanied the film's release.

Collateral Murder reveals the strengths and weaknesses of WikiLeaks' hybridity. Eager to make an immediate impression on professional news organizations, the
team forensically analyzed and edited the raw video material, even to the extent of
overlaying animated arrows highlighting key people and events. Assange directed
the team, acting as a kind of program producer. They made fine-grained editorial
decisions. For example, fragments of conversation were removed from the audio
soundtrack during the opening, to avoid encouraging viewers to "make an emotional
bond" with the helicopter pilots (Khatchadourian, 2010). They gave the film a highly
provocative title designed to draw attention to the casual use of "collateral damage,"
the military euphemism that has become common code for civilian injury and death.
And they prefaced the footage with a quotation from George Orwell's famous 1946
essay, "Politics and the English Language": "Political language is designed to make
lies sound truthful and murder respectable, and to give an appearance of solidity to
pure wind." Here was WikiLeaks acting something like a professional news organization, but one with a clear antiwar message. It had morphed from intermediary to
committed news producer.

This created new dilemmas. *Collateral Murder* was a significant media intervention, one that free speech advocates across the globe were quick to praise. It brought
global attention to the casual disregard for civilians' lives and it graphically revealed
the increasingly cool, detached nature of modern warfare, or at least how those with
superior military power could see it that way. The leak derived from a credible source
and unlike the other major leaks there were relatively few concerns that the film would
jeopardize the safety of military personnel on the ground. There were also immediate
reverberations across the U.S. media system. For example, Ethan McCord, the U.S.
soldier caught on camera lifting the wounded children to safety, left the army and
became a public figure after speaking out in support of the film on several television
shows.

Yet the same forces shaping the production and publication of *Collateral Murder*
also clouded its reception. Critics argued that the edited version decontextualized
the events. Although the footage makes it clear that the pilots had mistaken a journalist's long camera lens for a rocket-propelled grenade device, some of the men were in
fact armed. (Reuters would later announce that it had changed its policy in order to
forbid reporters from accompanying armed groups). These were U.S. military officers
in a battle zone operating according to their training. Although it has been argued by
Marjorie Cohn, a human rights lawyer, that the attack contravened several important

principles of international law (2010), the pilots' apparent relish for their grisly tasks, as revealed through their gung-ho language, was also framed as a reflection of the daily reality of warfare. But arguably the biggest problem was the obviously "packaged," professional nature of the WikiLeaks release. Even though the raw footage was published in its entirety alongside the edited version and several damning moments from the full video were actually omitted from the shortened edit, *Collateral Murder* symbolizes WikiLeaks' partial transformation from activist network and intermediary for whistle-blowers to ideologically committed documentary filmmaker. But this metamorphosis simultaneously threatened to undermine WikiLeaks as a legitimate journalistic enterprise. So from that point on, it adopted a different approach, one based on the profound interdependence of newer and older media logics.

Power and Interdependence

It is clear that from their very beginnings WikiLeaks planned to engage with professional media. In 2006 they asked Daniel Ellsberg, the famous whistle-blower who had released the Vietnam war Pentagon Papers to the *New York Times* in 1971, to act as the "public face" of the new initiative (Leigh & Harding, 2011: Ch. 3, para. 55). Relations between WikiLeaks and some sections of the German press, such as *Zeit Online* and the business paper *WirtschaftsWoche* were cordial long before the big leaks of 2010 and there were also early links with the British press. For example, in November 2008 WikiLeaks published a report on post-election political killings among members of Kenya's banned Mungiki sect. The story achieved greater impact through a temporary alliance with Jon Swain, a journalist at the *Sunday Times*. This collaboration was significant: Assange went on to win the 2009 Amnesty International New Media Award for his role (WikiLeaks, 2009b). WikiLeaks also tried various experiments to stoke interest in leaks. For example, in an early release of U.S. Army equipment lists the core team created an interactive searchable database that merged secret and freely available sources. They then issued detailed instructions to journalists on how to run reports against it (United States Army Counterintelligence Center, 2008).

Basic collaborative practices therefore started to emerge. WikiLeaks would provide the raw data to journalists, perhaps with some summaries and guidance about a leak's most significant elements; the journalists would publish selective excerpts but link back to the full data on the WikiLeaks site. But this model did not become embedded as a consensual norm and this is significant in explaining WikiLeaks' move toward a more integrated approach in 2010. Journalists quoting selectively and editors running stories without attribution were the subject of much concern and led to a sense of resentment about the hypercompetitive nature of contemporary news making. Some early experiences only heightened suspicions, such as when a journalist working for the German weekly magazine *Stern* covered a leak related to a Franco-German electronic toll road system without giving credit to WikiLeaks (Domscheit-Berg, 2011: Ch. 4, para. 16).

Despite their initial policy of publishing all leaks in the order in which they were received, WikiLeaks gradually learned the importance of sifting out the data most likely to make an impact. They wanted to avoid becoming too dependent upon the professional media but they also wanted to prioritize leaks for preparation and publication (Domscheit-Berg, 2011: Ch. 7, para. 2). It soon became clear that the mere publication of vast quantities of data did not by itself generate interest among professional journalists. WikiLeaks' perspective on this is intriguing and it suggests some ambivalence about their original goals and a further explanation of their switch to fully fledged collaboration with news organizations. According to Assange, the problem was one of oversupply. Journalists were swamped by too much data. The trick was to increase its value by restricting its quantity and then follow this up by collaborating more closely. This, it was believed, would generate greater interest, more manageable stories—and impact (Mey, 2010).

FROM THE NETWORK TO THE NEWSROOM

By the time of the Afghanistan release in summer 2010 WikiLeaks had decided that working closely with journalists would be its chief mode of operation. The core team "looked around for reliable partners" before settling on the New York Times, the Guardian, and Der Spiegel (Domscheit-Berg, 2011: Ch. 15, para. 12). Der Spiegel journalists held weekly meetings with WikiLeaks staff during the run-up to the publication of the stories. Meetings with the Guardian and New York Times staff were also a regular feature by this time, as participants shuttled between London and New York. Assange worked for a time alongside the journalists at the Guardian's London offices (Ellison, 2011). And as WikiLeaks' strategy evolved they began to involve broadcasters: in the run-up to the "exclusive" launch of the Afghan war logs, Assange offered interviews to Channel 4, Al Jazeera, CNN, and a freelance reporter, much to the chagrin of the newspaper partners (Leigh & Harding, 2011: Ch. 8, para. 29).

By mid-2010, then, the relationship between WikiLeaks and professional media was symbiotic. But the precise nature of the power relations in this context of interdependence is a matter for further analysis and interpretation.

Bill Keller, executive editor of the New York Times and one of those directly involved in brokering the arrangement that led to the publication of the 2010 leaks, argues that the press were the unequivocal leaders throughout. Describing Assange as "a self-important quasi-anarchist," Keller says that WikiLeaks was always treated as the outsider. In fact, so keen is he to depict the relationship in these traditional terms that, in a post-mortem describing the embassy cables release from the perspective of his editorial office, he pointedly and repeatedly refers to WikiLeaks as "a source." As Keller puts it:

> we have treated Julian Assange and his merry band as a source. I will not say "a source, pure and simple," because as any reporter or editor can attest, sources are rarely pure or simple, and Assange was no exception. But the relationship with sources is straightforward: You don't necessarily endorse their agenda, echo their rhetoric, take anything they say at face value, applaud their methods or, most important, allow them to shape or censor your journalism. Your obligation, as an independent news organization, is to verify the material, to supply context, to exercise responsible judgment about what to publish and what not, and to make sense of it. That is what we did (Star & New York Times Staff, 2011: Ch. 1, para. 68).

The other major partner in the 2010 stories was the *Guardian*. Its attitude was very different. The paper had used WikiLeaks data early on. During 2009 the British high court upheld so-called superinjunctions preventing the *Guardian* from reporting on Barclays Bank's alleged tax avoidance and oil trading company Trafigura's alleged dumping of toxic waste in the Ivory Coast. Superinjunctions forbid all media discussion of the injunctions they cover, so WikiLeaks agreed to host documents that British judges had ruled must be kept secret, undermining the court's decision. These cases demonstrated that mainstream media organizations had much to gain from forming an alliance with a group of activists who were not shaped by the regular routines of the news industry and much less likely to capitulate when faced with legal threats. In March 2010 the *Guardian* offered to reciprocate on WikiLeaks's role in the Trafigura affair by publicizing the *Collateral Murder* helicopter film (Leigh & Harding, 2011: Ch. 5, para. 16). In the event, WikiLeaks chose to launch at a high-profile press gathering at the National Press Club in Washington, DC. But the *Guardian*'s July 2010 publication of Afghanistan war documents is tellingly labeled a "Guardian/WikiLeaks publication" (Leigh & Harding, 2011: Ch. 9, para. 10). This was clearly seen as a collaborative endeavor.

It was the *Guardian*'s analysis of the predicament in which WikiLeaks found itself by mid-2010 that proved so important in shaping how the Afghanistan, Iraq, and embassy cables stories emerged. The newspaper's leadership argued to Assange that WikiLeaks was becoming weaker because it was under threat of legal action, black propaganda campaigns, and hacking attacks. They suggested some sort of multinational alliance of newspapers, WikiLeaks, and NGOs. Fearful that the American embassy in London would seek a legal injunction from British courts before the stories emerged, the *Guardian* also suggested that the aim would be to publish simultaneously on the WikiLeaks site and across several outlets in a range of countries.

WikiLeaks too, were contributing to the strategy at this stage. They suggested that simultaneous publication by the *New York Times*, where they had some contacts, would make it less likely that the alleged U.S. military source of the leaks, Bradley Manning, would be charged under the U.S. Espionage Act (Leigh & Harding, 2011: Ch. 7, para. 47). And although the *Guardian* was initially reluctant to accede to WikiLeaks' request that *Der Spiegel* be allowed into the Afghanistan collaboration, it soon became obvious that the Germans had a great deal of expertise that could be brought to bear in verifying the leaks, including access to secret supporting documents from the German Parliament's investigation into the war (Leigh & Harding, 2011: Ch. 8, para. 18). The outcome was a historic international collaboration involving WikiLeaks and several elite national news organizations: the *Guardian*, the *New York Times*, *Der Spiegel*, *Le Monde*, and *El País*. The ultimate prize was the embassy cables leak of November 2010.

While it is clear that the publication of these enormous leaks was heavily dependent upon the professional and organizational resources of traditional news organizations, a key point here is that this pool of resources evolved rapidly during the collaboration.

A custom search engine was coded by the *Guardian*'s in-house technology staff, enabling its foreign affairs team to run queries against the huge cables database of around three hundred million words of jargon-riddled text. An editorial decision was made to redact material that might endanger sources and military personnel, but deciding this was the easy part; following through, when faced with such huge amounts of textual data, proved far more difficult. The embassy cables were the equivalent of around two thousand printed books (Leigh & Harding, 2011: Ch. 11, para. 20).

Suspicion and differences of opinion bedeviled all involved. The journalists had several concerns: the status and credibility of the leaks, the possibility that the U.S. government and private individuals named in leaks might bring lawsuits against the editors of the European newspapers, the potential harm that might come to informants inadvertently named in secret documents, and Assange's claim to act as the sole intermediary between "his" sources and the media. The legal concerns were particularly acute with the embassy cables because these contained numerous descriptions of financial corruption involving not only politicians but also business leaders from around the world. In the British context, where high court injunctions have become more common in recent years, it was possible that some of these individuals might succeed in restricting publication before any of the stories saw the light of day. There was therefore a "safety in numbers" approach girded by simultaneous international publication, the linchpin of which was WikiLeaks' online publishing infrastructure.

The *Guardian's* and the *New York Times'* accounts of the 2010–2011 period both stress Assange's unpredictable behavior but also his desire to avoid becoming too dependent upon a narrow group of professional media actors. There were undoubtedly conflicting norms. With the Afghanistan documents, for example, WikiLeaks wanted to share the data more widely, including among known sympathetic freelancers. The *Guardian* and the *New York Times* wanted to retain exclusivity (Domscheit-Berg, 2011: Ch. 15, para. 16). The *Guardian's* Nick Davies said of Assange: "The problem is he's basically a computer hacker. He comes from a simplistic ideology, or at that stage he did, that all information has to be published, that all information is good" (quoted in Leigh & Harding, 2011: Ch. 8, para. 24).

For its part, WikiLeaks was eager to ensure that the usual journalistic norms for reporting insider information from government sources would not apply in the case of such enormous leaks, particularly in America. They had mixed results with this request. The *New York Times*, in a plan to avoid charges of unethical reporting, decided to inform the U.S. State Department before proceeding with each new set of revelations. This decision was made on the grounds that it would enable journalists to use reactions from officials to gain a better sense of the authenticity of the WikiLeaks documents. It would also enable them to identify the redactions necessary to safeguard U.S. informants and military personnel (Leigh & Harding, 2011: Ch. 14, para. 59). In its coverage, the *New York Times* exercised a cautious approach to redaction and it refused to link to WikiLeaks because it claimed the site contained sensitive information (Leigh & Harding, 2011: Ch. 8, para. 29). Bill Keller warned the White House of his plans in advance of the launch of the cable stories and four of his staff attended an off-the-record meeting with officials from the White House, the State Department, the CIA, the FBI, the Pentagon, and the Defense Intelligence Agency. The U.S. administration demanded that sources on the ground be protected but they also insisted that secret U.S. intelligence operations and any potentially embarrassing remarks made by top U.S. officials should be removed from the articles. Keller agreed to redact to protect on-the-ground sources but was "unpersuaded" by the other arguments. However, this initial meeting between journalists at the *New York Times* and the U.S. State Department was followed by a regular series of daily conference calls and ad hoc gatherings to discuss the content of forthcoming stories. The White House did not seek to prevent publication. As Keller says, "in our discussions before the publication of our articles, White House officials, while challenging some of the conclusions we drew from the material, thanked us for handling the documents with care. The Secretaries of State and Defense and the Attorney General resisted the opportunity for a crowd-pleasing orgy of press-bashing" (Leigh & Harding, 2011: Ch. 11, para. 64) The U.S. military and intelligence authorities, working through the "usual channels," therefore played an important role in shaping how the cables stories were handled at the *New York Times*. Meanwhile, the *Guardian* and the other press partners also indirectly considered State Department responses when deciding what to redact, because Keller and his team in New York constantly fed information across from their briefing meetings (Leigh & Harding, 2011: Ch. 14, para. 46).

The discourse that emerges from some of the professional journalists' accounts, particularly that of Keller, is of the need for professional news organizations to tame an "anarchist" WikiLeaks hell-bent on publishing everything in its possession. Yet there is little hard evidence that WikiLeaks had a cavalier attitude to sensitive information at this stage. As the *Guardian* journalists themselves admit, by the time of the embassy cables Assange was as eager as the professionals to be selective in what was published and to redact the documents, not only to protect sources but more pragmatically to avoid provoking unnecessary hostility to the project among professional journalists. Indeed, during the Afghan war documents release earlier in 2010 WikiLeaks had removed a batch of fourteen thousand files because they may have contained identifying information (Domscheit-Berg, 2011: Ch. 15, para. 25). The Iraq war logs of October 2010 were also heavily redacted (Leigh & Harding, 2011: Ch. 8, para. 25) And yet the perception that WikiLeaks was an irresponsible organization and "not journalism" was very widespread. According to a content analysis of newspapers from November 14, 2010 to January 28, 2011, some 60 percent of stories misleadingly referred to the "dumping" of "250,000" cables (Benkler, 2011). In fact, by the end of December 2010, a total of just 1,942 had been released.

In the day-to-day processes of news production the worlds of WikiLeaks and the journalists were sometimes uncomfortably far apart. The *Guardian's* David Leigh and Luke Harding reveal that there was a good deal of muddling through in handling data and digital tools. The sheer size of the two hundred million-word embassy cables database forced *Guardian* journalists to run keyword searches using TextWrangler, a rudimentary piece of Macintosh text editing software (Leigh & Harding, 2011: Ch. 11, para. 16). Terms that were too generic would produce thousands of results, so they would sometimes resort to searching for unusual phrases in the hope of hitting some bizarre description of events. In discussing how to publish stories based on the Afghanistan documents the *Guardian's* journalists spoke of coverage in the anachronistic language of paper and the old news cycle: "14 pages, on the day of launch" (Leigh & Harding, 2011: Ch. 8, para. 20). Far more readers would encounter this material on the paper's website, where "page" space was not a constraint. As if to force this digital media logic home, the official launch of the cables stories was actually scooped by an anonymous individual named freelancer_09, who tweeted page scans of all of the major headlines from a paper copy of *Der Spiegel* he or she picked up from a batch left by mistake at Badisher Bahnhof station on the Swiss-German border (Leigh & Harding, 2011: Ch. 15, para. 14).

But we also must recognize that, however much they struggled to come to grips with WikiLeaks' infrastructure and working practices, the journalists offered their own network resources. They improvised their own form of secure transnational network infrastructure, meshing their practices with those of WikiLeaks. E-mail was out of bounds; Skype video calls were used instead. During these sessions the code numbers of relevant cables would be silently held up to the camera as a means of evading interception. Access to the cables was also provided over encrypted VPN connections. The *Guardian*'s cables team were given temporary "burner" pay-as-you-go cell phones as a means of evading wiretaps (Leigh & Harding, 2011: Ch. 14, paras. 19–21).

Journalists adapted to the demands imposed by the huge volumes of data, some of which required great effort to verify. A team of experienced war reporters was assembled to undertake these tasks, including Jonathan Steele and James Meek of the *Guardian*, Eric Schmitt of the *New York Times*, and John Goetz and Marcel Rosenbach of *Der Spiegel* (Leigh & Harding, 2011: Ch. 8, para. 16). Their team also included Alastair Dant and Simon Rogers, whose role was to create compelling visual displays for the website, integrating leaked data with temporal and locational information.

The news organizations also provided a further set of resources: legal expertise, legitimacy, and widespread recognition among their publics. This helped the partnership as a whole resist political pressure in the run-up to publication. Two days before the launch, *Guardian* editor Alan Rusbridger fielded a conference call from senior figures in the U.S. administration, including the U.S. Assistant Secretary for Public Affairs Philip J. Crowley, Secretary of State Hillary Clinton's private secretary, and members of the Department of Defense and the National Security Council. The administration's aim was to establish precisely what was about to be leaked. Rusbridger conceded the broad themes of the first three days, but no details. Georg Mascolo, the editor-in-chief of *Der Spiegel*, took a similar call from the U.S. ambassador to Germany (Leigh & Harding, 2011: Ch. 14, para. 56).

This was in stark contrast with what happened to WikiLeaks. Assange wrote to U.S. ambassador Louis Susman in London to ask that the U.S. authorities produce specific examples of how publication of the embassy cables might put individuals in danger. The response came from Harold Koh, a legal adviser to the State Department. Koh ignored Assange's request, declared that the cable leak was "provided in violation of U.S. law," and demanded that WikiLeaks return the stolen files (Leigh & Harding, 2011: Ch. 14, para. 65).

These episodes are highly revealing. In contrast with WikiLeaks, the senior journalists had much experience of bargaining with elite government sources. Their editors possessed the legal resources that would enable them to craft stories to avoid provoking lawsuits. The news organizations also had clout: all of the partners were revered national institutions in their own right. Any decision by the governments of the United States, Britain, Germany, France, or Spain to attempt to suppress publication by the newspapers would have instantly provoked outrage among a significant section of each country's population. On the other hand, suppression would have proved futile in any case because the stories were scheduled to appear simultaneously elsewhere—on the WikiLeaks website. The likelihood of concerted action by five governments was minimal. Coordinated collective action by the newspapers, WikiLeaks, and its distributed networks was a safer bet.

The power of the traditional news organizations was thrown into sharp relief when Assange was first accused of alleged sexual misconduct in Sweden, during the publication of the embassy cables. Journalists instantly faced a significant problem. Even though Assange was a partner in their efforts, to downplay a potential personal scandal would have threatened their credibility. The *New York Times* started to shift their emphasis and ran a front page extended profile of Assange dealing in some detail with the sexual allegations. The *Guardian* and the other partners eventually followed suit, as Assange's personal character began to emerge as a strong part of the WikiLeaks narrative and an opportunity on the part of the *Guardian* and its partners to report a new human interest angle in the story.

This shift in power relations was exhibited during a fraught and revealing episode a few weeks before the embassy cable stories went public. Despite Assange agreeing that he would grant the press partners exclusive access (Leigh & Harding, 2011: Ch. 13, para. 12), WikiLeaks had itself started to leak. The entire embassy cables database had been acquired by Heather Brooke, a London-based freelance journalist and freedom of information campaigner. This led to a confrontation at the *Guardian*'s headquarters on November 1, 2010. During this meeting, involving Assange and his legal team, the *Guardian*'s senior editors and their lawyer, *Der Spiegel* and *Guardian* journalists, and the *New York Times*' Bill Keller (by phone), the interdependence among these actors was played out in vivid fashion.

Assange was angered by the hostile profile of him in the *New York Times* and now wanted the paper to be kept out of the deal. He mentioned potential collaboration with other papers, including the *Washington Post*. Meanwhile, the *Guardian* had been negotiating with Heather Brooke in an attempt to bring her into the fold to eliminate the risk that she might take her copy of the cables to another paper and spoil their scoop. The *Guardian* responded to Assange with the argument that the cables had in fact already been leaked and neither they nor the *New York Times* was now dependent on WikiLeaks for the data required to run their cables articles. But the *Guardian* could not be sure that they would be able to secure Brooke's compliance, nor would they have the WikiLeaks web publishing infrastructure to guarantee the worldwide availability of their evidence. Assange therefore still had power resources, derived from digital media, to deploy. Assange then asked that the embassy cables partnership be widened to include *El País* and *Le Monde* and that the *New York Times* publish on their front page his response to their unfriendly profile. Though Bill Keller refused Assange's request to have his say, the meeting did agree to include the Spanish and French papers. The original partners' exclusive was therefore diluted, but Assange failed to exclude the *New York Times* from the deal because the *Guardian* later passed the cables over to Keller in any case. This was, therefore, a victory through compromise for all involved. What follows is the revealing "10 bullet point" note on which *Guardian* editor Rusbridger agreed with WikiLeaks:

Publish on Nov 29 in a staggered form.
Run over two weeks or more up to just before Xmas.

Exclusive to G, NYT, DS (plus El País and ? Le Monde).

Subject matter to be co-ordinated between partners and to stay off certain issues initially. No veto to anyone over subjects covered over whole course of series (post-Jan). WL to publish cited documents at same time.

After Xmas the exclusivity continues for one more week, starting around Jan 3/4.

Thereafter WL will start to share stories on a regional basis among 40 serious newspapers around the world, who will be given access to "bags" of material relating to their own regions.

G to hire HB [Heather Brooke] on an exclusive basis.

If "critical" attack on WL they will release everything immediately.

If material is leaked to/shared with any other news organization in breach of this understanding all bets are off.

If agreed the team will commence work on a grid of stories for the first phase (Leigh & Harding, 2011: Ch. 11, para. 40).

The terms of this deal crystallized the interdependence among WikiLeaks and the professional news organizations. The first embassy cables articles went ahead as planned, save of course for the *Der Spiegel* accidental Twitter leak, on November 28, 2010.

FROM THE NEWSROOM TO THE NETWORK

This marked the end of an episode of collaboration, but in December 2010 WikiLeaks' polymorphous network resources came to the fore again in the immediate aftermath of the embassy cables launch, providing symbolic and physical reinforcement to the professional journalists. There erupted a sprawling, symbolically charged cyber conflict, pitting activists engaged in electronic civil disobedience against a group of politicians, public authorities, and private companies intent on weakening WikiLeaks' organizational capacity.

Faced with a series of massive distributed denial of service attacks originating from botnet armies of virus-infected computers assembled by hostile hackers, including one named "The Jester," WikiLeaks moved its main website to Amazon's web services cloud storage—the largest platform of its kind in the world. The cables website, meanwhile, remained on a server hosted in France. The denial of service attacks on WikiLeaks main site intensified, their sources becoming more diverse.

As with all such episodes, it is impossible to identify the origins of these hacking attacks with certainty, but they jelled with a domestic campaign by politicians in the United States to have the WikiLeaks site taken down. Senator Joe Lieberman led the charge by calling in public for Amazon to suspend its hosting and for other companies assisting WikiLeaks to end their relationship with the organization. Lieberman's office contacted Amazon to ask if there were "any plans to take the site down?" (Slajda, 2010). In an extraordinary move, Amazon acceded to these requests and closed down WikiLeaks' storage space on the grounds that it violated their terms of service. The company argued that customers may only publish content to which they hold the rights, referring to a clause originally designed to deter copyright infringement. But Amazon also invoked a much vaguer clause from its terms, stipulating that hosted materials should not "cause injury to any person or entity." They claimed that the "250,000 classified documents" that they wrongly said WikiLeaks had already published would put "innocent people in jeopardy" (Amazon Web Services, 2010).

Amazon's decision induced a climate of fear. The precise extent to which other companies came under direct political pressure is not known and probably never will be fully known. However, some details are publicly available. Following a public statement by Osama Bedier, a vice president of PayPal, we know that PayPal received a letter from the U.S. State Department on November 27, 2010, the day before the cables stories launched. The letter stated that WikiLeaks' activities were "deemed illegal" in the United States. In response, PayPal moved on December 4 to suspend WikiLeaks' account, thereby choking off donations to the organization at a time when it was most likely to attract funding (Arthur, 2010). December 3 saw EveryDNS suspend the wikileaks.org domain and its associated e-mail accounts. On December 6, Assange's Swiss bank account was frozen by PostFinance, on the grounds that he "provided false information regarding his place of residence during the account opening process." That same day, MasterCard blocked WikiLeaks' access to its credit card services; Visa followed suit the day after (Arthur, 2010). The Twitter accounts of Assange, Birgitta Jónsdóttir, and other WikiLeaks leaders were the subject of a subpoena from the Department of Justice on December 14. Under U.S. law, Twitter could not resist the subpoena without being prosecuted, but it made the order public after successfully applying to have its details "unsealed" and sent to those whose accounts were under investigation.

This unprecedented series of events led to "Operation: Payback" and "Operation Avenge Assange": decentralized online campaigns of politically motivated retaliatory hacking attacks aimed at the websites of the public organizations and companies that were suppressing WikiLeaks. The action was minimally coordinated by a loose, leaderless, memberless, and constantly shifting transnational collective of around ten thousand hacktivists named Anonymous, some of whom were associated with the "doing it for the lulz" culture of the libertine and irreverent web forum, 4Chan (Shapira & Warrick, 2010). Operation: Payback had started in September 2010 as an online protest against the Motion Pictures Association of America's attacks on the file-sharing site, the Pirate Bay (Coleman, 2011). To discuss tactics, Anonymous used Internet Relay Chat (IRC) channels, PiratePad (a web-based text editor that provides for simultaneous real-time document writing), and polls embedded in online Google forms. Within a few days, more than fifty thousand had downloaded the desktop software that allows a user to take part in the denial of service attacks, but Anonymous almost certainly used networks of virus-infected "zombie" computers as well (J. E. Dunn, 2010). Media reports at the time suggested that Anonymous's support for WikiLeaks was a new development, but in fact the group had played important supporting roles in the past. In 2008, for example, they had assisted with organizing website material for a leak detailing secret aspects of the Scientology movement (Domscheit-Berg, 2011: Chapter 3, para. 22).

This was, in part, a phony war, and reliable reports are thin on the ground. Anonymous cultivates an air of secrecy, describing itself simply as an "internet gathering," but MasterCard's website was briefly the victim of a successful distributed denial of service attack on December 8. It also appears that Anonymous briefly closed the website of PostFinance, Assange's Swiss bank, and caused some disruption to the Swedish government portal (Bloxham, 2010). ABC News reported that Sarah Palin had contacted them to allege that her website, SarahPAC.com, and her personal credit card details had previously been targeted by Anonymous hackers (Tapper, 2010). A number of new search engine interfaces to the cables database were launched, such as cablega-tesearch.net. In addition, "Operation Leakspin" was launched by, among others, users of the popular news sharing site Reddit: volunteers posted links to the cables and readers were encouraged to "vote up" those that were most important (Operation Leakspin, 2010). Anonymous's Facebook page was suspended on December 8 for violation of the company's terms of service (Bosker, 2010). Rumors of successful attacks on Amazon swirled during this intense period but at the time of writing there is little substantial public evidence that these attacks actually took place. And, in yet another bizarre twist of organizational hybridity, Anonymous itself issued a series of carefully worded formal press releases outlining that the denial of service attacks on PayPal, which it admitted were taking place, were electronic civil disobedience not aimed at critical infrastructure but at the "public face" of the companies and organizations (Anon Ops, 2010).

Hacktivism in itself is nothing new and goes back to the mid-1990s (Chadwick, 2006: 114–143), but the intensity and visibility of these reactions and counter-reactions to the cables leaks *was* new. This was part of an ongoing public drama in which WikiLeaks' networks of affinity were mobilized, mostly in support of Assange, but partly in support of the collaboration between WikiLeaks and the professional journalists. These actions were an essential aspect of the hybrid media system. They were a show of strength of sorts, by the members of an online "anti-leader" network who had become politicized and who were willing to take personal risks in order to demonstrate their support for transparency, freedom of expression, and the principle of whistle-blower anonymity. And those risks were very real: in July 2011 the U.S. State Department and the British and Dutch police announced that sixteen participants in the Anonymous denial of service attacks on PayPal had been arrested and charged with crimes (U.S. Department of Justice, 2011).

Conclusion

What are we to conclude about these fascinating episodes in the evolution of news making and political mobilization?

Part news producer, part social movement, part public information provider, part broadcaster, part direct action network, WikiLeaks has had an undeniable impact on public affairs. It leaks, it publishes, it produces, it mobilizes. Whether one admires or dislikes Julian Assange and whether one agrees or disagrees with WikiLeaks' political mission, the series of leaks in 2010 were arguably among the most important global political news scoops of the past few decades. As Charlie Beckett and James Ball succinctly put it, "instead of taking sides, we should be taking notice" (Beckett & Ball, 2012: 159). These scoops were all the more significant because they were the creative product of ongoing investigations, and not simply the reporting of unforeseen events like natural disasters, which journalists are always compelled to cover.

It is my argument that the overall impact of these news stories was achieved through interdependent power relations built upon the integration and exploitation of older and newer media logics. This involved the hybridization of professional investigative journalism and online volunteer activism, the recombination of established institutional power and what Manuel Castells has in other contexts termed distributed "network-making power" (Castells, 2009: 45).

No doubt there are strong opponents of this interpretation in the professional news industry. The WikiLeaks approach threatens traditional investigative reporting because in some ways it offers a more effective model. Some interpretations have been replete with phrases designed to construct a cordon sanitaire between the domains of journalism and WikiLeaks. For example, one journalist referred to the 2010 stories as simply a "collaboration of newspaper and Web site" (Ellison, 2011). WikiLeaks is not just a website, and it is more than "just a source," to revisit *New York Times* editor Bill Keller's formulation.

But while we need to look beyond self-justificatory dismissals of WikiLeaks by professional journalists we also need to recognize there are obvious weaknesses in the WikiLeaks approach. This is only partly a story of WikiLeaks' insurgency.

In many ways, as this analysis has shown, to depict WikiLeaks or professional journalists or, indeed, online hacktivist networks like Anonymous only in terms of each group's or network's power to "act upon" a preexisting set of media relations is to miss the truly important point. WikiLeaks constructed for itself and then occupied important boundary spaces between older and newer media practices and logics. It conducted technologically enabled raids across each side of these boundaries in a continual quest for resources that enabled it to exercise power. But these power resources were themselves always conditioned by relations of complex interdependence with other political and media actors, whether they were online or offline networks of activists, or professional news organizations.

WikiLeaks relied upon anonymous whistle-blowers for its source material and over time it built a leak infrastructure able to marshal huge quantities of data. It built a publishing operation and it produced important pieces of journalism from its own resources, as the process leading to the publication of the *Collateral Murder* film reveals. It has propelled the ethics and even the caché associated with hacktivism, internet libertarianism, and "data journalism" into the realm of mainstream politics and news media. It has even created a relatively novel online documentary genre (*Collateral Murder* again).

But it seems to me to be an inescapable fact that the information that has had the most decisive impact has been animated and mediated by professional journalism. This journalism has operated in environments where professional status, experience of investigations, and institutional resources have been decisive. Even *Collateral Murder*, an online viral success with more than thirteen million YouTube viewings, drew upon television genres. And it was embargoed until a relatively high-profile press release event in Washington, where Assange distributed a press kit to the gathered media before moving on to appear on the Colbert Report, a popular U.S. satirical television news show. Press and broadcast news media have both been essential to the WikiLeaks phenomenon.

Yet by the same token we should be wary of according too much power to professional news organizations. We might ask: if WikiLeaks must coexist in symbiosis with the press and broadcasters, is WikiLeaks powerful? Or we might reverse this question: if the press and broadcasters must coexist in symbiosis with WikiLeaks, are the press and broadcasters powerful? These are valid enough questions but they perhaps rest upon an inadequate conceptualization of power. For in the hybrid media system, as I have shown in this chapter, power is not always exercised in zero-sum games; it may emerge from physical and mediated interactions that are socially and technologically constructed and which evolve over time, in a diverse range of settings. What actually count as effective resources for powerful action in the hybrid media system have emerged from the interactions among WikiLeaks, the newspaper and broadcast media, and the online activists.

As I have shown, some of these interactions were shaped by power operating as resources for the issuing of ultimatums and vetoes among elite players in focused, discrete environments, often behind closed doors and with legal teams in tow. This was the case, for example, when Assange and the press partners came together at the last minute to hammer out the terms of the deal for the cables release. Sometimes power has been dispersed across a broader network, such as when WikiLeaks used its technological infrastructure to gather data leaks and channel these to the press; or when it has capitalized on the expertise of activists on the ground in various geographical locations. This broader network was also in flow when hacktivists came to the symbolic aid of both WikiLeaks and their press partners, as happened in the aftermath of the cables leaks.

As this book goes to press in the fall of 2012, WikiLeaks, in its role as a networked publisher, continues. In April 2011, for example, it partnered with the *Washington Post* on new cables releases detailing secret plans to depose the Yemeni president (Whitlock, 2011). All of the quarter of a million embassy cables were released by WikiLeaks in unredacted form in late 2011, as part of a new round of partnership deals with "over 90" media and human rights organizations around the world (WikiLeaks, 2011). This was a controversial move that WikiLeaks claims it was forced to make due to the *Guardian*'s leaking of the password to an encrypted copy of the cables database that had been uploaded via BitTorrent when Assange was arrested in December 2010 (Cablegatesearch, 2011). Bizarrely enough, the *Guardian*'s David Leigh and Luke Harding seem to have accidentally published the password in their book about the collaboration with WikiLeaks. They had assumed—wrongly it transpired—that WikiLeaks had changed the password once they had handed over the files to the paper (Ball, 2011).

Cooperation has by no means been a frictionless process. There are plenty of examples of when things turned conflictual. Much of this suspicion stemmed from WikiLeaks' capitalization on the resources offered by the hybrid media system. Assange's approach evolved to the extent that he personally began using the WikiLeaks' Twitter account to express his views, including his argument that he was becoming the victim of U.S. intelligence "dirty tricks." His use of Twitter to publicize the cause involved projecting his own persona to try to build a larger online support network and articulate connections among the other elements of the hybrid media system, particularly broadcasters. This became an important aspect of WikiLeaks' overall repertoire of behaviors during the embassy cables affair, and a simultaneous strength and weakness. Assange adapted quickly to the glare of publicity and he began to move more easily among celebrities. His December 2010 arrest pending extradition proceedings further amplified a growing cult of personality, as several wealthy publishers, actors, journalists, and film directors, including Ken Loach and Michael Moore, provided money to enable his release on bail. By the time he was freed from prison just before Christmas 2010, Assange was a global celebrity.

Unsurprisingly, the press partners involved in the big releases of 2010 were quick to attack WikiLeaks' publishing of the entire unredacted cables database in late 2011. Previously permeable boundaries between WikiLeaks and the professionals began to solidify. Elite professional journalists in Britain modulated their emphases back toward the importance of professional practices and norms, by intensifying their framing of WikiLeaks around the Assange personality cult and other human interest frames and generally drawing a cordon sanitaire ever more tightly around WikiLeaks in order to prevent it from assuming the status of a meaningful competitor to professional journalism. Meanwhile, WikiLeaks, too, modulated its emphasis back toward the networked online activism that had fueled its earlier, pre-embassy cables phase, albeit with a new inflection provided by Julian Assange's willingness to use his new celebrity status to attract mainstream media attention to his cause. Assange took the decision to publish all of the embassy cables after conducting an online poll of WikiLeaks' 1.5 million followers on Twitter, but the results of the poll were not published (Ball, 2011). In the spring of 2012 he was hired by the state-funded Russian television news channel *Russia Today* to conduct a series of high-profile interviews with political figures from around the world, further enhancing his persona and his identity as a journalist, but also contradicting WikiLeaks' fundamentalist approach to free speech. Assange's decision to seek political asylum in the Ecuadorian embassy in London in 2012 to avoid being extradited to Sweden and potentially on to the United States to face espionage charges before a grand jury generated further new frames for the professional journalists, who were quick to pick up the threads of the human interest narrative they had used when Assange was first arrested in December 2010 (Guardian, 2012).

Yet in 2012, despite having its credit card and Paypal donations system frozen by the United States, WikiLeaks' online supporter networks and publishing structure clearly remained in place, enabling it to publish over five million e-mails detailing the "web of informers, pay-off structure, payment laundering techniques and psychological methods" of Stratfor, a global "intelligence" company that provides services to companies and governments (WikiLeaks, 2012).

It is interesting to reflect on why the *New York Times*' discourse about WikiLeaks differed so markedly from that of the European press partners. In the uproar that followed publication of the embassy cables stories in the United States there was much debate about whether WikiLeaks was "really journalism" (see for example Adler, 2011; Benkler, 2011; Greenwald, 2010; Packer, 2010). There is more than principle at stake: if WikiLeaks can be publicly defined as journalism, any prosecution of Assange would need to overturn U.S. constitutional precedent because WikiLeaks would be subject to traditional First Amendment protections for the press under U.S. law. Fueling this discussion are differing views on whether WikiLeaks is responsible in its approach to redacting leaked data. As I have shown, the evidence in this area is mixed. WikiLeaks has often been selective in its approach to publication and it has taken redaction seriously, but it has been hampered by an inability to mobilize sufficient volunteer labor to systematically carry out these tasks and it steadily became frustrated with what it saw as journalists' cowardice in the face of elite pressure. WikiLeaks' view of political information was fundamentally different from that of the journalists, who are well used to protecting sources for the long term, cherry-picking the best pieces of evidence, and framing stories to generate the maximum possible short-term interest, before moving on to the next thing. Newer media logic conflicted with older media logic in this regard.

New York Times editor Bill Keller's dismissals were echoed across the American broadcast and press media and the wider debate about WikiLeaks' journalistic credentials were shaped there by the American broadsheet press's comparatively strong professional norm of objectivity and its related ambivalence toward advocacy journalism. In some respects, then, WikiLeaks' hybrid model of journalist, publisher, and mobilization movement is much more disruptive of the media system of the United States than it is of those in Europe, though there are of course many important differences across the European context. This goes some way toward explaining the distancing tactic of Keller and his allies.

But overall, WikiLeaks and the professionals innovated together, effectively blending their preexisting technologies, genres, norms, behaviors, and organizational forms to create new hybrid approaches to news making. They have shared these resources among themselves and, in some cases, with networked publics. The development of meaningful capacity for action in this new type of technology-enabled, not-quite-journalism has involved a process of learning, co-creation and co-evolution in the creative pursuit of new norms and working practices.

This is a story of interdependence among older and newer media logics in the gathering and production of information, and the exploitation of that information as news. WikiLeaks and their media partners in Britain, America, Germany, France, Spain and many other countries have together played an important role in the ongoing construction of a media system in which they have also developed the capacity to so decisively intervene: a hybrid media system.

6

Symphonic Consonance in Campaign Communication: Reinterpreting Obama for America

I am like a Rorschach test.
—Barack Obama[1]

Everything was synched up and working in symphonic consonance.
—David Plouffe, chief campaign manager, Obama for America, 2008[2]

The 2008 U.S. presidential election was momentous in the history of modern electoral politics. Much attention has focused on Barack Obama's use of the internet to engage supporters, register new voters, and mobilize them to turn out on election day. But while these aspects of the campaign are obviously important, this chapter offers a different interpretation of campaign communication in 2008. Online media were undoubtedly a key part of Obama's strategy, but this is far from the whole story.

My aim in this chapter is to explore the complex hybridity of the Obama campaign. My overarching argument is that the campaign's significance lies not in its internet campaigning, but in how it so ruthlessly integrated online and offline communication, grass-roots activism and elite control, older and newer media logics.

But 2008 is not only the story of Obama. Candidates and their staff, journalists, builders and maintainers of online platforms, volunteer activists, entertainment media, and many ordinary citizens together played crucially important roles in forging new political communication practices. These groups were pioneers in the construction and exploitation of a hybrid media system in election campaigning and the 2008 presidential campaign revealed much about the wider context in which struggles for political power now play out. So the chapter that immediately follows this one widens the scope in order to explore this system on a broader canvas.

Much will continue to be written about the Obama phenomenon, and irrespective of one's interpretation of President Obama's period in office, 2008 will long be seen as one of the most important elections in the history of liberal democracy. Here, while I certainly discuss how Obama's campaign constructed and, in turn, capitalized upon the evolving patterns of the hybrid media system more effectively than did opponent John McCain's, my main aim in this chapter and the next is to explore the textures of mediation that defined the campaign as a whole. I seek to reveal how the interdependence of older and newer media logics—their technologies, genres, norms, behaviors, and organizational forms—has become a key force in the power relationships among media, politicians, and the public during U.S. election campaigns.

Ascribing too much importance to campaigns can of course blind us to the long-term forces that inevitably shape all elections. After all, in 2008, the two traditional long-term predictors of American electoral outcomes—the incumbent's popularity and the state of the economy—were in alignment. Republican George W. Bush was one of the least popular presidents in the history of opinion polling and the economic downturn weighed heavily on the entire campaign, sharpening its intensity to dramatic effect during the run-up to election day as the financial crisis plunged confidence in the economy to depths not seen since the Great Depression.

And yet 2008 was still a remarkably close contest. The Democratic primary turned out to be an endurance test, as Obama and Senator Hillary Clinton ran neck and neck until the summer of 2008, causing a delayed start to the general election campaign. Just as significant is that McCain and Obama were effectively tied in their approval ratings for surprisingly long periods. Indeed, McCain was ahead right before the Democratic convention, which came at the end of August 2008. It was not until mid-September, with only six weeks to go before election day that Obama opened up a lead, and yet the polls narrowed once again during the final week (Kenski, et al., 2010: 4). Arguments about the "inevitability" of an Obama victory can therefore only be made in hindsight. As Jeffrey Alexander has convincingly argued, campaigns are "a flow, a stream of meaning making" characterized by attempts to actively shape the stage on which the entire political drama unfolds (Alexander, 2010: 163). Hazards and missteps abound. The 2008 campaign mattered, and because the campaign mattered, its mediation matters. As I will show, however, this mediation matters in a way that belies easy talk of the ascendancy of online communication in campaigns. The year 2008 was a crucial moment in the building of the hybrid media system. This is the story of how extraordinary newer media logics in campaigning were integrated with equally extraordinary older media logics.

Television-Era Campaign Logics Die Hard, but Also Coevolve with the Internet

Most of the commentary on the 2008 Obama campaign has focused on internet media. "If it were not for the internet," said Arianna Huffington, the founder of the *Huffington Post*, "Barack Obama would never have been elected president" (K. Anderson, 2009). But 2008 was, in many respects, much like any other television-era campaign, and to downplay this is to misunderstand the campaign's true significance. At the same time, to place the enduring influence of television-era campaigning in its proper context we must consider how campaigning now works in an increasingly integrated hybrid system.

Television-centric campaign strategy abounded in 2008. Obama's time was ruthlessly scheduled for maximum efficiency and impact, not least in the area of fundraising, where appearances were skewed toward "high-dollar" events. Public utterances were mostly scripted and actions were mostly stage-managed. David Axelrod, Obama's chief adviser, and David Plouffe, his campaign manager, were the most important individuals in this domain. Speeches were drafted by committee, with professional speechwriter Jon Favreau taking the lead, though several key speeches had significant input from Obama himself (Plouffe, 2010: 40, 49). The campaign had a large staff devoted to advertising and internal polling. It made heavy use of focus groups to test policy statements in advance of press releases, particularly on key issues such as healthcare. In keeping with television-era traditions, the campaign plowed massive resources into Iowa, the first contest of the primaries, to maximize the chances of establishing momentum and viability in the eyes of elite journalists. A terrible fear of the slightest mistake polluted the campaign for its entire duration, a fact that insider accounts betray in some detail, with, for example, tales of "systemic failure" and the inadequate "scouring" of potential problems like the Reverend Jeremiah Wright, Obama's controversial pastor whose interventions on race relations became more inflammatory as the campaign progressed. As David Plouffe put it: "I still kick myself for how terribly we mishandled our Wright work" (Plouffe, 2010: 41). The phrase "Wright work" reveals the time-honored practices of the war room: seeking out potential problems with a candidate's past and rendering these amenable to careful management. The campaign solicited the support of high-profile figures from the spheres of television entertainment, business, and sports, and it orchestrated their appearances in "high-roller events" for the maximum possible television exposure and impact on the news agenda. Participation in the early televised primary debates was accompanied by what the campaign called "visibility contingents"—supporters deliberately assembled to convey a sense of enthusiasm in front of the cameras (Plouffe, 2010: 61).

There was also classic "opposition research," which enabled the war room to feed to the press negative background information on competitors, in the hope of generating critical coverage. Notable examples include the information about rival Democratic candidate Senator John Edwards's "$400 haircuts," which was given to the press by an Obama researcher, and "Punjabgate," a story that tried to portray Hillary Clinton as soft on jobs outsourcing, but which backfired when the *New York Times* instead framed its report around the Obama campaign's attempt to smear opponents.

Control by the campaign war room also extended to what it perceived as equally important matters, such as the public's attitudes to celebrity endorsements. The most vivid example of this was Oprah Winfrey. "We…deployed our ace in the hole—the big O…," wrote Plouffe. "Her numbers among noncore caucus-goers and primary voters in the early states were even higher than among the general population. We tested this thoroughly before deploying her…" (Plouffe, 2010: 118). The campaign conducted opinion polls on all of its potential endorsers. The Reverend Al Sharpton's low approval ratings meant his support was not requested. The campaign also delayed the announcement of Senator John Kerry's endorsement of Obama for several weeks, after polling showed that it would distract attention from Obama's early gains (Plouffe, 2010: 125, 132). But Sharpton and Kerry were established political figures whom one would expect to receive such careful treatment; Oprah was not.

Oprah's cultural reach owes a great deal to her television career, but in recent years this has been augmented by three brand-building projects that have embedded her persona and values in American public life: the Oprah.com website, the Oprah book club, and *O, the Oprah Magazine*, which sells 2.4 million copies and has an estimated readership of some 16 million per month (Garthwaite & Moore, 2011). These provide a significant sphere of influence for companies and politicians fortunate enough to hitch themselves to the bandwagon. Celebrity endorsements are nothing new in electoral contests, but the extent to which the Obama staff integrated Oprah into their campaign is striking. Rather than hope in some vague sense that the sheen of America's biggest television celebrity might rub off on their candidate, the campaign saw it as a crucial part of their goal of expanding the electorate, particularly among young women and African Americans, and they succeeded in drawing into the electoral process groups less likely to respond to formal political appeals.

The big O endorsement paid off early. Thirty thousand people came to hear Obama, his wife Michelle, and Oprah speak at meetings in Des Moines and Cedar Rapids in early December 2007, just a few weeks before the Iowa caucuses. This amounted to 13 percent of the eventual record turnout of 240,000 in that state. And, in a remarkable shift, eventual turnout among the under-thirties was at the same rate as among those over sixty-five—a significant departure from previous caucuses, when older voters turned out at twice the rate of the young (Nagourney, 2008b).

NEWER MEDIA LOGICS ENCOURAGE OLDER MEDIA LOGICS: TELEVISION ADVERTISING

Barack Obama's 2008 campaign raised a total of around $750 million; around $500 million of this came through online donations. The amounts raised online were unprecedented in campaign politics worldwide, but precisely what role did this money play in the campaign?

The vast sums raised online paid for private planes and motorcades, essential resources for the system of symbols that has defined "presidentiality" since television emerged. They paid for a huge nomadic army of salaried staff who were deployed across the country like pieces on a chess board. Obama advertised across all possible media: television, radio, newspapers, internet, billboards, video games, ringtones, leaflets, bumper stickers, and text messaging. But most importantly, the money paid for historically unprecedented amounts of television advertising. Obama outspent all previous presidential campaigns in this area and by a large margin. According to its chief advertising manager, Jim Margolis, the campaign spent a total of $407 million on commercials: $93 million in the primaries and $314 million in the general election. John McCain spent $147 million in the general election (primary data are not available) (Margolis, 2009: 120). Obama sank around $250 million into television ads alone. Not only did this exceed McCain's television spending by around $100 million, it was $62 million more than what (at that time) was the record-breaking amount the Bush-Cheney campaign spent in 2004 (Toner, 2010: 154). During the final two months of the campaign, Obama spent almost $84 million more than McCain on television and radio (Kenski, et al., 2010: 266). Nielsen television data show that during September, October, and November of 2008, Obama comprehensively out-bought McCain in cable television units (2,092 to 1,518), network television units (432 to 345) and local spot television units (299,207 to 164,556) (Abramowitz, 2010: 96). The vast bulk of these local television ads were aired in the key battleground states. These were significant older media advantages for Obama, and they were bought with the online money.

Consider some of the sums spent to promote even the most basic messages of the campaign. The Obama campaign spent over $14 million on television ads aimed at associating McCain with Bush, including $6 million for a month of spots entitled "The Same." A similar ad, entitled "90 percent," cost a total of $8 million in national cable slots during the final two weeks of the campaign: it was so prevalent that paid media was transformed into earned media when the ad went on to be parodied in a *Saturday Night Live* comedy sketch starring actor Will Ferrell. The National Annenberg Election Survey found that heavier users of television, newspaper, and the internet for their campaign information were more likely to believe Obama's "McSame" arguments (Kenski, et al., 2010: 42).

In a move unprecedented for a major party candidate since the 1970s U.S. campaign finance reforms, Obama's internet donations allowed him to withdraw from public funding for the general election. This, in turn, freed his campaign to spend on its media and grassroots organizing at levels far beyond what would have been possible had it stayed within the federal limits. It could coordinate its media campaign with the Democratic party organizations in the key states, but it was not reliant on the party for funding a volunteer operation. It could massively increase its television advertising toward the end of the campaign, when McCain's campaign was running out of money. This financial advantage was demonstrated to remarkable effect late in the campaign, when Obama was able to run a series of two-minute commercials and an extraordinary thirty-minute hybrid documentary-advertisement on national television, laying out his economic policy in some detail, amid a context of growing financial crisis. The online money paid for all of this.

Due to a lack of money, McCain was forced to run ads funded jointly by his campaign and the Republican National Committee. These are regulated by the FEC to ensure that messages are focused exactly equally on the presidential campaign and broader party messages. They often produce confusing and ineffective ads at best and downright nonsensical ads at worst. Senior adviser to McCain, Steve Schmidt, described them as "like watching a Fellini film on acid" (Schmidt, 2009: 57). In the end, McCain's team abandoned the approach and fell back on their own rapidly dwindling supply of money.

For all the talk of the importance of the ground war and the establishment of a volunteer infrastructure assisted by the custom-built social network site, MyBarackObama.com, television advertising played an equally important role in building support, even as early as six months before the Iowa caucuses. When the campaign's record-breaking second quarter fundraising totals were published in mid-2007, the first response in the war room was to increase advertising. As Plouffe put it, the influx of money, much of it raised online, allowed them to "begin advertising earlier and more frequently ... because voters in these states knew very little about Obama at this point. Most of what they knew was surface information—he was a senator, gave a good speech in Boston in 2004, served in the Illinois legislature. We needed to fill in his life story, his values, accomplishments, and agenda. Now we had the resources to do a more thorough job" (Plouffe, 2010: 78). This theme—using television advertising to "do a more thorough job" in conveying the controlled, personalized narratives that are so crucial to a presidential campaign, and for which television is the best medium—is a powerful current in the story of Obama's 2008 victory. The approach continued throughout the post-Iowa primaries and into the general election campaign, when television advertising, and not just the internet, was seen as the most effective means of quickly establishing candidate recognition and even of spurring enthusiasm among local volunteers.

As the campaign moved into the general election, managing resources in the swing states required a careful balancing of priorities. On the ground, staffers and volunteer labor often plugged the gaps in states that were lower down the pecking order for advertising spending. Minnesota and Wisconsin fell into this category, for example. But overall, television advertising was seen as a better means of educating the electorate about the personal and family history of a relative newcomer to national politics (Plouffe, 2010: 250, 264). The idea that the internet was the only key to the ground campaign is wide of the mark: the picture is more complex.

Despite the obvious affordances of the internet for long-term campaign building, such as its suitability for integrating with the ground game and its capacity for rapid rebuttal (Anstead & Chadwick, 2009), once a campaign is underway, when candidates must deal with multiple contests in quick succession across a vast territory, television advertising is still seen as supremely advantageous. Obama sought to establish support bases in several states through advertising, particularly in the primaries immediately after Iowa and New Hampshire, when time was tight in the run-up to Super Tuesday, the day in 2008 when twenty-two primaries were held. And with the emergence of early voting rules that enable large states such as California to vote long before Super Tuesday itself, the time pressure in 2008 was even greater (Plouffe, 2010: 138). Record amounts of funds flowed into the campaign on the back of Obama's Iowa and South Carolina victories in early 2008. All but $4 million of the $32 million total for January 2008 was raised online, which meant that it could be quickly deployed in broadcast ads in the Super Tuesday states to "help fill the void" in the ground effort, even in very expensive advertising markets such as Los Angeles and New York (Plouffe, 2010: 167). New York was particularly important for the campaign's strategy of securing Democratic Party delegate votes even in those states where it did not stand to gain a majority of the popular vote.

Newer media logics enhanced older media logics, in a virtuous circle. Immediately after Super Tuesday, the Obama campaign increased its media buying on the expectation of a further influx of online donations. This gamble paid off: $55 million flooded in by the end of February (Plouffe, 2010: 177). As donations continued to increase, the campaign was able to increase its advertising across all older media: television, newspapers, and radio. For example, in the closing stages of the Indiana and North Carolina primaries it plowed all of its advertising resources into a television campaign about how to deal with rising gas prices. As attention turned to the Texas and Ohio votes, it ran full-page newspaper ads in all of the daily papers in these two states (Plouffe, 2010: 191).

It is often assumed that the internet enables campaigns to adapt quickly to unforeseen events (Chadwick, 2007), and this is undoubtedly the case. But we should also remember that the very same digital technologies and working practices that drive internet campaigning are also now deeply embedded in all campaigns' internal coordination mechanisms and they also penetrate the habitual practices of journalists' news production. In television news, there has been a shift toward real-time reaction and round-the-clock working. Campaign media staff now spend large amounts of their time in video processing rooms, using computers to rapidly produce and edit broadcast-quality video complete with sophisticated graphical overlays and animations. The completed files are transmitted digitally to the advertising agencies, who then liaise with the television companies. Television ads are therefore now just as much a part of the rapid-reaction, real-time campaign as e-mail, blogs, and social network updates. For example, in the midst of the financial crisis and on the day the Dow Jones index fell 500 points due to the Lehman Brothers collapse, John McCain remarked that "The fundamentals of our economy are strong." The Obama campaign responded within a matter of hours with a television ad, "Fundamentals," that was formally launched the morning after. Obama also mentioned "fundamentals" during the first televised presidential debate in Oxford, Mississippi (Kenski, et al., 2010: 196). McCain's selectively chosen seven-word remark became a major theme of the remainder of the campaign: it was included 668 times in newspapers and 303 times in broadcast news (Kenski, et al., 2010: 184).

Quickly prepared commercials like "Fundamentals" integrate and remediate the key turning points in the big real-time television events of the campaign. In another example, during the third televised presidential debate, McCain responded cuttingly to Obama's claim that McCain held the same views as Bush: "Senator Obama, I am not President Bush. If you wanted to run against President Bush, you should have run four years ago," he said. The following morning, the Obama campaign issued a commercial featuring archived video footage of McCain proudly stating that he "voted with the president over 90 percent of the time" (BarackObamadotcom, 2008a). The McCain campaign followed up soon after with a newspaper interview in the *Washington Times* and a television appearance on *Meet the Press*, both of which were aimed at distancing their candidate from the Bush era (Kenski, et al., 2010: 38).

Television and radio advertising are still perceived by campaign insiders as more effective than any other medium for persuading voters (Kaye, 2009: 14). They have become more, not less, valuable for campaigns because over the last few election cycles the broadcasting advertising system has itself evolved. The growth of cable television and satellite radio has fragmented audiences, as many viewers and listeners have switched from national broadcast networks to a range of new digital channels. Cable news is now watched at roughly the same levels as the nightly network news (Kenski, et al., 2010: 278). During the 2008 campaign, far greater numbers (44 percent) used cable news channels such as MSNBC, CNN, and Fox as their most important television sources of campaign information when compared with those (18 percent) who used network news, such as ABC, CBS, or NBC (Pew Research Center, 2008a).

Cable television creates new opportunities for effective and measurable advertising. Much of this is now targeted at the slots between a wider range of programming than "hard" news. Lifestyle and entertainment programs are now popular among campaign media buyers, because the buyers know with some precision the kinds of audiences that are likely to view certain types of niche cable content. Campaigns use their own data and those from the cable channels themselves, but they also buy data from market research companies such as Nielsen, MRI, and Scarborough Research. These data make it easier to target ads by gender, ethnicity, age, and likelihood of voting. The ad slots in between shows on stations like the Food Network offer advertisers a less competitive and cluttered environment for their messages than the more limited slots around the big network news shows. Cable ads are more likely to be influential as a result (Kenski, et al., 2010: 278). These developments have renewed television's role as a medium for political advertising in presidential campaigns.

In contrast with the $250 million spent on television advertising, Obama spent just $17 million on internet advertising and McCain a paltry $8 million (Fenn, 2009: 217). While much online space, like a Facebook page, is essentially "free" to fill with content, and online advertising is much cheaper than television advertising, these sums are still remarkably small. In 2008, most internet ad spending was channeled toward banner and video slots and the Google AdWords and AdSense systems. Though the sums spent were small, Google ads were an innovative departure from earlier campaigns, though even here these digital media strategies were integrated into the television strategies. Campaign staff began buying text ads that were automatically generated by Google's algorithms and displayed alongside relevant keywords that were entered by the public as they searched for information related to the campaign. These ads were also used in key states to attract volunteers. Because Google keyword purchases can be changed very quickly, Google ads were useful for intervening in synchrony with key television events, such as the presidential debates. For example, prior to the third television debate, the Republicans purchased many keywords related to a section of their campaign site they had established to capitalize on McCain's repeated mentions of "Joe the Plumber," a reference to a Republican supporter who famously confronted Obama about his tax plans in front of cameras during canvassing in Ohio. The Democrats countered this with a new online form on their site. Launched just a day before the televised debate, it featured a "Joe the Plumber Tax Calculator," which meant that it was likely to appear high up the text ads list as people went online to search the web after the debate. These techniques were clearly new to campaigns, and yet temporally they did not stand alone, but meshed with the older media logics of the televised debates.

Obama's huge financial resources also allowed the campaign to innovate in its television advertising. This further reinforced and renewed television's role in the contemporary campaign, but these ads also had an important web element. As the campaign moved toward its denouement in early September, and the global financial crisis started to dominate coverage, Obama's campaign decided to introduce a new series of economy-focused commercials. At an extra cost of some $6 million per week, and in a significant departure from the standard thirty-second television format, these new ads were two minutes long and integrated with further content on the web. These were huge expenditures, but the campaign raised a record $100 million of its $150 million for September online and it could deploy this money quickly. By that stage its e-mail list had swelled to more than 11 million supporters and it was seeing remarkably high levels of engagement, with around a third of supporters having donated and almost all of them having volunteered (Plouffe, 2010: 326–327).

If the two-minute ads were a departure from tradition, what came next was even more unusual. Six days before election day, at an estimated cost of $5 million, the Obama campaign produced a thirty-minute documentary-infomercial entitled *American Stories, American Solutions*. This aired across the major television networks (excluding ABC), as well as MSNBC, Fox, Univision, BET, and TV One (Fenn, 2009: 215). The professionally produced film had Obama as its narrator, but it was directed by Academy Award winning filmmaker David Guggenheim. However, as if to symbolically enshrine the principles of community organizing in this decidedly non-grassroots media genre, the focus was on examples of ordinary Americans and their stories of economic hardship and determination. There were multiple references back to the narrative themes of Obama's previous ads as well as personal testimony from renowned senators and U.S. military commanders. The film contained a detailed description—or certainly more detailed than is usual in campaign commercials—of Obama's policy agenda. The broadcast's final two minutes switched to a live transmission of a rally at which Obama was speaking that evening. The film integrated essential components of the campaign's strategy: community organizing at the grassroots, elite endorsement, liveness, the simultaneous physicality, theatricality, and mediality of representing rallies and crowds, and the symbolic projected power of a campaign that can afford to dominate so much of American prime-time television scheduling with its own media content. An estimated 33.5 million watched the live televised transmission (Fenn, 2009: 215) and the film was streamed live on the campaign website and quickly archived to YouTube (BarackObamadotcom, 2008b). It went on to dominate two days of news coverage as election day arrived. Not since independent multimillionaire candidate Ross Perot's series of thirty-minute films during the 1992 campaign had such a television onslaught been witnessed by American voters. The documentary-ad had a positive effect on Obama's favorability ratings and those who reported watching the film were more likely to vote for the Democrat (Kenski, et al., 2010: 246).

A further hybrid development in the 2008 campaign was the emergence of so-called "press ads"—commercials that were never destined to be aired on television but were shown on YouTube, the main campaign websites, and the temporary microsites. These ads also often found their way onto television, radio, and newspaper news websites (Fenn, 2009; Kaye, 2009: 29–68). As Jim Margolis, Obama's senior adviser on advertising revealed, campaign staff send these ads to newspaper and broadcast journalists late at night or in the very early hours of the morning to try to gain earned media coverage from a paid media artifact (Margolis, 2009: 130). The files come complete with professionally produced video and graphics and require little if any extra work to made fit for broadcasting. Faced with a shortage of money for television advertising during the primaries, in summer 2007 the McCain campaign decided to temporarily suspend its television spending and prioritize web video (Barko Germany, 2009). To the campaign's surprise, this tactic had much success, as journalists, especially those working the morning news shifts, were always eager for fresh visual material. The day after the third and final televised presidential debate, which saw McCain make headway with his repeated mentions of Joe the Plumber, McCain's team uploaded an internet-only ad entitled "Joe the Plumber." This gave television reporters something extra to add to their post-debate coverage and reinforced McCain's message in the debate. This remarkably cheap way of gaining broadcast media attention was joined a few days later by a traditional $5.7 million television ad, "Sweat Equity," which aired 12,750 times in the final two weeks before election day (Kenski, et al., 2010: 229). As Chris Mottola, McCain's senior adviser on advertising said, "we had to feed the beast, feed the media every day and give them something to cover and something to talk about … It was like leaving bright, shiny objects in front of the media to cover the next day or cover in a cycle" (Mottola, 2009: 111). Anita Dunn, senior press officer for Obama, has gone as far as to say that the regular made-for-television ads were actually *less* likely to be covered by reporters than the more sensational ones they uploaded to the web and sent directly to the news studios solely to get media coverage (Dunn, 2009: 145).

In addition to these press ads, the rise to prominence of YouTube during the 2008 campaign generated many "let's see what's happening online" side-features on television news. These often showed YouTube ads running inside web browsers that were in turn remediated on giant monitors in the television studios. This kind of coverage further encouraged campaigns to step up their online efforts as a means of capitalizing on television's insatiable appetite for novelty and the news media's more general "horse race" frame, which was just as dominant in 2008 as it had been in previous television-era campaigns (Owen, 2010).

Television therefore remains a powerful campaign medium, not only because the medium is itself still hugely important for reaching audiences, but also because the very nature of television is shifting, as its technologies, genres, norms, behaviors, and organizational characteristics are becoming hybridized with those of the internet. In the hybrid media system, campaign commercials are increasingly part of a circulation, repurposing, and mobilization circuit: made-for-television ads feature on YouTube, made-for-YouTube ads feature on television; both appear as paid video advertising on newspaper and television companies' websites; both link to campaign microsites channeling online donations or other online actions such as petition-signing. And citizen movements also solicit online content that they can repurpose in television advertising: MoveOn's "Obama in 30 Seconds" competition asked volunteers to create short films that the organization then showed as traditional paid television commercials in the campaign's final weeks.

TELEVISION AND THE INTERNET: THREATS AND OPPORTUNITIES

This hybridity compels campaigns to continually weigh the threats and opportunities presented by campaigning with older and newer media. The rise of cable and the fragmentation of television news audiences has altered campaigns' perception of television as a medium. The networks are still heavily shaped by time constraints, the cable news channels much less so. Meanwhile, YouTube has become a gigantic video hub whose digital media logic of archiving and repetition has the capacity even to transcend the always-on, real-time stream of cable news. Yet in 2007 and early 2008, cable news channels attracted surprisingly high audience figures for the televised Democratic primary debates and the channels continually pressed state parties to hold more debates. Campaign managers still clearly see televised debates as major campaign events and they now tailor their approach to the broader media system. Cable television news has taken up the slack left by the networks, and the internet provides ceaseless opportunities for debate coverage of varying kinds. There were more than thirty nationally televised candidate debates during the 2008 campaign (May, 2009: 81).

The power of television as a tool for campaigns to quickly and efficiently move the news agenda was obvious even during the primary's early skirmishes. There were persistent attempts to use high-profile television appearances to attempt to steer the "national narrative" in Obama's favor, especially during the build-up to the Iowa caucuses, when there was much traditional media skepticism about his viability (Plouffe, 2010: 75, 91–92). During a televised debate in Philadelphia in October 2007, Hillary Clinton's failure to clearly state whether she was in favor of providing illegal immigrants with driver's licenses became a big story for television news. This was followed in quick succession by revelations that Clinton was planting questions with audience members at televised rallies in Iowa. Cable news revealed video showing a questioner winking in sly recognition as she asked a planted question on climate change. The offending clip, taken from MSNBC's *Hardball*, was also uploaded to YouTube by "james1053." (james1053, 2007).

The national television networks have steadily reduced their coverage of the parties' conventions over recent decades. Nevertheless, in 2008 there was much anticipation of each party's gathering, and the conventions still provide excellent opportunities for campaigns to try to shift the news agenda, not least because the 2008 race demonstrated that the audiences for these events can still be enormous. A record-breaking 38.3 million people watched televised coverage of Obama's acceptance speech at the Democratic meeting in Denver. Twenty-four million watched Joe Biden's vice presidential speech. With figures of 38.9 million for McCain and 37.2 million for Palin, the Republicans even managed to top the Democrats. These audiences were much larger than for Bush and Kerry in 2004, who attracted 27.6 and 24.4 million respectively (Kenski, et al., 2010: 131). The big events during the conventions are carefully timed to coincide with key early evening television news bulletins. A good example was Hillary Clinton's carefully staged 6:30 p.m. interruption of the convention's formal vote counting process, in order to nominate Obama "by acclamation" from the floor of the convention. Annenberg election study data reveal that, after controlling for standard predictors of candidate preference, the convention acceptance speeches played a significant role in shaping perceptions of the candidates. Both Obama's and Biden's speeches improved their favorability ratings, as did those of McCain and Palin, though there were doubts expressed about Palin's "readiness" to be vice president (Kenski, et al., 2010: 123–148). Televised convention speeches are clearly here to stay. They play an important role in punctuating campaigns, in grabbing the attention of professional media, and in shaping voters' perceptions of candidates and their campaigns.

Having said all of this about the positive importance of television, the 2008 campaign was also infused with contradictory attitudes toward the medium. Now that online campaigning has become embedded in presidential campaigns, television may often loom as a less controllable threat. Long-form news shows such as the esteemed *Sixty Minutes* still have the resources to conduct investigative journalism. Live broadcast format shows such as ABC's *Good Morning America* also have considerable investigative resources, but their live nature can also catch candidates and their staff off-guard. Appearances on these shows require time and effort to be spent on preparation and staff must "war-game out how…to minimize the damage," as David Plouffe said of the "proctologic" exposé in early 2008 of Obama's previous real estate dealings with Tony Rezko, a Chicago-based property tycoon (Plouffe, 2010: 155). Late-night television comedy shows can slice and dice almost any news footage to achieve satirical effects. Obama's team responded by tightly controlling the political choreography of his appearances across as many public manifestations as possible (Cornfield, 2010: 213). Scheduled press conferences, such as the one held by Obama in order to defuse the Tony Rezko story, can turn into hostile feeding frenzies. It was not until a meeting behind closed doors with senior staff from the two major Chicago newspapers that were pushing the story had generated two positive editorials that the crisis was defused (Plouffe, 2010: 209–210).

Then there was Obama's televised chance encounter with a citizen, Joe Wurzelbacher, while street campaigning in Ohio during the closing stages. Wurzelbacher, or "Joe the Plumber," confronted Obama with a highly specific question about the effects of the Democrat's proposed tax increases for those earning more than $250,000 a year. Part of Obama's response included the phrase "when you spread the wealth around, it's good for everybody." This was leapt upon by conservative commentators (Associated Press, 2008). Widely reported as a rare moment of direct, unstaged interaction with the public, and one with concrete economic policy implications, the Joe the Plumber video became a leitmotif of the final weeks of the campaign. But what was initially lauded as a rare piece of authenticity on the campaign trail soon metamorphosed into televised politics as usual. Wurzelbacher was quickly integrated into the McCain campaign assemblage and appeared in several television news interviews, including an exchange with Diane Sawyer on *Good Morning America* during which he called Obama's tax plans "social-ist." This intervention was later picked up and repeated by McCain in a radio address (Kenski, et al., 2010: 226). Wurzelbacher also appeared at some Republican rallies, albeit briefly. McCain attempted to capitalize still further by injecting more than twenty refer-ences to Joe the Plumber during the final televised presidential debate at Long Island, whose audience numbered some fifty-six million. Investigative reports soon revealed that Wurzelbacher was not a registered plumber and that he was not going to be personally affected by the Obama tax plans, but this did not prevent the Republicans from making headway. By the close of the campaign McCain's favorability ratings were improving, as were voters' perceptions of his ability to handle the economy. These were related to the perception that Obama was a "tax and spend liberal": viewing the final television debate was positively correlated with this attitude (Kenski, et al., 2010: 219, 225).

The threats posed by the internet to a campaign are similar in some respects to those posed by television. The online environment sometimes looms as a vast, uncontrollable space populated by malicious rumors, ideologically charged bloggers, satirical viral vid-eos, and archival evidence of candidates' mistakes, all integrated and presented via a gigantic and convenient search interface called Google. But it is now equally obvious that campaigns can use the internet to discipline and control their campaigns in ways that can be difficult to achieve using television and newspapers. Campaigns often have direct access to the public online, unfiltered by news shows and journalism. They use the internet to bolster their ground efforts through carefully targeted fundraising. They now produce extraordinarily wide-ranging campaign assemblages that fuse technological means of control with the physical human labor required for door-knocking, canvassing, and phone-calling, in what Rasmus Kleis Nielsen calls "personalized political commu-nication" (R. K. Nielsen, 2012). The web allows campaigns to sidestep the media logics of televised events, to construct a campaign on their own terms, with a schedule that they can more easily control. More than ever, campaigns can harvest behavioral data under conditions that they themselves have generated. In short, campaigns have now tamed large swathes of the internet and they have integrated it into a hybrid approach focusing on all relevant media.

Even spikes in online fundraising are now closely linked to important real-time televised campaign events, such as victory and defeat in primary contests, and good and bad performances in televised debates. These older media-driven events provide timely opportunities for campaign activists to intervene using newer media. As with the convention speeches, in 2008 the audiences for these events were enormous. The average television audience across the three presidential debates was fifty-nine million. The vice presidential debate between Sarah Palin and Joe Biden was watched by seventy-three million, making it by far the most-watched vice presidential debate in U.S. history. Indeed, the Palin–Biden debate almost topped the first Carter–Reagan *presidential* debate of 1980, which was viewed by eighty-one million. In 2008 all of the debates were made available for viewing in multiple online environments.

The campaigns sent e-mails and text messages during the hours before each debate, urging supporters to share their views and donate online (Johnson, 2009: 12). Donations strengthen the ground campaign, but the donations that cluster around real-time televised events like debates are also a means of intervening in the flow of mainstream news. They are tangible signals to the mainstream media that the public is reacting. Campaigns try to capitalize on these new dynamics. The night of Sarah Palin's network-broadcast vice presidential nomination acceptance speech in St. Paul, the Obama campaign received a large influx of online donations, as people sent in money while watching Palin's speech. These real-time interventions also provide symbolic resources for the campaign press staff, who are able to generate authentically positive counter-narratives for the television and broadcast media that will inevitably become fixated on the big speech. Citizens are aware of this, and, acting in concert on the spur of the campaign e-mails, they now time their interventions carefully for the largest possible impact. It was these sorts of interventions during the televised primary debates that made it easier for Obama to actively consider withdrawing from public funding, not only because they provided a foretaste of the enormous sums that might be donated once the campaign entered its most intensive phase, but also because Obama's decision, for all the problems it portended for the unconstrained use of money in future presidential campaigns, could be presented, and not without warrant, as an affirmation of concerted democratic action by a supportive public eager to make its voice heard by proxy. As Nick Anstead has argued, internet fundraising is now embedded within broader historical traditions of civic voluntarism in American political culture (Anstead, 2008: 289).

Still, we must qualify these democratic aspects of online fundraising. Early reports made much of the claim that the amount Obama raised in small donations was only around the same as George W. Bush raised during the 2004 campaign and only marginally greater than McCain's 2008 record (Malbin, 2008). More detailed analysis carried out after the dust had settled on the election revealed a more significant achievement for Obama. Not only did he receive a far greater number of small donations than all of the other candidates in the primaries, the 33 percent of money he raised from donors giving a total of $200 or less was quite significantly ahead of Bush in 2004 (26 percent) and far outpaced McCain in 2008 (21 percent) (Corrado, et al., 2010: 17). Obama therefore raised more in small contributions than any other presidential candidate since meaningful records began.

And yet, these numbers do still mask a more complex picture. The sources of Obama's "early money," which is donated before primary voting begins and is the most crucial resource for demonstrating candidate viability, were heavily skewed toward large donors: 60 percent of donations between January and August 2007 were in amounts of $1,000 or more. Those working in the financial sector, pharmaceuticals, defense, and broadcasting featured prominently in the early money (Ferguson, 2008; Sifry, 2009). Like other recent presidential campaigns, Obama made use of "bundlers," usually wealthy individuals who collected together maximum donation amounts from their business and social networks (Corrado & Corbett, 2009). Only 32 percent of Obama's donations came from those who gave less than $200 *in total*. Many individuals made a large number of repeat donations. Indeed, they were strongly encouraged to do so by the campaign, and then to signal that they had done so to others in their online social networks by establishing online fundraising groups and displaying personal fundraising "thermometer" widgets on their MyBarackObama.com profile pages. These technologies translated the "bundling" principle into the online realm. There is a strong argument that the subscription model of fundraising enables poorer individuals to spread the costs of donating across several months. But there are other advantages for the campaigns. Not only does it avoid donor burn-out and secure steadier streams of income, it also allows the campaign to convey its grassroots credentials by targeting professional media and bloggers with stories about "small online donations" during key moments like televised debates.

The War Room Meets Structured Interactivity

It is easy to forget that Obama was an insurgent candidate in 2008. Hillary Clinton had been preparing for a presidential run for many years. She had a latent national network of activists and campaign staff, many of whom cut their teeth during her husband Bill Clinton's successful 1992 campaign. Hillary was remarkably well-known, a political brand in her own right, and widely expected to activate a large-scale fundraising effort at short notice. An Obama victory would be a major political upset. While certainly not unknown after his much-reported 2004 Democratic convention speech, Obama was an African American based in Chicago; a relative political outsider who lacked significant organization across the key swing states he would need to win to secure the presidency. Not only did Obama defeat Clinton, he went on to emphatically beat John McCain, one of the most experienced and popular Republican politicians of recent times, and, ironically, a man who had blazed the trail in online campaigning during a failed bid for the Republican nomination in the 2000 primaries.

As befitting an insurgent, Obama's campaign had to be built from scratch out of what were—initially—meager resources. The campaign's early internal polls in Iowa had him trailing well behind not only Clinton but also Senator John Edwards (Plouffe, 2010: 19). The first goal was to present Obama as the main alternative to Clinton as early as possible in the primary season, well in advance of the first electoral test. The second goal was to prevent Clinton from gaining momentum from victories in the early primaries. Following that, the third goal was to "expand the electorate" by creating a pool of newly registered primary voters, including young people, African Americans, Latinos, and those Republicans and independents who could be motivated to participate in the Democratic primaries. The hope was that these groups would then continue their enthusiasm into the general election. In the Iowa caucuses, not only would this involve encouraging larger numbers of young people to attend events that are traditionally dominated by older citizens, it would also involve Republicans and independents reregistering as Democrats in order to show their support for Obama. Campaign director David Plouffe and the team planned to build what Plouffe calls "a grassroots movement" based on a "ragtag army" of volunteers and small donors who could be mobilized through interpersonal communication, both online and offline. Word of mouth would create a "permission structure" that encouraged individuals to become involved (Plouffe, 2010: 94).

But the Obama campaign was also tightly controlled from the center. The internet was important for building momentum, but only in tandem with putting precinct captains and volunteers on the ground. Obama established a small, close-knit circle of senior advisers with whom he would issue the "big decisions" (Plouffe, 2010: 22). Avoiding leaks to journalists was a strong motivator of this approach, but so too was a widely held skepticism about the nature of recent internet-fueled presidential campaigns. While essential for pioneering the development of online campaigning (Chadwick, 2007), the memory of Howard Dean's chaotic and ultimately unsuccessful primary campaign of 2004 weighed heavily on the Obama team's collective mind (Kreiss, 2012).

The initial inner circle included just three individuals: David Axelrod, David Plouffe, and Robert Gibbs (Plouffe, 2010: 22). This classic television-era war room model was sustained throughout the campaign and proved remarkably watertight. There were media spectacles and there were slip-ups, but there were no hugely important insider leaks. Unlike the Dean campaign, disunity in the war room was rare.

In keeping with the electoral traditions of the last few decades, campaign resources were channeled ruthlessly into swing states. But by recent standards, these states were more numerous. Regions of the country previously regarded as out of bounds for the Democrats suddenly came into play (A. Berman, 2010). Rather than gamble on winning Florida and Ohio—a strategy that has developed into a mainstay of presidential campaigns since the 1990s—Obama's staff began by treating sixteen states as potentially up for grabs. As we saw above, these states were pummeled with television advertising, but the multiple-state strategy also required a large-scale ground campaign coordinated by experienced staff. Obama used portions of his huge central fund to reinforce state-level Democratic parties' ground efforts in the key states. The electoral penalties for being seen to be disengaging from even just one or two of the key states are severe. For example, when, due to lack of resources, John McCain announced his withdrawal from Michigan during the general election campaign, his poll ratings in the state quickly declined and he effectively conceded it to Obama. In Indiana, McCain did not even establish a headquarters and visited only once, for four hours in June (A. Berman, 2010: 170). As Obama's ground and internet operations revealed growing levels of volunteering and support, the campaign used its resources to increase television advertising but it also increased physical "candidate time" for real-space speeches and rallies. As we shall see in the next chapter, physical presence, if those real-space events are coordinated online and then mediated by local and national news outlets, still matters a great deal.

Obama's campaign organization built upon established models but it also innovated. A press and communications department was established, but in stark contrast with the model that emerged during the first wave of internet campaigning of the 1990s, the press office was not granted overall control of the new media department. Managed by former Dean campaign worker Joe Rospars, new media was much more tightly integrated with field operations than had previously been the case in American campaigns. New media reported directly to the campaign's chief, Plouffe (Kreiss, 2012). Unlike the McCain campaign, Obama's online media staff also worked closely with the rest of the

media and communications personnel and new media people played a role in influencing strategy across the board (Kaye, 2009: 5). This system meant that the norms and
practices of the new media staff constantly interacted with those of the field division
and the traditional press and communications team. However, overall control of campaign messages was firmly in the hands of the war room. Obama, Axelrod, Plouffe, and
Gibbs channeled their commands through a network of press and communications,
new media, and ground campaign managers.

The tight integration of new media and volunteer coordination in the ground campaign allowed the campaign leadership to use its power to reach down into localities and
challenge some traditional models of state politicking. South Carolina Democrats, for
example, have a longstanding tradition of paid political organizing: a system of patronage in which, in return for payment, local political and church elites offer their candidate endorsements and the safe delivery of support. In a rejection of what it termed
"old-school politics" and an affirmation of "organizing," the Obama campaign tried
to sidestep these traditions. Amid much criticism from local Democrats, it appointed
Anton Gunn, a community organizer, as political director for the state. This would not
have been possible without the online strategy. Gunn and Jeremy Bird from campaign
headquarters recruited volunteers using a combination of Facebook and in-person trips
to college campuses. The campaign's videographer Kate Albright-Hanna and its blogger
Sam Graham-Felsen were dispatched to the state to gather material for the website that
would serve to illustrate how they were breaking the mold (A. Berman, 2010: 130–131).
The campaign was successful in bypassing many of the South Carolina kingmakers and
in mobilizing younger white voters and newly registered African Americans. It meshed
online with offline, as internet content publicized thousands of house parties and a "bar-
bershop and beauty-salon outreach program" (Plouffe, 2010: 161). Obama carried the
South Carolina primary by 28 percent.

The war room engaged directly with the new media team over the design of key
elements of the online campaign. The best example of this in flow is e-mail. Building
on new media director Joe Rospars's previous experience in pioneering the genres of
the campaign e-mail during his time with Howard Dean, Plouffe was able to test and
calibrate the form and the content of this peculiarly powerful campaign medium. The
tone and length of e-mails were varied. There were experiments with formatting and
image placement, even font styles and colors (Kreiss, 2012). E-mails linking to video
were more likely to engage supporters and the campaign knew quite precisely how
much engagement was happening: "It was like having our own television returns,"
said Plouffe (2010: 297). The biggest responses tended to follow e-mails that were
signed by Obama himself, but to avoid diluting their impact "signed" e-mails were
kept to a minimum. By the close of the campaign each state had its own team solely
responsible for locally targeted e-mail messaging. In some cases targeting came right
down to county level (Plouffe, 2010: 77, 329). E-mail became a talisman of the ground
campaign. Among the panoply of digital media, it was long-established "mundane
tools" like this that proved to be more significant in harnessing volunteer efforts to the
broader goals of the campaign than newer environments like online social networks
(R. K. Nielsen, 2011, 2012).

E-mail took its place in a hybrid system of central managerial control and structured interactivity. This permitted only a *relatively* porous subsystem of netroots

mobilization (Cooper, 2011). And unlike the Dean campaign, this subsystem rarely if ever threatened—or, rather, flattered to deceive—those whose command and control pushed the core strategic objectives. The Dean campaign was an organizational hybrid of social movement and election campaign: its social movement repertoires ended up acting as a drag on its ability to deliver electoral gains (Chadwick, 2007). The Obama campaign was a similar organizational hybrid. Indeed, the campaign staff often had a social-movement-meets-campaign model in mind as they went about their work (Vaccari, 2010). But with Obama, the social movement repertoires—the educating, the empowering, and the mobilizing—were tightly integrated with the repertoires of the electoral campaign—the recruiting, the training, the motivating, the monitoring, and the coordinating.

Several examples illustrate this integration. Well in advance of the establishment of official state headquarters, local activists in Missouri used Facebook and MyBarackObama.com to establish a St. Louis for Barack Obama group. But when the campaign arrived in the state months later, it asked the St. Louis volunteers to make weekly road trips to Iowa instead (Plouffe, 2010: 175). Similarly, a supporter named Joe Anthony had established an unofficial MySpace profile for Obama in 2004, but in 2007 he was ordered by Obama's new media team to close the 160,000-follower account because it distracted attention from the official campaign. When Anthony refused, Obama's staff went directly to MySpace and asked the company to seize the profile (Sifry, 2007). MySpace, who no doubt saw Obama as a potential future president, quickly complied.

The Obama campaign was, in the words of Jon Carson, its national field director, a "highly structured, accountable system...." "Despite this decentralized system" he says, "I knew every single morning how many phone calls had been made, how many doors had been knocked, where, by whom, and if there was anything funky in the data" (Carson, 2009: 42). All of this pivoted on an important distinction between distributed labor and distributed power. As former Dean campaign worker Zephyr Teachout put it: "some very smart people have figured out how to organize your excitement" (2007).

From the outset, the Obama team had a clear strategy for online campaigning, the clearest since the internet first emerged as a force in American politics. The overarching aim was to develop the website into an important node in what they envisaged as a fairly tightly controlled network of nodes. Each node would ultimately belong to the campaign and would be designed to play a specific role. For example, live video of events and announcements on the main site were seen as a means of spurring people to log on to the social network site MyBarackObama.com to discuss these events with others.

MyBarackObama ("MyBO") ended up with more than two million user profiles and was the platform for organizing more than thirty-five thousand volunteer groups and two hundred thousand local face-to-face events across the country (Vargas, 2008). On its own, however, MyBO was insufficient. The campaign had profiles on fifteen social network sites, including niche forums like BlackPlanet and AsianAvenue. There were more than five hundred pro-Obama groups on Facebook before Obama even announced his candidacy (R. Davis, et al., 2009). One of Facebook's founders, Chris Hughes, was hired by the campaign for his expertise. It was no coincidence that when Facebook opened up its application programming interface in 2007 for all-comers to create new applications for the service, Obama's campaign was the first to take advantage of the new platform (Baumgartner & Morris, 2010: 56–58).

The approach across the country was to integrate and balance this often-spontaneous local organizing against central strategy: "When staff arrived bearing more resources and focused goals, followed by advertising and some candidate time, the foundational work of our supporters on the ground paid huge dividends," said Plouffe. "We made sure to stress to volunteers that they had standing behind them a national HQ...and would make sure their work was strategically sound and received adequate resources" (Plouffe, 2010: 181, 256).

The Camp Obama Assemblage

A significant chunk of the central campaign's "strategically sound" resources for volunteers came in the form of Camp Obama. These gatherings were held across the key swing states during 2007 and 2008 (for some examples of the typical program of each event from early in the campaign see Camp Obama, 2007). Camp Obama combined strict campaign goals with looser, though still focused, principles of community organizing that had been important in forming Obama's political identity in Chicago during the 1980s and 1990s. Campaign goals included targeting, registering, and turning out key voter groups, such as Latinos in Denver or African Americans in North Carolina. The community organizing principles were injected by Marshall Ganz, the renowned veteran of 1960s community movements, who acted as an adviser to the Obama campaign and who personally led several of the Camps.

The Camp Obama gatherings are best understood as unusual assemblages of organizational rules and capacities, mobile technologies, and goal-oriented coordinative behaviors. They integrated people, local community buildings, training manuals, and ideas about experiential learning. They also structured opportunities for personal self-discovery and the formation of emotional bonds among activists.

Consider the camp held in Denver, Colorado, a couple of months before election day (see the wonderful ethnographic account in Alexander, 2010: 45–59). Around two hundred Americans of Hispanic origin from across the state converged in a community center in a working-class neighborhood. They were joined by twenty of the Obama campaign's full-time salaried field organizers, around a dozen state organizers, and a similar number of national staff who were representatives from campaign headquarters in Chicago. The goal was to register twenty thousand new Hispanic voters in the twenty-six days before the state registration deadline. The means to do so was hundreds of small local teams, each of whose job it was to call, canvass, and complete registration forms for Hispanic voters in their neighborhoods. The national organizers distributed a detailed grid of tasks to the local field staff, but these were not handed to the wider gathering of volunteers for fear it would give the impression that orders were simply being handed down from the top; which was, of course, precisely what was happening.

There followed a day of workshops and breakout sessions in which the principles of community organizing were spelled out and personal stories were shared about what the campaign meant to each volunteer. As the leader of the sessions explained, organizing was not about "lecturing" people, but about sharing stories and quickly building trusting relationships with strangers. Written on the chalkboards at these meetings was a series of binary opposites that summarized Ganz's model in shorthand terms. Instead of allocating "tasks," participants were told that they should encourage "stories." Don't ask "what?," they were told; instead ask "why?" or "how?" But even in this intensely face-to-face context, older media logics intervened: motivational videos of Obama's most powerful speeches were shown to the group on television before they were handed their goals.

Canvassing was organized in shifts from 9:00 a.m. to 9:00 p.m. each day. Individuals signed up for shifts and agreed to meet face to face every week for the remainder of the campaign. Role-playing exercises provided opportunities for the newly educated to put these principles into practice before the watchful eye of the camp leader and the audience. The teams were instructed to give themselves distinctive names, to develop their own group poems or songs, and then to perform these in turn in front of the whole gathering. Despite the emphasis on the principles of indirectness and trusted relationships in community organizing, the Camp Obama teams were instructed to call up to fifty friends and family members on their cell phones right there and then and invite them to a house party for Obama. The field organizers told the volunteers that the parties should follow a common format: the inspirational Obama video should be shown, and this should be followed by group conversation and voter sign-ups. Each Camp Obama group then reported its phone contact statistics back to a meeting of the whole audience in the community center hall. Following a break for dinner, the meeting reassembled for a speech by a leader from the national campaign's Latinos for Obama division. The leader ended by reminding the group about the twenty-thousand newly registered Hispanic voters the Colorado campaign must acquire. Finally, a graduation ceremony was held and volunteers were awarded diplomas and T-shirts.

Crucially, and beyond the scope of Alexander's ethnography, the practices of the physical Camp Obama gatherings were transcoded into the online part of the campaign assemblage. A few days later, the national campaign launched "Neighbor-to-Neighbor," an online phone-banking platform produced by political consultants Blue State Digital. This enshrined in digital form many of the principles of community organizing at Camp Obama (BarackObamadotcom, 2008d). When a supporter joined an Obama group on Facebook, for example, they were soon contacted by a campaign volunteer asking for a phone number. Information from a person's profile was used to spark conversation as a prelude to a request for volunteer engagement (Cornfield, 2010: 224). Camp Obama and Neighbor-to-Neighbor thus constituted the hybrid integration of real-space and online community organizing.

Digital Media and Control

The more it progressed, the more Obama's campaign was animated by an impulse of control. As Daniel Kreiss has argued, it combined new digital technologies with "the bureaucratic objects that were part of the imaginary of the nineteenth century: the social organization, management structures, large-scale coordination, and meticulous planning" (Kreiss, 2012). This was an older organizational logic combined with a newer media logic of control. What Kreiss terms "computational management" enabled a shrewd awareness of the comparative opportunity costs and calculable returns associated with different types of campaign activity. During the primaries, the campaign's leadership used its polling and sign-up data combined with its estimated television and other paid media costs to devise "cost-per-delegate" formulas that assessed the utility of campaigning in one state versus another. After all, the primary was eventually decided, not by simple victories based on the share of the vote in each contest, but by the numbers of delegate seats each candidate had managed to accrue in each state.

The general election was similarly amenable to this newer media logic of control. Share of electoral college votes were what mattered in that context, but in 2008 there was also an unprecedented amount of early voting, sparked in large part by the Obama campaign's massive and continually calibrated education program encouraging young and sporadic voters to vote early. A third (34 percent) of the electorate cast their votes before election day, an increase of 14 percent on 2004 and 20 percent on 2000 (Kenski, et al., 2010: 255). Eleven of the fifteen key battleground states had some form of no-fault absentee voting or early voting. And these early voters broke decisively for the Democrat: of the 6 percent who cast ballots three weeks before election day, 62 percent supported Obama but only 37 percent supported McCain. Swing voters who voted early were also more likely to vote Obama. And those who received e-mails from the Obama campaign were significantly more likely to vote early. Receiving an e-mail from McCain made no difference (Kenski, et al., 2010: 260–262).

It was the extensive face-to-face ground campaign combined with targeted e-mails that created such a powerful advantage in the struggle to get people to vote early (Kaye, 2009: 17). This advantage was felt most keenly during late October, when McCain started to make inroads on tax policy. By that stage, large numbers of voters had already declared their preferences and the majority of these had voted for Obama. The Democrats thus exploited a huge financial advantage at ground level to run what was a effectively a rolling program of get-out-the-vote mobilization across the last two months of the campaign.

Higher quality data than had previously been available to Democratic campaigns proved remarkably useful for allocating technological and human resources. The Democrats had learned from the Republicans' approach in 2004, when George W. Bush's campaign chief Karl Rove had orchestrated the "72-hour strategy," a massive word-of-mouth get-out-the-vote drive that saw Bush supporters contact their friends and neighbors in the final hours before election day. By 2008, the Democrats had their first truly national voter file (Finney, 2009). This was built between 2004 and 2007, in large part by party chair Howard Dean and his team of assistants, including Joe Rospars. Dean aggregated the state-level party databases, provided a unified mode of access to the data, and offered it to all Democratic candidates during the 2008 race. Drawing upon three microtargeting, demographic, and supporter modeling databases—Votebuilder, Catalist, and Strategic Telemetry—the Democrats were much better equipped than they had been at any time since this type of tool made its debut in the 1990s (Kreiss, 2012). Rospars and the new media division capitalized on their previous experience with Dean, but by 2008 they had the resources to construct a set of robust practices for effective online campaigning. They focused on building direct relationships with individual voters and avoided having Obama's schedule dictated by appearances at events organized by local Democratic Party committees for the benefit of the party faithful.

These were not the kinds of electors to which Obama needed to appeal to defeat the Republicans. This created time for the campaign to create its own local events, many of which did not require donations as a condition of entry. Not only could these events attract those who would feel uncomfortable paying a donation to attend a political meeting, but also, more importantly, the campaign could use the information gathered through the sign-in process to build data profiles of those in attendance. These profiles were then compared against demographic targets that needed to be met if Obama was to have a chance of expanding the electorate in the key states (Plouffe, 2010: 71). The model proved its worth.

In addition to using e-mail as a means of spurring donations and volunteering, the war room issued several much more detailed text and video messages during the course of the campaign. Initially these were aimed at professional journalists as a means of convincing them of the viability of Obama's candidacy. But it soon became obvious that there was an appetite for them among the volunteer base and online blogger networks. These memos contained a mixture of stimulating rhetoric, historical facts from previous elections, snippets of internal polling data, surprisingly candid projections of the race ahead, and grainy video clips from inside the office (the slickly produced ones were criticized by supporters). They served to educate volunteers about the leadership's strategy and they generated interest by pulling back the curtain on what were supposedly the inner workings of campaign headquarters. Just as importantly, they softened the impact on donors and volunteers of journalists' narratives, whose skepticism about Obama's challenge to Clinton continued until very late in what was already an unusually long primary season. These e-mails also provided a counterpoint to the "poll-of-polls" information that now features in withering detail on websites like RealClearPolitics.com and Pollster.com. These sites emerged as important reference points for broadcast, newspaper, and online media players during the 2008 cycle. Providing credible counter-analysis and detailed projections complete with concrete numbers was an effective way for the campaign to try to reduce uncertainty and therefore the thresholds to participation for potential supporters. For example, as voting day loomed, the campaign sent out an extraordinarily detailed e-mail presentation in which they cataloged how it was going to spend all of its gigantic $38 million budget in Florida (Plouffe, 2010: 330). The risk that they would be spilling secrets to their opponents was perceived to be offset by the gains in commitment and trust that would come from a policy of transparency, even though it was made equally transparent that this was *not* an opportunity for the Florida grassroots to voice their opinions on precisely how the campaign's money should be spent.

As the primary campaign progressed, it became evident that even when he was losing in the headline-grabbing vote share contest, Obama was still picking up large numbers of state delegate votes: the real hard currency of Democratic primaries. The leadership's analytical e-mails then became part of a strategy to educate elite journalists about the need to focus on the details when reporting on primary results. The campaign tried to "shift the national narrative from raw votes to the question of delegates" to address the "electability" criticisms that were putting doubts in the minds of the superdelegates and the Democratic party leadership (Plouffe, 2010: 157, 200). Here was a case of using the internet, supposedly a medium primarily for mass mobilization and the ground campaign, to target messages to journalists and political elites using a newly invented genre: the detailed field report e-mail.

Yet the complexity of the delegate rules, which was further vexed by the potentially free-floating nature of the Democratic party superdelegates, seems to have defeated even the most experienced older media reporters, necessitating more traditional methods of intervention. Frustrated at the *New York Times'* miscounting of Obama's true support among delegates, the war room made direct contact with the paper's highly respected political reporter, Adam Nagourney. They suggested to Nagourney that learning from the campaign about the delegate race math might pay off in the form of a scoop for the reporter: Nagourney could get one step ahead of the press pack. Nagourney duly agreed to a conference call involving Obama's team, the paper's political editor, and its polling unit. During the call, Plouffe explained the intricacies of the delegate system and how Obama was pulling ahead of Clinton where it mattered, in numbers of "pledged delegates." He argued that the superdelegates would feel duty-bound to follow the lead given by the pledged delegates. Following the meeting, the *Times* agreed to start presenting the delegate counts differently. But more importantly, a few days later Nagourney published a big story that did much to force home the point that Obama had been picking up delegates even in those states where he had ostensibly "lost" to Clinton (Plouffe, 2010: 185–186).

This intervention—a good illustration of the enduring relations of interdependence that exist among campaigns and professional journalists—had an important educative effect, not just on public opinion but also on political elites in Washington. The message was reinforced inside the campaign through a flurry of e-mail memos. Nagourney's *New York Times* article was a genuine turning point in the race. It increased the pressure on the Clinton campaign by reframing the story around her need to "catch up" with Obama. It paved the way for a decisive television news intervention by another journalist in early June when ABC News' Charles Gibson was the first to declare that Obama had secured the nomination for president and that it was now impossible for Clinton to win enough support (ABC News, 2008). Meeting with Nagourney was a classic moment of older media logic for the Obama campaign, but one that was first made possible by newer media logic—the e-mail field reports.

Outcomes

What were the outcomes of this combination of older and newer media logics? Pinpointing campaign effects is a minefield, and is not my main purpose here. But we can identify some areas where the strategy of symphonic consonance is highly likely to have made a difference to the outcome of the 2008 presidential contest.

Obama won 52.9 percent of the popular vote in the general election. Second only to Lyndon B. Johnson's 1964 landslide, this was the largest Democratic majority of the modern era, and well ahead of McCain's 45.7 percent. Of the states won by Bush in 2004, Obama took back a total of nine: Colorado, Florida, Indiana, Iowa, New Mexico, Nevada, North Carolina, Ohio, and Virginia. Ohio, Nevada, Florida, and Colorado had not been in Democratic hands since the Bill Clinton era. The victories in North Carolina, Virginia, and Indiana were genuinely surprising. North Carolina had been Republican since 1980, but Virginia and Indiana had been solidly Republican since 1968. The national swing was 9.6 percent, and in some states, such as Indiana, Nevada,

Michigan, and Pennsylvania, the swings were large by historical standards. Turnout was 61.6 percent, a significant increase of 1.5 percent on 2004 and a revival of participation levels last seen in the 1960s, though turnout was perhaps not as significant as expected given Obama's ground campaign. The headline turnout figure conceals a more complex situation, however. The increase in turnout for the Democrats, up ten million votes from 2004, was undoubtedly real. But the overall increase in turnout was tempered by a two million-vote *decline* in turnout for the Republicans (Cook, 2010).

Young voter turnout (18–29-year-olds) increased by about 6 percent in absolute terms, though, again, this is not as impressive as it seems if it is considered as a proportion of the overall electorate (Sabato, 2010: 46). Still, 66 percent of 18–29-year-olds voted for Obama, against only 32 percent for McCain (Barr, 2009: 114). Seventeen percent of self-identifying conservatives voted for Obama, and 85 percent of African American conservatives did so. Seventeen percent of those who voted for Bush in 2004 switched to Obama, but only eight percent of those who voted for Kerry in 2004 switched to McCain (Kenski, et al., 2010: 22). Given that the goals of the campaign were to target these constituencies and expand the electorate, these were successes.

The Obama campaign eventually raised an unprecedented $750 million, more than twice the amount raised by George W. Bush in 2004 (Toner, 2010: 149). About $200 million out of a total of $414 million for the primaries alone was raised online (Toner, 2010: 149). McCain managed to raise $221 million during the primaries but he was constrained to just $85 million in the general election due to his necessary acceptance of federal funding. This meant that McCain was outspent by a ratio of almost 2.5 to 1. Obama had a total of six thousand employees working for him by the end of his campaign, 95 percent of whom were under thirty years old (Plouffe, 2010: 370).

By the summer of 2008, Obama's ground advantage was clearly established. In key states, Obama's field offices far outnumbered those of McCain. For example, in Ohio the ratio was 33 to 9; in Virginia it was 27 to 7 (Abramowitz, 2010: 103). Overall, the Obama campaign and the Democratic party had around 770 field offices and spent $56 million on paid staff. McCain's field offices numbered 370 and his staff expenditure just $22 million (Toner, 2010: 154). The results speak for themselves: the Democrats increased their registered supporters by 2.9 million, compared with the Republicans' increase of 1.5 million (Kenski, et al., 2010: 19).

By the close of the campaign, Obama's e-mail list had swelled to thirteen million addresses (Plouffe, 2010: 364). Around 24 percent of all voters were contacted via e-mail during the campaign, though e-mail came a poor second to a much older medium for direct contact—the phone, which was used to reach 53 percent of voters. CNN's national exit poll found that 26 percent of voters had been "personally" contacted by the Obama campaign, while 18 percent had been reached by the McCain campaign (Sabato, 2010: 71). By election day, Obama had 2.4 million friends on Facebook; McCain had 623,000. Across the top 200 online video platforms, 104,000 videos mentioned Obama; 64,000 mentioned McCain. The Obama campaign itself uploaded 1,822 videos to YouTube; McCain's campaign managed just 330. Twenty of Obama's videos received more than one million views by the campaign's close. McCain's performance on YouTube was less spectacular, with only three videos topping the one million mark (Alexander, 2010: 60; Rasiej & Sifry, 2008). The Annenberg Election Study (Kenski, et al., 2010: 306) found that those who self-reported acquiring political information online were more likely to vote for Obama, though the margin was very small—a clue to how the internet must be set in the context of the wider media system, particularly the deluge of television advertising I discussed earlier in this chapter. Overall, 68 percent of voters cited television as their main source of campaign news, compared with 26 percent who cited "the internet" (Pew Research Center, 2008a). This seldom-reported statistic should not come as a surprise if we consider the amount of television advertising generated during the campaign—funded, of course, by all of those internet donations.

Conclusion

The Obama campaign of 2008 was important in constructing a new model for the successful prosecution of the American presidential campaign. This novelty did not arise from the use of newer media but from an approach that simultaneously constructed and ruthlessly exploited the hybrid media system for the purposes of campaign communication. The campaign went beyond simple reactions to a preexisting context: it actively shaped the media system in which it could then play such a decisive role. This was a genuine breakthrough, but the breakthrough was not the sole result of the adoption of digital media.

The campaign clearly saw the internet as a tool for mobilization and the coordination of face-to-face contact activity such as canvassing and voter registration and mobilization. But the internet was not understood as a means of displacing television and newspapers. And despite the importance of the new media staff and their direct line of communication with the war room, it was clear from an early stage that the internet campaign would be tightly managed to ensure that it was fully integrated with the other divisions. Online interactivity, while encouraged, would, as much as possible, be on the campaign's own terms and harnessed in a way that fitted with this hybrid media campaigning model.

Obama's campaign was a calibrated and controlled response to long-term trends in the fragmentation of mediated politics. But the response was not quite as expected. Yes, the campaign ruthlessly sliced and diced the demographics and used targeted communication on a scale that had never before been witnessed. And yet 2008 also revealed the continuing importance of physical gatherings and big television events. The theatrical, the grandiose, and the televisual endure in importance. This is the wider context in which Obama's digital media campaign must be set. Televised debates, ads, newspaper interviews, web videos, and high-profile television appearances increasingly meshed together to create new campaign dynamics. In an important sense, then, as time passes it is becoming clearer that there is never likely to be such a thing as an "internet election." While the internet was undoubtedly of major significance, its position in a broader media system matters just as much. It is to analysis of that broader media system beyond the campaign that I now turn.

7

Systemic Hybridity in the Mediation of the American Presidential Campaign

Amy Rice and Alicia Sams's behind-the-scenes documentary *By the People: the Election of Barack Obama* (2009) vividly exposes what it now takes to run an American presidential campaign. Much of this revealing film is devoted to capturing the backstage maneuvers of Obama's senior staff: David Axelrod, David Plouffe, and Jon Favreau. Consider some typical scenes. As Axelrod and Plouffe enter elevators, they descend into silence and stare intently at their BlackBerry smartphones. They leave elevators and walk into campaign rooms where staff sit huddled around computer screens and multiple television screens. With Blackberrys still in hand, Axelrod and Plouffe often half look up at these televisions, which usually feature news bulletins from around six or seven different channels, before directing their gaze to multiple computer monitors. These monitors usually feature data—incoming results and projections of the night ahead—based on polling and digitally stored voter contact reports that are updated hourly (Plouffe, 2010: 170). Axelrod and Plouffe often appear to cross-reference this information against what they are reading in their Blackberry text messages and e-mails. Meanwhile, at another computer sits Jon Favreau, usually willing into submission the final draft of a speech he is writing for the candidate.

Vast amounts of time in the contemporary campaign is spent interacting with one screen or another, or several screens at the same time. This is campaigning in the hybrid media system.

Autobiographies and Premediation

Election campaigning now begins many years before the campaign itself and this is driven by a bastion of older media logic that has assumed even greater significance in the last decade: the candidate book. Almost all candidates in recent election cycles have used autobiographies to premediate their campaign, as far as possible on their own terms. Richard Grusin has written of the spread of premediation as "the cultural desire to make sure that the future has already been pre-mediated before it turns into the present (or the past)—in large part to try to prevent the media, and hence the American public, from being caught unawares...." "Premediation," he suggests, "is not about getting the future right, but about proliferating multiple remediations of the future..." (2010: 4). This concept can be transposed to the campaign environment. Obama's two bestselling autobiographies, *Dreams from My Father* (1995) and *The Audacity of Hope* (2006), together with John McCain's bestselling *Faith of My Fathers* (1999), played important roles in the run-up to the 2008 contest. These books provided professional journalists with an extended set of narratives about the candidates, ready-made well in advance of when the reporters' gaze would inevitably focus on personal character and past judgment. Given their importance for establishing early campaign momentum, it is no surprise that the visual lexicon of candidates' websites also heavily reinforced these narratives. This was particularly evident, for example, in the skillful use of what David Gliem and James Janack have termed "historiated" still photography. Such photography served to tie Obama visually to transformational moments in America's past, such as the Lincoln presidency, the Kennedy era, and the great speeches of Martin Luther King (Gliem & Janack, 2008). These historical themes were also reinforced by graphic design-ers and visual artists such as Shepard Fairey and Ron English, whose retro-style posters were important in augmenting the campaign's official visual style (Seidman, 2010).

As Jeffrey Alexander has argued, the autobiographies of potential future presidents usually conform with the classic tropes of heroic fiction. A candidate will present him-self as having overcome past hardships during unusual formative experiences that have come to shape his present character (Alexander, 2010: 64) These themes were dominant for each candidate in 2008. On the McCain side, it was how a military record in Vietnam equipped him to become a "fighter" and how an earlier career flouting party discipline in Congress made him a "maverick." As for Obama, it was how experience of community organizing in Chicago and an unusual mixed-heritage background had both made him particularly proud to be American. To force these narratives home, giant video screens featuring grainy archive images depicting a candidate's past life often formed the back-drop to rallies and speeches, but also websites.

During the early stages of the campaign, journalists working for elite media such as the *Washington Post* and the *New York Times* latched onto these books and presented readers with summary accounts of the candidates' histories. The 2006 book tour for Obama's *The Audacity of Hope* sparked off an independent grassroots campaign that urged him to announce a presidential bid. More importantly, it stoked television jour-nalists' incessant desire to speculate on likely entrants in the race. The success of the book tour led to an appearance in October 2006 on *Meet the Press*, during which Obama was questioned by Tim Russert. Although he would not formally announce his deci-sion to run until January 2007, this was the first public signal that Obama was seriously considering his candidacy.

Autobiographical narratives provide journalists with particularly important resources during times of surprise and crisis. As the U.S. financial meltdown closed in on the campaign in October 2008, several essays in the *New York Times* and the *Wall Street Journal* refracted the candidates' likely reactions through the prism of the autobiographies they had earlier established through their books (Alexander, 2010: 85). Books are therefore an effective means of influencing the long-term framing of the campaign. But they also carry risks. Should the context shift and public opinion swing dramatically away from support for a candidate's formative values and character, a candidate's personalized narrative may become anchorless. McCain's experience of military valor struck many chords, but in the context of his advancing years, the grow-ing unpopularity of America's involvement in Iraq, and the emergence of the economy as the most salient issue for voters in the campaign, his story was less resonant than Obama's. Yet even Obama had problems with the story of his books, as his rapid rise and limited experience in national politics fueled McCain campaign's attacks on him during the summer of 2008.

The Real-Space–Internet–Television Nexus

In line with the online announcements of rivals John Edwards and Hillary Clinton that they had decided to run, Obama launched his Democratic primary campaign with a video uploaded to YouTube on January 18, 2007. As David Plouffe said of this: "the fact that it feels more casual, not like an Oval Office address, is dead-on. It looks less contrived" (Plouffe, 2010: 32). The point, of course, is that it was contrived. Not only was it con-trived, it was also deemed insufficient: the video launch was followed by an "announce-ment tour" that began with a carefully managed outside rally in Springfield, Illinois, complete with a crowd of fifty thousand supporters and a carefully designed stage in front of the Old State Capitol that had been lit up in anticipation the night before.

These first major events of the campaign presaged what was to become a recurrent theme: the physicality and theatricality of journeying around the country to partici-pate in carefully orchestrated real-space spectacles was a crucial aspect of project-ing Obama to the public and of garnering professional journalists' interest. But the significance of these real-space campaign events must also be set in a wider context. Real-space spectacles integrated with the online effort. Tickets to attend rallies and speeches were issued via online sign-up forms. Attendees were asked to sign in to rallies and hand over their e-mail addresses. This is now essential in the early primary states, such as Iowa and New Hampshire, where relatively small electorates and pro-gressively refined voter information files make it possible for campaigns to know a great deal about the entire voting body. In Iowa, for instance, the Obama team was able to compare its attendance data with the voter data it had purchased, and it could then target its campaign efforts accordingly. Iowa meetings revealed that large num-bers of young voters, non-activist Democrats, and even Republicans and indepen-dents were attracted to participate in these real-space rallies (Plouffe, 2010: 42). And the individuals who attended could be tracked throughout the entire duration of the campaign. Donations, volunteering activity, and primary voting patterns were logged, enabling the campaign to adapt reflexively and calibrate the stimuli with which they attempted to mobilize support.

Many "low-dollar" real-space fundraising events were held, not only as a means of generating money and sign-ups, but also to spark interest among local newspapers. Such events were perceived as having a discrete function that was especially important during the early stages of the primaries, when there was a struggle to get the media to take Obama's candidacy seriously and to convey the impression of growing and enthu-siastic grassroots support. The campaign learned that the opportunity costs of devoting the candidate's time to internet-coordinated physical events that might produce com-paratively small donation returns would be offset by the increased likelihood that local media reports "would also include footage of Obama delivering his message speech and excited supporters at what looked like a rally" (Plouffe, 2010: 49). And the campaign leadership created a broader sense of affiliation when it live-streamed some of these events to supporters across the country, and when it granted successful low-dollar fundraisers occasional meetings and conference calls with Obama and other members of the senior team. This was a case of using the coordinative affordances of online media to organize physical gatherings. But those gatherings, in turn, produced beneficially credible website, television, radio, and newspaper coverage, and they also boosted the volunteer infrastructure of the campaign.

Physical campaign events therefore continue to shape the mediation of American presidential campaigns in powerful ways. They are a test of an organization's capacity to turn out committed supporters willing to invest time and effort in demonstrating support for a candidate, often in freezing weather during the most important early primaries. Bodies and money are the symbolic resources upon which performative success rests in the eyes of professional journalists. In-person attendance at rallies and reports of donation figures are relatively "hard" proxies for popular enthusiasm. A show of strength at a rally signals to reporters that the candidate should be taken seriously, even if they know all too well that the party has to varying extents manufactured the show. The location of rallies is more carefully chosen than ever. One in Delaware on Super Bowl Sunday turned out to be the largest in the state's history and it did much to secure the state's primary delegates for Obama on Super Tuesday. But Delaware was selected primarily for the coverage the meeting would inevitably receive in the Philadelphia television region (Plouffe, 2010: 169).

The physicality of an enthusiastic crowd can often be powerfully conveyed on television, but it can be difficult to convey in textual online mediation. However, the self-produced video footage that now plays such an important role in campaigns makes for good online content to e-mail to volunteers, post on the official campaign blog, and upload to YouTube. These real-space events are also useful for more concrete tasks, though these tasks are also made more achievable by digital media. At many rallies, including most spectacularly Obama's seventy-five thousand-strong convention speech at Denver, Colorado, impromptu phone banks were set up to spur a captive audience of activists to make calls for support. Attendees were invited to call names from specially prepared flyers handed out on entry (Cornfield, 2010: 225). If journalists use turnouts at rallies as a proxy for the broader commitment of supporters, events like the Denver speech phone banks add an extra layer of authenticity, physically demonstrating the existence of the wider networked campaign. Text-to-screen technology was also used on several occasions as a means of fusing real-space with digitally mediated space. The Obama Minute campaign organized by New York photographer Scott Cohen asked supporters to donate money and send text messages that were then displayed on a giant billboard in Times Square. Web users could also embed Cohen's widget on their websites displaying the constantly updated billboard (An Obama Minute, 2008).

Ironically, however, as the campaign progressed it became increasingly obvious that Obama was having fewer and fewer opportunities to be depicted interacting in smaller, calmer settings with voters (Plouffe, 2010: 142). This approach is regarded as essential for displaying humility, interpersonal skills, and a willingness to connect with the public on their own terms. These are quintessentially televisual moments: candidates are usually wearing a microphone and there is space for journalists to operate a camera and use close-up shots. This is a different kind of physicality from the rally, but one that has become an increasingly essential part of televised electoral campaigning since the 1960s. Even as early as the New Hampshire primary, the fear was that Obama would be depicted as a crowd-pleasing "rock-star" with a large devoted following of young people. Conveying too much grassroots enthusiasm might turn off potential voters whose evaluative criteria does not involve inspirational stump-speech performances. This fear generated a series of responses by the Obama campaign and these reveal television's unique advantages and its place in the assemblage of media, technologies, and human labor that make up the contemporary campaign.

An excellent example of the enduring power of the genres of television-centric campaigning came during the primaries. Behind in the opinion polls and about to go down to an unthinkable second defeat to Obama, Hillary Clinton gathered with a small group of sixteen voters, fourteen of whom were women, in a coffee shop in Portsmouth, New Hampshire. About one hundred journalists were crammed into the shop, out of view of the cameras (Breslau, 2008). ABC and many other television channels were there to film the occasion. Clinton was asked how she juggled the demands of running a campaign with her personal life and identity as a woman. She began her response and, suddenly, her eyes welled up with tears. With the tears held back, a few seconds later she continued, but her voice quavered as she struggled to control her emotions. The response was simultaneously fragile and defiant. To spontaneous applause of sympathy, she outlined her commitment to the nation and hinted at how difficult it was for a woman to campaign for president.

This was classic campaign television, but it also caused a hybrid media storm. The tears were replayed continually on cable news shows and multiple versions were uploaded to YouTube, where they quickly amassed hundreds of thousands of viewings. This one-minute, fifty-two-second clip dominated the rest of the New Hampshire primary, which Clinton went on to win. And yet, if the short-term effects of what many perceived to be a genuine moment of emotional authenticity were positive for Clinton, the hybrid media system also provided a context for deeper ambivalence to take root. Taking advantage of the instant archival properties of YouTube, viewers pored over the footage, strategically deploying the video frame's pause button to look for even the slightest signs of fake emotion, before telling the world about their own particular interpretation in the comments section—and taking some of the sheen off Clinton's New Hampshire "comeback" (Kantor, 2008).

FROM THE GRAND TOUR TO THE "C-WORD"

Important as this episode was, it pales into insignificance when compared with the grandest manifestation of the enduring importance of television in campaigns: Obama's tour of foreign leaders in July 2008.

Obama's campaign had long planned a series of overseas visits and a large outdoor rally as a way of marking the transition from the primaries to the general election. So in July 2008 Obama traveled to visit troops in Iraq, Afghanistan, and Kuwait, before heading to Israel, Jordan, Berlin, Paris, and finally London. This voyage was unprecedented in recent campaign history and ambitious even by U.S. presidential standards. But the key point is that Obama was not yet president. Flocked by cameras as he moved from one carefully chosen location to the next, to be greeted by yet another head of state, the televisual, even cinematic construction of presidential power became more and more obvious. The very nature of the journey, a multi-stop tour of several foreign countries, rendered this a decidedly older media spectacle. The resources required for journalists to cover it in person were substantial, ruling out contributions from bloggers, and it tapped into decades of established genres for covering televised presidential interventions on the international stage. Television news was in its element.

A trip of this importance would be guaranteed to get saturation media coverage back in the United States. The aim was to convey that Obama had international standing, counter charges that he lacked foreign policy credentials, and signal his willingness to engage afresh with European leaders whose support for U.S. foreign policy had wavered in recent years over issues such as the war in Iraq. Germany fitted the bill as the location for the outdoor rally. There was a good historical reason to choose Berlin: it had been the location of John F. Kennedy's famous speech at the Brandenburg Gate in 1963.

There were significant risks attached to this journey. Most obvious was the potential for missteps in countries whose media were unfamiliar with Obama and where the campaign could not rely on its own supporters to appear on cue for the cameras. While it might be predicted with some certainty that at least a few thousand Berliners would turn up to hear a presidential candidate's speech, there was much uncertainty about the size of the crowd and how negative coverage would be generated by a small showing. By the time of the speech it became clear that the crowd would be large—the campaign had secretly hoped for fifty thousand. As it transpired, over two hundred thousand people assembled at the Tiergarten—more than four times the number that heard Kennedy in 1963. Obama appeared before a vast crowd, many of whom were waving American flags, and announced himself as "a proud citizen of the United States, and a fellow citizen of the world" (BarackObamadotcom, 2008c). The television images were unique in post-war presidential campaign history. This was an event with obvious visceral power.

And yet the grand tour proved a double-edged sword. Reporting just after the Berlin rally, Fox News's David Asman spoke of "Barack Obama looking like a rock star in Germany today . . . " "Is the fact that they loved him there a red flag for Americans here?," Asman asked. Other conservative media followed suit, as the *Washington Times* and the *New York Post* weighed in with the "rock star" theme. The right-wing Media Research Center released a web video, "Obama Love 3.0," featuring a montage of positive comments from liberal journalists accompanied by Frankie Valli's "Can't Take My Eyes Off You" (Alexander, 2010: 170).

The stage was set. Two days after Obama returned from Europe, the McCain campaign countered with one of their most successful television attack ads of the campaign. An illustration of the enduring power of television advertising in the hybrid media system, the ad caused significant damage to Obama's reputation. Entitled "Celebrity," it was a "press ad" (see chapter 6) published to the campaign website the night before it was first aired on television, as a way of influencing the following morning's news agenda. It intercut Obama's Berlin speech with crowds chanting his name, but this was followed by images of musician Britney Spears and millionaire heiress television celebrity Paris Hilton. The strapline: "He's the biggest celebrity in the world. But is he ready to lead?"

The McCain Celebrity ad had an immediate impact on professional journalists, who were eager to report what they thought was the first significant blow to Obama's image as a gifted orator and crowd-puller. Television comedy shows soon joined the fray. Stephen

Colbert: "The big story is still Barack Obama's world tour. I've got to give him credit. Once again today he made history by being the first man to travel around the world in a plane propelled only by the power of the media's flash photography" (The Colbert Report, 2008). With over 2.2 million views, Celebrity became the McCain campaign's most popular ad on YouTube, enabling them to secure a foothold in an online arena which until then had been dominated by their opponents.

The success of Celebrity encouraged McCain's team to follow up with a series of variations on the theme. These included several public statements designed to stoke perceptions that Obama was a cultural elitist, such as the claim that he liked organic tea. McCain also gave an extraordinary speech at a motorcycle rally in South Dakota at which he said that he preferred "the roar of fifty thousand Harleys" to a "couple hundred thousand Berliners" (Ma3lst0rm, 2008). A blizzard of celebrity-themed coverage dominated news and entertainment programming. Broadcasting outlets as diverse as Fox News, CNN's *Showbiz Tonight*, NPR's *Morning Edition*, ABC's *World News*, and MSNBC's *Today Show* discussed the ad. Even relatively liberal MSNBC declared: "Fifty years ago, the charge being hurled around that would hurt any candidate was, you know, 'communist sympathizer.' There's another 'C' word out there today, celebrity…He's a celebrity!" (Alexander, 2010: 173–175). Meanwhile, the Republicans established a new initiative on their website, punning on the title of Obama's second book: they called it "audacity watch." In a bizarre twist, satire met reality and reality met satire, as the comedy website Funny or Die released an online "ad for the Paris Hilton Presidential Campaign." Hilton herself appeared in leopard-print swimwear, criticized McCain as a "wrinkly, white-haired guy," and, in a swipe at the Republicans' denigration of her as a celebrity bimbo, eloquently described a perfectly credible position on energy policy that inventively combined the two candidates' positions (Funny or Die, 2008). In later iterations of the Celebrity commercial, the Republicans dropped Hilton and Britney Spears from the imagery.

The traction gained by the Republicans' hybrid media success with Celebrity contributed to their closing the opinion poll gap with Obama to well within the margin of error. The Obama campaign became concerned that the large crowds they were drawing as they criss-crossed around the country would add further fuel to the mainstream media's growing "rock star" narrative. Bizarrely, they started to avoid rallies and began placing their candidate in smaller, more intimate settings, like diners, stores, and factories. They also decided to scale down some of the pageantry of the settings for Obama's biggest events. The Democratic party's Denver convention acceptance speech had been carefully planned to convey to the television audience the importance of appearing before a large crowd of seventy-five thousand people. Plans involved a stage set redolent of the Lincoln Memorial, complete with fake classical columns. Faced with criticism of Obama's hubris, the night before the speech campaign managers desperately proceeded to "rip out lights and all kinds of embellishments," as senior adviser David Axelrod described the process (Axelrod, 2009: 73). Parts of the stage were dismantled and camera angles tested to ensure that Obama was not filmed in front of the offending columns. The aim was to give the impression that Obama was positioned among the crowd, not rising imperiously above it.

The fake classical columns survived the makeover, though they were in the event rather understated, pushed to the edge of the stage and out of the close-up shots of

Obama speaking. The video filmed for the web by the Obama campaign team was a simple one-camera production, shot in precisely the way they wanted. The television news coverage, over which the Obama campaign had some influence but not total control, was quite different, with multiple cameras, sweeping shots across the crowd, and close-ups on supporters' jubilant and often tearful faces. And yet, during the most important sections of the speech the television news coverage's backdrop was also columnless and low-key. The speech managed to escape being tarnished by accusations of rock star arrogance. The Obama campaign eventually switched back to bigger outdoor rallies.

The Perfect Union of Internet and Television

Despite its enduring power in shaping campaigns, it is important to note that television today is not what it was a generation ago. It has been partially hollowed out, disaggregated, and scattered across a diverse array of platforms and technologies. The televisual still exists as a powerful set of campaign communication genres, but its modalities have shifted, as content migrates across the hybrid media system. Television's role in campaigns is increasingly complex and multi-layered, and there are now pockets of systemic integration between television and the internet.

The 2008 election was the first in which YouTube (founded 2005) played a major role. YouTube and other online video platforms like Dailymotion and Vimeo have hybrid media logics. They combine the potential reach of a mass broadcast medium with the interactive, horizontal, network affordances that have grown to be an essential part of internet media. But the emergence of YouTube has also encouraged much interdependence among the internet and television, and this can sometimes be decisive in shaping the campaign.

THE CNN–YOUTUBE DEBATES

The first signs of this in flow came with the CNN–YouTube debates, held in July and November 2007. The product of a unique collaboration between Google and CNN, these two live media events fused the genres and stagecraft of traditional televised candidate debates with the amateur authenticity that has become the dominant characteristic of the most popular YouTube content. Ordinary citizens were invited to submit thirty-second videos for consideration by a panel of CNN and party staff. A representative enough sample of the best of these was selected for presentation in their original form, and these were mediated live to the candidates and the studio audience via a giant screen. Each candidate was also given a single thirty-second slot in which he or she could screen an officially produced "YouTube-style" campaign video; these were interspersed with the citizens' videos. CNN presenter Anderson Cooper played the traditional role of moderator, channeling to candidates 39 video questions that were selected out of a total of 2,989 for the Democrats and 34 out of 4,927 for the Republicans. Following the live debates, an archive was established on YouTube.

Due to the show's format, watching the debates on live television involved several layers of remediation. But watching the debates *online* meant engaging in a remarkably kaleidoscopic media experience. Online viewers watched the remediated television images online at YouTube, but those television images prominently featured a giant video screen that remediated to both the studio audience and those watching from afar a series of videos that had started life as YouTube uploads. And, of course, those videos had been jointly solicited by a television news organization and the video division of an internet company.

The tensions and power plays in this hybridity are evident from a closer reading of the debates. As we saw in relation to broadcast media's treatment of the internet during Britain's prime ministerial television debates in chapter 4, CNN too sought to put YouTube in its place by prefacing each debate with a series of dismissive remarks about the videos they could not show because they were deemed unsuitable. Anderson Cooper was an active moderator who intervened with journalistic authority. He often injected detailed information, rephrased a video's question, and asked supplementary questions. At the same time, however, it is clear that CNN did not wish to drain YouTube of its distinctiveness. While serious and well-considered, the amateur videos had an unmistakable YouTube vérité. Shaky camerawork, bad lighting, and domestic locations like bedrooms and living rooms were much in evidence, and many of the videos were quirky and humorous. For example, an animated Alaskan snowman named "Billiam" asked a question about climate change. The studio audience had no formally assigned role, and yet they made several decisive interventions through their selective applause for both the questioners and the candidates. But the most decisive moment came when it was demonstrated how such a nontraditional event could have a significant long-term impact on the presidential campaign. As the debate turned to foreign policy, a YouTube video from Stephen Sorta of Diamond Bar, California, asked Obama and Clinton if they would be willing to meet "without precondition with the leaders of the authoritarian states of Iran, Syria, Venezuela, Cuba, and North Korea." Obama replied that he would, but Clinton made it clear that she would not. This line of division produced a flood of press commentary after the debate and an ongoing discussion among all of the Democratic candidates that rumbled on for several weeks during the primaries (Phillips, 2007). It also spurred the Clinton camp to increase their attacks on Obama's lack of foreign policy experience.

AMATEUR AND NOT-SO-AMATEUR ONLINE VIDEO

The 2008 election saw an explosion in the amount of online video produced by those working away from the direct control of the campaigns. Accurate measurements are difficult to obtain in this field and the closest thing there is to an overall count comes from Divinity Metrics, an online marketing firm. Its analysis of all videos uploaded across two hundred different platforms during four hundred days of the campaign found that there were around 104,000 videos about Obama and 64,000 about McCain (Aun, 2008). Several of these online videos will go down in history as the first important interventions of their kind in American politics. They are undoubtedly significant but their provenance and overall impact are in some cases less straightforward than headlines like "YouTube sensation" would suggest.

An early sign of what was to come was the "bomb Iran" video. An attendee at a Republican rally shot a cell phone video of John McCain singing about wanting to "bomb, bomb, bomb" Iran to the tune of the Beach Boys' song "Barbara Ann." The film was uploaded to YouTube by "mckathomas," but it was then reported by television news (mckathomas, 2007). Bomb Iran was also subsequently repurposed for professionally produced television commercials by MoveOn and for an online film by Robert Greenwald, which brought it to different audiences (Brave New Films, 2008; heyitsjoe, 2007). Many of the popular satirical videos were by amateurs and mashed up some well-established online memes with campaign news footage. There was "Baracky," which featured clips of McCain and Obama playing out the plot of the hit film, *Rocky*; the "Empire Strikes Barack," featuring clips of Obama and Clinton playing out plot lines from *Star Wars*; and Hugh Atkin's "BarackRoll," which tapped into the long-running "Rick Rolling" online meme that involves posting links that lure unsuspecting individuals into watching the video for Rick Astley's now-kitsch 1987 song, "Never Gonna Give You Up." The "Barack Roll" mash-up featured video footage of Obama dancing on *The Ellen Degeneres Show*, underlaid with spliced-together phrases from speeches to give the impression of Obama "singing" along to Astley's song (disappointme, 2008; HollaAtYoDaddy, 2008; Humanitainment, 2008).

The most important of the unofficial videos were not, however, made by amateurs. Their presence reflected a broader assemblage of creativity, entertainment, and political education, comprising professional artists and designers (like Shepard Fairey) who played significant roles in producing symbolic resources such as street art, logos, posters, and illustrations that were important in framing Obama's public persona (Seidman, 2010). "Vote Different," the well-known film depicting Hillary Clinton as the Big Brother figure in Apple Computer's famous "1984" television ad, was created by Phil De Vellis, an established political public relations professional. Website Barely Political's equally well-known video "I Got A Crush . . . on Obama" was the idea of an experienced advertising executive named Ben Relles and it took three weeks in production with professional filmmakers Kevin Arbouet and Larry Strong (L. S. Miller, 2008). Actress Amber Lee Ettinger, the star of "I Got A Crush . . . ," appeared on Fox and MSNBC and was subsequently hired by the Obama campaign to do voice-overs for its "robocall" voter contact (L. Powell, 2010: 94).

"Yes We Can," the mash-up of music, rap, and Obama's New Hampshire primary concession speech—the most popular web video of the entire campaign—was a celebrity endorsement professionally produced by Jesse Dylan (the son of Bob) and Will.I.Am of the globally popular group The Black Eyed Peas. The film featured renowned Hollywood actress Scarlett Johansson and successful musicians John Legend and Herbie Hancock, among several others. "Yes We Can"'s release was coordinated with the Obama campaign team and orchestrated for mainstream media appeal. It has often been forgotten that it first appeared, not on YouTube, but on television's *ABC News Now* (Wallsten, 2010: 169), though, given that *ABC News Now* is simultaneously streamed to the internet and mobile devices, "television" is, of course, a relative term. The campaign and Democratic bloggers were also crucial in creating the conditions for the virality of "Yes We Can." Statements from the Obama campaign drawing attention to the video acted as spurs to a wider network of bloggers. As online viewing increased, television and newspaper journalists started to report the video's popularity. This in turn brought further attention to it and it further increased the online viewings (Wallsten, 2010). By the end of the campaign "Yes We Can" had received almost twenty million viewings and more than 87,000 comments. Given its origins among musicians and Hollywood actors it should come as no surprise that this hybrid political–entertainment video so readily migrated to television.

THE REVEREND WRIGHT AFFAIR

The CNN–YouTube debates and the complex provenance of successful online campaign videos were important, but nothing quite illustrates how television content wends its way through online media as well as the Reverend Wright affair. This episode reveals how personalized, media-driven scandals can take on new dynamics in the context of the hybrid media system. This was a decisive episode in the campaign, one that almost fatally damaged Obama's candidacy. High televisual drama across the national networks and the power of moving images became integrated with the migration and viral recirculation of those images across the internet, as YouTube became a central archival hub for content remediated from broadcast and cable news shows. Claims that broadcast television is "becoming a sideshow" in election campaigns (Cornfield, 2010: 209) are wide of the mark. The interdependent recombination of television and online video is what matters.

The affair's origins were online. In late 2006, Fran Eaton, a conservative blogger who wrote for the online citizen journalism outlet the *Illinois Review* visited Reverend Jeremiah A. Wright Jr.'s Trinity Church in Chicago. Eaton published a blog post on December 31, 2006, criticizing what she saw as the church's militantly pro-African American ethos. In mid-February 2007, Eaton appeared on WVON radio in Chicago, where she termed the church "black supremacist" and this sparked some national media coverage later that month. ABC News's early coverage of Obama prominently featured Trinity Church. Then, Sean Hannity of Fox News decided to conduct a televised interview with a conservative New York blogger, Erik Rush, to discuss the matter. The following day, there was a fraught encounter between Hannity and Reverend Wright on Fox News. Wright was also mentioned in a headline-grabbing profile of Obama in *Rolling Stone* magazine and in an April 30 article in the *New York Times* (May, 2009: 83–85). At this stage, however, nobody had video footage of Wright's sermons. Without pictures, the national networks—ABC, CBS, and NBC—would not touch it.

The story of Obama's pastor's radical views about race relations in America therefore effectively lay dormant for eight months. Then, in January 2008, a column in the *Washington Post* discussed a lifetime achievement award Wright's church had presented to controversial minister Louis Farrakhan. This development was also taken up by CNN. Within a few days CBS ran a minor story—the first on this by a national television network—about the links between Wright and Obama (May, 2009: 85). But again, no videos of Wright's sermons were shown.

A print article in the *Wall Street Journal* of March 10, 2008, was the first to mention the existence of sermon videos (May, 2009: 85). At around the same time, a set of amateur-made videos of Wright's sermons were being openly sold to members of the Trinity congregation and were bought independently by Fox News and the team of ABC's chief investigative reporter Brian Ross. Fox aired an extended excerpt from one of the videos on March 12, 2008, and it published an accompanying text story on its website (Goldblatt, 2008). Brian Ross's team at ABC were more thorough. They pored over the tapes and were given approval to run a three-minute package on the morning news the following day—March 13. Ross's news sequence was the first time excerpts from several of the sermon videos were shown on a national network. Fox News then began running a wider variety of clips, and the Fox News and ABC sequences were soon remediated on YouTube, as individual users uploaded files and began to remix the clips with other content as a way of putting their own spin on Wright's remarks. This mixture of television, television website video, YouTube television video, and remixed YouTube mash-ups was further circulated across e-mail, Facebook, and Twitter via simple links, but it was also syndicated as embedded video clips on political blogs.

Unsurprisingly, the ABC story—"Obama's Preacher: the Wright Message?"—used heavily edited clips from the sermons. These clips provided the fuel for the majority of the YouTube content. Wright was exposed using fiery rhetoric to attack racism: "America's chickens are coming home to roost" was his reaction to 9/11; "Not God Bless America. God Damn America!" and "US of KKKA" were his statements on the treatment of African Americans (facts44, 2008).

The Pew Research Center's weekly News Interest Index poll a couple of weeks after the ABC story found that 51 percent of the American public had heard "a lot" and a further 28 percent "a little" about Wright's sermons (Pew Research Center, 2008c). Annenberg survey data show that Obama's favorability ratings also declined quite steeply as a result (Kenski, et al., 2010: 84–86).

This was a big moment for television but it was also an important moment for internet media. Fox and ABC broke the story on television, yet it had originated with Fran Eaton and her fellow conservative bloggers. And once televised it quickly acquired an internet dynamic, which in turn served to amplify television journalism's contribution. By August 2008 there were more than two thousand Jeremiah Wright videos of one kind or another on YouTube, yet around 60 percent of these were simply clips from ABC and the three main cable television news channels (May, 2009: 81). A detailed content analysis of four hundred of the YouTube videos reveals an interdependent relationship between television and YouTube (May, 2009). Spikes in YouTube traffic were closely correlated with the release of new clips from the sermons and interventions by Obama and Reverend Wright. But these spikes tended to occur the day *after* the previous day's television news stories. YouTube viewings continued to rumble through the remainder of the campaign, increasing the story's longevity and audience reach. Television was also responsible for occasionally jolting the Wright affair back to life. The importance of YouTube was quickly recognized by older media. For example, when Bill Moyers interviewed Wright in late April, PBS decided to scoop themselves by posting their film on YouTube the day before it aired on television (May, 2009: 89).

Similarly, the Wright affair met with older media logic from the Obama campaign, but the campaign's response also soon acquired a newer media logic that unsettled some long-held assumptions about what makes for effective communication in election campaigns. Obama decided to address the issue head-on, out of a fear that the sermon tapes would inflict irreparable damage to his prospects by putting racism at the center of the campaign. Rather than merely stage a traditional press conference as an attempt to fend off the accusation that he shared Wright's views, Obama sought to reshape the news agenda by delivering a lengthy and complex speech at the National Constitution Center in Philadelphia. The venue was chosen for its relatively small size because the campaign wanted to avoid the feverish atmosphere of an open rally. There were fewer than one hundred ordinary audience members in the room; the rest were journalists. This was a speech aimed at the television-viewing public; an event made for television in the classic mold. Significantly, however, the event was not staged for *live* television. While it would be broadcast live on CNN, it would take place on a Tuesday morning, when few would be watching. The aim was to influence the lunchtime and evening television and radio news bulletins, the newspaper websites and political blogs, and the following day's commentary cycle in the elite newspapers. The "more perfect union" speech did indeed receive a highly favorable editorial response in newspaper outlets.

But just as significant is what happened when the Obama campaign uploaded the CNN video to YouTube. Within the space of a day, Obama's speech had attracted 1.3 million viewings and had appeared on Google's "most-blogged" list. Within ten days the YouTube viewings had jumped to 3.4 million, then to more than 4.5 million as the primaries reached their crescendo in June. The speech symbolizes the new power of instant archiving and interpersonal sharing of online video. This was a hybrid media response: URLs and embedded links to the YouTube version of the television video, on which the CNN logo and even its news ticker were proudly emblazoned were circulated among family, friends, and work colleagues. It was a television moment, and yet it was also a rejection of the televisual approach to political sound-bites. The speech was thirty-seven minutes long and departed in significant ways from a traditional campaign speech. Its structure was relatively complex and it was delivered in a calm and reflective style. There was applause, but the audience—not a crowd—was small, and could barely be heard. And the web video was watched in its entirety by vast numbers—more than six million by the close of the campaign. On the *New York Times* website, full transcripts of the speech were e-mailed at higher rates than the story about the speech (Stelter, 2008).

In telling parallels with the awareness levels for Reverend Wright's sermon videos a couple of weeks earlier, Pew's News Interest Index poll for March 27 found that 54 percent of Americans had heard "a lot" and 31 percent "a little" about Obama's reaction speech (Pew Research Center, 2008c). Annenberg election survey data also show that Obama's favorability ratings improved markedly following this response (Kenski, et al., 2010: 84–86).

Wright made a further explosive intervention later in the campaign, when he appeared before assembled journalists at the National Press Club in Washington, DC to speak of how he believed that the U.S. government may have spread HIV among African Americans. This time Obama responded with outright condemnation. An assortment of Republican Political Action Committees and "527" groups, such as Our Country Deserves Better, ran television commercials during the final weeks of the general election campaign, rekindling the Wright issue for television news, online news sites, and bloggers (Kenski, et al., 2010: 87–88). But these were minor revivals. Obama's earlier hybrid media response defused the scandal.

The Wright affair and the Philadelphia speech gave the Obama campaign important experience of the power of the web to bypass some of the traditional dictates of television's reporting of politics. It demonstrated the effectiveness of longer, more reflective responses to media-driven scandals and it capitalized on YouTube's growing role as an outlet for long-form as well as short-form genres in politics—a surprisingly important aspect of its role in the hybrid media system.

Fear and Loathing and "Citizen Journalism": "Bittergate"

The Reverend Wright affair was soon joined by a further important episode illustrating the complex interdependence of older and newer media. This became known as "Bittergate" and it came as the 2008 primaries entered their final decisive phase.

During a wide-ranging discussion at a San Francisco fundraising meeting on April 6, 2008, Obama turned to discuss the plight of small-town America. He said "You go into some of these small towns in Pennsylvania, and like a lot of small towns in the Midwest, the jobs have been gone now for 25 years and nothing's replaced them...And it's not surprising that they get bitter, they cling to guns or religion or antipathy to people who aren't like them or anti-immigrant sentiment or anti-trade sentiment as a way to explain their frustrations" (Fowler, 2008).

This fundraising meeting was closed to the press and the discussion was deemed "off the record." On this rare occasion, the press staff had not enforced its own policy of recording their candidate's every utterance (Plouffe, 2010: 216) Unknown to them, an audio recording of the meeting was being captured on a handheld voice recorder by an amateur blogger and citizen activist named Mayhill Fowler. Part of a distributed team of "amateur" citizen journalists who were following the campaign under the *Huffington Post*'s "Off the Bus" program, Fowler was in fact an experienced Democratic party supporter and had even donated to the campaign. Self-described as a "teacher, editor, and writer," Fowler had followed Obama for a year, writing for her blog and filing opinion pieces for the *Huffington Post*, on an unpaid basis.

Fowler was not a journalist, nor was she a straightforward blogger or campaign volunteer. She had gained entry to the San Francisco event because she was known to the campaign, but she did not ask permission to record Obama's remarks and she was not treated as a journalist by the press staff. Fowler had her own personal blog, but her involvement with the *Huffington Post* meant that there soon followed some internal editorial discussions with *Post* editor Arianna Huffington about the news value of the material Fowler had gathered. Following those editorial discussions, Huffington authorized publication in the certain knowledge that Obama's remarks would have a huge impact on the news. "We recognized it was a politically volatile story and thought it would create news," said Marc Cooper, one of *Huffington Post*'s deputy editors (Bradley, 2008). Cooper was right. CNN International picked up the story and started to broadcast packages featuring the most controversial section of Fowler's audio file. Within a few hours the story had spread across the media system to cable and national network news shows, blogs, newspaper websites, Facebook, and Twitter. It played a major role in the Pennsylvania primary's televised debate, as moderators Charles Gibson and George Stephanopoulos repeatedly questioned Obama about his comments.

Bittergate reveals further key aspects of the hybrid media system in political campaigns. Anita Dunn, chief communications officer to the Obama campaign has described 2008 as a tipping point in news media's treatment of politics. Cable television and the internet, she said, created "a bizarre national narrative" that was divorced from the "real campaign" (Dunn, 2009: 140). The picture she paints is of semi-professional bloggers covering the campaign from outside the official press corps, scanning YouTube and social media sites for leads, uploading multiple stories throughout each day, and requiring immediate responses to each story from the campaign. Professional journalists were compelled to compete in this febrile environment.

Bittergate was enabled by the affordances of small, difficult-to-detect recording devices and the ease with which audio files can be transmitted and manipulated, but these are not its most significant aspects. Fowler occupied an uncertain boundary space at the intersection of professional journalism, blogging, and political activism. The *Huffington Post* was a group blog, albeit one with aspirations to become a more fully fledged organization (a vision that was realized when it was bought by AOL in 2011 for $315 million). It was led by an editorial staff with experience of journalism and a keen awareness of what would raise the profile of the blog. But the Obama press team had no intention of treating Fowler as a journalist and it is not clear that she saw herself as one. A professional journalist, even if he or she had managed to gain entry to an event that was not for the press, would more than likely not have reported the remarks, because the meeting was categorized as off the record. On the surface, this was about conflict between the norms of older and newer media journalism, but its ultimate impact actually turned on the hybrid integration of these norms.

Rumors and Lies and Myths about the Internet

Similar dynamics are in play if we consider further the evolving division of labor among media in campaign reporting. A recurrent theme in recent election coverage is that the internet is an unaccountable rumor mill populated by extremists able to inject invective and misinformation into public discourse free from the usual journalistic norms of professionalism and objectivity. In 2008, there were many examples of this in viral e-mails (for a long list see Castells, 2009: 483–486). The best example is the rumor that Barack Obama "is a Muslim." But while a small number of right-wing blogs featured speculation about Obama's religious faith as early as the summer and fall of 2006 (Google Blog Search, 2011), the emergence and popularization of the "Muslim" myth was far from a simple case of unaccountable and anonymous online zealotry.

The first recorded U.S.-sourced entry in Google News's archive for "Obama is a Muslim" is from a February 4, 2007, story labeled "Obamaphobia" that appeared in the student-run *Harvard Crimson* (Google News Search, 2011). The *Crimson's* piece was commentary on an earlier story, because in fact it was *Insight*, a well-known conservative print and online magazine owned by News World Communications (who, until 2010, also owned the *Washington Times*) that first sparked broad interest in the falsehood. In January 2007 *Insight* published a story claiming that an unnamed source in the Clinton campaign had revealed that Obama "had been educated in a Madrassa as a young boy and has not been forthcoming about his Muslim heritage" (Insight, 2007). The Clinton campaign officially denied that it was the source for this article, but this was not enough to deter Fox News's *The Big Story*, which ran the story two days later (Fox News, 2007). There then followed a period of intermedia conflict, as CNN ran an investigative piece debunking *Insight's* (and now Fox News's) findings. Such public discord over the basic facts of a story only served to raise its profile, and it rumbled on across blogs, YouTube, and online social network sites as the primary campaign progressed. We will never know the extent to which links to posts and viral e-mails were responsible for keeping the issue alive; the e-mails seem to have been particularly important (see Emery, 2011). But we can say with some certainty that two further older media interventions made a significant contribution to the circulation of this information.

The first intervention was the publication in July 2008 of the *New Yorker* magazine's controversial front-page cartoon depicting Barack Obama wearing Islamic dress alongside his wife Michelle, who was depicted as a Black Panther with combat fatigues and a rifle. Originally intended as the liberal magazine's satirical attack on conservative rumor-mongers, it soon became evident that the cartoon was a misfire. Given the unsettling context of misinformation that had hung over the campaign, the cartoon was neither humorous enough nor ludicrous enough to be effective as satire. The Obama campaign officially condemned the cover as "tasteless and offensive" (Zeleny, 2008). Predictably, however, the vivid images dominated campaign coverage across television and newspapers for several days.

The second older media intervention was the publication on August 1, 2008, of *The Obama Nation*, a book by Jerome R. Corsi. Corsi is one of the authors of *Unfit for Command*, the book that inspired the conservative Swiftboat Veterans for Truth campaign against Democratic presidential candidate John Kerry in 2004. Among *The Obama Nation*'s many unsubstantiated allegations was the claim that Obama was hiding his Muslim religion. Corsi's book was an instant bestseller and went on to ship more than a million copies, guaranteeing it earned media coverage in the form of tie-in news articles, both negative and positive, across broadcast and newspaper media.

The "Obama is a Muslim" myth demonstrates that even the most extreme online information can now become hybridized in some way with professional news reporting. What had started out as a subterranean rumor circulating on a small subset of right-wing conservative blogs entered the mainstream as a result of *Insight*'s story and the Fox News–CNN dispute in January 2007. It then began circulating through e-mails, social network sites, and blogs, before occasionally erupting back into the mainstream under the pressure of new events: the publication of the *New Yorker*'s cover cartoon and the television and newspaper reception of Jerome Corsi's book. And the individual effects of this rumor were probably substantial. Those who received greater numbers of e-mails (of all kinds) during the closing period of the campaign were more likely to believe that Obama was a Muslim (Kenski, et al., 2010: 100). By the end of the campaign, 19 percent of respondents believed this to be the case. While only a quarter of these individuals voted for Obama, 64 percent voted for McCain (Kenski, et al., 2010: 98).

Be the First to Know…After the Associated Press

In common with the presidential campaigns of 2000 and 2004, the 2008 contest saw campaign staff use candidate websites and e-mail lists to selectively bypass traditional news gatekeepers and try to get one step ahead of the daily news cycle. As I have shown, this involved issuing new videos and press releases via e-mail to supporters in advance of sending them to journalists, in order to create a sense of excitement and solidarity. Fundraising announcements were usually first released on campaign websites. For example, the Obama campaign announced to its supporters that it would not be accepting public funding for the general election campaign via an e-mail linking to a video clip of Obama explaining why he had taken the controversial decision. There were also concerted efforts to capitalize on the real-time affordances of the mobile web, which had by 2008 finally become important due to the growing penetration of smartphones. While the use of Twitter was still in its early stages in 2008 and the practice of displaying hashtags at the start of television shows was in its infancy (though CNN experimented with this), abbreviated SMS text message codes were in abundance and a regular feature on web and television commercials.

In August 2008, the Obama campaign planned a historic first in using mobile media to bypass professional journalists. Things did not quite go as planned. The announcement of the vice presidential running mate Joseph Biden was to be delivered by phone text message. The procedure leading up to Biden's selection was just as secretive and elite-driven as it has always been, and the plan to use text messaging was spurred in large part by a desire to attract reporters' attention and to increase the campaign's cell phone numbers database, which was then in the "low six figures," in stark contrast with its much larger e-mail list. Within two weeks of the VP announcement, that phone list had grown to more than two million numbers (Plouffe, 2010: 295). But the way the announcement almost backfired provides further insight into the perpetual power struggles between older and new media logics, even in this supposed moment of triumph for digital campaigning.

Supporters were encouraged to sign up to "be the first to know" of Obama's choice. Traditionally, television and newspaper reporters are the first to know of the vice presidential selection: this has evolved over the decades into one of the big media events of the campaign. The decision to announce via text message was not popular among journalists, and some of them decided to blunt its impact. The competition to break the news ahead of the formal announcement was intense and eventually global news agency the Associated Press (AP) managed to find out from an unnamed source inside the Democratic party that Joe Biden had been chosen as the vice presidential candidate. Eager to intervene before the Obama campaign sent its text messages, AP published the story on its website and its syndicated news feed shortly after midnight on August 23. Minutes later, broadcast news started reporting the story that had just been handed to them by one of their most important wire agencies. In a race to deliver the messages before too many supporters would see the news and realize that the plan had been thwarted, the Obama campaign began sending the messages to their cell phone subscribers. But this was the middle of the night across most of America and not part of the carefully timed delivery that the campaign had in mind. Older media's revenge, in this case exacted of all things by a wire service established in the nineteenth century.

Hard News and Soft News, Offline and Online: Framing Sarah Palin

The vice presidential nomination message was an interesting example of older media's power, but it was a skirmish when compared with my final exhibit of this chapter: the troubled reception of the Republicans' 2008 vice presidential nominee Sarah Palin.

In this case, television entertainment's influence was partly made possible by the intensification of trends in the production and consumption of political information that have now been observed for around a decade: the growing importance of "soft" news and "entertainment" genres—particularly but not exclusively late-night comedy shows—for the acquisition of political knowledge and for political engagement (Williams & Delli Carpini, 2011: 1–16). During 2007 and 2008, McCain and Obama made a combined total of nineteen appearances on the major late-night comedy shows that are now so important for reaching younger voters and those who pay less attention to straightforward news media (Gulati, 2010: 192). The use of entertainment-as-news is an important aspect of the hybrid media system in election campaigning. At the same time, however, contrary to the view that Sarah Palin's "story was not defined by professional journalists" (Williams & Delli Carpini, 2011: 3) we need to recognize the role played by professional political reporters in driving the story and creating a context in which the satire could flourish.

Immediately after the formal announcement of Palin as the Republican vice presidential nominee on August 29, as if surprised by their own decision the McCain campaign effectively cocooned her for an extended period as they scrambled to prepare for a convention speech and a series of high-profile television interviews. In the run-up to the nomination speech, the McCain campaign decided not to release the news that Palin's unmarried teenage daughter was then five months pregnant, electing instead to "flush the toilet," as Tucker Eskew, one of Palin's senior advisers described it, on the Labor Day holiday (August 31) (Nagourney, 2008a).

In the days between the Palin announcement and the Republican convention, McCain's staff also found themselves having to defend the campaign against a series of revelations, including that Palin's husband had been convicted of driving while drunk in 1986; that, as governor of Alaska, Palin had fired a senior official because he had refused to fire a state trooper who was Palin's ex-brother-in-law and with whom the Palin family had fallen out; and that Palin's image as a reformist did not tally with her initial lobbying for federal pork-barrel funding for the construction of a bridge to Gravina Island, Alaska (the so-called "bridge to nowhere").

Suddenly the narrative of Palin as an outsider and a family centered conservative populist began to falter. As the doubts and critical commentary began to pile up, the McCain team went on the offensive, seeking to attack television and newspaper journalists for what seemed like a growing refusal to take the Palin candidacy seriously. This set in train a crucial set of interactions between professional journalists and the McCain campaign. These interactions reveal the enduring power of professional media—and of investigative journalists in particular—in using their considerable resources to hold campaigns to account and legitimize critical framing among entertainment media.

The Republicans' first attempt to reframe the vice president was when McCain spokesman Tucker Bounds appeared on CNN's Election Central to argue that Palin's period as governor of Alaska meant that she had more experience of political decision making than Obama. When asked for an example of when Palin had taken an important decision, Bounds floundered and an argument broke out between him and the show's host Campbell Brown. In protest at what was perceived by the Republicans to be Tucker Bounds's harsh treatment by Campbell Brown, McCain pulled out of a prescheduled interview with CNN's veteran presenter Larry King. The campaign issued a press release: "After a relentless refusal by certain on-air reporters to come to terms with John McCain's selection of Alaska's sitting governor as our party's nominee for vice president, we decided John McCain's time would be better served elsewhere" (Rutenberg, 2008). The McCain campaign's response to such a minor event was extraordinary. However, behind the scenes, journalists from what McCain campaign director Steve Schmidt pointedly described as "national media" had started to ask questions of a highly personal nature about Palin's recent pregnancy and the parentage of her then five-month-old child, who was born with Down Syndrome (CBS, 2008).

The Republicans' attack on the credibility and legitimacy of senior CNN journalists did not play well. Frustrated at being denied direct access to a candidate about whom ordinary voters knew very little, newspaper and television journalists started to grumble in public. McCain's boycott of CNN was framed as a broadside attack on journalism in general in a piece by Howard Kurtz of the *Washington Post* (Kurtz, 2008). The *Post*, the *Wall Street Journal*, and the *New York Times* all called for the McCain campaign's news blackout to end. But McCain campaign manager Rick Davis then inflamed things still further when he stated on Fox News Sunday that reporters would not be granted access to Palin unless they began to treat her "with some level of respect and deference" (Dionne, 2008).

The response by the nation's most prestigious and well-resourced media organizations was to send teams of investigative reporters to Alaska to unearth stories about Palin's personal history and her record as Alaska governor. Facts emerged that allowed reporters to substantiate the story that Palin was involved in the improper firing of her ex-brother-in-law—it was revealed that an ethics committee of the Alaska state legislature was investigating the incident. (The committee later found that she had acted improperly.) A series of revelations also emerged regarding alleged improper expenses claims, the alleged withholding of e-mails from the public record, the alleged firing of a librarian who resisted the governor's attempts to have books removed from the Wasilla public library, and Palin's exaggerated claims that she had cut unnecessary costs in the governor's office. The three major television networks weighed in with synchronicity on September 9 and 10 with reports summarizing these and more of the fruits of the newspaper journalists' endeavors (Alexander, 2010: 226–230). On September 14, the *New York Times* completed the picture, with a piece by senior reporters Jo Becker, Peter S. Goodman, and Michael Powell that proudly proclaimed that it was based on "a review of public records and interviews with 60 Republican and Democratic legislators and local officials" (Becker, et al., 2008). In a process that in fact differed from what has been variously described as the recycling of "viral slurs" (Kenski, et al., 2010: 137) "the hardwiring of the crazy left-wing blogs into newsrooms" (Wallace, 2009: 33), and an illustration of "the precipitous decline in the power of journalists" (Williams & Delli Carpini, 2011: 6), these Palin revelations emerged from a well-researched article produced by experienced and respected political reporters working for America's most prestigious traditional news organization.

The McCain team relented and proceeded as planned with extended interviews with Charles Gibson of ABC News and Katie Couric of CBS News. Palin's performance during these two events, particularly the Couric interview, set in train an extraordinary period of negative commentary and satire, the likes of which, in terms of its impact and modalities, had never before been witnessed in U.S. presidential campaigns. But it was the negative newspaper coverage that had been provoked by the McCain campaign's attacks on journalists during the interregnum between the vice presidential announcement and the Charles Gibson interview that legitimized what turned out to be such damaging satirical treatment.

An important line of inquiry for journalists was Palin's lack of foreign policy experience and this was tested in both interviews. Palin was working against the context of low expectations and did not perform disastrously, but there were some damaging exchanges over economic and foreign policy. One line would come back to haunt the Republicans. In response to a question about Russia during the Gibson interview, Palin responded: "They're our next-door neighbors and you can actually see Russia from land here in Alaska" (SaveOurSovereignty2, 2008). Palin's suggestion was that Alaska's proximity to Russia somehow equipped her with valuable foreign policy insight.

These were odd remarks: folksy and down-to-earth but basically irrelevant to Palin's foreign policy credentials, not to mention the broader state of United States–Russia relations. They were soon picked up by political columnists, but by this time mainstream television satirists were also circling. In the first show of *Saturday Night Live*'s new season comedian Tina Fey embarked on a series of heavily trailed comedy sketches in which she played the Alaska governor. In the opener, she uttered with uncanny precision the line "I can see Russia from my house!" The offending clip was replayed across television news shows, but because the new season of *Saturday Night Live* is traditionally an important event in the American television calendar, coverage also spilled over to soft news and talk shows like *Today* and a raft of cable entertainment and celebrity gossip programming.

Matters were made worse two weeks later, when Palin was interviewed by Katie Couric of CBS. After Couric pressed her to explain her remarks in the Gibson interview, Palin provided a longer response, but one that was confusing and even less credible. This too was the subject of critical commentary and the embedded video clip from the CBS News website became instant blog fodder (Pitney, 2008). It provided further fuel for Tina Fey, whose corresponding *Saturday Night Live* sketch was extraordinary, not because of its imagination, but because so much of its content was directly lifted from the replies Palin provided in the real interview with Couric (johny boy, 2008).

The Couric interview spoof clips caused traffic to spike on the NBC website. The Fey sketch from September 13 led to 5.7 million views within four days on NBC's site alone (Wallenstein, 2008), providing a boost to *Saturday Night Live*, one of NBC's most important shows and very much a bastion of television entertainment. On October 18, with barely more than a couple of weeks to go before election day, Fey and her colleagues received the largest television audience for *Saturday Night Live* in fourteen years—seventeen million (Williams & Delli Carpini, 2011: 4).

And yet the online audiences for the Fey sketches greatly exceeded those from television. By October 23 NBC had streamed the sketches forty-three million times from its website and its joint venture Hulu.com (Snider, 2008). Spread virally through links to online video as well as consumed through paid-for iTunes downloads, these clips played an important role in the framing of Palin, spanning the gaps between the weekly television installments of *Saturday Night Live*.

A mid-October Pew Research Center survey reported that 72 percent of the American public had heard about Tina Fey's portrayal of Palin (Pew Research Center,

2008b). Annenberg election study data reveal that regular viewing of *Saturday Night Live* (the data do not distinguish between television and web viewing) was associated with skepticism about Palin's suitability for the vice presidency, and this was particularly strong among all-important independent voters (Kenski, et al., 2010: 157). But Pew's mid-October survey also reveals that 78 percent of Americans reported hearing about the Palin-Couric CBS news interview. Hard news, soft news, and entertainment; bloggers, elite broadcast and newspaper journalists; NBC.com, Hulu.com, YouTube, and iTunes: it was the hybrid media system that did so much damage to Palin.

Conclusion

This analysis of key episodes during the 2008 U.S. presidential campaign reveals an evolving system of interconnected and interdependent older and newer media logics. Politicians, professional political staff, journalists, citizen activists, and sometimes only momentarily engaged members of the public competed and cooperated in mediated environments as they attempted to use both older and newer media logics to exert their power. Actors in this system are articulated by complex and evolving power relations based upon adaptation and interdependence. They create, tap, or steer information flows in ways that suit their goals and in ways that modify, enable, or disable others' agency, across and between a range of older and newer media settings.

The consumption of campaign news from online sources has increased massively in less than a decade, and yet television remains the most important overall source of information for citizens, as print media organizations repurpose their content and reposition it at the center of the online news system. Candidates attempt to premediate the framing of their individual character and judgment through the strategic use of autobiographies; reporters fall back on these books as a resource. The physical spectacles of candidate appearances on the campaign trail continue to generate important television, radio, and newspaper coverage, as Obama's grand tour of foreign nations and his Denver acceptance speech demonstrate. But these televisual spectacles also integrate newer media logics of data-gathering, fundraising, tracking, monitoring, and volunteering, as well as the conveying of enthusiasm, movement, authenticity, and common purpose.

These older and newer media logics now constitute a system for producing and reproducing a campaign's important events, combining the powerful genres and modalities of political television with the networked coordinative power of internet media. Sometimes these older and new media logics are fused in real time, as occurred with the phone banks at speeches and the online fundraising drives that occur during televised debates. Sometimes the temptations to campaigns of orchestrating and projecting power in these large-scale televisual campaign moments are too great, as Obama's Denver speech again makes clear. Yet events based on smaller, more intimate moments of televisual campaigning are also risky because they are also subjected to a newer media logic, as activist citizens are now able to scour remediated television clips of slip-ups using YouTube's archive.

This chapter has revealed growing systemic integration of the internet and television in American election campaigning. There is conflict between older and newer media power but there is also a great deal of interdependence. The CNN/YouTube debates illustrate how older media seek to extend their power by making online media practice conform as far as possible to the safe and controlled environment of a televised candidate debate, though the domestication can never be complete, as many of the citizens' questions were based on classic YouTube amateur genres. The exuberant outpouring of online amateur video is an important trend in campaigns, but one that must be understood in the context of the power resources of those who are able to produce the successful online videos. Virality can never be fully predicted, but establishing linkages among previously well-known celebrities and organizations is more likely to produce it. The most successful online videos are created by those who already have cultural capital and network power from the entertainment field. "Yes We Can" was coordinated with the Obama campaign and it was produced by global celebrities. The Reverend Wright affair owes its origins to conservative bloggers and it became a YouTube phenomenon in part due to the wide variety of amateur-produced mash-up videos, but the Wright sermon videos first broke on Fox and ABC television, the majority of the YouTube content was simply remediated from television clips, and viewings on YouTube tended to be responses to new information on television news. Obama's response, the "more perfect union" speech, was designed as a supremely televisual intervention, but once uploaded to YouTube the video soon acquired a newer media logic, one that capitalized on the power of the online archive to circumvent the sound-bite constraints of television.

The case of Bittergate reveals the uncertainties but also the impacts on news that can occur when the boundaries between older and newer reporting norms begin to blur. The rumors that Obama "is a Muslim" spread across e-mail networks during the campaign but they are best understood not as the product of a wild and untamed internet, but of complex interactions between a conservative magazine, Fox News, CNN, a million-selling book by a conservative author, and an ill-judged satirical cover of the *New Yorker*. Newer media logic drove the Obama campaign's attempt to enthuse its supporters, boost its cell phone number database, and bypass political reporters by releasing news of the vice presidential nominee by text message, but the impact was diluted by AP's leaking of the story before the vast majority of the messages had been sent.

Entertainment media played important roles in the critical reception of Sarah Palin, but these attacks were sparked and legitimized by professional reporters who reacted negatively to the McCain campaign's complaints that they were not giving Palin a chance to establish her credentials. Senior reporters at the *New York Times* and the *Washington Post* used their considerable investigative resources to establish the credibility of several negative stories about Palin's governorship of Alaska. The news reports and the satirical treatments fed off each other, as the NBC websites, the iTunes store, YouTube, and, of course, the public through their downloads and sharing of links gave the comedy a viral life cycle in between the punctuating weekly doses of *Saturday Night Live*. In short, we end this chapter where we began: the campaign of many screens.

8

Hybrid Norms in News and Journalism

So far in this book, I have sought to demonstrate how power relations based on conflict, competition, and interdependence among older and newer media logics operate across a range of fields: technologies, genres, norms, behaviors, and organizational forms. While I have drawn upon some important insider evidence to demonstrate these processes in action, for instance from key political and communication staff working for the Obama 2008 campaign in chapters 6 and 7, and from journalists and WikiLeaks activists in chapter 5, most of the evidence has been drawn from publicly available data. In order to demonstrate, for example, the importance of the interactions between television and online video in American election campaigns or the hybrid assemblages of real-time news-making in the cases of the British Bullygate scandal and televised prime ministerial debates, it was essential to reconstruct the publicly available traces of these phenomena.

But a thorough examination of the norms that animate a media system—which I understand as contestable, shared meanings that are socially sanctioned and which inform legitimized and regularized patterns of thought and behavior—requires a different research strategy. To explore norms we need to get inside the textures of meaning that give life to the settings—the organizations and networks—that matter in political communication. In short, we need to understand how people make sense of their daily practice as actors in the hybrid media system.

The challenges here are numerous. Studying a single organization like a newspaper or a political campaign by exploring the beliefs of its key actors is difficult enough. Exploring norms in the hybrid media system requires that we focus on a wider range of actors than is usually the case with insider studies of media and politics. Indeed, the very idea that there are easily identifiable, organizationally granted roles when it comes to the creation of mediated politics is becoming increasingly problematic. As I have shown throughout this book, political communication now occurs in complex, hybrid assemblages of older and newer media, as a diverse array of actors, ranging from large professional news organizations to elite politicians to engaged citizens, participate in an incessant struggle to shape public discourse and define the political agenda.

This and the following chapter therefore switch to a different mode of research. In these chapters I explore the evolving norms of the hybrid media system by considering the meanings actors ascribe to their roles. These actors are drawn from a range of relevant older and newer fields of political and media practice. The aims of this and the following chapter, then, are to try to get under the skin of how and why these actors behave as they do, to assess the extent to which new norms are being forged, and to identify the extent to which these norms are becoming embedded in routine practice in political communication. In short, this and chapter 9 are concerned with *sense making* in the hybrid media system.

My raw materials here are interviews I conducted personally among people operating at the very heart of Britain's media–politics nexus in London, during 2010, 2011, and 2012. Happily, this period included Britain's momentous general election of May 2010. During my fieldwork I interviewed party communication staff; journalists, program-makers, and editors working in radio, television, newspaper, magazine, and news agency organizations; independent bloggers; the director of a prominent public relations company; senior regulatory staff at the Office of Communications (OFCOM) and the Press Complaints Commission (PCC); communications staff working inside government departments and in the Prime Minister's Office in Number 10 Downing Street; and members of the renowned million-member progressive political activist network, 38 Degrees. The interviews ranged in length from forty-five minutes to two hours and forty-five minutes.[1]

I chose these interviewees because I wanted to "sample" a range of different political and media settings: those associated with formal organizations but also those working in nonorganizational settings, or settings whose precariousness, contingency, or what we might term "boundariness" were what made them interesting as subjects of study, given the initial research questions that fueled this book. It helped that several of my interviewees had, in previous careers, moved between the different but deeply interconnected worlds of media, politics, public advocacy, and citizen activism; indeed, some had done so shortly before the interview.

This fieldwork sample is not, of course, meant to be representative of the hugely diverse media system of contemporary Britain. No set of in-depth qualitative interviews could ever achieve that status and it would be unwise to assume that it might. However, my interview subjects, and the norms they reveal as important, add up to what I believe is a convincing *figurative* representation of daily practice in the hybrid media system.

In this chapter I focus on evidence from the field of news and journalism. In the chapter that follows I turn my attention to political activism, election campaigning, and government communications.

The Evolution of Westminster Lobby Journalism: "the Whole Works"?

Britain's Westminster "lobby" is infamous for being one of the most secretive and restrictive systems in the liberal-democratic world for managing interactions between senior politicians and journalists. Around two hundred lobby-registered journalists are drawn from elite newspaper and broadcast organizations and enjoy access to political and communications staff working at the highest levels of government. Among the many controversial aspects of the lobby rules is the norm of non-attributability that surrounds the reporting of the twice-daily press briefings chaired by the prime minister's press officer. But lobby norms extend, tentacle-like, through the rest of Britain's system of political reporting. Despite recent developments that have weakened the lobby, such as the opening up of the morning's (but not the afternoon's) prime ministerial briefings to all accredited journalists, source confidentiality based on "lobby terms" remains a well-established weapon that can be deployed strategically by politicians, senior civil servants, and of course journalists themselves (Gaber, 2011). The lobby came into its own during the heyday of broadcast-mediated politics from the 1960s to the 1990s (Cockerell, et al., 1984). And yet we know next to nothing about how the emergence of digital media is influencing the norms of lobby correspondents.

To gain an insider perspective on what is still a secretive world, I interviewed two lobby correspondents: David Stringer, the Westminster correspondent of the Associated Press (AP) news agency, and Laura Kuenssberg, former chief political correspondent at BBC News and now Business Editor at ITV News (Interview 25, October 2010; Interview 31, January 2012).

Kuenssberg and Stringer, who are both in their thirties, work for what are, in many respects, two of the most traditional institutions of journalism anywhere in the world. They operate according to the routines and expectations of elite political reporting, in Kuenssberg's case at the very highest professional level in Britain. Yet both are avid users of the web and both were among the first generation of journalists to use Twitter. Indeed, Kuenssberg was an early adopter of the service and before she began to use it for reporting had to write a paper for senior management at BBC News, justifying its virtues as a tool for political correspondents (Interview 31, January 2012).

Kuenssberg and Stringer both express enthusiasm and optimism about how social media have enhanced journalists' ability to connect with the public and hold politicians to account. Stringer speaks of how Facebook and Twitter provide monitorial resources for political journalists eager to react quickly to stories as they develop throughout the day. He uses the example of instantly getting "about twenty" MPs' initial responses to the election of Ed Miliband as the new leader of the Labour Party in September 2010. "How groups of people are thinking, how they're responding to events" is important for getting a quick sense of the significance of a potential story. Stringer also suggests that there has been a broadening of sources beyond the usual Westminster "bubble" and that he is now able to identify networks of activists keen to try to engage with journalists online. In the process, these distributed publics reveal grassroots opinion to journalists in ways that previously were very difficult to trace. This has changed reporting, by making it essential for journalists to get a sense of how events are playing out among a broader network rather than simply relying on biased proxies like government or party press officers. Stringer cites his experience during the 2010 general election, when he says reporters were able to get a "richer sense of how the Labour Party felt, the pessimism within the party." "Without the web you traditionally wouldn't have got a handle on it," he adds (Interview 25, October 2010).

At the same time, Stringer has developed a certain measured skepticism about how the online environment has evolved. He identifies signs that party spin doctors are now settling on a range of effective new approaches to strategic communication. He points to the shrewd use of the online personas of Gordon Brown's wife, Sarah, and David Cameron's wife, Samantha, during the 2010 election. Sarah Brown was very active on Twitter and Samantha Cameron had her own YouTube channel. Then there was Labour's recruitment and integration into their election campaign of Ellie Gellard, a blogger with the pen name Bevanite Ellie. Gellard, a Labour activist and at that time an undergraduate student at the University of Bristol, described herself on her blog as the "stilettoed social-ist." She amassed a large Twitter following after her successful campaign to have a video, "Fighters and Believers," shown nationally as one of Labour's allocated television election broadcasts. During the run-up to the election it became obvious that Gellard was one of Labour's more prominent online supporters and she was invited by Gordon Brown to give a speech at the formal launch of the party's campaign. Stringer suggests that this was a case of the "party hierarchy taking someone who has built herself a following, and using her as a PR tool." She went from "independence and her ability to express herself to essentially becoming a party official," he says (Interview 25, October 2010). Stringer also points out that the Conservatives' senior press officer during the campaign, Henry McCrory, used Twitter to target a select group of political journalists with a "super-fast form of rebuttal." And more broadly across government there is now an embedded aware-ness of what works strategically in the digital environment, with, for example, depart-ments like the Foreign Office launching new digital diplomacy initiatives designed to frame foreign policy in softer terms for both domestic and foreign audiences.

Stringer works for AP, a successful and long-established global news agency. AP feeds a great deal of content to British media organizations and its reputation for factual accuracy is an important part of its status and power. Stringer is keen to stress that news agencies like his are an oasis of high-standards journalism in a desert of often dubious practice at tabloid newspapers. This should come as no surprise. But news agencies like AP, Reuters, and the Press Association (PA) have come under pressure in recent years as a result of the internet's impact on breaking news. The news agencies have adapted, of course, and the most important strategic move in this process of adaptation is the argument that not only must agencies be the first to break news, they must do so with the highest standards of accuracy and journalistic judgment. So Stringer is keen to draw a boundary between the agency model and his lobby routines, on the one hand, and the frenzied, hypercompetitive digital news environment, on the other. The rush to break news and compete with bloggers, online activists on Twitter, and digital-only media organizations like the *Huffington Post* has led to older news organizations often churning out insubstantial stories based on PR releases, in order to stay in the game, he says:

> For an agency journalist there is no capacity to be wrong. It would damage the reputation of the company. Ourselves, Reuters, PA, AFP, their whole rationale is to be fast, to be first, yes, but also to be accurate. And if you don't have both, essentially there's no point. So it does bring incredible pressures on getting things right. It brings incredible pressures on attempting often to corroborate news, particularly in the political sphere, [where] there may be news broken by the BBC who may quote unnamed, unattributed sources....It means to me and my colleagues, yes you have to move very quickly, you have to have the access and the ability to attempt to find those people and corroborate stories, but you have to have a very, very clear sense of what your company's standards are, what your sourcing standards are; you have to have a very clear sense of whether something is correct or not. Otherwise, the reputational damage you could do could be really corrosive (Interview 25, October 2010).

In this perspective, sourcing properly and not following the online "herd" is a key aspect of what defines professional journalism. Here, the traditions of the lobby emerge as an important bulwark against what Stringer describes as "a huge cluster of new noise that may or may not be useful to journalists and may not be instructive." The agency model and the lobby are thus mobilized as a way of articulating an argument about older media standards in the digital era.

Yet lobby reporters are still compelled to compete with each other to be the first to frame an unfolding story and to reveal important breakthroughs as a story develops. As I argued throughout this book, preemption has become an important aspect of exercising power in the hybrid media system, as the temporal rhythms of the fast-moving online environment have been adapted and adopted by traditionally "slower" media forms, particularly print media. I ask Stringer if he sees it as important to use online tools to try to frame stories early in the day, as some television and radio reporters now do, to preempt their own scoops with blog posts and Twitter updates that come before their appearances in a news bulletin. He talks about the peculiarities of putting out in the open what was previously a relatively private process "between a reporter and his notepad" or in the journalists' "huddle at the end of a big speech." He also suggests that there are commercial pressures that compel elite media organizations to compete across all platforms and that having senior reporters blogging and tweeting is as much about "getting value for money" from a big-name reporter as it is about attempting to seize a story early in the day. The point, though, is that these two aims—preemption and getting value for money from journalism brands—are interconnected. But above all, for Stringer it is broadcast media that are still the most powerful in political reporting. Interviews on BBC Radio 4's morning *Today* program often dictate the news agenda across all media during the rest of the morning, and *Today* is joined soon after by the rolling television news channels, he says. Of the latter he adds: "Their influence is absolutely huge. I wouldn't go so far as to say that it's dictating the news agenda, but it's not far off it. There is a sense now, and particularly for journalists and people working in newsrooms, who invariably have multiple news channels on and dozens of TVs in their office, when there is a breaking news flash across Sky News or the BBC News channel there is a scramble."

At the same time, Stringer mentions that in his experience there are always examples that contradict the power of broadcasters. Bloggers may post "something salacious" that gets followed up by professional journalists. And in any case, as I will demonstrate when I discuss the *Guardian* later, "print" media and the wire organizations are using digital tools to enable them to compete with television in new ways, and very much on television's own turf as the preeminent real-time medium. Stringer has integrated social media into his routines and in AP he works for a company that requires journalists to extend their repertoires, to provide what he describes as "the whole works." "I don't feel personally threatened," he says, "because my company is using these platforms. During the [2009] Copenhagen climate talks, we had people blogging. Our reporters, in addition to their normal duties, were posting pictures, doing blog posts on Facebook, Twitter updates, the whole works. We worked across that whole range. You see that with dozens of traditional news outlets." (Interview 25, October 2010). There is a recognition among journalists, he says, that "we're not the only dog in the race...Members of the public can see the process of stories develop in a way they never could before...You can see the workings. Perhaps that's a good thing."

The sense that it was when the internet became an important real-time medium that its role in shaping political news became more powerful is borne out strongly in my interview with former BBC political correspondent, now ITV business editor Laura Kuenssberg. Kuenssberg describes the transition from a time in the early 2000s when the online environment was essentially oriented around retrieving information, to the mid-2000s when the expectation emerged that television reporters should write companion pieces for the BBC website, to the "complete transformation" of the last two years and "the kind of journalism where essentially you're filing stories all the time" (Interview 31, January 2012). In contrast with David Stringer, Kuenssberg is more forthright about how print and broadcast journalists have adapted to the digital environment and how they now see these tools as an important part of their attempts to be first to frame the news agenda. Broadcast journalists can now break stories "off air" through blog posts and Twitter updates and, as Kuenssberg says, "you get credit for your story." This is in contrast with the older temporal logics of "the papers," where "the instinct is you save it for the splash" and older broadcasting logics, where the tradition was that you work toward the flagship evening bulletins: "you get as many goodies as you can and you keep them for the time when you're going to have the most eyeballs on them." This older temporality made sense in the days of media scarcity, but for Kuenssberg this is "fading away very, very fast because news cycles have sped up. People don't wait for their news, so it doesn't make sense any more to make your stories wait."

Kuenssberg argues that, contrary to many predictions, broadcast journalism has resisted becoming the hapless victim of online competition from bloggers and online news sites and she believes that political bloggers like Guido Fawkes are now essentially a part of the Westminster bubble and not the radical upstarts that they once were. And at the same time she says the "main players have moved online in a very healthy, big, serious way." Indeed, if anything, the internet is allowing broadcast journalists to further enhance their personal brands. In 2011, Kuenssberg left BBC News for its old television rival, ITV News. When she decided to change her Twitter username from @BBCLauraK to @ITVLauraK, she instantly took her 59,000 followers with her to her new job. The episode caused a mini-storm, as journalists speculated on what this meant for the independence and power of those reporters who have been able to build big personal brands online. Kuenssberg says that the move was "genuinely very amicable" and that she "took a risk" that people would stop following her account. However, she also reveals that the reputational damage to the BBC would have been potentially quite significant had the organization decided to try to force her to switch accounts and start afresh at ITV without her follower base.

With Kuenssberg, there is a sense that despite elite broadcast media's uniquely privileged position in reporting political news, particularly its huge audiences, the trappings of the broadcast environment can be inhibiting for journalists. She speaks of having witnessed the freedom that Twitter provided to reporters during the 2008 U.S. presidential election, and of enjoying the ability to "just file" without needing a satellite link or camera operator. This idea of an individual reporter having the freedom to post immediately to the internet without the usual collective editorial processes that shape broadcast news caused some initial "nervousness" at the BBC when she asked for permission to start tweeting as part of her daily routine. Kuenssberg says it "took a few months" for a paper she wrote for the BBC news board to be approved after the BBC news managers "had to sit down and think quite seriously about what it was going to do on that new platform."

Kuenssberg decided early on to be highly strategic about her use of Twitter. She integrates it into her real-time television reporting routines, focuses on breaking new information, adding color to evolving stories, and layering-in details (though "not gossip" or anything "personal") that will never find a way into the television bulletins. She recounts the story of when she tweeted from backstage at the Labour Party conference that Lord Mandelson had lost his security pass and had been refused entry because the police officers did not recognize the former cabinet minister. In this sense, Twitter is seen as something like a public version of mobile text messaging, which Kuenssberg says has been crucial for Westminster journalism for more than a decade: "I've lost count of the number of times that somebody texted me while I was on air and I would look down and read it—not read it out—but that would then inform what I was then saying" (Interview 31, January 2012). Still, fitting digital media into the rhythms of rolling television news is what is most important for Kuenssberg. As I have argued at several points throughout this book, television and the internet now share family resemblances as real-time monitorial media. Kuenssberg reports with some enthusiasm how the 2010 general election was a "TV election" dominated by the televised leader's debates and the live reporting of Gordon Brown's off-camera remarks after his troubled encounter on the streets of Rochdale with disenchanted Labour voter, Gillian Duffy.

Twitter also fits with an approach to political journalism that is quite distinctive in its emphasis on pulling back the curtain on the hidden world of the lobby. As we saw in chapter 4, Kuenssberg tweeted from behind the scenes in the "spin room" during Britain's first televised prime ministerial debates in 2010. These fragments of the backstage processes of negotiation that take place among politicians, their communications staff, and elite journalists were an important part of the hybrid mediated experience of the debates. Kuenssberg says that she has never treated the lobby as a secret realm that ought to be protected and instead sees it as the journalists' duty to "bust the doors open and tell people as much as you possibly can."

At the same time, Like David Stringer, Kuenssberg also discerns the rise of a new approach to digital media among politicians and spin doctors: a diminishing fear of losing control of the online political space and a growing confidence in using social media to bypass professional journalism. Those running for high office must still put themselves up for scrutiny in broadcast media, but they now also have vast swathes of the media system—Facebook, Twitter, YouTube, Flickr, direct e-mails, their own websites—that are relatively free from these traditional constraints, though not from citizen monitoring. Kuenssberg is quick to defend the standards of professional journalism and the importance of television media in holding politicians to account. While she suggests that journalists should move away from the role of gatekeeper and try to become online "curators" that assemble news as part of an ongoing process throughout the day, she contextualizes this with reference to the "avalanche of information" that must now be effectively filtered. As such, curation is here still very much a professional role requiring skill and knowledge, a role that is mostly seen as the preserve of journalists. This is therefore an assertion of the power and identity of broadcast journalism in the context of an abundance of information and a perceived scarcity of attention and skills among the broader public.

Occupying Boundaries Between "Professional" Journalism and "Amateur" Blogging

In chapter 4 I discussed the hybrid news-making assemblages during Britain's Bullygate scandal of 2010, which centered on allegations that Gordon Brown had mistreated staff working inside Downing Street. Recall that a key actor in that episode was London-based blogger Adam Bienkov. Since 2008, Bienkov has published at blogger.com under the title *Tory Troll*. It was Bienkov who responded decisively to one of the key turning points in Bullygate: the BBC News channel's report that staff in the prime minister's office had allegedly called a bullying charity "helpline" to complain about their treatment. Within a few hours, Bienkov posted what turned out to be an explosive late-night article to his blog revealing the dubious credentials of this bullying "helpline." By the following morning the bullying claims were well on the way to being discredited. About a month after Bullygate, I interviewed Bienkov about his role in the affair, but I also wanted to learn more generally about his practices as a blogger, his interactions with politicians and professional journalists, and how he positions his work in the context of the broader media system (Interview 1, March 2010). The interview proved highly revealing. The norms by which Bienkov operates situate his practice in a liminal space at the boundary of professional journalism and amateur blogging.

Bienkov's *Tory Troll* blog was established during the Spring of 2008 and focused on London Assembly politics in the run-up to the city's third mayoral election. In that campaign, London's daily paper, the *Evening Standard*, favored the Conservative candidate Boris Johnson and it ran a particularly hostile campaign against incumbent Labour mayor, Ken Livingstone. This spurred left-of-center activists to think about establishing an alternative voice online. *Tory Troll* and another blog, *Mayorwatch*, were the products of this context and, following Boris Johnson's election as mayor, Bienkov went on to establish himself as an independent source of news about London politics.

Bienkov's approach is striking in its fusion of the genres and norms of blogging—independence, irreverence, and narrowly focused content—with those of professional journalism: the importance of breaking stories, attention to sourcing, and writing in a broadly accessible, at times almost tabloid style. When he started the blog, Bienkov deliberately sought to avoid becoming another commentary blog—there were already many of those in British politics. Instead, he decided he would try to write original stories and break news. "If you want to break through and get your stories into the news," he says, "you need to be breaking something that is new, not just saying 'this is my opinion about X'...You'll never get noticed." This was easier to achieve in what was effectively a new and rapidly evolving political system that emerged in the aftermath of the capital's first few mayoral elections. It soon became clear that reporting on the London Assembly was not going to run on the same lines as the tightly controlled lobby system that operates at the Westminster parliament. As a result, Bienkov was able to make an impact inside the bureaucracy and build up networks of contacts. Relations of journalist–source reciprocity emerged. As London Assembly members and their press officers and civil servants started to notice Bienkov's blog posts they sensed that he might play a role in shaping the news. They began to feed him information. A division of labor of sorts has emerged. Press officers are more likely to send him the detailed policy documents that professional journalists might ignore, but they do so in the hope of indirectly catching the eye of professional media: "They read the blog, they know that when I write stories there's a chance it will be picked up by the *Evening Standard* or by the BBC, whereas if they'd sent a link to a 20-page document to a time-strapped journalist at the BBC they probably wouldn't have had the time or the interest to look into it," he says (Interview 1, March 2010).

While it might not always be possible, breaking news is seen as central to "getting noticed" by professional news organizations. This logic is what drives *Tory Troll* and is key to its integration into the hybrid media system. It results in regular interactions between Bienkov the blogger and sources inside City Hall, as well as professional journalists at the BBC, the *Guardian*, and the *Evening Standard*. Bienkov speaks highly of journalists at the *Guardian* who will often link to his stories and give credit, and of some broadcast journalists whom he says "sometimes tip [him] off about things." He goes on: "Through doing the blog I've built up relationships with them and I pass them stories, they pass me stories, so it's not so much the direct influence that it has on the public, it's the influence it has on the people in the mainstream media who then bring it to a wider audience" (Interview 1, March 2010). "Influencing the influencers" is how Bienkov describes it. For example, a story he posted to the blog after he issued a Freedom of Information Request to the mayor's office asking for details of letters sent by Prince Charles to Boris Johnson was picked up and splashed across the front page of the *Evening Standard*, complete with a quote from Bienkov. Elsewhere, norms of credit-giving among professional journalists are less clear, though Bienkov is also quick to suggest that "it's got a lot better" recently (Interview 1, March 2010). Bloggers, then, are influenced by some of the norms of professional journalism, but some of the norms of blogging have also started to move in the other direction, and now influence professional journalism. Credit-giving is one example of this process of norm diffusion, as bloggers are presented here as the savior of journalistic standards:

> That's something that the blogosphere has changed. It's brought this new culture of openness, of giving credit for stories, of backing up your stories with documents, of linking to your sources, and blogs get a lot of criticism from some journalists, who say "they can just say what they like, they don't have to back it up with facts." In a lot of cases, I think the opposite is true. A lot of newspapers don't back up their facts, they don't link to documents, they cherry pick quotes from them without you being able to see the original source. And when they get things wrong, often it never gets corrected…In some ways I think blogs are improving the behavior of journalists (Interview 1, March 2010).

Bienkov goes along to public committee meetings at City Hall, only to find that journalists stay away from all but the monthly mayor's question time. He downloads long policy documents from the Greater London Authority website and pores over the details, hoping to pick up stories that professional journalists do not have the time to gather. Paradoxically, he marks the distinctions between himself and professionals by trying to uphold what he considers to be older, "proper" values of journalism that he thinks have been lost as a result of commercial pressures in newsrooms. He fills the gaps now left by the mainstream: "It's what journalism used to be before the big cutbacks at newspapers, before journalists got tied to their desks as they do these days. It's just simply because I've got the time to do it, I guess, whereas they've got to turn over five stories a day or whatever. They haven't got time to get down there, whereas bloggers can do that" (Interview 1, March 2010). Trained as a journalist at a local vocational college, Bienkov earns income from a mixture of paid shorthand work, freelancing, and helping out with local news websites in southeast London. Some of his freelance pieces are for the *Guardian*'s network, *Comment Is Free*, which is a hybrid that brings together professional journalists from the paper with a distributed network of thousands of part-time contributors. This serves to further integrate his practice into the system of professional news media, though in a way that still distances him and other bloggers from the authentically "professional." Blogging is seen here as a way of getting a paid job in professional journalism, but on one's own terms, unlike the classic trainee route. While Bienkov admits that most of his research takes place online, he adheres to the professional norms and routines of news-gathering in more traditional journalism. He has a beat and he usually sticks to it. The sources on his beat provide him, through face-to-face meetings or e-mail tip-offs, with the best stories, because these are people to whom he can sometimes gain exclusive access.

Bienkov's intervention in the Bullygate crisis was born of a different context and method, however (for a full analysis of Bullygate see chapter 4). The story was away from his regular beat and his blog post about the claims of the National Bullying Helpline was written and published in a couple of hours on a Sunday evening. As I documented in chapter 4, the article emerged from a combination of resources: a skeptical reaction to the BBC News Channel's reporting of the story, some expertise in online fact-finding, some real-time monitoring of social media for quick feedback, and an assessment of a few tweets and e-mails that arrived from friends and acquaintances urging him to look deeper into the story. Bienkov's blog condensed and provided some fixity to what had, until then, been a dispersed and fragmented set of messages and counter-messages on Twitter. As he describes it, "I did all of those checks and put it together in a blog post, spent about two or three hours on it, put it onto Twitter and literally within seconds it just went completely crazy. It was retweeted by ten people, then twenty people, then a hundred people....And what's interesting about Twitter, my blog was quite a well-known blog, but you can be anybody, you can be a person who's only written two blog posts, but if you write something that touches a nerve like that it can snowball and before you know it, it gathers its own momentum" (Interview 1, March 2010).

The morning after his blog post about the bullying helpline, Bienkov was bombarded with e-mails providing tip-offs and urging him to examine the story further. But he chose not to, due to a lack of time and resources. By then, the story had shifted and a new skepticism toward the bullying allegations had spread across broadcasters and the newspapers (Interview 1, March 2010). Bienkov did not have contact with the BBC at the time, but a few weeks later, while attending an event at a central London university, he ended up chatting with a senior BBC journalist, whose name he did not want to divulge to me. He was surprised to hear the journalist say that he "could not believe" that the BBC had run the story without adequate checks and that Bienkov had been "absolutely spot on" with his blog post. As this book goes to press, Bienkov's blog continues, but he has also authored several further pieces about the 2012 London mayoral contest for the *Guardian*'s *Comment Is Free* network.

Bienkov clearly had the resources required to make a powerful intervention in the Bullygate affair. He is a "citizen journalist" of sorts, but one whose norms and practice blur the boundaries between blogger and professional. In turn, professional journalists have been influenced by his norms and practice. This boundary position has also enabled him to play a significant role in the reporting of London politics. Yet this position can be precarious. He is often dependent upon mainstream journalists' goodwill in linking to his stories, and as a lone individual he does not have the resources required to follow up big stories, even when he has played a pivotal role in bringing them to the attention of a wider public.

Similar forces are in play with another blog, *Left Foot Forward*. Established in 2009 by Will Straw, the son of former Labour home office minister Jack Straw, *Left Foot Forward* is a group blog that quickly grew to have around forty contributors. I interviewed Straw a couple of weeks after the 2010 British general election, a period when he and his fellow writers had emerged as one of the important blogs of the campaign (Interview 10, May 2010). (Straw left the blog to join the Institute for Public Policy Research think tank at the end of 2010.) What I found at *Left Foot Forward* was an intriguing hybrid. *Left Foot Forward* is a blog, a think tank, "serious" journalism, activist group, and partisan blog. It aims to mobilize progressive activists, but under Straw's leadership it has also become partly, though certainly not wholly, integrated into the Westminster lobby and Britain's national political reporting system.

Left Foot Forward's funding model is unusual. Describing himself as one of probably only "a dozen professional bloggers" in Britain, Straw tells me how a small group of wealthy donors paid for his modest part-time salary and a small office in Kennington, just across the River Thames from Westminster. These include YouGov pollster Peter Kellner, former chairman of Green and Black's chocolate and human rights advocate Henry Tinsley, and millionaire Labour peer Pat Carter. These donations included "a £5000 cheque here, a £10,000 cheque there"; several other individuals established bank standing orders. Two trade unions also provided funding: the communications union Connect and Britain's largest general union, Unite. Straw also managed to broker occasional advertising deals with broadcaster ITV and left-wing magazine *Tribune*, as well as event sponsorship from London think thanks like the Smith Institute and the Institute for Public Policy Research. *Left Foot Forward* encourages individual donations but at the time of the interview only a few thousand pounds had been raised this way. Straw supplements his income by writing the occasional paid article for professional media organizations.

Left Foot Forward was established with a mission to conduct "evidence-based blogging" with a progressive bent. The meaning of evidence-based blogging is important in understanding the blog's role in the hybrid media system. Like Adam Bienkov, Will Straw wanted to avoid the blog becoming another outlet for reactive commentary. Instead, he wanted to conduct background news gathering and break the occasional story. But more importantly, he wanted to provide rapid factual rebuttal to stories in Britain's right-of-center dominated newspaper media, on a daily basis. Key to this aim was presenting *Left Foot Forward* as legitimately expert enough to meet the norms and expectations of professional media: "something a little bit different, a bit more highbrow, I suppose, a bit more policy-focused, and with a bit more credibility in the policy community," Straw says (Interview 10, May 2010). Yet despite the blog's think tank identity it also has strong links with the Labour Party and the trade union movement. Straw speaks of having worked "very closely" with Labour's communications team to get information about the campaign and material for factual rebuttals during the 2010 general election (Interview 10, May 2010). The Labour press officers send Straw ideas for stories that will benefit the party, especially during periods when the blog is generating interest from big media, as it was during the 2010 election, when "live blogs" on the websites of the *Guardian* and the *Financial Times* routinely linked to articles on *Left Foot Forward* and other blogs. Echoing Adam Bienkov's notion of "influencing the influencers," Straw says the Labour headquarters "knew that getting stories up on *Left Foot Forward* was a good way of getting into wider elite media. I think if we'd had a readership of a couple of thousand a month, and rather less impact, they wouldn't have bothered." Straw filters story suggestions on the basis of how well they fit with the blog's mission of using evidence-based blogging to expose news articles hostile to Labour. During the general election the blog was drawing an audience of ninety-two thousand unique visitors per month; the average is around thirty thousand per month. As a rough comparison, *Prospect* magazine, whose managing editor I interviewed (see below), has a monthly circulation of around twenty thousand copies. "When the BBC's technology correspondent, Rory Cellan-Jones, talks about us we get a massive spike," says Straw.

The *Left Foot Forward* blog's visibility has also been enhanced by a number of television and radio appearances by Straw, though these are less than straightforward. The mention of the BBC's Rory Cellan-Jones provides a hint. Though Straw made nothing of this, he is often asked to appear on broadcast news packages that are driven by frames about the novelty of the internet and blogging in election campaigns. He is presented as a representative of the online political community. The policy-related stories and statistical rebuttals published by *Left Foot Forward* are often downgraded in these appearances, as if that is the more serious material that only "proper" and "legitimate" journalism and think-tanks can provide. This is an important aspect of the power relations among political bloggers and professional political journalists in Britain. Straw's broadcast media appearances often fit a "medium is the message" logic that is part of a process of boundary-drawing by broadcast journalists, as journalists often seek to position online media as intriguing but marginal to the production of political news. The focus is the "whizz-bang" new technology of blogs and social media in the campaign, not the substance of the blog's content. As we saw in chapters 5, 6, and 7, these logics have played a role in older media's representation of internet activism in U.S. presidential campaigns, and in some journalists' approach to WikiLeaks.

On the other hand, this framing does not always work. Straw is clearly plugged into London's networks of professional political journalism; a legacy, he says, of his days as president of the Oxford University Students' Union and spending a year as a press officer at the Treasury. He describes how he approaches stories that he thinks are most likely to attract journalists' interest. He e-mails journalists from an extended list. Among the most receptive are Andrew Sparrow, the *Guardian*'s senior political correspondent; Jim Pickard and Alex Barker, who run the *Financial Times Westminster* blog; Paul Waugh, once of the *Evening Standard* but now of the *Politics Home* website; and Sam Coates, chief political correspondent at the *Times*. Straw also finds some lobby correspondents to be receptive, particularly Michael Savage at the *Independent* and Allegra Stratton, then at the *Guardian* and now a television reporter for the BBC's *Newsnight*. In common with most political journalists, when in the office Straw is permanently tuned to the rolling news coverage on television. He monitors this coverage so that he can time his attempts to intervene with *Left Foot Forward* stories: "I tend to have BBC News and Sky News on all day. So I get a sense of what they're talking about. If there's a journalist talking about a particular story and we've got a particular angle on it, I might send them a direct message by Twitter or text or an email flagging our particular angle to them...and try and get our stuff out that way" (Interview 10, May 2010).

Straw clearly interacts with professional journalists but how is he received by them? Like Adam Bienkov's, the experiences have been broadly positive, but this is not the whole story. Straw recounts examples of friendly journalists who seek information from bloggers, but there have also been episodes of conflict that reveal his relatively precarious structural position in the news-making system. For example, a story he posted in March 2010 about contradictory statements by senior Conservative politicians, including then-party-leader and now prime minister David Cameron, over plans to introduce a banking levy, almost backfired. The editor of the Conservative *Spectator* magazine, Fraser Nelson, wrote an article attacking Straw's argument, but Nelson's piece was also framed as a general criticism of poor standards of research among bloggers. Straw responded later in the election campaign by exposing the highly selective statistics behind a *Spectator* article claiming that "98%" of the new jobs in the British economy since 1997 had gone to "foreigners." The *Daily Mail* and the *Daily Express* had lifted the *Spectator* story for their front pages and BBC Radio 5 used it as the basis for their popular morning phone-in show. Straw asked two researchers at the Trades Union Congress to examine the data. In fact, the *Spectator*'s figures were less straightforward than they appeared. It transpired that the story referred to British citizens born abroad as "foreigners," it did not include workers of pensionable age, and it only included private sector jobs—a point about which the *Spectator* was clear but the *Mail* and the *Express* were not. By lunchtime the same day the *Spectator*'s editor was forced to issue a clarification on the magazine's website. "The story died because we killed it," says Straw.

This competition and precariousness in the context of integration and interdependence is a thread that runs through even the most successful moments for *Left Foot Forward*. To take another revealing example, during the 2010 election campaign the blog was the first to break the story of allegedly homophobic remarks made by a Conservative shadow cabinet minister at the time, Julian Lewis, in a speech he delivered at a meeting in his Hampshire constituency of New Forest East. One of the audience, a local student named Andrew Tindall, tweeted that he had "just spent an hour listening to the scaremongering of a corrupt, paranoid homophobe" (Tindall, 2010). Straw picked this up on Twitter and sent a private message to Tindall asking for an e-mail describing the details. Tindall replied and Straw then wrote a story on the basis of Tindall's account and posted it to the *Left Foot Forward* blog. As Straw says: "I was the first news outlet, if I can call myself that, to put the quote up" (Interview 10, May 2010). This was, in reality, Straw's scoop and another example of how fragments of information gathered online can now be integrated into the news-making process. However, professional journalists were soon circling. Michael Savage, the lobby correspondent at the *Independent*, saw the story on *Left Foot Forward* and decided to call the candidate Julian Lewis to ask him about his remarks. Lewis responded by sending Savage a letter he had written earlier to a constituent, outlining in more detail his opposition to sixteen as the age of consent for gay men. The following day's *Independent* ran with Savage's story on its front page, but Straw did not get a mention. When asked privately by Straw why this was the case, Savage was apologetic but argued that he did not "need" Straw's blog post or even the tweet from Andrew Tindall to run the story because he had better evidence in the form of the letter from Julian Lewis himself.

The Julian Lewis story is revealing in several respects. *Left Foot Forward* clearly "broke" the story, but in what Straw himself describes as "only a technical sense." As Straw says: "I don't think putting up a tweet or a blog post is breaking a story, except in some technical sense.... The point at which it's broken is by the mainstream media, not the tweet but the whole story." Professional journalists eager for the latest piece of news during a campaign now see blog stories as fair game, especially when those stories have broken on the basis of publicly available fragments of information found online on social media services such as Twitter or Facebook. There is a residual but still powerful hierarchy of sourcing in political reporting and it relies on the idea that a story is a packaged entity that goes beyond a simple blog post or tweet. In short, even among some bloggers, it is seen as something that can only really be meaningfully produced by a professional journalist.

Integrating Broadcast and Online

Bloggers like Adam Bienkov and Will Straw occupy an increasingly important liminal space between the logics of older and newer media in news making, but they move into this space from positions that are formally outside of mainstream media organizations. But how do things look from the perspective of those working within elite broadcast media? I turn now to explore an illuminating example of an attempt by television news journalism to integrate the internet into its practice: Channel 4 News' *FactCheck*.

FactCheck began shortly before the 2005 British general election campaign and was originally inspired by the FactCheck.org website at the University of Pennsylvania's Annenberg Public Policy Center. Annenberg's center first came to prominence during the 2004 U.S. elections as a result of its regular debunking of claims made by presidential and congressional candidates. Channel 4 relaunched their own feature as *FactCheck with Cathy Newman* in time for the 2010 general election, and this time they added a new section of the Channel 4 News website with a blog that allows user comments. Cathy Newman was then a well-known political correspondent for Channel 4 News and she has since joined the studio presenting team.

During the 2010 election campaign the *FactCheck* team were responsible for two particularly important news stories. First, in March 2010, then-prime-minister Gordon Brown appeared before the Chilcot Inquiry into the Iraq war and claimed that U.K. defense spending had increased in real terms every year under the Labour government. Official Ministry of Defence figures obtained by *FactCheck* showed this to be untrue. Second, on the day after the election campaign's first live televised prime ministerial debate on April 15, *FactCheck* debunked a claim made by David Cameron during the debate that he had visited a police station "the other day" that was about to buy a "£73,000 Lexus" car. It transpired that Cameron's supposed example of public sector inefficiency was not all that it seemed. *FactCheck* revealed that he had visited the station eight months earlier and that the car cost closer to £50,000 ($80,000) (Interview 18, June 2010).

FactCheck's rebranding as *FactCheck with Cathy Newman* is indicative of how it has developed as a hybrid form of political news making, because it positioned a well-known presenter alongside a team of back-room web journalists. As Alice Tarleton, a longstanding member of the *FactCheck* team told me when I interviewed her in June 2010, the editors "wanted to personalize it a bit more … you're working with Cathy Newman and it's in her name and it's her brand" (Interview 18, June 2010). *FactCheck*'s significance lies in its hybrid recombination of some totemic practices of television journalism and online journalism. It is best interpreted as a shrewd reaction to the challenge presented by the rapidity and multiplicity of online news. It is about asserting broadcast media's power to maintain a certain form of investigative reporting, despite the unfavorable context of newsroom cuts. But this has not been achieved by pumping significant financial resources into long-term background investigations. Instead, *FactCheck* takes accelerated newsgathering and hypercompetition as its starting point, while seeking to position Channel 4's television news at the center of political information cycles. In one sense, *FactCheck* is skeptical and investigative reporting of a high standard. But the stories that it produces are usually reactive and they are often researched and written in the space of just a few hours. *FactCheck* is news designed for broadcast television and yet the stories appear first on the web, most often in the late afternoon. This is based upon a recognition among journalists that such news can often be better presented online, because the genres of television news dictate that stories designed to debunk politicians' claims with statistical analysis are not likely to work well in the packaged, fast-edited environment of contemporary broadcast news.

FactCheck therefore gets around what "Tony," a former senior executive at ITN told me was a basic hindrance during broadcast journalism's adaptation to the web era: "The fact is, broadcasters don't own many words … there just isn't enough of it" (Interview 23, July 2010). The BBC, with massive resources at its disposal, solved this problem in the early years by buying in large quantities of textual news agency content that it could place on its website. Then, when online video took off after the emergence of YouTube in 2005, the BBC successfully transposed its power to the new audiovisual web, with the launch of its iPlayer web television platform in December 2007. Lacking the financial underpinnings enjoyed by the BBC, Channel 4 has found other, more sporadic models for integrating the web and television.

FactCheck reports are produced through a process of collaboration involving members of Channel 4's web and television news teams. This collaboration is signaled symbolically by the way Channel 4 television presenters integrate the stories into their news packages by pointing viewers to the website for more information on a scoop. This practice of highlighting tie-in websites at the end of broadcast news bulletins has of course become extremely common over the last decade, but it is the tightness of the integration between television and the web that makes *FactCheck* different. Sometimes a *FactCheck* story will drive an entire package in the news bulletin, but even when it does not, reporters will make a point of mentioning the *FactCheck* blog in their pieces to camera and news anchors will often mobilize evidence from that day's *FactCheck* when they interview government ministers; this happened, for example, when presenter Jon Snow interviewed shadow deputy prime minister Harriet Harman in 2010 (Interview 18,

June 2010). Once the live television bulletin has ended, the news editors close the hybrid loop by embedding the television video clip featuring the *FactCheck* evidence at the foot of the textual online version of the story.

As Alice Tarleton explains, *FactCheck* is about "having the small scoop" by puncturing the bubble of politicians' often selective use of statistics. This is achieved by having skilled journalists spend time calling insider sources in government departments and interrogating the data in its raw form, usually in dense official reports from the Treasury, the Office of Budget Responsibility, or the Office for National Statistics (Interview 18, June 2010). Tarleton explains how inserting a small scoop from an online story into a television bulletin extracts the maximum value from a story that might not match the news editor's idea of an eye-catching television piece:

> It can be a tricky thing, because actually with *FactCheck* you're often looking at a lot of very detailed, boring tables and trying to make that into an interesting article and then to translate that into interesting TV is another step again. So what makes a good *FactCheck* may not necessarily make a good package on TV. But then again it might actually make a 30-second segment. Cathy [Newman] may be doing a live piece and may be able to say at the end "and my *FactCheck* team have also been looking and have found out that the speech I've just been telling you about from David Cameron actually contained a big untruth. Here's the real truth."

An important function of *FactCheck*'s website is building momentum on a story as Channel 4 News moves toward its important live early evening television show. Tarleton monitors social media "to gauge reaction to a story through the day," deliberately targeting bloggers and Twitter users in the hope that they will "do the work" of spreading a story virally in order to build anticipation before the show. The online audience, especially on Twitter, can often provide a boost when an activist community engages with stories that are "about as worthy and number-crunching as we want to get," she says. Blogs with large readerships, particularly Guido Fawkes, "will often send a decent chunk of readers your way," she says, though there is an acute awareness that the big blogs are also in the business of breaking "small scoops." As Tarleton says of a story about the Conservative MP John Bercow's expenses claims, to which Guido Fawkes beat them:

> Once, during the election, I'd spotted an election leaflet that John Bercow had put out which we thought had a slightly dubious expenses claim. Didn't have time to look at it that day and thought it will keep, we'll look at this later. But then Guido Fawkes had done a less comprehensive job than we'd done, he'd just kind of flagged it up and said it looked a bit strange. And I think you could then have made the judgement that we could do a more comprehensive job on it. In that case we thought well, he's got the line on it. He's done it first so that makes us less keen to do it. You always do want to have things first (Interview 18, June 2010).

Tarleton is also keen to draw boundaries between sourcing stories online and what *FactCheck* does: "I'd say it all overlaps. But certainly it's not the case that you just look at Twitter all day rather than doing old-fashioned journalism…For many stories I'd use Twitter to gauge reaction to a story through the day but all of the research is going to be speaking to researchers, speaking to the Treasury, reading official Treasury forecasts, reading research papers that are available online and can be emailed to me…of course that is part of good journalism in general. That does make it important that you have normal press office channels and experts" (Interview 18, June 2010).

If *FactCheck* constitutes one mode of boundary-blurring between the logics of older and newer media, a different though related mode has emerged at the BBC's flagship radio news show, the *Today* program. Kevin Marsh has worked in broadcast journalism for close to forty years and in 2011 he retired as the head of the BBC's College of Journalism, a role he took on after having worked as editor of *Today* from 2002 to 2006. During his career, Marsh has edited what are arguably the three most important news shows in post-war British radio—*Today*, the *World at One*, and *PM*. He also had a spell in the 1980s working for ITV's most important television bulletin, the *News at Ten* (Interview 27, June 2011).

A central theme in Marsh's discussion of the rise of online media is how growing torrents of audience feedback have come to shape the style and ethos of the BBC's approach to political coverage. The rise to ubiquity of e-mail during the 1990s meant that by the time Marsh became editor of *Today* in 2002 he was receiving around "50,000 emails a year" from listeners who "wanted to push back about stories." This was before the explosion of user comments on the BBC's websites, before the launch of the iPlayer online video platform, and before BBC news' increasing integration with social media during the late 2000s. However, Marsh suggests that the reality of massive audience feedback soon began to affect the culture of the big news shows. Marsh narrates how, during the 1980s and 1990s, the development of a more professionalized approach to media management among politicians, together with a decline in routine parliamentary reporting among elite print and broadcast media, opened up a space for more "serious" political news programs like *Today* to emerge as the main challengers to official power. By the time of Tony Blair's election as prime minister in 1997 the political parties and broadcast journalists had arrived at a modus vivendi. On the one hand, there was a recognition among journalists that politicians would attempt to exert as much control as possible over news. On the other hand, reporters and interviewers were now expected to expose attempts to mislead, control, and manipulate the media through the use of new, more aggressive forms of what Marsh terms "on-air interrogation." This led to the increasingly confrontational style that made BBC presenters like Jeremy Paxman and John Humphrys household names during the 1980s and 1990s.

Marsh argues, however, that the growth of online news and digital forms of engagement with the public around the basic news product have created the need for gentler and more intelligent "conversational" styles of political journalism. No longer is it about the model presenter as being a "ranting, frothing lunatic…shambling around the ring…looking for the next punch to land" from a position of some professional privilege. Instead, while a new generation of presenters like Evan Davis at *Today* and Eddie Mair at *PM* are certainly trying to preserve the preeminence of professional journalism at the BBC, not to mention broadcasting's dominance in the coverage of politics, they also recognize that the public has not been well-served by the older, elite-driven game of confrontation and "attack journalism." This is by no means a frictionless transition.

Marsh mentions how mobilizing audience e-mails as evidence of public sentiment during interviews on *Today* has often met with resistance from government press officers. And the same experiments also provoke hostility from some presenters who fear that their status as the arbiters of relevant lines of inquiry during interviews is under threat.

Marsh's is a narrative of the gradual incursion into elite broadcasting's treatment of politics of some of the norms of informal online media discourse. These new norms privilege conversational styles of expression and a certain communicative egalitarianism. They are based upon the idea of the journalist who speaks from a position of parity with an informed audience rather than as a member of a detached elite that has more in common with the politicians the journalist is supposed to hold to account than the public he or she ought to serve. But at the same time there is a powerful residual norm of professional status and prestige. The norms of online discourse and the mobilization of online opinion are fused with the older, more obviously elitist norms of traditional broadcast journalism at BBC Radio 4. As Marsh says: "It's still about saying 'I'm the lucky journalist who has access to this guy. Nobody else has access. I'm the guy who can formulate the questions.' Not everybody out there would know exactly how to formulate the best questions. So I've got these skills that I as a journalist can bring—the patrician approach if you like—the access, the skills, the application, the intelligence to ask the right questions. But I'm also listening to what's out there."

Despite the boundary-drawing that rests upon distinctions between the routines of professional journalists, bloggers, and social media audiences, *FactCheck* is a story of successful integration of the internet and broadcasting, while *Today* is adapting to the norms and expectations generated by the emergence of online media over the last decade. Experiences in the traditional magazine and newspaper sector are less straightforward, however. My interviews revealed diverse patterns of adaptation, resistance, and renewal.

Adaptation, Resistance, and Renewal in Evolving Newspaper Media

At the time of my interview, James Crabtree was *Prospect* magazine's managing editor. I ask him if the web has changed the way the magazine works. Tellingly, he replies, "In a big sense, no, though I probably shouldn't admit that." He argues that the monthly magazine sector has largely been insulated from the impact of the web. Yet *Prospect* runs its own blog, records and publishes its own podcasts, and regularly offers unpaid online versions of articles that appear in its print edition; hybrid media in action. However, Crabtree still draws what he sees as a clear boundary between *Prospect*'s "more considered, long-form" journalism and what he calls the "what's-new-in-the-last-ten-minutes" political journalism that was pioneered by *Politico* in the United States and now finds its equivalent in Britain in sites like *Politics Home* (Interview 7, April 2010).

"Frank" is a senior journalist at the *Independent* whose role involves integrating a digital strategy into the paper's daily practice (Interview 5, April 2010). During a long interview he tells me in some detail about the realities of working inside a resource-starved newsroom that was forced to adapt to the rise of hypercompetition in online news.

The *Independent* went through a period of deep cuts in the late 2000s, including a 25 percent staff reduction in early 2009. Frank tells amusing folklore tales of older journalists who are used to the pre-CNN and pre-internet rhythms of the newsroom and who "bugger off and come back at about four o'clock with purple lips" after having had a "couple of bottles of red." It has taken such characters a "while to settle down to the 'and where are your other four stories today?' process that we're up against," Frank says.

Frank speaks of resistance among all journalists, even the new recruits, to writing stories for the web. In 2010, unlike other British papers, particularly the *Guardian* and the *Telegraph*, the *Independent* had still not moved to an integrated print-and-web newsroom. There are still entrenched divisions between the paper's web operation and its print edition. Powerful norms of resistance to the culture of online news have been established. In time-honored traditions of the pre-digital era, even when stories break early in the day, some journalists will deliberately hold copy back until around six o'clock in the evening, in the hope of catching the editor's eye with a story as the print edition is being finalized and the British online audience have gone home for the evening. The attitude is "well, there's not much point in me doing this, because it will never get in the paper, so I won't do it at all…Some people would just blatantly and unashamedly ignore it and refuse to deal with it," Frank says. Senior journalists still want a "front-page splash" and will resist "top of the website," which they see as second-best. Even in papers where the distinction between web and print journalists is not formalized, Frank speaks of an informal hierarchy of medium that remains particularly strong in political reporting. He also reports editorial apathy about the website, manifested in senior staff "never speaking" about the site and asking for a story to be removed "only once" (Interview 5, April 2010).

Even though the audience for the *Independent* website far exceeds that for the print edition, the fragmented nature of audience attention in the online realm weakens further the internal argument for publishing on the web. Frank makes a great deal of the "granular" nature of online news. The assumption among editors specializing in digital news is that individuals are much more likely to arrive on the website from a Google search or by clicking through from Twitter or Facebook or a news aggregator like Google News or Reddit. When the "average number of pages per user per month is only eleven" and when "most people will read only one story per month and they've got that through search" and they will probably "have read about it yesterday on the BBC website anyway," reader loyalty is not convincing as an argument about the importance of blogging and publishing stories to the web among a community of already skeptical professional newspaper journalists. This context explains why the paper tends to populate a good proportion of its website with unchanged news agency stories from PA, for fear of diluting its print edition. Not only are PA stories already sub-edited for clarity, they have also been pre-screened for potential legal complaints. Each day, the aim is to start replacing PA stories with those written by in-house reporters as the paper moves toward its print deadline in the late afternoon, but some columnists resist the "web-first" approach and want to see their stories debut in print. Frank suggests that a lack of staff time at the *Independent* means that resources for sub-editing and legal checks are both stretched. Ironically, digital technologies make it much easier to integrate agency stories and stock images and make them look like they are the product of your own reporters, but as Frank jokes, "with no journalists, a fairly limited PA feed, and a bunch of pictures off Getty, it's a bit like one of those funny cookery programs: you've got a pepper, you've got a potato, and an orange—make something out of that. There's a fairly limited amount of recipes you can concoct..." (Interview 5, April 2010).

Agency content on the newspaper website stands in stark contrast with the commentary and campaigning stories which usually break in the print edition and for which the *Independent* has become well known. When it comes to basic reporting, however, the picture presented by Frank is bleak, especially in areas like foreign news. There is gallows humor. For example, the paper's "one bloke in America" covered the aftermath of the 2010 Haiti earthquake but also Hollywood. "He flies in from Haiti, a major disaster, to the red carpet...so in the morning it's death, disaster, and pulling bodies out of rubble, and then he's brushing the dust off himself and trying to do the Oscars. Nobody can sustain that. It's just putting people in stupid positions..."

I move from the *Independent* to the *Guardian*, where things are different. The organization began its transition to a "web-first" approach to publishing in the mid-2000s and this accelerated under the force of editor Alan Rusbridger's "digital first" announcement in 2011. From 2007 to 2008 the *Guardian*'s print and online editions became much more closely integrated and it became the norm to publish important stories and break news to the web in order to compete with other media organizations, including the television news channels. The *Guardian* now effectively runs a global twenty-four-hour news desk for at least five days a week, made possible by editorial staff based in America and Australia. As "Carol," a young member of the senior editorial team at the paper summarizes: "We went from having a web desk and a paper desk that had no interaction, to having an integrated desk which had a small proportion of people working on more web-focused stuff, with a majority of news editors still working on the paper. Now we're in a situation where there are still specialists dealing with each platform but the desk as a whole is just creating content and more and more of that is being focused on the website than on the paper" (Interview 30, September 2011).

It is clear that there has been a concerted editorial push from the very top at the *Guardian* to adapt to the multiple challenges of online news. Over recent years this has gone beyond making journalists aware that they should be publishing their stories to the web, toward a more holistic approach in which staff are strongly encouraged to reach out to the audience in real time using social media. Twitter has been a particularly important part of this transition. Almost all of the *Guardian*'s reporters use the service. What has been the impact of this shift on the news production process?

Early examples of journalists sourcing from Twitter led to it becoming quickly embedded in routine practice at the *Guardian*, not only as a way of disseminating stories but also as a mechanism for sourcing. A key early moment came in April 2009 when, in an exposé of alleged police brutality, investigative reporter Paul Lewis used Twitter to source eyewitness accounts of the death of an innocent bystander, Ian Tomlinson, during the G20 protests in London. Within a matter of a few days Lewis had spoken to twenty reliable witnesses and had secured controversial video footage from an American tourist showing that a police officer had struck Tomlinson with a baton, causing him to fall to the ground and injure himself. (The officer was later charged with manslaughter and was acquitted in July 2012.)

Carol speaks of Twitter as meshing with the *Guardian*'s "comfort with breaking stories during the daytime" and she argues that it has increased the visibility of news editors, primarily because it is they who preside over the streams of information entering and exiting the newsroom. But there is a more significant underlying shift here, and it is one that is very much about positioning the *Guardian* as a more powerful actor in shaping the news agenda in the hybrid media system. The belief is that far from weakening its position, the website, when integrated with social media, can serve to enhance (former) print journalists' influence. Not only can traditional print outlets now adapt in order to outdo new online news players like bloggers and web-only news sites, they can also start to compete more closely with the old enemy: broadcasters. Carol explains how this has started to shape strategic decisions in particularly powerful ways, with scoops such as the July 2011 revelation by veteran investigative reporter Nick Davies that *News of the World* journalists had illegally hacked the voicemail of murdered school-girl Milly Dowler during the police investigation of her disappearance in 2002. Davies' Milly Dowler story, which won the 2011 Paul Foot award for investigative journalism, was published in the late afternoon and immediately spread via a Twitter campaign that was seeded by *Guardian* journalists. The story set off a series of reverberations that led, a few days later, to News Corporation boss Rupert Murdoch deciding to close down the 168-year-old *News of the World* after alleged evidence of widespread illegal phone hack-ing was revealed among some of its journalists. The *Guardian* editorial team knew that this was a major new development in their ongoing investigation of the phone-hacking scandal and they saw publishing to the web first as a way of gaining an upper hand over broadcast news. But only through the mechanism of Twitter did the story have the imme-diacy they sought—an indication of how social media networks have only very recently reshaped the context of online journalism. "We broke it at 4:29 p.m.," Carol says. "You're doing it at a point in time where we could drop it and probably cause mayhem in other peoples' newsrooms when they had everything sorted out and then there was 'oh God, the *Guardian* have gone and done this.' That ability to put it out helps us ... People then identify that story as being something that is the *Guardian*'s because that's how the TV stations are reporting it. So the next day they probably go out and buy the paper ... It's allowed us to compete in ways we never could before."

Although dependent upon resource-intensive background investigations to produce the big stories in the first place, the expectation emerging here is that if former print media organizations can adapt to the new temporal rhythms of the web they can gain new advantages over the twenty-four-hour television news channels that have been pre-eminent in breaking news since they emerged in the 1980s. Here, the web emerges as savior of what were once just print media by putting newspapers in the same temporal real-time game as broadcast media.

WIKILEAKS AND THE "SONNY AND CHER THEORY"

If enhancing former print media's power in relation to broadcast media has helped spur the *Guardian*'s adoption of digital tools, there have recently been more radical changes in the organization of journalism at the paper. As I argued in my interpretation of WikiLeaks in chapter 5, the key to understanding that entity is to avoid reducing it to a simple case of how professional journalists used an online activist movement as "just another source." At the same time, however, WikiLeaks is a movement whose ability to act with meaningful power has been fundamentally shaped by its negotiated interdependence with the logics of professional older media. James Ball is one of only a few individuals in the world to have experienced both sides of this stormy collaborative relationship—what he half-jokingly described to me as the "Sonny and Cher Theory," in honor of the tempestuous creative tension inside pop music's famous "power couple" of the 1960s and 1970s.

Ball worked directly for WikiLeaks from late 2010 to early 2011 and was an assistant to Julian Assange and the WikiLeaks core team during the release of the embassy cables in December 2010. Prior to that, he had spent several months assisting WikiLeaks as a volunteer during the busy summer leading up to the release of the Iraq War logs in October 2010. Ball also performed some public duties for WikiLeaks while Assange was briefly imprisoned in December 2010 after the allegations of sexual misconduct against Assange by the Swedish prosecutor. When he left WikiLeaks in early 2011, Ball landed a full-time job as a journalist in the *Guardian*'s investigations team, working with David Leigh, the longstanding investigative reporter who played a major role in the *Guardian*'s WikiLeaks team (for more on WikiLeaks see chapter 5). (After our interview Ball went on to co-author a book about WikiLeaks with journalism scholar Charlie Beckett (Beckett & Ball, 2012)). I was keen to learn more about the practices inside WikiLeaks, as well as the alliance between WikiLeaks and its media partners. Due to his experience of crossing the boundary between activism and professional journalism, Ball was well-positioned to act as an informant.

Ball's role inside WikiLeaks speaks further to the organization's complex and contradictory nature, which I discussed in chapter 5. A large part of his work involved making the data releases accessible and usable as story material for WikiLeaks' extended network of partners around the world. This included journalists in the formal alliances Assange forged during 2010, but it also encompassed a bigger, distributed global network of writers and activists (Interview 29, September 2011). Ball spent a great deal of time sifting through the material, helping volunteer engineers test the computerized redaction systems, and suggesting stories to a wide range of media partners. The existing accounts of WikiLeaks make little of these informal connections, but Ball tells me how Assange would ask staff to give "sneaky first looks" to those outside the formal partnerships, "to try to keep them on side." Although WikiLeaks was chaotic in most respects, it had a fairly sophisticated view of its own precarious position in the hybrid media system and of how to enhance its own influence. Its aim was to try to play professional media companies off against each other, in the hope that it would avoid becoming over-dependent on any single organization. But this was also about minimizing a potential competitive backlash among those frozen out of the big-leak "exclusivity" deals that had been struck with the *Guardian*, the *New York Times*, *Der Spiegel*, *Le Monde*, and *El País*. Fearing that a broader media backlash would reduce the impact of the big leaks, there were "little rogue side deals...done to keep other outlets interested." For example, Ball gave Channel 4 News a "five-hour heads-up" on a cable revealing that the U.S. Government believed that President Rajapakse of Sri Lanka was allegedly guilty of war crimes (Interview 29, September 2011). Channel 4 News has a strong tradition of reporting on Sri Lanka, so it leapt at the opportunity to craft a scoop package for its television news and website (Channel 4 News, 2010e). WikiLeaks also gave basic hints to inquiring journalists about what the next day's cables stories would feature and Assange sent "bunches of cables to an Australian newspaper" with which he had informal links.

This approach may have made sense to WikiLeaks but it infuriated those on the other side of the agreement. There was a conflict of norms, as the long-term relationships built on reciprocity and trust that are seen as essential for "good" political journalism were severely weakened by that fact that, in Ball's words, "You couldn't trust what WikiLeaks said. You really couldn't" (Interview 29, September 2011). After all, the professional journalists were providing their expertise, without which they thought WikiLeaks would flounder.

Having said that, it is also clear from Ball's account that despite Assange's view that simply putting unannounced data releases on the WikiLeaks website would not garner the impact he craved, and despite the important role of professional journalists in crafting stories on the basis of often-impenetrable collections of data, some of this work was done in advance by Assange, his core team, and the broader network of WikiLeaks volunteers. This came "probably as a relief more for mainstream journalists than anyone else because the impact of just dropping the stuff is nowhere near [what you have] when you've had a team of people with some privileged access doing [spending] the time," says Ball. For example, Ball and his colleagues at the Bureau for Investigative Journalism were responsible for finding and then cataloging over several weeks the war logs that revealed that the United States had turned a blind eye to systematic torture and abuse inside the Iraqi military. The Bureau found twelve hundred cases. This proved to be an important story for the professional media during the official launch of the war logs in the autumn of 2010. Such details put something of a dent in the stories of heroic newspaper journalists spending weeks combing through huge databases from scratch. The "professionals" clearly had pointers from the WikiLeaks "amateurs"; indeed, given the role of the wider global network of professional journalists who were pulled in at various times to assist WikiLeaks, "amateurs" is not the most appropriate term.

The distinctions between journalism and activism, and the broader question of whether WikiLeaks constitutes a fundamental rupture with previous traditions of political reporting provokes some intriguing reflections. Ball's move to the *Guardian* changed his impression of WikiLeaks and it was clear during the interview that he was eager to draw boundaries between the norms of professional practice and those of renegades like Assange. WikiLeaks was very able in technical terms but it had an unclear grasp of its own stated principles. Ball stressed that he was a paid member of staff at WikiLeaks; he invoiced for his time and expenses as he does for all freelance work: "I'm a journalist, not an activist," he says. He feels more accountable to the public at the *Guardian* than he ever did at WikiLeaks, due to established ethical and organizational norms such as internal editorial oversight, giving individuals the right to reply in advance of publication, and responding to complaints when stories are factually incorrect: "With WikiLeaks it was transparency for everyone except itself," he says.

Ball is dubious about WikiLeaks's future following its decision to release the entire embassy cables database in unredacted form in late 2011. He sees a role for online "uncensorable publishers," but only if they work as sources that supply journalists with information. Partnerships of the kind established in 2010 are too fraught with difficulties, but if "leaks came on the quiet from newspapers trying to avoid various laws, it would do alright and someone like Julian Assange could cheerfully take credit for the scoops," he adds. In other words, this would be a return to the basis on which WikiLeaks operated in its initial guise from 2006 to 2009.

Ball reveals the latest installment in the evolution of the "Sonny and Cher Theory" of interdependence among WikiLeaks and professional media. The *Guardian*'s "open journalism" initiative launched in 2011 "actually tallies incredibly closely with Julian Assange's 'scientific journalism,'" he says. Linking to the sources of stories such as official documents, publishing databases for others to mine, and incorporating online contributions into article narratives are all aspects of this. The *Reading the Riots* project, which brought together journalists from the paper and scholars from a range of universities in Britain and America to explain the London riots of summer 2011 is a good example. In such cases the *Guardian* will "publish the data before we've even worked on it ourselves," says Ball. But then he adds a telling qualifier, revealing professional journalism's power in the context of online volunteerism—"we keep bits back."

The New Politics of Regulation

I move, finally, to the field of media regulation in Britain. Here, unsurprisingly, there is much uncertainty surrounding the development of online media. Part of the problem for actors in this domain is that the understandings originally developed for print and broadcast media only partially apply to online media, and online media has evolved a great deal since internet use first started to diffuse in the 1990s. Ed Richards, the chief executive of the Office of Communications (OFCOM), which is the closest thing Britain has to a unified broadcast media regulator, describes his agency as a "converged regulator," but explains that "government more broadly probably has a long way to go to understand the opportunities and the consequences of convergence" (Interview 4, April 2010). Britain's 2003 Communications Act was hatched during a period when the internet was only just beginning to reach the levels of popularity that have necessitated responses from policymakers over issues such as intellectual property rights and harmful online content. Yet despite this uncertainty there is also the view that OFCOM has adapted to the online media environment, in large part because it was created at the end of a long period of deregulation in broadcasting. Jay, a former senior official at OFCOM is keen to stress that "don't forget that we license 2,000 broadcasters here" (Interview 22, July 2010). Experience gained during the era of multi-channel television is here seen as providing guidance for the future regulation of the internet.

Whether this is a convincing argument remains to be seen, but it is one that finds similar expression at the center of what is, at the time of writing (the fall of 2012), the closest thing Britain has had to a print media "regulator": the Press Complaints Commission (PCC). The PCC was derided by critics as a toothless body from its beginnings in 1991 as a means of forestalling a then-emerging government agenda to regulate newspaper media. Lacking statutory powers, the PCC was essentially a system of self-regulation sanctioned by those news organizations that chose to join it—principally the tabloid-dominated national newspaper and magazine sector. As such, it had a reputation for regulatory capture. In 2012, the PCC was thrust into the spotlight as one of the players in the News Corporation phone-hacking scandal when, during witness hearings in Lord Justice Leveson's inquiry into press standards, it came under heavy criticism for failing to properly investigate previously alleged malpractice at the *News of the*

World. I interviewed Stephen Abell, the PCC's director, in April 2010. Abell joined the organization in January 2010 and moved on to work for a public relations company in February 2012. In Lord Justice Leveson's report of November 2012, the PCC received heavy criticism, and its role in the future of newspaper journalism is highly uncertain.

Like the senior staff at broadcast regulator OFCOM, Abell argues that the principles developed in the pre-internet era are being transposed now that newspapers are online. In fact, he suggests that the PCC's model of self-regulation is even better suited to the online realm because it is based upon "cooperation and collaboration" and "flexibility and transparency." He continues: "we offer a model of self-regulation where people voluntarily buy into it. Now that model actually fits online very well because of shifting jurisdictions, because of the ease of self-publication. Any form of top-down regulation doesn't really fit... The model of self-regulation fits new media really, really well" (Interview 6, April 2010).

Despite this perceived fit between the older principles of press self-regulation and what he sees as the organizing culture of online news, Abell is very keen to draw boundaries around the PCC's regulatory domains. Only those organizations that are paid-up members of the PCC are subject to its code of practice, so this rules out almost the entirety of the blogosphere. When the *Huffington Post* established its British organization in 2011 it asked to join the PCC, but that is the only exception to date, and it said more of the *Post*'s desire to blend "amateur" online news with "professional" journalism than it does of the PCC's remit. Only the online editions of the PCC's members are of interest to the PCC, which rules out vast swathes of online content.

Abell speaks of how, as newspapers and magazines moved online during the 2000s, the PCC developed a rough consensus on how it would seek to apply the principles of self-regulation to the internet; but, he adds, it has trodden gingerly during a time when print media are under commercial threat. As the interview with Abel progresses, it becomes clear that these boundaries are becoming more difficult to maintain due to the increasingly hybrid character of the production and consumption of news and the campaigns by online activists eager to score points against what is seen as a protective bastion of not only "old" media in general, but also a British newspaper sector dominated by right-wing tabloids.

In 2009, for example, there was a concerted campaign by bloggers who sought to expose unethical practice at Express Group newspapers after journalists there sourced material, including pictures, from the Facebook profiles of survivors of the Dunblane shootings of 1996. The PCC issued a ruling critical of the way the *Scottish Sunday Express* handled online sourcing. Also in 2009, the PCC received numerous complaints about an article on the *Spectator* magazine's blog by a columnist, Rod Liddle. Liddle had argued that "the overwhelming majority of street crime, knife crime, gun crime, robbery and crimes of sexual violence in London is carried out by young men from the African-Caribbean community," but the PCC found that there was insufficient evidence for this assertion. This was the first time that the PCC had sought to directly regulate a blog. The *Spectator*, sensing that it might avoid censure, argued that its blog should not be treated in the same way as the other sections of the publication (both web and print) because a blog was "conversational" in nature and the editor permitted critical comments to be published under the original article. That same year an article by *Daily Mail* journalist Jan Moir speculated that drug abuse may have been responsible for the death of gay musician Stephen Gateley, formerly of the popular group Boyzone, even though an inquest indicated that he died of an untreated heart defect. Moir's article sparked outrage among equal rights activists and led quickly to an online campaign to have the *Mail* withdraw the piece. Twitter and Facebook played important roles in coordinating the activists' protests and their subsequent complaints—twenty-five thousand of them—to the PCC. But the PCC's investigation eventually rejected the complaints and upheld Moir's right as a journalist to comment on matters of public concern. This in turn sparked another online campaign, this time against the PCC on the grounds that it was in the pocket of the *Mail*, one of Britain's most popular papers and now by far Britain's most popular news website.

Despite Abell's attempts to narrate how the PCC's older rationale has been effortlessly extended as the digital era has progressed, as he recounts these episodes it is clear that there are deeper uncertainties about how to deal with the realities of the hybrid media system. The Jan Moir case in particular provided the PCC with a missed opportunity to side with the online activist networks and bloggers that sought not only to make a point about intolerance, prejudice, and dubious ethics at tabloid papers, but also to push the PCC toward acting as a conduit for public pressure calling for better standards of journalism in general. In this sense, while Abell is keen to stress how the PCC had already adapted to the challenge of online news, in fact, it is these new dynamics in the online environment, as news becomes increasingly contested by online activist networks, that added to the climate of hostility toward the PCC by the time the Leveson Inquiry into British press standards opened in 2012.

Conclusion

The overarching theme that emerges from this fieldwork is that political news making in Britain is now characterized by incessant processes of boundary-drawing, boundary-blurring, and boundary-crossing, as the logics of older and newer media interact, compete, and coevolve. The fact that these actors constantly engage in rhetorically asserting the importance of "where they draw the line" between older and newer media practices is an important symptom of this underlying flux. The secret world of the Westminster lobby system, very much a bastion of older media practice, is to some extent under challenge from the more fluid context of political journalism that has been encouraged by the rise of the internet. Yet lobby journalists are adapting. They are building personal brands and transposing the practices of filtering and judgment-making that buttressed their professional status in broadcasting and print lobby journalism into the newer domain of online social media. Lobby journalists are also becoming attuned to the new ways in which political elites now seek to use online media to communicate directly with the public and news makers outside the lobby. In turn, those political elites are transposing strategies to control the flow of political information as they also operate across older and newer media—a development I consider in more detail in the next chapter.

These processes of boundary-drawing, boundary-blurring, and boundary-crossing are prevalent among bloggers and professional journalists, and often in surprising ways. Bloggers and activists can adopt what they consider to be the "genuine" norms of old-style, professional journalism as a way of asserting their identity and power. Professional journalists, meanwhile, can adopt some of the norms of the new-style "amateur" online domain, though with some reservations about standards and account- ability, not to mention some understandable fears about ceding their power to new competitors. Some bloggers occupy hybrid liminal spaces as semi-professional or semi-amateur journalist-activist-experts, and this enables them to occasionally inter- vene to break important political news and to interact with politicians and professional journalists in sometimes decisive ways. Such actors can maintain close links with the world of Westminster journalism and are able to tap insider sources for information on the grounds that, since the emergence of social media, a blog post can quickly cir- culate and become the subject of a professional journalist's story. Hybrid news spaces like the *Guardian's Comment Is Free* network often provide an organizational focus for what is mostly networked action, though it is important to stress that the professionals often react negatively to increased competition and the growing status of online players. Some journalists have developed norms of resistance inside "print" newsrooms, even though they are increasingly drawn into the unremitting logic of hypercompetition in online news.

Despite these forces of integration, the position of political bloggers is still precari- ous. They are often marginalized, for example, by professional media stories that frame blogging in general as being about new technologies in politics rather than about the substantive news that bloggers themselves may unearth and the new standards of pro- bity and monitorial accountability that bloggers contribute to the hybrid media system. And bloggers and online activists on social media sites are also increasingly outflanked by broadcasters who have integrated the quick temporal rhythms and conversational genres of the online news and social media domains into their routine practices, while still retaining their credibility and prestige as "investigative" journalists who have the organizational status, the resources, and the access required to hold politicians to account, even in the context of a rapidly pluralizing and fragmenting media system. Regulatory agencies like OFCOM and the PCC (which was unraveling as this book went to press) may claim that they have adapted to the new media environment, but they are increasingly drawn into a new politics that is about the symbolic differences between the logics of a fast-fading era, in which print and broadcast media ruled the roost, and a newer era of online networked activism that points to a more egalitarian but also more ethical set of norms for organizing the production, consumption, and regulation of political news.

Still, in the hybrid media system there is always another line to be drawn, some more terrain to be staked. I close this chapter with a final, particularly poignant illustration of boundary-drawing through establishing norms of resistance. This comes from an inter- view with "Jim," a former very senior journalist at the BBC. Jim ends our wide-ranging interview by arguing that a secure future for professional journalism lies in its asserting itself as something entirely distinct from what he calls the "insane Jeff Jarvis route where you have a fucking free-for-all and nothing actually emerges from it" (Interview 28, June 2011). As Jim explains, "You need to say, hang on a minute, new media is doing *this* over here, mainstream media, big media, whatever you want to call it, is doing *this* over here."

The remainder is worth quoting at length, because it illustrates very vividly what I mean by boundary-drawing as a response to the threat of newer media logics:

> Unless journalists start to wake up to what it is that differentiates them from the rest of the information universe we'll probably be exactly where we are now but slightly more confused and a bit more frayed at the edges...Because we're so neurotic about journalism—all journalists are neurotic about the trade—we've found it really, really difficult as each new web onslaught has hit us. First of all it was just search engines, for Christ's sake, which started to blow everything apart. Then it was news aggregators. Then it was Twitter. Then it was Facebook. Then it was YouTube. As each thing has hit us, we've been so neurotic about what it is we do, or the fact that we don't really know what we do or we've never really thought about it. Most practitioners don't really think about it. We thought, well, shit, we need to get a piece of this. This is going to change us. This is changing everything we do. 'Oh, we must change.' And of course you have the web gurus telling you you've got to change. At the same time, you look at some of the worst of journalism. You look at the Madeleine McCann case [of the reporting of the abduction of a British child during a family vacation in Portugal in 2007], where 106 times the *Daily Express* and the *Daily Star* just made things up about the McCanns. You look at phone hacking. And you think, actually, if I want to defend journalism as a distinct and discrete part of this universe, everybody's going to laugh at me because we're shit at things. News International, who own the *News of the World*, they see rumor and gossip as a revenue stream for them. Therefore for them gossip and rumor is what their business is all about. Now, when people like me stand up and say we must defend the rights of journalists in Syria and China and Zimbabwe because if you don't have journalists all you have is gossip and rumor, then you think, oh shit, hang on a minute, what about the *News of the World*? So we've got this kind of neurosis about who we are, what we are, what we can do...Real-time searching...You click real-time results. The first things you're getting are going to be the last things put out there. Someone retweets it, someone blogs it, and you think, yes, this is getting a head of steam behind it and it's all in real time. That looks like news. It *looks like* news. I think unless we can define journalism much more closely than we have, we'll be where we are now but worse...I think we've got to shape up now. We've got to get our act together, because the weight of stuff that's out there now is just too great....It's about getting a very clear understanding of what journalism is and how it's different from everything else" (Interview 28, June 2011).

Here, Jim makes the case that political journalism should become a unique and specialized professional domain based upon rigorous ethical standards, where the line of separation between itself and other, non-journalistic practice—the online information that "*looks like*" news—is supposedly made clear.

9

Hybrid Norms in Activism, Parties, and Government

You have to master the grid, you have to master the agenda...but unless
you're mastering it in old media you can't master it in new media.
—"Mary," senior campaign official, the British Labour Party[1]

In this chapter we move from sense making in the field of British news and journalism to that in the fields of political activism, election campaigning, and government communications. I begin by analyzing how things work at 38 Degrees, a well-known British activist movement that rose to prominence in the late 2000s and by 2012 had more than a million members. I show how 38 Degrees has created a distinctive space for itself by hybridizing norms of mobilization associated with older and newer media logics. Then I move on to explore evidence I gathered from interviews with senior campaign staff in the Conservative and Labour parties in the aftermath of the 2010 British general election, and from a number of senior officials in British government, including those who have worked at the very top, in the Office of the Prime Minister. Finally, I explore practices at the London office of an international public relations agency specializing in political campaigns.[2] Here, too, though the issues and contexts differ from those in the previous chapter, the fieldwork uncovered a variety of different sense-making strategies based upon the hybridity of older and newer media logics.

From "Building the Actions" to "Being in the Moment" in a Hybrid Mobilization Movement

The British movement 38 Degrees provides an excellent illustration of how political activists increasingly hybridize older and newer media logics in their attempts to shape news and policy agendas. Modeled in part upon America's MoveOn (see Chadwick, 2007; Karpf, 2012) and Australia's GetUp!, 38 Degrees has run several highly visible campaigns in a wide range of areas, including the environment, the National Health Service, media reform, and constitutional reform. By November 2012 it had a membership of over one million.

38 Degrees is best understood as a hybrid mobilization movement (Chadwick, 2007), but it has extended this organizational type in important ways. It emerged in

2009 from an international network coordinated by British career activists David Babbs and Hannah Lownsbrough. Ben Brandzel, who played a pivotal role in establishing MoveOn, and Jeremy Heimans, who co-founded GetUp!, performed outside advisory roles. Startup funding came from Gordon Roddick, husband of the late Dame Anita Roddick, the businesswoman and lifelong environmentalist behind the successful Body Shop retail brand. Hannah Lownsbrough had worked for several NGOs before joining 38 Degrees but had most recently helped found the London office of Avaaz, the transnational campaigning organization that has taken the MoveOn/GetUp! hybrid model of online–offline organizing and applied it internationally. Babbs, meanwhile, had previously organized Friends of the Earth's "Big Ask," which in 2006 was part of a successful broad-based campaign to introduce Britain's first significant climate change legislation. Significantly, Babbs describes Friends of the Earth as "a very traditionally constituted NGO with a very different feel" from 38 Degrees.

The third founding leader, Johnny Chatterton, arrived via a less conventional route, one highly revealing of 38 Degrees' organizational culture. Chatterton had been hired by the Burma Campaign U.K. after he "helped seed," as he puts it, one of the early examples of political activism in social media: the Support the Monks Protest Facebook group that was set up in 2007 to highlight the Burmese state's crackdown on anti-government protests led by the country's Buddhist monasteries. This experience of being a young, technologically literate online activist was important in shaping Chatterton's attitudes to organizing and mobilizing, but it was not only the power of Facebook for quickly raising awareness of international human rights abuses that fascinated him, but also how the interactions among internet and broadcast media went on to shape the evolution of that campaign. "The Support the Monks protest was incredible," he says, "because of these blurred boundaries. We had the BBC giving me a special number to call and an e-mail address to e-mail if I heard anything out of Burma, so I could pass the news straight on to these" (Interview 12, May 2010). Established NGOs such as Amnesty International also joined forces with the Facebook group activists and together they launched a Global Day of Action to raise awareness of Burma. Chatterton left to become 38 Degrees' digital campaigns manager soon afterward.

Internet-enabled experimentalism combined with efficient and strategic organizational leadership animates all 38 Degrees' activity. Babbs speaks of the need to get the technical details of the website "absolutely right" and of how important it is that the leadership provide a coherent and efficient set of mechanisms enabling members to have an influence on emerging policy agendas. There are repeated references to "providing a service" and "high standards" for members while trying to strike a balance between being "disciplined and professional" and "relaxed and experimental." Without strong strategic leadership from above and "an agenda of some sort," says Babbs, it "gets ragged and falls to bits—you lose focus and everyone feels dispirited" (Interview 12, May 2010).

A key element of this leadership-driven "service" to members is what constitutes the key organizational resource of 38 Degrees: the "actions." The organization has only four paid staff and around a dozen unpaid interns who undergo short periods of volunteering in its central London headquarters. When I visited, headquarters consisted of a couple of rooms in a slightly scruffy but functional office building off Kingsway. A small

advisory board comprising its original startup funders and some staff from other campaign organizations meets once a month for a couple of hours. 38 Degrees does not hold
real-space conferences open to members and there are no formal bureaucratic means
by which members can expect to influence the leadership's decision making. The leaders even acknowledge that the decision to call those on its e-mail list "members" was
a deliberate attempt to encourage a sense of shared identity in the absence of organizational mechanisms, though there is also an awareness that becoming a member of a
political organization raises the bar too high for many, so they talk about people "being
involved" or "joining in."

But it is the "actions" that move 38 Degrees. Actions is a totemic word because it
provides identity and collective meaning. And the construction of actions rests upon
the hybridization of older and newer media logics.

The 38 Degrees headquarters team speaks of "building the actions," "trying out the
actions," and "getting members to do the actions." On one level, actions has a simple
meaning: they are specific activities that the leadership aims to structure for its members to enable them to exert influence on the mainstream news media, online networks,
and the policy agenda. On another level, actions form the entire organizational basis
of the movement. Actions are technological enablers but they often combine online
and real-space behaviors and impacts. The website, the e-mail list, the social media
presence on Facebook and Twitter, together with the leadership team's interactions
with, and judgments about, emerging news stories are the mechanisms through which
actions are developed. Actions go beyond the simple expression of opinion in online
environments; they are constructed by the leadership team to have specific and defin-
able outcomes. Members are asked to sign online petitions or send e-mails and make
phone calls to their MPs. They are asked to show up physically at lunchtimes to protest in front of buildings around the country, as they did in 2010 against proposed cuts
to the BBC. They are asked to organize flash mobs at parties' local constituency campaign gatherings, as they did in several targeted seats during the 2010 general election,
to raise awareness of the lobbying industry (Interview 15, May 2010). The 38 Degrees
website enables these actions by providing form e-mails and online petitions that may
or may not be personalized by individual members, together with information generated from tailored web databases. Alternatively, members may be asked to very quickly
contribute donations to pay for prominent newspaper and billboard advertising. These
ads suddenly migrate messages across media settings and are designed to put pressure
on elite media and policymakers; in other words, those more likely to pay attention
to a full-page ad in a national newspaper and be spurred to call the 38 Degrees office
for more information or interview David Babbs for a television or radio package. The
ultimate aim of the actions is to send coherent, legitimized, and representative messages
to government and legislators at Westminster. Only through the ongoing construction
and modification of actions can 38 Degrees lay claim to being an "organization" in any
meaningful sense of the word.

A typical working day at 38 Degrees begins before the team arrive at headquarters.
Staff conduct "media checks" and often discuss these checks via e-mail, during the night
and in the early morning. If an important news story emerges overnight that fits with 38
Degrees' underlying progressive agenda, the leadership will then try to construct actions
to engage members as quickly as possible. The processes through which actions emerge

is therefore based upon the hybrid integration of online and offline media practices, the recalibration of strategy on the basis of perpetual online feedback from members, and a mixture of long- and short-term routines that often revolve around sharing information with other NGOs. 38 Degrees engages in rapid reaction to emerging news agendas, but it is able to do so with legitimacy because it also engages in continuous background research on its members' views. It exhibits many of the features of the classic single issue "cause" group, but its technological infrastructure allows it to rapidly switch focus from one issue to the next, run campaigns across several issues at any given time, or quickly drop campaigns that do not strike a chord with members. Timeliness is essential to this mode of operation. As Chatterton puts it: "There will be moments when people really care about something, maybe they've just seen it on the news and thought, damn I want to do something about that. We hope to be in that moment and make it easy" (Interview 14, May 2010).

E-mail underpins everything. Each month, the leadership conducts a web poll of one-twelfth of its e-mail list. At the time of my visit, the most recent of these polls had generated over five hundred responses and this was seen as a typical number (Interview 14, May 2010). The aim of the monthly poll is to provide 38 Degrees headquarters with an understanding of issues emerging among its membership base. But the poll also contains a series of tracker questions that can inform adjustments to a campaign as it evolves, as well as a free block of questions that the leaders use to "insert some questions that are just relevant to that time, stuff that we're particularly concerned about" (Interview 14, May 2010). In addition, the team issues specific polls on campaigns that they would like to see run, or it offers members a set of clear choices on how to approach a particular issue (Interview 15, May 2010). The leadership also "seed" ideas to Twitter and Facebook to get a rough sense of the levels of concern. They harvest comments on their online petitions, analyze them quantitatively, and then use the evidence in broadcast media appearances. Though Babbs expresses ambivalence about the "interview circuit" and recounts the tale of when very favorable coverage on national television news led to "only about 70 people taking an action," he regularly appears on Britain's major television and radio news shows (he fielded a call from Radio 4's *PM* in the middle of my interview). When he appeared before a House of Lords committee investigating the Digital Economy Bill in 2010, Babbs presented thematically organized aggregated evidence: over twenty thousand comments from those who signed 38 Degrees' online petition opposing the legislation.

Volunteers in 38 Degrees' headquarters continually monitor suggestions sent to them through the organization's Facebook and Twitter profiles, the website's contact form, and by e-mail. Campaigns director Hannah Lownsbrough "runs a bit of a filter" on those and then she distributes them to the other team members. The results of all of this are discussed at the weekly staff meeting, where the team take strategic decisions. Actions often emerge from these weekly meetings, but the process is not straightforward. Often members will convey strong opinions in a monthly poll but an action suggested by the leadership will fall flat. Before deciding to "go full-list" to all e-mail subscribers with a new action, the leadership usually sends out test e-mails to just a sample. It then analyzes click-through rates and conducts experiments with subject lines and framing, with the aim of generating more enthusiasm with the e-mail's next iteration. Sometimes actions continue to fail during testing and are simply abandoned. While this process is reminiscent of older-style campaign message testing in broadcast environments, the timeframes here are sometimes extraordinarily compressed, the matter of only a few hours. The whole ritual is often conducted in real time, as the team click on their automated mass e-mailer (provided by public relations agency Blue State Digital) and watch for the responses and metrics as they flow in. As Chatterton describes it: "It's fairly rapid. We can see those numbers coming in. When things go really fast you can tell. You can see it going and you think, we're fine, we can go. If you're not sure, you need to keep on waiting, and then, if you're still not sure after two hours, chances are … So we examine what's gone wrong there. Maybe the subject lines are wrong, maybe the framing was wrong, maybe the e-mail structure was wrong, or maybe there's another story that just exploded" (Interview 14, May 2010).

A good example of these micro-cycles of mobilization was the Trafigura affair of October 2009, which has gone down in recent British political history as a victory for freedom of expression over media censorship. The Trafigura affair ended with a successful campaign to overturn a superinjunction forbidding the *Guardian* newspaper from reporting a question in the House of Commons regarding allegations that a multinational oil trading company had been responsible for the illegal dumping of toxic waste in the Ivory Coast. Members of 38 Degrees played an important role alongside the *Guardian* and other British and Norwegian media organizations in quickly mobilizing a flash campaign of concerned activists focused largely around Twitter. As Chatterton reveals, victory came quickly:

> The Trafigura injunction was very interesting. We came into the office that morning and thought, what is going on here, it's dreadful being censored in this way. What can we do? We looked around and we couldn't find out through conventional networks and then Twitter started bubbling up that it was Trafigura. It probably took us about 90 minutes from coming into the office, knowing something had to be done, and getting an action out and starting to test it. And after about 15 minutes after we launched, and we'd had a crisis meeting with the volunteers, we'd all sat around, figured out what to do—the positioning. We got the e-mail ready, got the tech ready, got people writing to their MPs saying "this can't happen, you're censoring Parliament as well"— because they weren't letting people report what was being said in Parliament. And then Trafigura folded, and their lawyers Carter Ruck rescinded the superinjunction and it could be freely reported. That was an incredible two hours for us….Conventional NGOs couldn't have responded in that time frame and got that out (Interview 14, May 2010).

Speed of reaction to emerging news agendas thus plays a hugely significant role in 38 Degrees' approach to mobilization. When I suggest that this approach might put them at risk of becoming a reactive organization whose goals are defined by the headline writers of the professional media organizations, it sparks some fascinating responses. The team is keen to stress the importance of the ongoing processes of member consultation and testing, the advantages of following the mainstream media's agenda, and the significance of a particular understanding of authentic representation in contemporary political campaigning.

The leadership of 38 Degrees argues that campaigns do not simply emerge from the "back of an envelope" on a given day. It is clear that "scenario planning" for different potential outcomes, "power analysis" to determine where to apply pressure, and identifying "members' concerns" through polling and monitoring of social media takes up a great amount of daily effort (Interview 13, May 2010). Citizen organizations often have very little routine power when it comes to scheduling, particularly in spheres of politics where timeliness is important, such as when legislation enters Parliament, a public figure delivers an important speech, or the editor of a newspaper launches an investigative campaign. Babbs argues that the internet has allowed activists to "catch up with the 24-hour news cycle, which, in the 1990s, politicians had learnt to control" (Interview 15, May). As Lownsbrough puts it: "I, as a citizen, am unable to determine the parliamentary timetable. Not being an editor of a national newspaper, I am unable to determine what goes on the front page at any given time. But I am able to have an understanding of the fact that on a day when that's climate change, for example, a substantial number of our members will want to get in on that....I don't think that's allowing other people to set your agenda. I think that's just being responsive to the circumstances in which we find ourselves" (Interview 13, May 2010).

It became clear that several of the big campaigns run by 38 Degrees did not emerge from simple reactivity but from a confluence of long-term planning and nimble responses to particular events—being "opportunistic within a strategic framework," as Babbs puts it (Interview 15, May 2010). A good example is the campaign against cuts at the BBC in 2009 and 2010. This had been identified as an evolving priority but was only fully launched when James Murdoch, who was at that time the News Corp chairman and chief executive, used a high-profile speech to criticize the BBC. "We thought okay, now's the time. Let's start," says Babbs (Interview 15, May 2010). Another example is when 38 Degrees ran a series of newspaper ads calling upon its members to e-mail the Liberal Democrat MPs involved in the coalition talks during the aftermath of the 2010 general election. The aim was to pressure the party into making electoral reform a condition of entering into a coalition with the Conservatives or Labour. As I discuss in this book's opening vignette (see the Introduction), at that time 38 Degrees was also part of a networked alliance of web-enabled activist campaigns, including Take Back Parliament, Unlock Democracy, Vote for Change, Avaaz, and Power2010. Together, these groups organized a real-space demonstration in front of the nation's entire broadcast media in central London, just as the coalition talks began in earnest. Babbs live-blogged the demonstration on 38 Degrees' Facebook page using his smartphone, but he also became enmeshed with television media that day and ended up participating in a hostile interview with Sky News' Kay Burley that quickly went viral on YouTube.

But when it comes to reactivity, by far the most intriguing norm I encountered is that, in an era in which the instantaneous communication of ideas via digital technologies is increasingly the expectation, it is the duty of any activist organization to engage with the public on a real-time basis. This is because the reactive, real-time nature of a campaign is important for conveying to the public an organization's responsiveness and authenticity. Launching quick responses to the daily news agenda is more likely to convey that the leadership are adequately representing their members' concerns. This is all the more important in the absence of real-space decision-making mechanisms. Lownsbrough: "[We] ... communicate with people in a medium which they know and you know to be almost instantaneous ... If somebody sends you an e-mail and it doesn't resonate with what you're experiencing that day then that feels a bit inauthentic because it's an instantaneous form of communication. So in the interests of authenticity, when you're communicating with people over the internet I do think an awareness of what's happening that day is absolutely critical" (Interview 13, May 2010). Lownsbrough goes on to describe speed as "the contribution that online activism can bring to the activism table" and a force that can restore to those who have become disengaged from politics "some of the excitement that comes from being right in something when the decision's getting made" (Interview 13, May 2010). Thus, the belief is that reacting to the mainstream media's news reporting increases the likelihood of successful online mobilization because this will resonate temporally with members' feelings and provide symbolic rewards. Real-time response is *itself* a mechanism that generates the substantive resources of authenticity and legitimacy required by the leadership, as well as an ethic of solidarity between the leadership and 38 Degrees members. The medium again becomes the message, in a process reminiscent of what Erik Bucy and Kimberly Gregson (2001) have elsewhere termed "media participation." But still, this ability to react in real time is shaped in advance by planning and preparation. Seemingly loose, flexible, and "spontaneous" mobilization, which takes place in some cases within just a couple of hours, depends upon a blend of viral messaging across its online supporter networks, ongoing organizational capacity through online polling, a keen awareness of the policy and news cycles, and a degree of interconnectedness with the news values and temporal rhythms of older media.

These are 38 Degrees' contributions to the hybrid media system. They have enabled the movement to recruit a million members in little more than two years and, on occasion, to influence policy. In 2011 38 Degrees mobilized 530,000 people to sign an online petition, 100,000 people to e-mail their MPs, and 220,000 people to share a campaign on Facebook to stop the British government from introducing plans to privatize more than quarter of a million hectares of the nation's public forests. In a move that was based on the understanding that certain information signals are more likely to be taken seriously than others by professional journalists and political elites, it also raised funds to commission the professional polling company YouGov to ask a representative sample of the British public about their views on the government's forest proposals. The results revealed that 84 percent were opposed to the plans. To reinforce the poll's findings, the 38 Degrees members then raised £60,000 from members to pay for a series of full-page ads publicizing the poll's findings in national newspapers. Babbs and Lownsbrough also made several television and radio appearances. Within a few weeks, the government's plans were withdrawn.

As this analysis reveals, 38 Degrees employs a careful division of labor in its approach to media. Online media are perceived as better for tight feedback loops, coordination, more active engagement, and representing the movement to itself. But being able to publicize its action through broadcast and print media helps target policy elites, validate the movement, and create highly visible signs of its efficacy for wider publics. This norm of a division of labor in media logics also underpins emerging practice in the fields of election campaigning and government, to which I now turn.

Blurring the Boundaries Between "New Media," "Press," and "Communications"

In the run-up to the 2010 British general election there was a frenzy of commentary about the role the internet might play in the campaign. This was fueled by the view that the medium had decisively shaped the 2008 American presidential campaign. As I showed in chapters 6 and 7, such an interpretation is only partly correct: the internet's role in 2008 is better understood if it is set in the context of its interactions with older media, particularly television. With this in mind, I was eager to explore insider views of election campaigning and government communications in the British context. I wanted to learn about how those working inside parties and government were making sense of claims about the growing role of online media in their fields of practice. My analysis in this section draws upon interviews I conducted with senior officials who were work-ing (or who had recently worked) inside Labour and Conservative party headquarters, senior officials working at the Cabinet Office and the Foreign and Commonwealth Office (FCO), former senior officials in the Prime Minister's Office, a director of the London office of an international public relations agency dealing with political cam-paigns, and a former press officer for the trade union movement. Across these fields, I identified an overarching process of transition from organizational norms that depend upon quite clear divisions between the roles of "new media" and "press," toward a newer, more integrated set of norms based upon what those working in these fields often sim-ply label "communications." However, this is a process riddled with tensions and contra-dictions. There are significant differences of emphasis in how things are evolving across different organizational fields, and it is clear that much is up for grabs. Still, "communi-cations" is now increasingly deployed to provide an overarching identity for a diverse range of roles and to enact an integrated approach to persuasive strategic communica-tion in the fields of election campaigning and government communications.

Craig Elder worked as a senior member of the Conservative Party's communications team from 2006 to 2011. I interviewed Elder soon after the 2010 general election. He sums up the Conservatives' campaign as being about the integration of "new media" personnel with the senior decision-making team. A previous distinction between "IT" and "communications" is now disappearing, he argues, as communications is becoming a realm that encompasses strategic decisions about online campaigning but no longer includes the daily grunt work that is now carried out by IT staff. As he puts it:

> Basically the internet used to be this thing, it was over there, it was in a cupboard, it was the guys who fixed your mouse who were the same guys who updated the stuff on the website. The guys in the press office would churn out a press release, it would be slapped up on the website, it would have a little picture put next to it, and that was the way you ran a website. What our team, which was brought in very early in David Cameron's leader-ship, was in essence brought in to do was really to wrestle that responsibil-ity away from an IT department, which has a very particular function, and move that across to a more communications-focused team. Essentially we are a marketing team, an advertising team, a communications-focused team.

We have technical skills within our team but it's not our predominant reason for being.... That's the overwhelming change within the organization
(Interview 9, May 2010).

The Conservatives' new media staff went from being "out in the cold, excluded," to having
their leader, Rishi Saha, present at every senior campaign war room meeting during the
2010 campaign. The online staff had their own budget and reported directly to the party
leader. In some respects, this is remarkably similar to the model of online campaigning
established by Obama in 2008 (see chapter 6). And as we shall see, this approach was also
adopted by the British Labour Party in 2010, though with a different inflection.

How has this approach embedded itself in the practices of campaign headquarters?
First, the Conservatives sought to use the internet as part of a broader attempt to "mod-
ernize" how they presented themselves to the electorate. The party's then director of
strategy, Steve Hilton, clearly saw the symbolic power of internet communication as
useful for softening and "humanizing" the party leadership and conveying a new ethos
of openness and willingness to engage with the public. The newer medium and its logic
became part of the newer message. Elder continuously refers to the importance of being
"honest" and "transparent" and speaks of the party making "big, big efforts to communicate in different ways and emphasize different qualities." The web is central here
because "it makes you look fresh and modern and innovative." While this approach had
a direct impact on the party's presence on the web, it was also aimed at newspaper and
broadcast media, who were looking for evidence of Cameron's attempt to move the
Conservative Party away from the "nasty party" image it acquired during the 1990s.
Inside the top echelon of the party, the web has therefore become totemic of an important cultural shift.

Second, the party has sought to integrate online opinion-formers into the orbit of
its press relations. It did this by actively encouraging the formation of a network of elite
bloggers and online activists that constitute an important part of what amounts to a new
extended and distributed "Westminster village." Organized around high-profile blogs
like those of Guido Fawkes and Iain Dale, and the activist community *Conservative Home*
led by Tim Montgomerie and Jonathan Isaby, this network began to provide important
lines of communication between the grassroots and the leadership. From the party's
2006 annual conference onward, bloggers were given press passes and were encouraged
to organize fringe meetings. While Conservative multimillionaire donor Lord Ashcroft
bought a majority stake in a new parent company he established for *Conservative Home*
in 2009 (M. Bell, 2009), thereby putting beyond any doubt that Montgomerie and his
team were seen as a select elite, the relationship between central office and these new foci
for grassroots discourse has not always been harmonious. Elder speaks of Montgomerie
as being "treated like a journalist" and likens dealing with *Conservative Home* to "herding cats," a term that implies that headquarters has sometimes attempted to steer and
control. But Elder goes on to put it in a way that implies a more equal balance of power:
"the centre-right blogosphere has been a critical friend rather than necessarily a mouth-
piece," he says. These prominent websites are seen as a tremendous resource for the
party but they are also rivals for attention, especially during election campaigns, when
the party leadership wants to target floating voters with its own website (Interview 9,
May 2010).

Integrating online opinion with traditional "press" functions also works in another way. It is significant how party central office staff used online media throughout the campaign. Twitter use cut across the divide between new media and press officer staff inside Conservative headquarters, but there were interesting residual logics at play in each camp. The Conservatives' chief press officer Henry Macrory used Twitter as a rapid rebuttal and propaganda tool to communicate in real time with a large though still select group of political journalists. This stridently partisan approach owed a great deal to the traditions of behind-the-scenes spin doctor practice and targeted private text messaging that I discussed in the previous chapter. Several journalists and bloggers commented on the often-caustic nature of Macrory's tweets (Political Scrapbook, 2010). Yet Elder and some of his colleagues took a gentler approach, one shaped by the informal, conversational, and eclectic genres of discourse in online social media environments. They tweeted very regularly in support of their party's position, but seldom did they use personal attacks, and they also interspersed their political tweets with nonpolitical content. These messages provided resources for retweeting among time-pressed Conservative leaders and candidates. When I ask him about the extent to which this was consciously planned, Elder says it was not, though he does admit that they "know what the rules of the game are" and were all "playing the safety-first rule" during the campaign.

A third way in which the Conservatives came to integrate the internet into their campaigning took the form of a number of prominent experiments in online engagement. Yet the logic of these experiments is to influence coverage in older media. In March 2010, the party organized its own "crowd-sourced" response to the Labour government's pre-election Budget, but the more than a thousand public comments this attracted were not published on the web in real time, out of fear that the exercise might be hijacked by supporters of the other parties or even give advance notice to the government of what the Conservative leadership might use in their post-Budget critique. Thus, what seems on the surface to be a model exercise in democratic engagement using the affordances of the internet actually becomes disciplined by the logics of control and spin and the temporal rhythms of broadcasting.

For the 2010 election the Conservatives launched MyConservatives.com, a tailor-made online social network site modeled loosely on the U.S. Democrats' MyBarackObama.com (see chapter 6). Central office encouraged candidates to establish profiles on "MyCon" and use it to raise funds for specific issues. They also saw it as a way to energize local volunteers, including, unusually for British politics, those who were not paid-up party members. The results were mixed. Elder says that around a hundred candidates (out of 650) "used it really well," that "thousands" of volunteers were involved and it was "a moderate success." MyCon also caused some internal friction between the party treasurer, who wanted to use traditional fundraising methods, and the communications team, who were more interested in experimenting with online engagement as a route to fundraising (Interview 9, May 2010).

But to what extent do the stated aims of these types of experiments actually matter at all? An important theme of these interviews with party and government personnel is the value that is ascribed to using the internet to gain exposure in older media. The MyCon online social network received mainstream coverage from the BBC's technology correspondents. The crowd-sourced budget response resulted in a story in the *Evening Standard* about planned changes to the pension system. "I don't think in our wildest

dreams we ever thought we were going to get a story out of what came out of there..."
says Elder. In other words, the criteria for success in these experiments in online engagement are not necessarily those associated with the participatory logics of digital media.
Instead, they often derive from the strategic logics of the "press" campaign practices that
evolved with older media. There is a need to be seen by broadcast and newspaper media
as eye-catching, fresh, and different and to offer visible evidence of such, which professional journalists can then use in their stories about the campaign.

These hybrid newer media–older media logics also run through the fourth way in
which the blurring of the distinctions between "new media," "press," and communications is being played out: the growth of a much more carefully considered approach to
the online campaign and a growing awareness of what are becoming the settled realities of web use among mass publics. Integrating digital media into the campaign is now
about proving online campaigning's worth as a system of practices based upon "specialist" or even "hidden" expertise that can deliver hard, calculable results. (I explored
this in relation to the 2008 Obama campaign in chapter 6). In this sense, social media
engagement, apart from its value in attracting elite media coverage to the campaign
along the lines I just discussed, is often window-dressing. What really matters now are
the dark arts of Google AdWords, search engine optimization, and the geodemographic
targeting of online messages. All of this is now situated in the context of a media system
in which it is acknowledged that broadcasters usually have mastery over the temporal
rhythms of the campaign, so the online campaign will do better if it synchronizes with
those rhythms even though online campaign professionals are the only ones able to
provide the high levels of technical expertise and insider knowledge required to master
these new technologies.

The biggest overall shift in 2010 (across all parties) was the amount of time and financial resources devoted to rebuilding websites to tap into the advantages gained by writing copy that ensures a site will appear prominently in Google's search results, so-called
"search engine optimization." These advantages can also come from buying Google
AdWord keywords so that web users searching for information are more likely to be
presented with links to the party's main website. The AdWord campaigns are planned
in advance to coincide with the big older media-driven events of the campaign, which
in 2010 were the televised prime ministerial debates. But AdWords are also changed
in response to unforeseen developments, such as breaking news stories. Just as television messaging became obsessively focused around targeting the undecided voter from
the 1980s onwards, now online strategy is being targeted away from the activists and
toward those larger sections of the public likely to be quickly Googling the election,
often during or soon after a big broadcasting moment, or even on election day itself.
Elder explains:

> The center of the project was we took a decision in 2008 to rebuild
> Conservatives.com around 26 key policy areas, to make sure that everything on
> the site pointed via a database to reference those 26 key policy areas, to make
> sure that the Conservative Party first and foremost won on search, so people
> could search "Conservative education," "Conservative immigration" and find
> that... Google search, Google ads, were a massive, massive part of our strategy
> as well, for reasons that I won't sort of [go into]... We used it both strategically,

on days like the budget, to make sure our message was out there and then when it came round to the election campaign we used far more of a blanket approach, so if you're searching for anything from your local Labour MP all the way through to terms like "hung parliament," "polling booth," "where's my polling station?," you would see messages from us and we would tailor that very much accordingly, and I think that history will show that to be a success. So that's not sexy stuff, if you like, but for me it's the reason we won the digital war. The fact is that we had digital media correspondents...from the BBC and the *Financial Times*...who were working on this and they always want to know about the buzzy thing, they always want to know what you're doing on Facebook, what you're doing on Twitter. And the fact is that if you pay too much attention to these things, if you get pulled into whatever the fashion of the day is, you lose.... You end up speaking to people that aren't your key audience. So we were all about floating voters. Our website was designed for one group of people, floating voters, on one particular day—May 6 as it turned out to be (Interview 9, May 2010).

This new approach to online campaigning has also become embedded in the Labour Party, though here there are important differences of emphasis. Labour had its own Google AdWords campaign in 2010. Though less lavishly funded than the Conservatives', it was still strategically oriented around the broadcast-mediated events of the campaign. As "Mary," a senior campaign official based in Labour headquarters explains:

We did a lot around the debates in particular and had a really great guy working on AdWords who understood quality scores, and we were getting awesome value for money and positioning was working really well for us. We were competing with the Conservatives because we spent a lot of time thinking about quality score and making sure that the keywords on the landing page matched the keywords in the AdWord itself. All that stuff that Google rewards you for with better positioning and lower CPC [cost per click], we were mastering that. They [the Conservatives] obviously had one thing they were putting on the AdWords and they were just blasting them out to thousands of keywords. If you understand how AdWords work, Labour's got a far more sophisticated strategy on this, by virtue of the fact that we had to—rewriting the copy, testing it, doing different variations, and constantly updating and changing it to reflect what was and wasn't working. That was good (Interview 21, June 2010).

Like the Conservatives, Labour worked for several years before the 2010 election to optimize its websites for maximum impact on Google. Even local candidate sites were subjected to this logic, as central staff advised constituency parties to try to raise their profiles by piggybacking on the search terms that local people might be using to find out about services in their areas, such as the rebuilding of schools and hospitals—a policy area that Labour was keen to stress. Labour also integrated its new media staff into the main campaign war room. Every morning, a senior figure from the new media team attended the 7:00 a.m. meetings, which usually consisted of about ten people, including Peter Mandelson, Alistair Campbell, Douglas Alexander, and longstanding party pollster Philip Gould. By the close of the election Labour had a historically large number of headquarters staff—twelve in total—working on the online aspects of the campaign, though as we shall see, what precisely counts as "online" is becoming more difficult to distinguish.

The central difference between Labour and the Conservatives is that Labour placed much more emphasis on attempting to integrate the web with their ground campaign. The Labour staff I interviewed all speak of their background in "organizing" as well as "communications" and of the need to energize their own supporters rather than use the web to appeal to undecided voters, a goal they believe is better achieved by other media, particularly television (Interview 21, June 2010; Interview 26, January 2011). Indeed, this is a source of pride, a rejection of what "David," a senior campaign official, sees as the inauthentic "PR" ethos of the Conservatives (Interview 26, January 2011). So Labour also sought to learn from the Obama model, but it had an advantage over the Conservatives because as early as 2006 it had established Membersnet, a rudimentary online social network of sorts. Labour also managed to embed an Obama-style virtual phone banking system early on, which allowed party members to call members of the public in key constituencies and instantly submit the responses online to a central database. "Cynthia," a former campaign official for Labour describes Membersnet and the online phone bank as "the big successes of the 2010 election" (Interview 20, June 2010). But as we saw in chapters 6 and 7, the Obama model is as much about older media as it is about the internet, and the internet is most powerful when it is used—by parties, journalists, celebrities, or members of the public—in consonance with television. Labour sought to use the same approach in the 2010 British campaign. As David says: "As a digital unit we have to face both ways and have an understanding and ability to move on both fronts. The relationship between the new media team and the press team has always been a good one … Working together, there's not a barrier to it as much as there was years ago … It's now a fairly inclusive process." (Interview 26, January 2011). But how does this relationship actually work in practice and what are the outcomes?

"Strategy" and "Tactics"

Mary, a senior campaign official for Labour, makes an important distinction between what she terms "strategy" and "tactics." By *strategy* she means embedding the internet in field operations—gathering e-mails, creating and refining databases, targeting and mobilizing activists via Membersnet to spread the word about the party's policies and its candidates, and spurring people to take real-space action such as door-knocking, canvassing, and driving voters to the polls. By *tactics*, she means using the internet, and social media in particular, to attract attention from broadcasters and newspapers in the hope of "influencing the media and influencing the story" (Interview 21, June 2010). Mary believes that using the internet for field operations is much more likely to produce concrete results, but there is always a strong temptation among senior politicians and press officers to use the internet for merely tactical purposes, to get a quick hit from broadcast media coverage. Labour had its own share of tactical behavior in 2010, such as consulting on their manifesto via Twitter, and asking young activist blogger "Bevanite Ellie" Gellard to speak at the televised rally to launch the campaign. Mary is keen to stress that Gellard "wasn't manufactured, she was genuine," but acknowledges that the party communications team were "still playing old media's game." Older media logics are here presented as diluting the potential of newer media.

This distinction between the norm of strategy and the norm of tactics has deep roots in British parties' web use and it goes right to the very top of government. "Bill," a senior official in the Cabinet Office, speaks of "a big divide" between the "strategic communications" people and the "news" people inside government departments. While the strategic communications staff have integrated digital communication into their approach, he says, the press teams still tend to "think in terms of print and broadcast media" and of how the internet might fit into their universe (Interview 11, May 2010). Bill tells the story of how strategic communications staff, unhappy with the large number of silent television screens constantly tuned to Sky News and BBC News in government offices, introduced a social media monitoring tool provided by web company Netvibes. Interestingly, these skirmishes were recounted to me in another interview—with "John," a senior official in the Foreign Office: "for some reason, I'm getting more and more TV screens put in my office, and I don't want another bloody TV screen, thank you very much. I don't need it, I don't want that, but they keep putting them in" (Interview 2, April 2010). Bill at the Cabinet Office argues that the shifts have come in those departments where ministers have become attuned to online communication and have instructed their communications staff to integrate it into their daily work. He says of his own job: "This isn't an IT role."

"Neil" and "Kate" are both former officials from the Prime Minister's Office who worked under Tony Blair during the closing years of his premiership and then for a period under Gordon Brown when he took over as prime minister in 2007. Neil tells me about the power of the traditional press officers inside Number 10 and the broader Labour Party. While Labour occupied Number 10, the press officers were risk-averse veto players who had the power of sign-off over all media activity: "So it was quite a battle with press. That was evident straight away. Everything we wanted to do, we had to talk to press about it. And as press people are, they were very conservative about taking risks." In those days, there were clear boundaries between the small group of three or four individuals working on new media projects at Number 10 and the prime minister's larger press team, not to mention the broader legions of press officers in the Cabinet Office. Neil speaks of the "old structure set up in '97 that was there to service traditional media, quite rightly, and that was what worked." But this structure strongly influenced the approach to online media. The website became dominated by "a collection of press releases...that were only useful for certain types of people—journalists" (Interview 19, June 2010).

During the final year of Blair's premiership, the emphasis shifted somewhat, as a new experimental culture began to develop at Number 10, driven in large part by Ben Wegg-Prosser, who became Blair's Director of Strategic Communications. Wegg-Prosser led a small team that introduced the Downing Street e-Petitions site and launched the prime minister's YouTube channel, the first of its kind in the world for a government head. Wegg-Prosser was quite close to Blair and convinced him that online engagement might be used strategically by Number 10. But the reasons behind this are revealing. As Neil explains, "I think he understood that the press goes in new media's favor also. If we do something good, the press picks up on it and it becomes a story and that happened with the YouTube thing" (Interview 19, June 2010). Kate, meanwhile, explains that the decision to start promoting Number 10 on the web stemmed from a desire to "see some level of control" over messaging in the hostile media environment that characterized the late period of Blair's premiership and almost the entirety of Brown's: "Basically, the theory became, that with media fragmentation, that everyone's a publisher...you might as well try and take control of the media, and become a primary source" (Interview 3, April 2010). In this approach, self-publishing via online media comes to be seen as a means of bypassing an increasingly truculent broadcast and newspaper media. Revealingly, Kate on several occasions uses the term "broadcasting" to describe what they were trying to achieve with the changes to the Number 10 website from 2007 onward.

The Number 10 YouTube experiments were often amateurish. Neil tells the story of how, when professional filmmakers were in Downing Street shooting other footage, Blair mocked the new media team's "rubbish little video camera." Some of Number 10's videos nevertheless struck a chord and had the desired effect with older media, such as Blair's French-language video congratulating Nicolas Sarkozy upon his election as French president in May 2007. Kate explains how this changed traditional press officers' views of the internet inside Number 10:

> Then people like David Hill, who at first was very doubtful about this—and I don't mean this pejoratively—but where a man of his generation kind of got it—is on that holiday weekend, when we did this Sarkozy thing, we were second on the BBC teatime news, with the medium *and* the message: "Blair's got a YouTube channel, Blair's congratulating Sarkozy." Now, Blair congratulating Sarkozy wouldn't merit a mention on any TV news without that mechanism. So then they kind of understood that we were having control and we were having impact and there was a ripple effect from what we were doing (Interview 3, April 2010).

While press officers were still resistant, due to what they saw as the inherently risky nature of online political communication, they were now able to see benefits in terms they more clearly understood. Brown's press team also understood the power of the political bloggers, Kate says, but only because these were perceived as simply an extension of the political gossip networks of the Westminster village. This was the press officers' way of integrating the internet into their practice. But it is clear that they were not interested in online engagement for any other reason. Instead, they sought to use the internet to try to place positive stories about the prime minister on television and radio.

A certain logic of integration has thus emerged. Elite politicians, their press staff, and their special advisers can see online communication working when it gets them mainstream media coverage on television, radio, and in newspapers. The online communications staff seem happy because these stories invariably highlight their innovative use of the internet. When this logic falls apart, as it did when an online petition protesting government plans to introduce a national road charging scheme quickly secured 1.7 million signatures on the Downing Street e-Petitions website in 2007, the press officer "firing squad," as Kate describes them, "line[d] up" to insist that the "measure of success is the message" (i.e., not the medium) and that they should not just make the news because "we're doing something online" (Interview 3, April 2010). The risks on that occasion were seen as too great. The government quickly abandoned its road-pricing scheme and the online petition was the cause, though this was never pub-licly admitted (Interview 3, April 2010).

When Gordon Brown took over from Blair as prime minister in 2007, the experi-mental phase inside Number 10 wound down and Brown employed his own team of communications staff. Wegg-Prosser and several others left and new personnel arrived, such as Damian McBride, who became a special adviser to Brown and handled much of media relations. This period saw the intensification of the tactical approach to online media. The new team continued with the attempts to use YouTube for what they thought would be headline-grabbing interventions that would put Brown in a positive light. The "nadir" of this approach, as Kate describes it, was what became known simply as the "*Countdown* video." *Countdown* is a long-running, moderately popular, but low-budget British daytime television quiz show that celebrated its twenty-fifth anniversary in 2007. Like other daytime television shows, it has something of an ironic "cult follow-ing" among the young. McBride had the idea to make a Downing Street YouTube video featuring Brown congratulating *Countdown* on reaching this milestone. The new media staff were opposed but they were overruled by McBride. The result was something of a minor disaster. Brown delivered an extraordinarily wooden speech direct to the camera, in which he reminisced over the show's contribution to British national culture. The video fell flat and the sense emerged that these "softer" online forms of communication exposed Brown to ridicule by professional political journalists who liked nothing better than new hooks for stories about the government's attempts to influence their coverage. As a consequence, Brown's team put "digital way down the pecking order" and in the run-up to the 2010 poll went "back to the old ways" of targeting elite journalists with stories that they wanted to be placed in friendly newspapers (Interview 3, April 2010). In 2009, the "Smeargate" affair saw it emerge that McBride and another Labour adviser, Derek Draper, had been planning to launch a new "gossip blog" called Red Rag that would publish details of the private lives of leading Conservatives. This episode, which led to Damian McBride's resignation from Number 10, was a signal of the colonization of the new media strategy by the "old ways" of spin and misinformation that had plagued the Labour government's dealings with the media since it first came to power in 1997.

Still, this tactical approach is understandable if we consider the other forces at play. It should come as no surprise that political journalists often respond with derision to gov-ernment's attempts to use digital media tactically, not least because they wish to protect their status as gatekeepers. Bill, a senior official in the cabinet office, revealed how, in his experience, journalists become unhappy if news is released via Twitter or a blog post rather than a formal press release. This happened during the launch of a new website and a new initiative to release government data in 2010, for example: "we launched with a single tweet...that was the only breaking of the news...and we had complaints from the press that we'd announced something without a press release!" (Interview 11, May 2010).

"Joined-Upness"

Despite these significant conflicts between the norms of older and newer media logics inside government and the Labour party, and despite Mary's moderate dismay about the prevalence of tactical online campaigning inside Labour's communications team, her distinction between tactical and strategic integration of the internet can only take us so far in understanding the party's approach to communication. This is because, in Mary's perspective, a strategic approach to the internet is defined mainly in terms of the contribution it makes to the ground campaign. There is, however, a good deal of evidence from these interviews that if strategy is understood in a more expansive sense, a strategic set of norms is indeed emerging. Much of this revolves around the ongoing integration of internet and broadcast media campaigning, and this is occurring on lines that are strikingly similar to those I discussed in relation to the American campaign context in chapters 6 and 7.

For Labour, this process began around 2007, when the mobile web took off and MPs, cabinet ministers, and their press staff and special advisers started to use social media. Mary suggests that smartphones made the web appealing to those among the Westminster elite who have staff to process their paperwork and who are "on the go all day" as they move between meetings, television studios, and parliamentary debates. The online team began asking senior politicians to use their television and radio appearances as opportunities to point the public to their websites. As part of this approach, Labour started to use a variety of new "microsites" tied to specific single-issue campaigns spearheaded by individual cabinet ministers. Two good examples are the "Ed's Pledge" site and "Back the Ban." Ed's Pledge was designed to tie in with then climate change secretary Ed Miliband's activities in the run-up to the 2009 U.N. Climate Change Conference in Copenhagen. Back the Ban was launched in 2009 but was given a boost in February 2010 when environment secretary Hilary Benn organized the mass online signing of a letter to David Cameron asking him to drop his party's opposition to the ban on fox hunting. As Mary says: "That's something we've spent a lot of time working on. One of the things that we kept saying was this online stuff only works if it's integrated with offline...We did do a lot of work with the press officers and with ministers themselves to say if we are launching a campaign you need to promote it offline....It wasn't perfect but that was definitely where we trying to get to in terms of joined-upness" (Interview 21, June 2010). These microsites were also useful for harvesting e-mail addresses from those who might be drawn into the party's orbit on a single issue but less likely to join as a dues-paying members.

During the 2010 campaign itself, Labour put its own inflection on the real-time integration of broadcasting and social media, a process that, as I show above, was also prioritized by the Conservatives. Labour "spent a lot of time thinking, in the run-up to the election, that the television debates were going to be really important and how we could maximize that online" (Interview 21, June 2010). Party staff established a social media dashboard on the main Labour website during each live televised debate, with the aim of harnessing the energy of those who Mary describes as "dual-screening"; watching the debate on their televisions while simultaneously engaging with others in social media environments using a smartphone, tablet, or laptop. The goal was to provide a common pool of information and opinion on what was said during the debates in the hope that this would prove useful for party activists as they went back to their constituency work the next day. There was also the hope that party members would be able to forward links and opinion from the online dashboards to their family and friends soon after each debate. At the same time, the party's research and policy units were on Facebook and Twitter during the debates, pushing out rapid rebuttals and reinforcements to journalists in real time as the debates progressed, under the heading "Get the Facts." A real-time media war room was established specially for each debate and this accompanied the frenzy of interaction among politicians, party staff, and journalists that I documented in chapter 4.

This did not always run smoothly: Mary speaks frustratedly of many senior politicians failing to sign off on news releases, even individual tweets, quickly enough for them to have impact in the real-time news environment. Unlike the Conservatives, Labour has rules that strongly discourage back-room staff from being named in press releases, so they were unable to adopt the strategically informal approach to social media at which the Conservatives' central office staff excelled. Frustrations also arose due to what were often still-entrenched divisions of labor among the senior press team and the new media team. It is clear that the press officers were the gatekeepers when it came to interacting with journalists. New media staff briefed journalists, but only with the approval of the press officers. And then there were the big unscheduled television moments of the campaign, such as Sky News's recording of Gordon Brown's supposedly "off-mic" comments about his awkward encounter with voter Gillian Duffy on the streets of Rochdale. As Mary says, "You have to master the grid, you have to master the agenda. And then if you know you're master of the agenda and you know you've got a story on Friday that is campaignable and is something you can be successful online about, then you can get ready…but unless you're mastering it in old media you can't master it in new media" (Interview 21, June 2010).

I turn, finally, to "Mike," the director of the London office of an international public relations agency. Mike's agency's practice exhibits the same tension between tactical and strategic integration of the internet that can be found in Number 10 and the Labour Party, but again, if we push this distinction too far, it starts to dissolve, to reveal an emerging set of practices that strategically blend older and newer media logics.

Around half of Mike's agency's clients are progressive political organizations; the rest are companies and other public bodies. The agency has established a reputation for innovation in digital campaigning and it offers clients tools such as mass e-mail databases, a website builder, a fundraising platform, an event planner, an online petition generator, and integration with Facebook and Twitter. But during the interview it soon became clear that much of what Mike's agency does involves blending online and offline action of various kinds. In common with several of the other domains I cover in this book, a division of labor in media logics is emerging in political public relations.

Mike tends to focus efforts online during the early stages of a campaign, as a means of building a base for future action and harnessing activist enthusiasm. The internet also enables a permanent and intense campaign, one that also allows the leadership to quickly switch emphasis without disorienting their networks of supporters. But during the closing stages of a campaign, Mike says, almost all effort shifts to interacting with broadcast and newspaper media and professional journalists. By the same token, the internet is seen as useful for structuring online activism using petitions, consultations, and social media sharing, yet it is also seen as useful for negative campaigning, or what Mike prefers to call "contrast" campaigning, because "You can put information into the public domain much more easily than you could before—anonymously." Mike used to feed bloggers stories that he needed to be circulated quickly, and he would recognize that what he sacrificed in terms of simple audience reach he might make up for in virality and speed of circulation. But now, Mike says, he feeds bloggers and journalists in the same way, because if the vast majority of professional journalists are publishing their stories online throughout the day, there is often little point in distinguishing between them and bloggers. By the same logic, when Mike targets broadcast and newspaper journalists with pieces of information, he will specifically suggest that a broadcast or newspaper journalist tweet it or mention it in a blog post rather than save it for the television or the next day's paper.

Thus, Mike's organization is developing a sense of what is likely to play well across different media, but this is, he says, increasingly driven not by audience size, but by audience type, together with an awareness of the circulatory and amplifying logics of the hybrid media system. He may try to influence a blogger, safe in the knowledge that the blog will also be read regularly by professional journalists. He may ask a professional journalist with a large following on Twitter to tweet a piece of information, safe in the knowledge that online activists will be exposed to it and spread it through interpersonal networks (Interview 16, June 2010).

Conclusion

This chapter has explored how those working in the fields of political activism, parties, and government in Britain are forging and adapting to the hybrid media system. I have shown how activist movement 38 Degrees cannily switches between older and newer media logics in its attempts to mobilize supporters and influence policy. It uses a division of labor between older and newer media to structure the "actions" that serve as its only meaningful organizational basis, but as David Karpf has argued in the U.S. context, this is not "organizing without organizations" but "organizing *with different* organizations" (Karpf, 2012: 3). The leadership engages in constant monitoring of the views of its members through a variety of sophisticated digital tools and it uses the knowledge gained from these processes to prepare for the launch of campaigns that are often timed for when an issue is prominent in broadcast and newspaper media. There is also a strong normative attachment to being able to react extraordinarily quickly to issues that rise to prominence in the "mainstream." Responsiveness produces and reproduces identity and solidarity because it meets expectations of authenticity and connectedness that have become embedded as cultural values among activists online. And yet the actions that 38 Degrees' leadership asks its networks of supporters to perform, like donating money for ads in newspapers and commissioning opinion polls, are often far removed from what we might think of as online activism. Indeed, they rest upon and capitalize upon an acceptance of broadcast and newspaper media's enduring roles. These new democratic forms of politics are carved out of the hybrid interstitial spaces between older and newer media.

We have seen how, in the field of parties and election campaigns, there is a contested blurring, but a blurring nonetheless, between the practices of "new media" and "press" staff. This is being enacted by the integration of both of these domains under the umbrella of "communications," as part of a general shift toward bringing digital practices into the core decision-making structures of British election campaigning. There are differences in emphasis across the two largest parties. Labour's approach rests more heavily on integrating the internet into the ground war, while the Conservatives have placed greater emphasis on targeting the undecided voter through effective online messaging. Yet online campaign teams in both of these parties have now settled on a range of back-room practices that provide resources for staking their claim to a seat in the war room, such as the use of Google AdWords campaigns. There are clear divisions between the self-described strategic and tactical aspects of integrating the internet, and those expecting hybridity in these particular fields to generate unbridled new opportunities for citizen engagement should prepare to be disappointed, especially when compared with the fields of news and journalism that I discussed in chapter 8. These fields therefore stand in contrast with the hybrid mobilization typified by 38 Degrees.

As the evidence in this chapter from those working at the very top of British government reveals, "tactical" rather than "strategic" integration provides the most powerful logics for combining broadcast-era control and spin with the fluidity of the internet, primarily because it does not unduly threaten the identity, routines, and therefore the power of traditional press staff. Tactical integration has, nevertheless, enabled hybridity to emerge, as it did during the 2010 election when all parties sought to run their online campaigns in consonance with broadcast media coverage dominated by the televised prime ministerial debates, in echoes of the developments we saw in the U.S. context in chapters 6 and 7. Even those working at the forefront of public relations and advertising, who see themselves as putting digital tools at the center of their campaigning practice, have a strong sense of the appropriateness of a division of labor between older and newer media. And the very idea of a division of labor, is, after all, based on the premise of systemic interdependence.

Conclusion: Politics and Power in the Hybrid Media System

That was the river, this is the sea.
—Mike Scott[1]

In this book, I have endeavored to show that political communication in Britain and the United States is now shaped by what is best described as a hybrid media system. By exploring a range of examples of this systemic hybridity in flow, in interactions and exchanges in the fields of news making, election campaigning, citizen activism, and government, I have shown how the interactions among older and newer media logics—where logics are understood as technologies, genres, norms, behaviors, and organizational forms—shape the power relations among political actors, media, and publics. Power in the hybrid media system is exercised by those who are successfully able to create, tap, or steer information flows in ways that suit their goals and in ways that modify, enable, or disable others' agency, across and between a range of older and newer media settings.

The hybrid media system is based upon conflict and competition between older and newer media logics but it also features important pockets of interdependence among these logics. Actors in the interpenetrated fields of media and politics simultaneously generate and shape the very hybridity that they then seek to exploit. As I argued in chapter 1 and have shown throughout, systems must be constructed, enacted, and reenacted, in ongoing acts of modification that over time become significant. Power in political communication is relational. It is shaped by hybrid networks of social and technological actants whose agency derives from their interdependence with other social and technological actants in interactive exchanges.

Political communication actors constantly mobilize but also constantly traverse the networks and logics of older and newer media to advance their values and interests. They do this in order to access the network power that resides in the norms and practices that animate these networks (Grewal, 2008, see also chapter 1 herein). To revisit my definition from chapter 1, power in the hybrid media system should be understood as the use of resources of varying kinds, that in any given context of dependence and interdependence enable individuals or collectivities to pursue their values and interests, both with and within different but interrelated media.

As I have demonstrated, the patterns of interaction between older and newer media logics are complex, heterogeneous, and variegated, both within and across fields. Hybridity empowers and it disempowers. But what, then, are the implications of all this for the different fields upon which I have focused?

In the field of news making, hybridity is creating an emergent openness and fluidity, as grassroots activist groups and even lone individuals now use newer media to make decisive interventions in the news-making process: in real-time assemblages in the case of the political information cycles I identified in chapter 4; through a mix of sociotechnical assemblages and elite/insider negotiation in the case of WikiLeaks, which I covered in chapter 5; and through the emergence of new hybrid norms among amateur bloggers and professional journalists that I identified in chapter 8. The hybrid media system exhibits a balance between the older logics of transmission and reception and the newer logics of circulation, recirculation, and negotiation.

And yet, all of this must always be set in the context of the ongoing power of professional broadcasting and newspaper organizations, who are in many respects successfully co-opting newer media logics for their own purposes while at the same time restating and renewing the logics that sustained their dominance throughout the twentieth century. While actors associated with newer media have come to see that they can exert power by adapting their norms and practices as a route to embedding themselves in positions of fruitful and negotiated engagement with actors associated with older media, this process also works in the other direction: older media have found important resources in newer media and will continue to do so. Hybridity also empowers those associated with older media logics, provided they are willing to restate their significance—and adapt.

Grassroots activism fueled by newer media logics must be set in the context of the broad and continuing power of the political and media elites who have carved out reserved domains that enable them to control what are still the main vehicles for politics in a liberal democracy: organized parties, candidates' campaigns, and of course the extremely powerful, and increasingly renewed, mass medium of television. These political and media elites had much to lose from the emergence of newer media logics at the end of the twentieth century, not least because these logics disrupted what had, even with the onslaught of media fragmentation that began during the late-1980s, become relatively fixed and settled patterns of interaction among elite political actors and elite broadcast and newspaper media. Older media's adaptation means that while power in the hybrid media system is relational and based on cooperation, divisions of labor, and interdependence with newer media, this interdependence is often asymmetrical (Keohane & Nye, 1989, see also chapter 1 herein). In some areas, older media logics continue to powerfully shape practice, though it is important to stress that this dominance is newly contingent and prone to fracture. The key point is that this contingency is now integrated into the media systems of Britain and the United States and it is not going to disappear in the near future.

Asymmetrical interdependence is most evident in the field of parties and election campaigning. Here, as I showed in my reinterpretation of the momentous 2008 U.S. presidential election in chapters 6 and 7 and the ethnography of hybrid norms in chapter 9, not only must the power-diffusing aspects of digital media be set alongside the rationalizing and centralizing aspects, the overall systemic balance in campaigning is still skewed toward older media logics, particularly the televisual styles of campaigning and the war-room practice, the ascendancy of which dates from the 1960s. There is a growing systemic integration between television and the internet that sometimes empowers online expression but this also renews war-room televisual logics. Those able to decisively intervene in the online flows of political information are often drawn from the official campaigns or are professional journalists. There is now an established role for online activism at the grassroots, but this is often on the campaign leadership's own terms. Perhaps this would have been a more difficult argument to make in the immediate aftermath of Barack Obama's 2008 victory, when the overwhelming weight of commentary was about how the internet had revolutionized election campaigning and how the Obama model would go on to inform a new style of governance based on openness, transparency, and grassroots mobilization. These ideas proved difficult to fully embed in government and on the campaign trail in 2012. The Obama administration and the 2012 presidential campaign are beyond the scope of this book, but, as I have argued, we might question whether newer media logics of transparency and grassroots empowerment were ever in fact the whole story of the 2008 election. Putting 2008 and Obama in the context of the hybrid media system draws attention to how it is perfectly possible to run an internet campaign that uses all relevant media, most notably television, to blend centralization, control, and hierarchy with decentralization, devolution, and horizontality. It also enables us to see how the impact of newer media are always shaped by assumptions carried forward from the use of older media.

This asymmetrical interdependence between older and newer media logics is also evident in British parties and campaigns. Here, my fieldwork revealed the increasing integration of older and newer media campaign roles, and this is an important development. But also evident are new lines of division between "strategic" and "tactical" norms about the uses of the internet. Strategic norms position the idea of internet-fueled grassroots engagement at the center of the party's ground campaign and appeal to the new media divisions; tactical norms, where the internet is used to grab the attention of older media, appeal to senior politicians and their traditional press officers. In my assessment, the prospects for power diffusion in this field are much less certain than in the fields of news making. This is not to say that the tactical norms cannot lead to important patterns of integration between the internet and older media, particularly real-time television integration that encompasses citizen activism. But as I showed in chapter 9, this is often driven by the logics of the broadcast-era war room in any case.

Today, we might ask whether the average citizen interested in influencing politics but without ambitions for high political office should join a party or create a Twitter account and start interacting with others in the diverse assemblages that now increasingly make political news and set the agenda. Then again, perhaps this, too, is missing an important part of the hybrid picture. For, as I showed in my discussion of political activist movement 38 Degrees in chapter 9, the hybrid media system creates new opportunities for such citizen groups to combine older and newer media logics in compelling and effective new ways. It is not a case of "either/or" but of "not only, but also."

I started this book from the perspective that hybrid thinking could be useful for moving beyond dichotomous modes of thought to understand how the older and the newer are layered into each other in political communication. The key to this, I believe, is to try to be as specific as possible about the combination of media logics in flow in any given event, process, or context. I have shown how newer media practices in the interpenetrated fields of media and politics adapt and integrate the logics of older media practices in those fields; and, conversely, how older media practices in the fields of media and politics adapt and integrate the logics of newer media practices. There is complexity and there is mess. Overall, though, it seems to be inescapable that political communication in Britain and the United States is more polycentric than during the period of mass communication that dominated the twentieth century. Though there are important constraints on the power of non-elites, and the logics of older media continue to be powerful in shaping politics, the opportunities for ordinary citizens to use the hybrid media system to influence the form and content of public discourse are, on balance, greater than they were during the stultifying duopoly of broadcasting and newspaper logics.

This goes beyond the simple fact that citizens are now able to express themselves online in public forums. In the hybrid media system it is older media's systemic integration and expectation of citizen expression occurring in newer media environments that often makes the difference. Internet-driven norms of networking, flexibility, spontaneity and ad hoc organizing have started to diffuse into our politics and media and these norms are generating new expectations about what counts as effective and worthwhile political action. Changing practices in the world of older media, particularly television, increasingly mesh with these online norms. Nobody should pretend that these behaviors are equally distributed; it is primarily political activists and the politically interested who are able to make the difference with newer media and/or inventive combinations of older and newer media. But the logics of digital media have been genuinely disruptive, even though that disruption has been modulated by the logics of older media.

Many of the shifts in political life that have occurred since the 1950s were based upon an acceptance of the power of the broadcasting-newspaper duopoly. During the heyday of the broadcast era from the 1960s to the 1990s, this preeminence hardened into an increasing self-confidence and self-awareness, particularly among television media, that they were revealing to publics what was self-evidently important about politics. But the duopoly's preeminence has now become partially undermined, as we have seen throughout this book. Indeed, when those associated with older media seek to co-opt the practices of newer media, they always face the risk that they steadily sow the seeds of their own destruction by granting legitimacy to newer media logics.

The complex interactions among media logics matter more now than the preeminence of a single media logic. Political communication has entered a new, more complex and unsettled era, in which power has become more relational, fragmented, plural, and dispersed. The hybrid media system exhibits chaos, nonlinearity, and disintegration but also surprising new patterns of integration. This is the "particulate" idea of hybridity that I introduced in chapter 1. Older and newer media logics sometimes flow independently, but increasingly flow together, creating arrangements for the conduct of political communication that are, on balance, more expansive and inclusive than those that prevailed during the twentieth century.

Interviews

Interviewees disguised by pseudonyms requested anonymity. The gender of anonymous interviewees should not be implied from their pseudonyms.

1. Adam Bienkov, blogger at *Tory Troll*, March 2010.
2. "John," senior official, Foreign and Commonwealth Office, April 2010.
3. "Kate," former official, the Prime Minister's Office, April 2010.
4. Ed Richards, Chief Executive, Office of Communications (OFCOM), April 2010.
5. "Frank," journalist, the *Independent*, April 2010.
6. Stephen Abell, Director of the Press Complaints Commission, April 2010.
7. James Crabtree, senior editor, *Prospect* magazine, April 2010.
8. "Oliver," former official, Cabinet Office, April 2010.
9. Craig Elder, Conservative Party communications team, May 2010.
10. Will Straw, founding editor of the *Left Foot Forward* blog, May 2010.
11. "Bill," senior official, Cabinet Office, May 2010.
12. Staff, 38 Degrees (group discussion), May 2010.
13. Hannah Lownsbrough, Campaigns Director, 38 Degrees, May 2010.
14. Johnny Chatterton, Digital Campaigns Manager, 38 Degrees, May 2010.
15. David Babbs, Executive Director, 38 Degrees, May 2010.
16. "Mike," director of the London office of an international public relations agency, June 2010.
17. "Jean," former trade union press officer, June 2010.
18. Alice Tarleton, journalist, Channel 4 News, June 2010.
19. "Neil," former official, the Prime Minister's Office, June 2010.
20. "Cynthia," former campaign official, the Labour Party, June 2010.
21. "Mary," senior campaign official, the Labour Party, June 2010.
22. "Jay," former senior official, OFCOM, July 2010.
23. "Tony," former senior executive, ITN, July 2010.
24. "Karen," former editor, Channel 4 News, July 2010.
25. David Stringer, Westminster Correspondent, the Associated Press, October 2010.
26. "David," senior campaign official, the Labour Party, January 2011.
27. Kevin Marsh, former editor, BBC Radio 4 *Today* program, June 2011.

28. "Jim," former senior journalist, BBC News, June 2011.
29. James Ball, journalist, investigations team, the *Guardian*, September 2011.
30. "Carol," an editor at the *Guardian*, September 2011.
31. Laura Kuenssberg, former Chief Political Correspondent, BBC News; Business Editor, ITV News, January 2012.

Notes

Introduction

1. For a full list of interviews, see page 211.

Chapter 2

1. Marvin (1988: 3).
2. Bolter and Grusin (1999: 271).
3. McLuhan (1964: 8).

Chapter 3

1. This section on Britain draws in part upon a paper I co-authored with James Stanyer, and which we presented to the Annual Meeting of the American Political Science Association in August 2010 (Chadwick & Stanyer, 2010).

Chapter 4

1. Quoted in Marvin (1988: 193).
2. A note about method. Studying political information cycles presents a significant challenge to researchers. Newspaper journalists now frequently post multiple updates to stories throughout the day and night and news sites have widely varying archive policies. The technological limitations of journalists' content management systems as well as editorial policy determine whether and how updates, additions, headline alterations, and picture replacements are signaled to readers. Most blogs and a minority of mainstream news outlets, such as the *Guardian* and the *Financial Times*, are transparent about an article's provenance. However, practices vary widely and it is common to see outdated time stamps, the incremental addition of paragraphs at the top or bottom of stories, and headline and URL changes to reflect new angles as they emerge. Sometimes entire stories will simply be overwritten, even though the original hyperlink will be retained. All of these can occur without readers being explicitly notified.

Several "forensic" strategies were used to overcome these problems. In addition to monitoring key political blogs and the main national news outlets' websites, the free and publicly available Google Reader was used to monitor the RSS feeds and the timings of article releases from February 20 to February 25, 2010, for the following outlets: *BBC News* (Front Page feed), *Daily Express, Daily Mail, Daily Mirror, Daily Star, Daily Telegraph, Financial Times, Guardian, Independent, Independent on Sunday, Mail on Sunday, News of the World,*

Observer, Sun, Sunday Express, Sunday Mirror, Sunday Telegraph, Sunday Times, and the *Times*. Links were followed back to newspaper websites to check for article modifications, updates, and deletions. Google Reader consists of an effectively unlimited archive of every RSS feed dating back to when a single user first added it to Google's database. Evernote, free and publicly available software, was used to store selected newspaper articles: see http://www.evernote.com.

The broadcast media archiving service, Box of Broadcasts, was used to store content from Channel 4 News, BBC News at Ten, the BBC 24-Hour News Channel, and ITV News, enabling the analysis of pivotal moments during the flow of events on February 20, 21, and 22. This service is available to member institutions of the British Universities Film and Video Council. See http://bobnational.net. Where they exist, links to public transcripts of television and radio shows have been provided.

The Twitter search function at http://search.twitter.com was monitored in real-time using a number of queries, such as "national bullying helpline," "#rawnsleyrot," and "#bullygate." From when the Twitter search service began and the time of the fieldwork, Twitter only made public the results from approximately three weeks prior to running a query, and, at the time of the fieldwork no robust and publicly available means of automatically extracting and archiving individual Twitter updates existed. To circumvent these limitations, screen outputs of selected Twitter searches were captured in real time and stored in Evernote. Readers may e-mail the author for a link to this online archive. In April 2010, after the initial fieldwork was conducted, Google launched its Google Replay Search, which later became Google Real-Time Search but was withdrawn in July 2011. This enabled searches of the Twitter archive going back to early February 2010 and it presented the results in a timeline format, though it cannot automatically account for changes to the names of individual Twitter accounts; these must be followed up manually. Where possible, the Google Replay Search service was used to track and present publicly available links to key Twitter updates. Twitter updates are reproduced throughout in their original, often ungrammatical and incorrectly punctuated form.

Chapter 5

1. Rusbridger (2011).
2. Quoted in Khatchadourian (2010).
3. Leigh & Harding (2011: Ch. 11, para. 19).
4. Collateral Murder was published in two versions—a seventeen-minute edited package uploaded to YouTube and released to the press, complete with guidance notes, and a thirty-nine-minute "full-version." The video footage, taken from the on-board camera of a U.S. Apache helicopter, captured that aircraft's role in events during a July 2007 attack on a small group of people in a residential area of Baghdad. Two of these people were armed with rifles; one was carrying a camera lens that appears to have been mistaken for a rocket-propelled grenade launcher. Two Reuters journalists, Saeed Chmagh and Namir Noo-Eldeen, were killed during the attack—Chmagh as he sought to crawl from danger into a van that arrived to rescue the wounded following the first phase of the attack. Ten others lost their lives and two young children, who were passengers in the van, were badly wounded and later taken to hospital. After the event, in a bid to find out what had happened to their staff and to learn more about the extent to which the Apache helicopter had been under threat, Reuters asked the U.S. military to release the video. This was repeatedly refused. Reuters staff were eventually permitted to watch an edited version of the footage, but this omitted the crucial second phase of the attack when the van containing the children, which was trying to evacuate the wounded, was destroyed by gunfire.

Chapter 6

1. M. Powell (2008).
2. Plouffe (2010: 277).

Chapter 8

1. See page 211 for the list of interviews. Several of these interviews were conducted on the basis that a subject's remarks could be attributed. Several were conducted on the understanding that most of the remarks were attributable but others were not. The rest were conducted on a completely confidential basis and on condition that I would preserve the subject's anonymity at all times. Where I cannot name an individual due to a confidentiality agreement I use basic terms to convey a sense of that person's professional role and typical working practices.

Chapter 9

1. Interview 21, June 2010.
2. See page 211 for the list of interviews.

Conclusion

1. The Waterboys, "This is the Sea." Chrysalis Records, 1985.

Bibliography

ABC News. (June 4, 2008). Transcript: Charles Gibson Interviews Barack Obama. *ABC News Website*. Retrieved January 31, 2012, from http://abcnews.go.com/WN/story?id=5000184&page=1#.Tyf2-0w9Ww5

Abramowitz, A. I. (2010). How Obama Won and What It Means. In L. J. Sabato (Ed.), *The Year of Obama: How Barack Obama Won the White House* (pp. 91–114). London: Longman.

Adam, B. (1990). *Time and Social Theory*. Cambridge: Polity.

Adams, R. (September 18, 2010). Jon Stewart and Stephen Colbert Ape Glenn Beck with "Rally to Restore Sanity." *Guardian Website*. Retrieved March 2, 2012, from http://www.guardian.co.uk/world/richard-adams-blog/2010/sep/18/jon-stewart-stephen-colbert-rally-to-restore-sanity-reddit

Adler, B. (January 4, 2011). Why Journalists Aren't Standing Up for WikiLeaks. *Newsweek Website*. Retrieved January 4, 2011, from http://www.newsweek.com/2011/01/04/why-journalists-aren-t-defending-julian-assange.print.html

Agence France-Press. (September 17, 2010). US Comics Unveil Dueling DC Political Rallies. *AFP News Website (Hosted by Google)*. Retrieved March 2, 2012, from http://www.google.com/hostednews/afp/article/ALeqM5gkOsOs61eFqq5znyHyVThYNAGTDw

Alexander, J. C. (2010). *The Performance of Politics: Obama's Victory and the Democratic Struggle for Power*. New York: Oxford University Press.

Altheide, D. L. (2004). Media Logic and Political Communication. *Political Communication*, 21 (3), 293–296.

Altheide, D. L., & Snow, R. P. (1979). *Media Logic*. London: Sage.

Altheide, D. L., & Snow, R. P. (1991). *Media Worlds in the Postjournalism Era*. New York: Aldine de Gruyter.

Altheide, D. L., & Snow, R. P. (1992). Media Logic and Culture: A Reply to Oakes. *International Journal of Politics, Culture, and Society*, 5 (3), 465–472.

Amazon Web Services. (December 3, 2010). Message. *Amazon Web Services Website*. Retrieved July 22, 2011, from http://aws.amazon.com/message/65348/

Amin, A. (2004). Regulating Economic Globalization. *Transactions of the Institute of British Geographers*, 29 (2), 217–233.

An Obama Minute. (October 6, 2008). An Obama Minute. *An Obama Minute Website*. Retrieved December 19, 2011, from http://anobamaminute.com

Anderson, B. (February 22, 2010). Bullying, Tantrums and Brown. *Independent Website*. Retrieved February 22, 2010, from http://www.independent.co.uk/opinion/commentators/bruce-anderson/bruce-anderson-bullying-tantrums-and-brown-1906506.html

Anderson, C. W. (2013). *Rebuilding the News: Metropolitan Journalism in the Digital Age*. Philadelphia: Temple University Press.

Anderson, K. (July 1, 2009). Arianna Huffington: Obsessiveness is the Greatest Strength of Online News. *The Guardian Website*. Retrieved May 9, 2012, from http://www.guardian.co.uk/media/pda/2009/jul/01/arianna-huffington-activate-conference

Angus Reid Public Opinion. (April 15, 2010). Angus Reid Real Time Reporting: First Debate. *Angus Reid Public Opinion Website*. Retrieved April 15, 2010, from http://www.angusreidelec-tions.co.uk/2010/04/debate/

Anon Ops. (2010). Anon Ops: A Press Release. *Dump.no Website*. Retrieved December 10, 2010, from http://dump.no/files/467072ba2a42/ANONOPS_The_Press_Release.pdf

Anonymous. (February 21, 2010). *The Bullying Helpline Blog*. Retrieved February 21, 2010, from http://thebullyinghelpline.blogspot.com/

Anstead, N. (2008). The Internet and Campaign Finance in the U.S. and the U.K.: An Institutional Comparison. *Journal of Information Technology and Politics*, 5 (3), 285–302.

Anstead, N., & Chadwick, A. (2009). Parties, Election Campaigning and the Internet: Toward A Comparative Institutional Approach. In A. Chadwick & P. N. Howard (Eds.), *The Handbook of Internet Politics* (pp. 56–71). New York: Routledge.

Anstead, N., & O'Loughlin, B. (2011). The Emerging Viewertariat and BBC Question Time: Television Debate and Real-Time Commenting Online. *The International Journal of Press/Politics*, 16 (4), 440–462.

Arnold, A.-K., & Schneider, B. (2007). Communicating Separation?: Ethnic Media and Ethnic Journalists as Institutions of Integration in Germany. *Journalism*, 8 (2), 115–136.

Arthur, C. (January 8, 2010). WikiLeaks Under Attack: the Definitive Timeline. *Guardian Website*. Retrieved January 8, 2011, from http://www.guardian.co.uk/media/2010/dec/07/wikileaks-under-attack-definitive-timeline

Ashcraft, K. L. (2001). Organized Dissonance: Feminist Bureaucracy as Hybrid Form. *Academy of Management Journal*, 44 (6), 1301–1322.

Ashcraft, K. L. (2006). Feminist-Bureaucratic Control and Other Adversarial Allies: Extending Organized Dissonance to the Practice of "New" Forms. *Communication Monographs*, 73 (1), 55–86.

Ashley, J. (February 22, 2010). A Month Ago, This Might Just Have Buried Brown. Not Now. *Guardian Website*. Retrieved February 22, 2010, from http://www.guardian.co.uk/commentisfree/2010/feb/21/brown-temper-elections-labour-tories

Assange, J. (2011). *The Unauthorized Biography*. London: Canongate.

Associated Press. (October 15, 2008). "Joe the Plumber" Becomes Focus of Debate. *YouTube*. Retrieved August 10, 2012, from http://www.youtube.com/watch?v=PUvwKVvp3-o

Associated Press. (February 28, 2012). Number of iPads Sold by Apple by Quarter. *ABC News Website*. Retrieved February 29, 2012, from http://abcnews.go.com/Technology/wireStory/number-ipads-sold-apple-quarter-15810416#.T05kCKA9Ww4

Aun, F. (November 7, 2008). Over Long Campaign, Obama Videos Drew Nearly a Billion Views. *Clickz Website*. Retrieved December 16, 2011, from http://www.clickz.com/clickz/news/1711540/over-long-campaign-obama-videos-drew-nearly-billion-views

Auslander, P. (2008). *Liveness: Performance in a Mediatized Culture* (Second ed.). Abingdon: Routledge.

Axelrod, D. (2009). Comments on Campaign Organization and Strategy. In K. H. Jamieson (Ed.), *Electing the President 2008: The Insiders' View* (pp. 55–83). Philadelphia: University of Pennsylvania Press.

Bäckstrand, K. (2006). Democratizing Global Environmental Governance? Stakeholder Democracy After the World Summit on Sustainable Development. *European Journal of International Relations*, 12 (4), 467–498.

Ball, J. (September 2, 2011). WikiLeaks Publishes Full Cache of Unredacted Cables. *Guardian Website*. Retrieved June 8, 2012, from http://www.guardian.co.uk/media/2011/sep/02/wikileaks-publishes-cache-unredacted-cables

BarackObamadotcom. (October 16, 2008a). 90 Per Cent. *YouTube*. Retrieved December 5, 2011, from http://www.youtube.com/watch?v=PluoMotgl2w

BarackObamadotcom. (October 29, 2008b). American Stories, American Solutions: 30 Minute Special. *YouTube*. Retrieved November 30, 2011, from http://www.youtube.com/watch?v=GtREqAmLsoA&noredirect=1

BarackObamadotcom. (July 24, 2008c). Barack Obama in Berlin. *YouTube*. Retrieved February 9, 2012, from http://www.youtube.com/watch?v=OAhb06Z8N1c

BarackObamadotcom. (September 10, 2008d). MyBO: Neighbor to Neighbor Canvassing. *YouTube*. Retrieved November 30, 2011, from http://www.youtube.com/watch?v=tt9JKIIs9Sw&noredirect=1

Barker, A. (February 21, 2010). Ministers Rally to Brown Over "Bullying" Claims. *Financial Times Website*. Retrieved February 21, 2010, from http://www.ft.com/cms/s/0/df7300b8-1eef-11-df-9584-00144feab49a.html?ftcamp=rss

Barko Germany, J. (2009). The Online Revolution. In D. W. Johnson (Ed.), *Campaigning for President 2008: Strategy and Tactics, New Voices and New Techniques* (pp. 147–159). Abingdon: Routledge.

Barnett, S., & Gaber, I. (2001). *Westminster Tales: The 21st Century Crisis in British Political Journalism*. London: Continuum.

Barr, K. (2009). A Perfect Storm: the 2008 Youth Vote. In D. W. Johnson (Ed.), *Campaigning for President 2008: Strategy and Tactics, New Voices and New Techniques* (pp. 105–125). Abingdon: Routledge.

Bartlet, J. (2011). Josiah Bartlet (@Pres_Bartlet) on Twitter. http://twitter.com/Pres_Bartlet. Retrieved December 2, 2011, from http://twitter.com/Pres_Bartlet

Baumgartner, J. C., & Morris, J. S. (2010). Who Wants to Be My Friend? Obama, Youth, and Social Networks in the 2008 Campaign. In J. A. Hendricks & R. E. Denton Jr (Eds.), *Communicator-in-Chief: How Barack Obama Used New Media Technology to Win the White House* (pp. 51–65). Plymouth: Lexington.

Baym, G. (2005). *The Daily Show*: Discursive Integration and the Reinvention of Political Journalism. *Political Communication*, 22 (3), 259–276.

BBC2. (2010a). Newsnight, April 15.

BBC2. (2010b). Newsnight, April 21.

BBC. (February 21, 2010a). Andrew Marr Show: Lord Mandelson Transcript. Retrieved June 18, 2010, from http://news.bbc.co.uk/1/hi/uk_politics/8526896.stm

BBC. (2010b). Several people working in Gordon Brown's office contacted an anti-bullying helpline, its boss tells the BBC. http://bit.ly/c7srZ4. *Twitter.com/bbcpolitics*. Retrieved February 21, 2010, from http://twitter.com/bbcpolitics/status/9437632216

BBC. (2010c). The Politics Show, February 21.

BBC News. (2010a). BBC News Special: BAFTA February 21.

BBC News. (2010b). BBC News, February 21.

BBC News. (2010c). BBC Ten O'Clock News, February 22.

BBC News Online. (April 30, 2010a). 8.4 Million Watch Final Prime Ministerial Debate. *BBC News Website*. Retrieved May 10, 2010, from http://news.bbc.co.uk/1/hi/uk_politics/election_2010/8653551.stm

BBC News Online. (February 21, 2010b). Helpline Enters Brown "Bully" Row. *BBC News Website*. Retrieved February 21, 2010, from http://news.bbc.co.uk/1/hi/uk_politics/8527193.stm

BBC News Online. (January 10, 2012). Leveson Inquiry: Telegraph Expenses Scoop Explained. *BBC News Website*. Retrieved March 5, 2012, from http://www.bbc.co.uk/news/uk-16494872

BBC Radio 4. (April 16, 2010a). Today. *Today Programme Archive Website*. Retrieved April 17, 2010, from http://news.bbc.co.uk/today/hi/today/newsid_8624000/8624275.stm

BBC Radio 4. (April 19, 2010b). Today. *Today Programme Archive Website*. Retrieved April 20, 2010, from http://news.bbc.co.uk/today/hi/today/newsid_8628000/8628896.stm

BBC Radio 4. (2010c). Today, February 22.

BBC Radio 4. (2010d). The World at One, February 22.

Becker, J., Goodman, P. S., & Powell, M. (September 13, 2008). Once Elected, Palin Hired Friends and Lashed Foes. *New York Times Website*. Retrieved December 2, 2011, from http://www.nytimes.com/2008/09/14/us/politics/14palin.html?pagewanted=all

Beckett, C., & Ball, J. (2012). *WikiLeaks: News In The Networked Era*. Cambridge: Polity.

Belam, M. (April 15, 2010). General Election Debate: the Digital Experience. *Martin Belam's Website*. Retrieved April 15, 2010, from http://www.currybet.net/cbet_blog/2010/04/general_election_debate_digital_experience.php

Bell, A. (1995). News Time. *Time & Society*, 4 (3), 305–328.

Bell, M. (September 27, 2009). Meet the New Media Mogul: Why Tories Fear Lord Ashcroft. *The Independent Website*. Retrieved May 14, 2012, from http://www.independent.co.uk/news/media/online/meet-the-new-media-mogul-why-tories-fear-lord-ashcroft-1793737.html

Beniger, J. R. (1986). *The Control Revolution: Technological and Economic Origins of the Information Society*. London: Harvard University Press.

Benkler, Y. (February 8, 2011). A Free, Irresponsible Press: WikiLeaks and the Battle over the Soul of the Networked Fourth Estate. *Yochai Benkler's Website*. Retrieved July 15, 2011, from http://benkler.org/Benkler_Wikileaks_current.pdf

Bennett, W. L. (1994). Constructing Publics and Their Opinions. *Political Communication*, 10 (2), 101–120.

Bennett, W. L. (2003). Communicating Global Activism: Strengths and Vulnerabilities of Networked Politics. *Information, Communication and Society*, 6 (2), 143–168.

Bennett, W. L. (2003a). New Media Power: The Internet and Global Activism. In N. Couldry & J. Curran (Eds.), *Contesting Media Power: Alternative Media in a Networked World* (pp. 17–37). Oxford: Rowman and Littlefield.

Bennett, W. L. (2005). News as Reality TV: Election Coverage and the Democratization of Truth. *Critical Studies in Media Communication*, 22 (2), 171–177.

Bennett, W. L., & Segerberg, A. (2012). The Logic of Connective Action. *Information, Communication and Society*, 15 (5), 739–768.

Berman, A. (2010). *Herding Donkeys: The Fight to Rebuild the Democratic Party and Reshape American Politics*. New York: Farrar, Strauss, and Giroux.

Berman, P. S. (2007). Global Legal Pluralism. *Southern California Law Review*, 80 (6), 1155–1237.

Bhabha, H. K. (1994). *The Location of Culture*. London: Routledge.

Bienkov, A. (February 21, 2010). Who are the National Bullying Helpline? *Adam Bienkov's Website*. Retrieved February 21, 2010, from http://torytroll.blogspot.com/2010/02/who-are-national-bullying-helpline.html

Bimber, B. (2003). *Information and American Democracy: Technology in the Evolution of Political Power*. Cambridge: Cambridge University Press.

Bimber, B., Stohl, C., & Flanagin, A. J. (2009). Technological Change and the Shifting Nature of Political Organization. In A. Chadwick & P. N. Howard (Eds.), *The Handbook of Internet Politics* (pp. 72–85). London: Routledge.

Bjørkan, M., & Qvenild, M. (2010). The Biodiversity Discourse: Categorisation of Indigenous People in a Mexican Bio-Prospecting Case. *Human Ecology*, 38 (2), 193–204.

Bloomfield, B. P., & Hayes, N. (2009). Power and Organizational Transformation Through Technology: Hybrids of Electronic Government. *Organization Studies*, 30 (5), 461–487.

Bloxham, A. (December 9, 2010). WikiLeaks Cyberwar: Hackers Bring Down Swedish Government Site. *Daily Telegraph Website*. Retrieved December 9, 2010, from http://www.telegraph.co.uk/news/worldnews/wikileaks/8190871/WikiLeaks-cyberwar-hackers-bring-down-Swedish-government-site.html

Blumler, J. G., & Gurevitch, M. (2005). Rethinking the Study of Political Communication. In J. Curran & M. Gurevitch (Eds.), *Mass Media and Society* (pp. 104–121). London: Hodder Arnold.

Boczkowski, P. J., & De Santos, M. (2007). When More Media Equals Less News: Patterns of Content Homogenization in Argentina's Leading Print and Online Newspapers. *Political Communication*, 24 (2), 167–180.

Bogard, W. (2009). Deleuze and Machines: A Politics of Technology. In M. Poster & D. Savat (Eds.), *Deleuze and New Technology* (pp. 15–31). Edinburgh: Edinburgh University Press.

Bolter, J. D., & Grusin, R. (1999). *Remediation: Understanding New Media*. Cambridge, MA: MIT Press.

Boorstin, D. (1964). *The Image: A Guide to Pseudo Events in America*. New York: Harper & Row.

Booth, J. (February 22, 2010). Gordon Brown Faces Calls for Inquiry Over Bullying Claims. *Times Website*. Retrieved February 22, 2010, from http://www.timesonline.co.uk/tol/news/politics/article7036094.ece#cid=OTC-RSS&attr=797084

Booth, R., & Borger, J. (November 28, 2010). U.S. Diplomats Spied on U.N. Leadership. *Guardian Website*. Retrieved June 20, 2011, from http://www.guardian.co.uk/world/2010/nov/28/us-embassy-cables-spying-un

Born, G. (2003). Strategy, Positioning and Projection in Digital Television: Channel Four and the Commercialization of Public Service Broadcasting in the UK. *Media, Culture and Society*, 25 (6), 773–799.

Bosker, B. (December 8, 2010). Operation Payback: Facebook BANNED Our Page. *Huffington Post Website*. Retrieved December 8, 2010, from http://www.huffingtonpost.com/2010/12/08/operation-payback-faceboo_n_794076.html

Bourdieu, P. (1984). *Distinction: A Social Critique of the Judgement of Taste*. Cambridge, MA: Harvard University Press.

Bradley, B. (April 15, 2008). Deep Inside "Bittergate." *RealClearPolitics Website*. Retrieved November 25, 2011, from http://www.realclearpolitics.com/articles/2008/04/deep_inside_bittergate.html

Brave New Films. (2008). John McCain's Chart-Topping Single "Bomb Iran." *YouTube*. Retrieved February 28, 2012, from http://www.youtube.com/watch?v=y2kyXN4ZVQg&feature=player_embedded

Breslau, K. (January 6, 2008). Hillary Tears Up. *The Daily Beast Website*. Retrieved November 23, 2011, from http://www.thedailybeast.com/newsweek/2008/01/06/hillary-tears-up.html

Brian, M. (December 13, 2010). Wikileaks.org Domain Comes Back Online, Helped by New DNS Providers. *The Next Web Media Website*. Retrieved December 13, 2010, from http://thenextweb.com/media/2010/12/13/wikileaks-org-domain-comes-back-online-with-the-help-of-new-dns-providers/

Briggs, A., & Burke, P. (2009). *A Social History of the Media: From Gutenberg to the Internet* (Third ed.). Cambridge: Polity.

Brogan, B. (February 21, 2010). Gordon Brown: "Psychological Flaws" is Starting to Look Like an Understatement. *Sunday Telegraph Website*. Retrieved February 21, 2010, from http://www.telegraph.co.uk/news/election-2010/7286123/Gordon-Brown-psychological-flaws-is-starting-to-look-like-an-understatment.html

Brown, J. A. (February 21, 2010). Try thebullyinghelpline.blogspot.com @jonswaine—Nat Bullying Helpline just a cheapy front for this commercial litigation "consultancy." *Twitter. com/DignityWorks*. Retrieved February 21, 2010, from http://twitter.com/DignityWorks/status/9438118357

Brownlee, J. (2009). Portents of Pluralism: How Hybrid Regimes affect Democratic Transitions. *American Journal of Political Science*, 53 (3), 515–532.

Bruns, A. (2008). *Blogs, Wikipedia, Second Life, and Beyond: From Production to Produsage*. New York: Peter Lang.

Bucy, E. P. (2004). Interactivity in Society: Locating an Elusive Concept. *The Information Society*, 20 (5), 373–383.

Bucy, E. P., & Gregson, K. S. (2001). Media Participation: A Legitimizing Mechanism of Mass Democracy. *New Media and Society*, 3 (3), 357–380.

Bulkeley, H. (2005). Reconfiguring Environmental Governance: Towards a Politics of Scales and Networks. *Political Geography*, 24 (8), 875–902.

Bullying UK. (February 21, 2010a). @bbcnickrobinson Our Statement regarding todays Gordon Brown and The National Bullying Helpline story http://buk.cc/9ehHVR *Twitter. com/bullyinguk*. Retrieved February 21, 2010, from http://twitter.com/bullyinguk/status/9447128169

Bullying UK. (February 21, 2010b). National Bullying Helpline Breach of Confidentiality Over Gordon Brown Complaints. *Bullying UK Website*. Retrieved February 21, 2010, from http://

www.bullying.co.uk/index.php/201002221235/blog/uk-news/national-bullying-helpline-br each-of-confidentiality-over-gordon-brown-complaints.html

Cablegatesearch. (July 27, 2011). Cablegate's Cables: Full Text Search. *Cablegatesearch Website*. Retrieved July 27, 2011, from http://www.cablegatesearch.net/search.php

Callaghan, K., & Schnell, F. (2001). Assessing the Democratic Debate: How the News Media Frame Elite Policy Discourse. *Political Communication*, 18 (2), 183–212.

Camp Obama. (September 25, 2007). Camp Obama on Blip.tv. *Blip.tv Website*. Retrieved November 29, 2011, from http://blip.tv/camp-obama

Cappella, J. N., & Jamieson, K. H. (1997). *Spiral of Cynicism: The Press and the Public Good*. New York: Oxford University Press.

Carson, J. (2009). Comments on Campaign Management and Field Operations. In K. H. Jamieson (Ed.), *Electing the President 2008: The Insiders' View* (pp. 34–54). Philadelphia: University of Pennsylvania Press.

Castells, M. (2004). *The Power of Identity: The Information Age: Economy, Society and Culture Volume II* (Second ed.). Oxford: Blackwell.

Castells, M. (2007). Communication, Power and Counter-power in the Network Society. *International Journal of Communication*, 1, 238–266.

Castells, M. (2009). *Communication Power*. Oxford: Oxford University Press.

CBS. (September 2, 2008). Transcript of Campaign '08: Republican National Convention. *Campaign '08: Republican National Convention*. Retrieved December 8, 2011, from http://docs.cbsconventionpress.com/0902.doc

Cellan-Jones, R. (April 22, 2010). It's All Nick Clegg's Fault. *BBC News Online*. Retrieved April 23, 2010, from http://www.bbc.co.uk/blogs/thereporters/rorycellanjones/2010/04/its_all_nick_cleggs_fault.html

Chadwick, A. (2006). *Internet Politics: States, Citizens, and New Communication Technologies*. New York: Oxford University Press.

Chadwick, A. (2007). Digital Network Repertoires and Organizational Hybridity. *Political Communication*, 24 (3), 283–301.

Chadwick, A. (2009). Web 2.0: New Challenges for the Study of E-Democracy in an Era of Informational Exuberance. *I/S: Journal of Law and Policy for the Information Society*, 5 (1), 9–41.

Chadwick, A. (2011a). Britain's First Live Televised Party Leaders' Debate: From the News Cycle to the Political Information Cycle. *Parliamentary Affairs*, 64 (1), 24–44.

Chadwick, A. (2011b). The Political Information Cycle in a Hybrid News System: the British Prime Minister and the "Bullygate" Affair. *The International Journal of Press/Politics*, 16 (1), 3–29.

Chadwick, A. (2012). Recent Shifts in the Relationship Between the Internet and Democratic Engagement in Britain and the United States: Granularity, Informational Exuberance, and Political Learning. In E. Anduiza, M. Jensen & L. Jorba (Eds.), *Digital Media and Political Engagement Worldwide: A Comparative Study* (pp. 39–55). Cambridge: Cambridge University Press.

Chadwick, A., & Howard, P. N. (2009). Introduction: New Directions in Internet Politics Research. In A. Chadwick & P. N. Howard (Eds.), *The Handbook of Internet Politics* (pp. 1–9). New York: Routledge.

Chadwick, A., & Stanyer, J. (August 31, 2010). Political Communication in Transition: Mediated Politics in Britain's New Media Environment. *American Political Science Association Annual Meeting Website*. Retrieved August 31, 2010, from http://papers.ssrn.com/sol3/papers.cfm?abstract_id=1642858

Chandler, D., & Munday, R. (2011). Ontology. In D. Chandler & R. Munday (Eds.), *Oxford Dictionary of Media and Communication*. Online version. Oxford: Oxford University Press. Retrieved November 21, 2011, from http://www.oxfordreference.com/view/10.1093/acref/9780199568758.001.0001/acref-9780199568758-e-1921?rskey=iiSGzg&result=4&q=ontology

Channel 4 News. (2010a). Channel 4 News FactCheck on Twitter. *Twitter.com/FactCheck*. Retrieved May 12, 2010, from http://twitter.com/FactCheck

Channel 4 News. (2010b). Channel 4 News, February 20.

Channel 4 News. (2010c). Channel 4 News, February 21.

Channel 4 News. (February 20, 2010d). Gordon Brown Denies Angry Outburst Claims. *Channel 4 News Website*. Retrieved February 20, 2010, from http://www.channel4.com/news/articles/politics/domestic_politics/gordon+brown+denies+angry+outburst+claims/3553242

Channel 4 News. (December 1, 2010e). WikiLeaks: US Memo Accuses Sri Lanka President of War Crimes. *Channel 4 News Website*. Retrieved May 3, 2012, from http://www.channel4.com/news/wikileaks-sri-lanka-leadership-responsible-for-crimes

Chapman, J. (April 19, 2010). Is This Really the End of Two-Party Politics? *Daily Mail*.

Chivers, C. J. (December 1, 2010). Below Surface, U.S. Has Dim View of Putin and Russia. *New York Times Website*. Retrieved July 18, 2011, from http://www.nytimes.com/2010/12/02/world/europe/02wikileaks-russia.html

Chung, A. (April 16, 2010). Clegg Up: Lib Dem Leader Wins TV Debate. *Sky News Website*. Retrieved April 16, 2010, from http://news.sky.com/skynews/Home/Politics/Sky-News-Instant-Leaders-Debate-Poll-With-Fizzback-Panel-Texts-Feedback-For-Faster-Results/Article/201004315603598?f=rss

Churcher, J. (February 21, 2010). Mandelson: Brown is Not a Bully. *Independent on Sunday Website*. Retrieved February 21, 2010, from http://www.independent.co.uk/news/uk/politics/mandelson-brown-is-not-a-bully-1906172.html

Clegg, S., & Courpasson, D. (2004). Political Hybrids: Tocquevillean Views on Project Organizations. *Journal of Management Studies*, 41 (4), 525–547.

Coates, S. (February 21, 2010a). Downing Street Officials Try to Play Down Brown's Alleged Bullying. *Sunday Times Website*. Retrieved February 21, 2010, from http://www.timesonline.co.uk/tol/news/politics/article7035738.ece

Coates, S. (February 21, 2010b). Mandelson: Gordon Brown Doesn't Bully His Staff, He Is Just Demanding. *Sunday Times Website*. Retrieved February 21, 2010, from http://www.timesonline.co.uk/tol/news/politics/article7035272.ece#cid=OTC-RSS&attr=797084

Coates, S. (February 22, 2010c). Q&A: Gordon Brown, Downing St and "Bullying." *Times Website*. Retrieved February 22, from http://www.timesonline.co.uk/tol/news/politics/article7036008.ece#cid=OTC-RSS&attr=797084

Cockerell, M., Hennessy, P., & Walker, D. (1984). *Sources Close to the Prime Minister: Inside the Hidden World of the News Manipulators*. London: Macmillan.

Cohn, M. (September 19, 2010). Bradley Manning: An American Hero. *Marjorie Cohn's Website*. Retrieved July 21, 2011, from http://www.marjoriecohn.com/2010/09/bradley-manning-american-hero.html

Coleman, G. (April 6, 2011). Anonymous: From the Lulz to Collective Action. *The New Everyday Website*. Retrieved April 6, 2011, from http://mediacommons.futureofthebook.org/tne/pieces/anonymous-lulz-collective-action

Collins, N., & Blake, H. (April 15, 2010). Leaders' Debate Live Blog. *Daily Telegraph Website*. Retrieved April 15, 2010, from http://www.telegraph.co.uk/news/election-2010/7585859/TV-Election-Debate-live.html

ComRes. (April 16, 2010). ITV News Instant Poll Results 15 April 2010. *ComRes Website*. Retrieved April 16, 2010, from http://www.comres.co.uk/page184332236.aspx

Conservative Home. (2010a). Conservative Home: Friday 16th April 2010. *Conservative Home Website*. Retrieved April 16, 2010, from http://conservativehome.blogs.com/frontpage/2010/04/friday-16th-april-2010.html

Conservative Home. (2010b). Sunday 21st February 2010. *Conservative Home Website*. Retrieved October 21, 2010, from http://conservativehome.blogs.com/frontpage/2010/02/sunday-21st-february-2010.html

Cook, R. (2010). From Republican "Lock" to Republican "Lockout"? In L. J. Sabato (Ed.), *The Year of Obama: How Barack Obama Won the White House* (pp. 75–89). London: Longman.

Cooper, M. (2011). Structured Viral Communications: The Political Economy and Social Organization of Digital Disintermediation. *Journal on Telecommunications and High Technology Law*, 9 (1), 15–80.

Cornfield, M. (2010). Game-Changers: New Technology and the 2008 Presidential Election. In L. J. Sabato (Ed.), *The Year of Obama: How Barack Obama Won the White House* (pp. 205–230). London: Longman.

Corrado, A., & Corbett, M. (2009). Rewriting the Playbook on Presidential Campaign Financing. In D. W. Johnson (Ed.), *Campaigning for President 2008: Strategy and Tactics, New Voices and New Techniques* (pp. 126–146). Abingdon: Routledge.

Corrado, A., Malbin, M. J., Mann, T. E., & Ornstein, N. J. (2010). *Reform in an Age of Networked Campaigns: How to Foster Citizen Participation Through Small Donors and Volunteers.* Washington, DC: Campaign Finance Institute, American Enterprise Institute, and the Brookings Institution.

Couldry, N. (2002). Playing for Celebrity: Big Brother as Ritual Event. *Television and New Media,* 3 (3), 283–293.

Couldry, N. (2012). *Media, Society, World: Social Theory and Digital Media Practice.* Cambridge: Polity.

Courpasson, D., & Dany, F. (2003). Indifference or Obedience? Business Firms as Democratic Hybrids. *Organization Studies,* 24 (8), 1231–1260.

CoveritLive. (2010). *CoveritLive.com Website.* Retrieved May 19, 2010, from http://www.coveritlive.com

Crawford, S. (1983). The Origin and Development of a Concept: the Information Society. *Bulletin of the Medical Library Association,* 71 (4), 380–385.

Crowston, K., & Williams, M. (2000). Reproduced and Emergent Genres of Communication on the World Wide Web. *Information Society,* 16 (3), 201–215.

Cryptome. (March 29, 2011). WikiLeaks Donor Relations. *Cryptome.org Website.* Retrieved June 22, 2011, from http://cryptome.org/0003/wl-donors.htm

Dahl, R. (1961). *Who Governs? Democracy and Power in an American City.* London: Yale University Press.

Dahlgren, P. (2009). *Media and Political Engagement: Citizens, Communication, and Democracy.* New York: Cambridge University Press.

Daily Express. (February 20, 2010). I Have Never Hit Anyone, Insists PM. *Daily Express Website.* Retrieved February 20, 2010, from http://www.dailyexpress.co.uk/posts/view/159499/I-have-never-hit-anyone-insists-PM/

Daily Mirror. (February 20, 2010a). I Have Never Hit Anyone, Insists PM. *Daily Mirror Website.* Retrieved February 20, 2010, from http://www.mirror.co.uk/news/latest/2010/02/20/i-have-never-hit-anyone-insists-pm-115875-22057223/

Daily Mirror. (February 22, 2010b). 'No Concerns' Over PM Bully Claims. *Daily Mirror Website.* Retrieved February 22, 2010, from http://www.mirror.co.uk/news/latest/2010/02/22/no-concerns-over-pm-bully-claims-115875-22062636/

Daily Star. (February 22, 2010a). Brown's Staff 'Rang Bully Helpline.' *Daily Star Website.* Retrieved February 22, 2010, from http://www.dailystar.co.uk/latestnews/view/123369/Brown-s-staff-rang-bully-helpline-/

Daily Star. (February 21, 2010b). Brown's Staff Rang Bullying Helpline. *Daily Star Website.* Retrieved February 21, 2010, from http://www.dailystar.co.uk/latestnews/view/123293/PM-staff-called-bullying-helpline-/

Daily Star. (February 20, 2010c). I Have Never Hit Anyone, Insists PM. *Daily Star Website.* Retrieved February 20, 2010, from http://www.dailystar.co.uk/latestnews/view/123181/I-have-never-hit-anyone-insists-PM/

Daily Star. (April 19, 2010d). Rivals Do an Add Lib. *Daily Star,* p. 6.

Darnton, R. (1995). *The Forbidden Bestsellers of Pre-Revolutionary France.* London: W. W. Norton.

Davies, N. (2008). *Flat Earth News: An Award-Winning Reporter Exposes Falsehood, Distortion and Propaganda in the Global Media.* London: Chatto & Windus.

Davis, E. (April 22, 2010). Extraordinary. Twitter parodies undercut media attacks on Clegg (#nickcleggsfault). Telegraph ends up defending itself. http://bit.ly/dmd6eA. Twitter.com/EvanHD. Retrieved April 22, 2010, from http://twitter.com/EvanHD/status/12633467781

Davis, R. (2009). *Typing Politics: The Role of Blogs in American Politics.* New York: Oxford University Press.

Davis, R., Baumgartner, J. C., Francia, P. L., & Morris, J. S. (2009). The Internet in U.S. Election Campaigns. In A. Chadwick & P. N. Howard (Eds.), *The Handbook of Internet Politics* (pp. 13–24). Abingdon: Routledge.

de la Torre, C., & Conaghan, C. (2009). The Hybrid Campaign: Tradition and Modernity in Ecuador's 2006 Presidential Election. *International Journal of Press/Politics,* 14 (3), 335–352.

DeLanda, M. (2006). *A New Philosophy of Society: Assemblage Theory and Social Complexity.* London: Continuum.

Deleuze, G., & Guattari, F. (2004). *A Thousand Plateaus: Capitalism and Schizophrenia* (B. Massumi, Trans. New ed.). London: Continuum.

Deuze, M. (2004). What Is Multimedia Journalism? *Journalism Studies,* 5 (2), 139–152.

Deuze, M. (2006). Participation, Remediation, Bricolage: Considering Principal Components of a Digital Culture. *Information Society,* 22 (2), 63–75.

Deuze, M. (2007). Convergence Culture in the Creative Industries. *International Journal of Cultural Studies,* 10 (2), 243–263.

Diamond, L. (2002). Thinking About Hybrid Regimes. *Journal of Democracy,* 13 (2), 21–35.

Dionne E. J., Jr. (September 9, 2008). Pulling the Curtain on Palin. *Washington Post Website.* Retrieved December 2, 2011, from http://www.washingtonpost.com/wp-dyn/content/article/2008/09/08/AR2008090801907.html

disappointme. (August 9, 2008). BarackRoll. *YouTube.* Retrieved February 9, 2012, from http://www.youtube.com/watch?v=wzSVOcgKq04

Doesfollow. (February 21, 2010). Search Query: krishgm and caroleharry. *Doesfollow Website.* Retrieved February 21, 2010, from http://doesfollow.com/krishgm/caroleharry

Domscheit-Berg, D. (2011). *Inside WikiLeaks: My Time With Julian Assange at the World's Most Dangerous Website* (Kindle ed.). New York: Crown.

Drezner, D., & Farrell, H. (2008). The Power and Politics of Blogs. *Public Choice,* 134 (1–2), 15–30.

Dunn, A. (2009). Comments on the Campaign and the Press. In K. H. Jamieson (Ed.), *Electing the President 2008: The Insiders' View* (pp. 135–150). Philadelphia: University of Pennsylvania Press.

Dunn, J. E. (December 10, 2010). Wikileaks DDoS Tool Downloads Grow Rapidly. *Techworld Website.* Retrieved December 10, 2010, from http://news.techworld.com/security/3252826/wikileaks-ddos-tool-downloads-grow-rapidly/

Dunn, T. N. (April 19, 2010). It's Lib Dems in Front. *Sun,* p. 1.

Easton, D. (1957). An Approach to the Analysis of Political Systems. *World Politics,* 9 (3), 383–400.

Easton, D. (1965). *A Systems Analysis of Political Life.* London: University of Chicago Press.

Economist. (February 22, 2010). Interview With Gordon Brown. *The Economist Website.* Retrieved February 22, 2010, from http://www.economist.com/world/britain/displayStory.cfm?story_id=15570484

Economist. (March 17, 2012). Online Newspapers: News of the World. *The Economist Website.* Retrieved March 29, 2012, from http://www.economist.com/node/21550262

Eisner, M. A. (2004). Corporate Environmentalism, Regulatory Reform, and Industry Self-Regulation: Toward Genuine Regulatory Reinvention in the United States. *Governance,* 17 (2), 145–167.

Ekman, J. (2009). Political Participation and Regime Stability: A Framework for Analyzing Hybrid Regimes. *International Political Science Review,* 30 (1), 7–31.

Ellison, S. (January 6, 2011). The Man Who Spilled the Secrets. *Vanity Fair Website.* Retrieved January 6, 2011, from http://www.vanityfair.com/politics/features/2011/02/the-guardian-201102

Elmer, G. (2012). Live Research: Twittering an Election Debate. *New Media and Society,* OnlineFirst Version at http://nms.sagepub.com/content/early/2012/09/23/1461444812457328.full.pdf (September 23, 2012).

Emery, D. (March 4, 2011). Is Barack Obama a Muslim? *About.com Urban Legends Website*. Retrieved November 30, 2011, from http://urbanlegends.about.com/library/bl_barack_obama_muslim.htm

Erjavec, K. (2004). Beyond Advertising and Journalism: Hybrid Promotional News Discourse. *Discourse and Society*, 15 (5), 553–578.

Esser, F., Reinemann, C., & David, F. (2001). Spin Doctors in the United States, Great Britain, and Germany: Metacommunication About Media Manipulation. *Harvard International Journal of Press/Politics*, 6 (1), 16–45.

Facebook. (2010). Facebook Democracy UK Page. *Facebook Website*. Retrieved April 15, 2010, from http://www.facebook.com/democracyuk

facts44. (March 15, 2008). Jeremiah Wright. *YouTube*. Retrieved November 24, 2011, from http://www.youtube.com/watch?v=36T1fnIafC0

Fairclough, N. (1992). *Discourse and Social Change*. Cambridge: Polity.

Farhi, P. (November 29, 2010). WikiLeaks Spurned New York Times, but Guardian Leaked State Department Cables. *The Washington Post*. Retrieved June 17, 2011, from http://www.washingtonpost.com/wp-dyn/content/article/2010/11/29/AR2010112905421.html

Farrell, H. (2003). Constructing the International Foundations of E-Commerce—The EU–U.S. Safe Harbor Arrangement. *International Organization*, 57 (2), 277–306.

Fawkes, G. (January 31, 2010). Labour Will Have a Khrushchev Moment of Truth in the End. *Guido Fawkes' Blog*. Retrieved June 15, 2010, from http://order-order.com/2010/01/31/labour-will-have-a-khrushchev-moment-of-truth-in-the-end/

Fawkes, G. (April 16, 2010). Clegg: Winning Here! *Guido Fawkes Website*. Retrieved May 17, 2010, from http://order-order.com/2010/04/16/clegg-winning-here/

Fenn, P. (2009). Communication Wars: Television and New Media. In D. W. Johnson (Ed.), *Campaigning for President 2008: Strategy and Tactics, New Voices and New Techniques* (pp. 210–221). Abingdon: Routledge.

Ferguson, T. (April 17, 2008). Financial Regulation? Don't Get Your Hopes Up. *Talking Points Memo Website*. Retrieved December 23, 2011, from http://tpmcafe.talkingpointsmemo.com/2008/04/17/financial_regulation_dont_get/

Fidler, R. F. (1997). *Mediamorphosis: Understanding New Media*. Thousand Oaks, CA: Pine Forge Press.

Fimreite, A. L., & Lægreid, P. (2009). Reorganizing the Welfare State Administration: Partnership, Networks and Accountability. *Public Management Review*, 11 (3), 281–297.

Financial Times. (April 13, 2012). About Us. *Financial Times Website*. Retrieved April 13, 2012, from http://aboutus.ft.com/corporate-information/ft-company/#axzz1rvwWuONs

Finney, K. (2009). Comments on Political Party Panel. In K. H. Jamieson (Ed.), *Electing the President 2008: The Insiders' View* (pp. 151–167). Philadelphia: University of Pennsylvania Press.

Foss, N. J. (2003). Selective Intervention and Internal Hybrids: Interpreting and Learning From the Rise and Decline of the Oticon Spaghetti Organization. *Organization Science*, 14 (3), 331–350.

Fowler, M. (2008). Obama: No Surprise That Hard-Pressed Pennsylvanians Turn Bitter. *Huffington Post Website*. Retrieved November 25, 2011, from http://www.huffingtonpost.com/mayhill-fowler/obama-no-surprise-that-ha_b_96188.html

Fox News. (January 22, 2007). Hillary Clinton Drops Madrassa Bomb on Barack Obama (Transcript of "The Big Story with John Gibson" January 19, 2007). *Fox News Website*. Retrieved November 30, 2011, from http://www.foxnews.com/story/0,2933,245582,00.html

Fraser, E. (February 20, 2010a). Exclusive: Gordon Brown refutes allegations he hit an adviser—says he's never hit anyone in his life …. http://bit.ly/byZ7Dl. Twitter.com/frasereC4. Retrieved February 20, 2010, from http://twitter.com/frasereC4/status/9399836988

Fraser, E. (February 20, 2010b). Observer Rawnsley alleges Brown received an unprecedented reprimand from the head of the Civil Service for abusive behaviour to staff. *Twitter.com/frasereC4*. Retrieved February 20, 2010, from http://twitter.com/frasereC4/status/9399836988

Fraser, E. (February 20, 2010c). Observer story on brown sensational—just read pre release. *Twitter.com/fraserC4*. Retrieved February 20, 2010, from http://twitter.com/fraserC4/status/9399177332

Freedland, J. (February 22, 2010). Revelations About Brown are Damaging, but They Hold no Surprises for Voters. *Guardian Website*. Retrieved February 22, 2010, from http://www.guardian.co.uk/politics/2010/feb/22/revelations-brown-damaging-voters

Funny or Die. (2008). Paris Hilton Responds to McCain Ad. *Funny or Die Website*. Retrieved December 2, 2011, from http://www.funnyordie.com/videos/64ad536a6d/paris-hilton-resp onds-to-mccain-ad-from-paris-hilton-adam-ghost-panther-mckay-and-chris-henchy

Gaber, I. (2011). The Slow Death of the Westminster Lobby: Collateral Damage from the MPs' Expenses Scandal. *British Politics*, 4 (4), 478–497.

Galtung, J., & Ruge, M. H. (1965). The Structure of Foreign News: The Presentation of the Congo, Cuba, and Cyprus in Four Norwegian Newspapers. *Journal of Peace Research*, 2 (1), 64–90.

Gans, H. J. (1979). *Deciding What's News: A Study of CBS Evening News, NBC Nightly News, Newsweek, and Time* (25th Anniversary 2004 ed.). New York: Pantheon.

Garcia Aviles, J., Leon, B., Sanders, K., & Harrison, J. (2004). Journalists at Digital Television Newsrooms in Britain and Spain: Workflow and Multi-Skilling in a Competitive Environment. *Journalism Studies*, 5 (1), 87–100.

Garthwaite, C., & Moore, T. J. (January 1, 2011). Can Celebrity Endorsements Affect Political Outcomes? Evidence from the 2008 U.S. Democratic Presidential Primary. *Craig Garthwaite's Website*. Retrieved December 20, 2011, from http://www.kellogg.northwestern.edu/faculty/garthwaite/htm/celebrityendorsements_garthwaitemoore.pdf

Gershuny, J. (2000). *Changing Times: Work and Leisure in Postindustrial Societies*. Oxford: Oxford University Press.

Gibbon, G. (April 30, 2010). What the Post-Debate Reaction Polls Tell Us. *Channel 4 News Website*. Retrieved May 4, 2010, from http://blogs.channel4.com/snowblog/2010/04/30/what-the-p ost-debate-reaction-polls-tell-us

Gibson, J. (April 15, 2010). Note to Lib Dem HQ. We can see what you're doing to our tracker and @bruntonspall can stop it. You're barred! http://bit.ly/bU4UVQ. *Twitter.com/janinegibson*. Retrieved April 15, 2010, from http://twitter.com/janinegibson/status/12243055856

Gillespie, M. (1995). *Television, Ethnicity and Cultural Change*. London: Routledge.

Gilroy, P. (1993). *The Black Atlantic: Modernity and Double Consciousness*. London: Verso.

Gitelman, L. (2006). *Always Already New: Media, History, and the Data of Culture*. Cambridge, MA: MIT Press.

Gliem, D. E., & Janack, J. A. (2008). A Portrait of a Transformational Leader: An Analysis of Text and Image on BarackObama.com. *American Communication Journal*, 10 (3).

Glynn, K., & Tyson, A. F. (2007). Indigeneity, Media and Cultural Globalization: The Case of Mataku, or The Maori X-Files. *International Journal of Cultural Studies*, 10 (2), 205–224.

Goad, R. (June 10, 2008). Blog Traffic Reaches All Time High. *Hitwise Website*. Retrieved May 24, 2010, from http://weblogs.hitwise.com/robin-goad/2008/06/uk_blog_traffic_reaches_all_ time_high.html

Goldblatt, J. (March 12, 2008). Barack Obama's Controversial Pastor Puts Church In Hot Water. *Fox News Website*. Retrieved December 6, 2011, from http://www.foxnews.com/story/0,2933,337308,00.html

Golding, P., & Elliott, P. (1979). *Making the News*. London: Longman.

Goodin, R. E., Rice, J. M., Parpo, A., & Eriksson, L. (2008). *Discretionary Time: a New Measure of Freedom*. Cambridge: Cambridge University Press.

Google Blog Search. (November 30, 2011). Google Blog Search: "Obama is a Muslim" for the year 2006. *Google Blog Search*. Retrieved November 30, 2011, from http://www.google.co.uk/sea rch?aq=f&sourceid=chrome&ie=UTF-8&q=Obama+Muslin#q=%22Obama+is+a+Muslim %22&hl=en&prmdo=1&tbs=sbd:1,cdr:1,cd_min:1/1/2006,cd_max:1/1/2007&tbm=blg& prmd=imvns&ei=elTWTpa9CoP1sgbQvNXODg&start=10&sa=N&filter=0&bav=on.2,or .r_gc.r_pw.,cf.osb&fp=6f0b926da9d13bd3&biw=1391&bih=1015

Google News Search. (November 30, 2011). Google News Search: "Obama is a Muslim" for the Year 2007. *Google News Search*. Retrieved November 30, 2011, from http://www.google. co.uk/search?aq=f&sourceid=chrome&ie=UTF-8&q=Obama+Muslin#q=%22Obama+is+a +Muslim%22&hl=en&tbs=sbd:1,cdr:1,cd_min:2007,cd_max:2007&tbm=nws&prmd=imv ns&ei=N1HWTvWpNsiyhAeew6R2&start=20&sa=N&bav=on.2,or.r_gc.r_pw.,cf.osb&fp= 31a082becceaa79f&biw=1391&bih=1015

Google Replay Search. (April 15, 2010a). Google Replay Real-Time Search Archive for "krishgm." *Google Replay Search*. Retrieved May 19, 2010, from http://www.google.co.uk/search?q= krishgm&hl=en&prmd=u&source=lnms&ei=SuTzS6uNNYmM0gTL4dWWDQ&sa=X &oi=mode_link&ct=mode&ved=0CAwQ_AU&&tbs=mbl:1,mbl_hs:1271286000,mbl_ he:1271372399

Google Replay Search. (2010b). National Bullying Helpline. *Google Replay Search*. Retrieved June 23, 2010, from http://www.google.co.uk/search?q=national+bullying+helpline&hl=en& prmdo=1&prmd=n&filter=0&tbs=mbl:1,mbl_hs:1266710400,mbl_he:1266796799,mbl_ rs:1266769607,mbl_re:1266772015

Goss, K. A., & Heaney, M. T. (2010). Organizing Women as Women: Hybridity and Grassroots Collective Action in the 21st Century. *Perspectives on Politics*, 8 (1), 27–52.

Grabe, M. E., & Bucy, E. P. (2010). *Image Bite Politics: News and the Visual Framing of Elections*. New York: Oxford University Press.

Greenwald, G. (December 2, 2010). Joe Lieberman Emulates Chinese Dictators. *Salon.com Website*. Retrieved December 2, 2010, from http://www.salon.com/news/opinion/glenn_ greenwald/2010/12/01/lieberman/index.html

Grewal, D. S. (2008). *Network Power: The Social Dynamics of Globalization*. New Haven, CT: Yale University Press.

Grice, A. (April 19, 2010). Clegg's Popularity Soars on Two Fronts; Lib Dem Leader's Stock Rises with Voters, While Mandelson Concedes Possibility of a Coalition. *Guardian*, p. 8.

Grusin, R. (2010). *Premediation: Affect and Mediality After 9/11*. Basingstoke: Palgrave Macmillan.

Guardian. (November 2, 2009). Investigate Your MP's Expenses. *Guardian Website*. Retrieved March 2, 2012, from http://mps-expenses.guardian.co.uk/

Guardian. (February 22, 2010). Gordon Brown: Brought to Book. *Guardian Website*. Retrieved February 22, 2010, from http://www.guardian.co.uk/commentisfree/2010/feb/22/andrew -rawnsley-gordon-brown-temper

Guardian. (August 24, 2012). Who Is Julian Assange? By the People Who Know Him Best. *Guardian Website*. Retrieved August 29, 2012, from http://www.guardian.co.uk/media/2012/aug/24/ who-is-julian-assange

Gulati, G. J. (2010). No Laughing Matter: The Role of New Media in the 2008 Election. In L. J. Sabato (Ed.), *The Year of Obama: How Barack Obama Won the White House* (pp. 187–203). London: Longman.

Guru-Murthy, K. (February 21, 2010). been looking into "National Bullying Helpline" after their Downing Street claim. they have 2 Tory Patrons and Cameron quote on website. *Twitter.com/krishgm*. Retrieved February 21, 2010, from http://twitter.com/krishgm/ statuses/9437279195

Habermas, J. (1989). *The Structural Transformation of the Public Sphere*. Cambridge, MA: MIT Press.

Hallin, D. C., & Mancini, P. (2004). *Comparing Media Systems: Three Models of Media and Politics*. New York: Cambridge University Press.

Heeks, R., & Stanforth, C. (2007). Understanding E-Government Project Trajectories From an Actor-Network Perspective. *European Journal of Information Systems*, 16 (2), 165–177.

Helm, T., & Asthana, A. (February 21, 2010a). Civil Service Chief Warned Gordon Brown Over Abusive Treatment of Staff. *Observer Website*. Retrieved February 21, 2010, from http://www. guardian.co.uk/politics/2010/feb/21/gordon-brown-abusive-treatment-staff

Helm, T., & Asthana, A. (April 18, 2010b). Nick Clegg Appeals to Youth Vote and Liberal Democrats Maintain Poll Surge. *Guardian Website*. Retrieved April 18, 2010, from http://www.guardian. co.uk/politics/2010/apr/18/election-liberal-democrat-surge-nick-clegg

Herbst, S. (1993). *Numbered Voices: How Opinion Polling Has Shaped American Politics.* Chicago: University of Chicago Press.

heyitsjoe. (April 20, 2007). MoveOn.org Ad Against McCain: "Bomb Iran" Song. *YouTube.* Retrieved February 9, 2012, from http://www.youtube.com/watch?v=U39zae4IxUA

Hodgson, D. E. (2004). Project Work: The Legacy of Bureaucratic Control in the Post-Bureaucratic Organization. *Organization,* 11 (1), 81–100.

HollaAtYoDaddy. (April 22, 2008). Baracky The Movie. *YouTube.* Retrieved February 9, 2012, from http://www.youtube.com/watch?v=s4sDlVFlOfk

Holton, R. J. (1998). *Globalization and the Nation–State.* Basingstoke, UK: Palgrave Macmillan.

Hoskins, A., & O'Loughlin, B. (2010). *War and Media: The Emergence of Diffused War.* Cambridge, UK: Polity Press.

Howard, P. N., & Chadwick, A. (2009). Conclusion: Political Omnivores and Wired States. In A. Chadwick & P. N. Howard (Eds.), *The Routledge Handbook of Internet Politics* (pp. 424–434). New York and London: Routledge.

Howe, J. (2008). *Crowdsourcing: How the Power of the Crowd is Driving the Future of Business.* New York: Crown.

Huffington, A. (March 28, 2007). News 2.0: The Hybrid Future is Kicking Down the Door. *Huffington Post Website.* Retrieved August 2, 2012, from http://www.huffingtonpost.com/arianna-huffington/news-20-the-hybrid-future_b_44401.html?

Humanitainment. (May 1, 2008). The Empire Strikes Barack. *YouTube.* Retrieved February 9, 2012, from http://www.youtube.com/watch?v=a8lvc-azCXY&feature=related

Insight. (January 17, 2007). Hillary's Team Has Questions about Obama's Muslim Background. *Insight Website.* Retrieved November 30, 2011, from http://web.archive.org/web/20070121201523/http://www.insightmag.com/Media/MediaManager/Obama_2.htm

International Telecommunication Union. (2011). *Measuring the Information Society, 2011.* Geneva: International Telecommunication Unit.

Ipsos MORI. (April 16, 2010). The Leaders' Debates: Immediate Public Reaction—Clegg Wins the First Round. *Ipsos MORI Website.* Retrieved April 20, 2010, from http://www.ipsos-mori.com/Assets/Docs/News/ipsos-mori-public-reaction-to-leaders-debate.pdf

Irvine, C. (February 22, 2010). Gordon Brown under Pressure to Explain Anti-Bullying Chief's Allegations. *Daily Telegraph Website.* Retrieved February 22, 2010, from http://www.telegraph.co.uk/news/newstopics/politics/gordon-brown/7289856/Gordon-Brown-under-pressure-to-explain-anti-bullying-chiefs-allegations.html

ITV, Sky, & BBC. (April 15, 2010). Programme Format Agreed by All Parties 1st March 2010. *ITV Website.* Retrieved April 29, 2010, from http://www.itv.com/utils/cached/common/ProgrammeFormat2.pdf

ITV News. (April 15, 2010a). The Election Debates. *ITV News Website.* Retrieved April 15, 2010, from http://www.itv.com/electiondebate/

ITV News. (2010b). ITV News at Ten, April 15.

ITV News. (2010c). ITV News, February 21.

james1053. (November 12, 2007). Hillary's Ringer Winks After Planted Question. *YouTube.* Retrieved November 22, 2011, from http://www.youtube.com/watch?v=MGvRkeiX8G4&feature=related

Jenkins, H. (2006). *Convergence Culture: Where Old and New Media Collide.* New York: New York University Press.

Johnson, D. W. (2009). An Election Like No Other? In D. W. Johnson (Ed.), *Campaigning for President 2008: Strategy and Tactics, New Voices and New Techniques* (pp. 1–28). Abingdon: Routledge.

johny boy. (September 28, 2008). SNL Tina Fey Sarah Palin interview with Katie Couric. *Metatube Website.* Retrieved December 2, 2011, from http://www.metatube.com/en/videos/15750/SNL-Tina-Fey-Sarah-Palin-interview-with-Katie-Couric

Jones, A. S. (2009). *Losing the News: the Future of the News That Feeds Democracy.* New York: Oxford University Press.

Kantor, J. (January 9, 2008). A Show of Emotion That Reverberated Beyond the Campaign. *New York Times Website*. Retrieved November 30, 2011, from http://www.nytimes.com/2008/01/09/us/politics/09moment.html?pagewanted=print

Karl, T. L. (1995). The Hybrid Regimes of Central America. *Journal of Democracy*, 6 (3), 72–86.

Karpf, D. (2012). *The MoveOn Effect: The Unexpected Transformation of American Political Advocacy*. New York: Oxford University Press.

Kaye, K. (2009). *Campaign '08: A Turning Point for Digital Media*. Jersey City, NJ: Virilion.

Keen, A. (2007). *The Cult of the Amateur: How Today's Internet Is Killing Our Culture and Assaulting Our Economy*. London: Nicholas Brealey.

Kenski, K., Hardy, B. W., & Jamieson, K. H. (2010). *The Obama Victory: How Media, Money, and Message Shaped the 2008 Election*. New York: Oxford University Press.

Keohane, R., & Nye, J. (1989). *Power and Interdependence: World Politics in Transition* (Second ed.). London: Scott, Foresman.

Khatchadourian, R. (June 7, 2010). No Secrets: Julian Assange's Mission for Total Transparency. *New Yorker Website*. Retrieved June 5, 2011, from http://www.newyorker.com/reporting/2010/06/07/100607fa_fact_khatchadourian?printable=true&currentPage=all

Kickert, W. J. M. (1993). Autopoiesis and the Science of (Public) Administration: Essence, Sense and Nonsense. *Organization Studies*, 14 (2), 261–278.

Kilborn, R. (2003). *Staging the Real: Factual TV Programming in the Age of "Big Brother."* Manchester: Manchester University Press.

Kim, E.-G., & Hamilton, J. W. (2006). Capitulation to Capital? OhmyNews as Alternative Media. *Media, Culture and Society*, 28 (4), 541–560.

King, O. (February 20, 2010). Channel 4 News interview with Gordon Brown on his election launch. Tonight 1910. Only network TV interview he giving today. *Twitter.com/oliverjamesking*. Retrieved February 20, 2010, from http://twitter.com/oliverjamesking/status/9381529327

Kitschelt, H. (1986). Political Opportunity Structures: Anti Nuclear Movements in Four Democracies. *British Journal of Political Science*, 1 (16), 57–85.

Klinenberg, E. (2005). Convergence: News Production in a Digital Age. *Annals of the American Academy of Political and Social Science*, 597, 48–64.

Kovach, B., & Rosenstiel, T. (1999). *Warp Speed: America in the Age of Mixed Media*. New York: Century Foundation Press.

Kraidy, M. (2005). *Hybridity, or the Cultural Logic of Globalization*. Philadelphia: Temple University Press.

Kreiss, D. (2012). *Taking Our Country Back: The Crafting of Networked Politics From Howard Dean to Barack Obama*. New York: Oxford University Press.

Kress, G. (2010). *Multimodality: A Social Semiotic Approach to Contemporary Communication*. Abingdon: Routledge.

Kuenssberg, L. (February 22, 2010a). David Cameron calls for an inquiry into no 10 bullying allegations. *Twitter.com/BBCLauraK*. Retrieved February 22, 2010, from http://twitter.com/BBCLauraK/status/9469476919

Kuenssberg, L. (February 22, 2010b). Lord Mandelson tells me the bullying row has "acquired an odour" of a political operation directed at PM. Accuses Tories of directing jo … *Twitter.com/BBCLauraK*. Retrieved February 22, 2010, from http://twitter.com/BBCLauraK/statuses/9472417887

Kuenssberg, L. (February 22, 2010c). One of the patrons of the bullying charity has just resigned. *Twitter.com/BBCLauraK*. Retrieved February 22, 2010, from http://twitter.com/BBCLauraK/status/9469476919

Kuenssberg, L. (February 22, 2010d). PM's spokesman says Sir Gus O'Donnell has never raised concerns with Brown over bullying of staff. *Twitter.com/BBCLauraK*. Retrieved February 22, 2010, from http://twitter.com/BBCLauraK/statuses/9482433951

Kuenssberg, L. (February 22, 2010e). Tory sources totally reject idea they had anything to do with charity allegations—she contacted BBC direct not through tories yesterday. *Twitter.*

com/BBCLauraK. Retrieved February 22, 2010, from http://twitter.com/BBCLauraK/statuses/9474573735

Kuenssberg, L. (April 29, 2010f). Twitpic Photo. *Twitpic.com*. Retrieved May 18, 2010, from http://twitpic.com/1jghho

Kurtz, H. (September 8, 2008). Palin & Press: A Testy Start. *Washington Post Website*. Retrieved December 2, 2011, from http://www.washingtonpost.com/wp-dyn/content/article/2008/09/07/AR2008090702646.html

Kwak, H., Lee, C., Park, H., & Moon, S. (2010). What is Twitter, a Social Network or a News Media? *Proceedings of the 19th International World Wide Web (WWW) Conference*, 19, 591–600.

Labourlist. (2010). Election 2010. *Labourlist Website*. Retrieved May 17, 2010, from http://www.labourlist.org/topics/Election2010/

lanerobertlane. (May 8, 2010). Kay Burley Bullies a Protester in the Name of "Journalism." *YouTube*. Retrieved June 14, 2012, from http://www.youtube.com/watch?v=ELJh2bTK1ew&feature=plcp

Langlois, R. N., & Garzarelli, G. (2008). Of Hackers and Hairdressers: Modularity and the Organizational Economics of Open-Source Collaboration. *Industry and Innovation*, 15 (2), 125–143.

Latour, B. (1993). *We Have Never Been Modern*. Cambridge, MA: Harvard University Press.

Latour, B. (2005). *Reassembling the Social: An Introduction to Actor Network Theory*. Oxford: Oxford University Press.

Left Foot Forward. (2010). *Left Foot Forward Website*. Retrieved May 17, 2010, from http://www.leftfootforward.org/page/13

Leigh, D. (December 3, 2010). Diplomatic Cables: Gaddafi Risked Nuclear Disaster After UN Slight. *The Guardian*. Retrieved June 17, 2011, from http://www.guardian.co.uk/world/2010/dec/03/wikileaks-cables-libya-enriched-uranium

Leigh, D., & Harding, L. (2011). *WikiLeaks: Inside Julian Assange's War on Secrecy* (Kindle ed.). London: Guardian Books.

Levine, E. (2008). Distinguishing Television: The Changing Meanings of Television Liveness. *Media, Culture and Society*, 30 (3), 393–409.

Levinson, P. (1998). *The Soft Edge: A Natural History and Future of the Information Revolution*. New York: Routledge.

Levitsky, S., & Way, L. (2010). *Competitive Authoritarianism: Hybrid Regimes after the Cold War*. New York: Cambridge University Press.

Libdemvoice. (April 22, 2010). Sky News Debate: Nick Clegg Opening Statement. *YouTube Website*. Retrieved April 22, 2010, from http://www.youtube.com/watch?v=5EFnJ_pQ2hI&feature=youtu.be&a

Liberal Democrat Voice. (2010). Monthly Archives: April 2010. *Liberal Democrat Voice Website*. Retrieved May 17, 2010, from http://www.libdemvoice.org/date/2010/04

Livingstone, S., & Lunt, P. (1994). *Talk on Television: Audience Participation and Public Debate*. London: Routledge.

Lockwood, M., & Davidson, J. (2010). Environmental Governance and the Hybrid Regime of Australian Natural Resource Management. *Geoforum*, 41 (3), 388–398.

Lukes, S. (2004). *Power: A Radical View* (Second ed.). Basingstoke, UK: Palgrave Macmillan.

Lulka, D. (2009). The Residual Humanism of Hybridity: Retaining a Sense of the Earth. *Transactions of the Institute of British Geographers*, 34 (3), 378–393.

Luntz, F. (April 16, 2010). U.S. Pollster Uses Instant Response Method to Rate Politicians Debate. *Sun Website*. Retrieved April 16, 2010, from http://www.thesun.co.uk/sol/homepage/news/election2010/2934852/US-pollster-uses-Instant-Response-method-to-rate-politicians-debate.html

Luvaas, B. (2009). Dislocating Sounds: The Deterritorialization of Indonesian Indie Pop. *Cultural Anthropology*, 24 (2), 246–279.

Lyons, J., & Beattie, J. (April 19, 2010). Crush Clegg: Desperate Tories Fightback Panic. *Daily Mirror*, pp. 10–11.

Ma3lst0rm. (2008). The Sound of Freedom. *YouTube*. Retrieved August 6, 2012, from http://www.youtube.com/watch?v=6-lDEEs9ipw

Macdonald, T. (2008). What's So Special About States? Liberal Legitimacy in a Globalising World. *Political Studies*, 56 (3), 544–565.

Maguire, K. (April 22, 2010). So bad for the Cons spinner Paul Stephenson's trying to brief hacks in the Bristol centre while debate's on. Poor form. *Twitter.com/Kevin_Maguire*. Retrieved April 22, 2010, from http://twitter.com/Kevin_Maguire/status/12658132770

Malbin, M. (November 24, 2008). Reality Check: Obama Received about the Same Percentage from Small Donors in 2008 as Bush in 2004. *Campaign Finance Institute Website*. Retrieved December 13, 2011, from http://www.cfinst.org/Press/PReleases/08-11-24/Realty_Check_-_Obama_Small_Donors.aspx

Mann, M. (1986). *The Sources of Social Power, Volume 1: A History from the Beginning to 1760 AD*. Cambridge: Cambridge University Press.

Manning, L. (February 21, 2010). National Bullying Helpline tells ITV News they have had several calls from staff at Downing Street complaining about bullying culture. *Twitter.com/lucymanning*. Retrieved February 21, 2010, from http://twitter.com/lucymanning/status/9435675183

Manovich, L. (2001). *The Language of New Media*. Cambridge, MA: MIT Press.

Margolis, J. (2009). Comments on Advertising. In K. H. Jamieson (Ed.), *Electing the President 2008: The Insiders' View* (pp. 108–134). Philadelphia: University of Pennsylvania Press.

Marvin, C. (1988). *When Old Technologies Were New*. New York: Oxford University Press.

Massanari, A. L., & Howard, P. N. (2011). Information Technologies and Omnivorous News Diets Over Three U.S. Presidential Elections. *Journal of Information Technology and Politics*, 8 (2), 177–198.

Mast, J. (2009). New Directions in Hybrid Popular Television: A Reassessment of Television Mock-Documentary. *Media, Culture and Society*, 31 (2), 231–250.

May, A. L. (2009). The Preacher and the Press: How the Jeremiah Wright Story Became the First Feeding Frenzy in the Digital Age. In D. W. Johnson (Ed.), *Campaigning for President 2008: Strategy and Tactics, New Voices and New Techniques* (pp. 78–101). Abingdon: Routledge.

Mazzetti, M. (November 28, 2010). U.S. Expands Role of Diplomats in Spying. *New York Times Website*. Retrieved June 20, 2011, from http://www.nytimes.com/2010/11/29/world/29spy.html

Mazzoleni, G., & Schultz, W. (1999). "Mediatization" of Politics: A Challenge for Democracy? *Political Communication*, 16 (3), 247–261.

McCarthy, K. (February 21, 2010a). RT @AdamBienkov New Post: Who are the National Bullying Helpline? http://bit.ly/cd8hYJ < incl link to this http://bit.ly/92bpMy. *Twitter.com/KerryMP*. Retrieved February 21, 2010, from http://twitter.com/KerryMP/status/9450210148

McCarthy, K. (February 20, 2010b). RT @mickswales: Getting sick of journos who made careers on back of links to Lab now trashing us to curry favour with Tories. <#rawnsleyrot. *Twitter.com/KerryMP*. Retrieved February 20, 2010, from http://twitter.com/KerryMP/status/9403106398

mckathomas. (April 19, 2007). Bomb Bomb Bomb, Bomb Bomb Iran. *YouTube*. Retrieved December 19, 2011, from http://www.youtube.com/watch?v=o-zoPgv_nYg

McLuhan, M. (1964). *Understanding Media: The Extensions of Man*. New York: McGraw-Hill.

McNair, B. (2006). *Cultural Chaos: Journalism, News and Power in a Globalized World*. London: Routledge.

McQuail, D. (1992). *Media Performance: Mass Communication in the Public Interest*. London: Sage.

Messner, M., & DiStaso, M. W. (2008). The Source Cycle: How Traditional Media and Weblogs Use Each Other as Sources. *Journalism Studies*, 9 (3), 447–463.

Metcalfe, N. (April 15, 2010). Leaders' Debate—As It Happened. *MSN UK Website*. Retrieved April 15, 2010, from http://msnuknews.spaces.live.com/Blog/cns!93FC6ECA7DF64076!17170.entry

Mey, S. (January 4, 2010). Leak-o-nomy: The Economy of Wikileaks *Medien-Ökonomie-Blog*. Retrieved July 22, 2011, from http://stefan-mey.com/2010/01/04/leak-o-nomy-the-economy-of-wikileaks

Miller, C. R., & Shepherd, D. (2004). Blogging as Social Action: A Genre Analysis of the Weblog. In L. Gurak, S. Antonijevic, L. Johnson, C. Ratliff & J. Reyman (Eds.), *Into the Blogosphere: Rhetoric, Community, and Culture of Weblogs*. St. Paul: University of Minnesota. Retrieved October 21, 2012, from http://blog.lib.umn.edu/blogosphere/

Miller, L. S. (May 16, 2008). Obama Girl Directors Get Feature Gig. *Gigaom Website*. Retrieved December 14, 2011, from http://gigaom.com/video/obama-girl-directors-get-feature-gig

Mitchell, G. (2011). *The Age of Wikileaks: From Collateral Murder to Cablegate (and Beyond)* (Kindle ed.). New York: Sinclair Books.

Molotch, H., & Lester, M. (1974). News as Purposive Behavior: On the Strategic Use of Routine Events, Accidents, and Scandals. *American Sociological Review*, 39 (1), 101–112.

Montgomerie, T. (February 20, 2010a). Andrew Rawnsley's Revelations About Gordon Brown. *Conservative Home Website*. Retrieved February 20, 2010, from http://conservativehome.blogs.com/leftwatch/2010/02/andrew-rawnsleys-revelations-about-gordon-brown.html

Montgomerie, T. (February 22, 2010b). BREAKING: Cameron suggests Sir Philip Mawer, custodian of ministerial code, runs an inquiry to get to bottom of bullying allegations #pbage. *Twitter.com/TimMontgomerie*. Retrieved February 22, 2010, from http://twitter.com/TimMontgomerie/status/9471176686

Montgomerie, T. (January 30, 2010c). Brown Accused of Violence Against Staff in Damaging New Revelations. *Conservative Home Website*. Retrieved June 15, 2010, from http://conservative-home.blogs.com/leftwatch/2010/01/brown-accused-of-violence-against-staff-in-damaging-new-revelations.html

Montgomerie, T. (2010). Twitpic photo. *Twitpic.com*. Retrieved May 18, 2010, from http://twitpic.com/1jgg15

Moreno, J. (December 9, 2010). WikiLeaks Cables Had a Huge Impact in Spain, Says El Pais Editor-in-Chief. *Guardian Website*. Retrieved December 9, 2010, from http://www.guardian.co.uk/world/2010/dec/09/wikileaks-cables-huge-impact-spain/print

Mottola, C. (2009). Comments on Advertising. In K. H. Jamieson (Ed.), *Electing the President 2008: The Insiders' View* (pp. 108–134). Philadelphia: University of Pennsylvania Press.

Nagourney, A. (September 2, 2008a). In Political Realm, "Family Problem" Emerges as Test. *New York Times Website*. Retrieved November 30, 2011, from http://www.nytimes.com/2008/09/02/us/politics/02assess.html?pagewanted=print

Nagourney, A. (January 4, 2008b). Obama Takes Iowa in a Big Turnout as Clinton Falters; Huckabee Victor. *New York Times Website*. Retrieved February 10, 2012, from http://www.nytimes.com/2008/01/04/us/politics/04elect.html?pagewanted=all

Nederveen Pieterse, J. (2001). Hybridity, So What? The Anti-hybridity Backlash and the Riddles of Recognition. *Theory, Culture, and Society*, 18 (2–3), 219–245.

News of the World. (February 20, 2010). PM Denies He Hit Aide. *News of the World Website*. Retrieved February 20, 2010, from http://www.newsoftheworld.co.uk/news/735212/Brown-I-have-never-hit-anyone-in-my-life.html

Nielsen. (March 22, 2010). Americans Using TV and Internet Together 35% More Than A Year Ago. *Nielsen Website*. Retrieved May 30, 2012, from http://blog.nielsen.com/nielsenwire/online_mobile/three-screen-report-q409

Nielsen. (2011a). The Cross-Platform Report, Quarter 1, 2011. *Nielsen Website*. Retrieved March 2, 2012, from http://www.nielsen.com/us/en/insights/reports-downloads/2011/cross-platform-report-q1-2011.html

Nielsen. (2011b). The Cross-Platform Report, Quarter 3, 2011. *Nielsen Website*. Retrieved March 2, 2012, from http://www.nielsen.com/us/en/insights/reports-downloads/2012/cross-platform-report-q3-2011.html

Nielsen. (2012). The Cross-Platform Report, Quarter 4, 2011. *Nielsen Website*. Retrieved May 30, 2012, from http://nielsen.com/us/en/insights/reports-downloads/2012/the-cross-platform-report-q4-2011.html

Nielsen, R. K. (2011). Mundane Internet Tools, Mobilizing Practices, and the Coproduction of Citizenship in Political Campaigns. *New Media and Society*, 13 (5), 755–771.

Nielsen, R. K. (2012). *Ground Wars: Personalized Political Communication in Political Campaigns.* Princeton: Princeton University Press.

Nord, L. W. (2006). Still the Middle Way: A Study of Political Communication Practices in Swedish Election Campaigns. *Harvard International Journal of Press/Politics*, 11 (1), 64–76.

Nuttall, S. (February 21, 2010). Oh dear & the Patron of the National Bullying Helpline is .... wait for it ....Ann Widdecombe. Be afraid. Be very afraid Mr Brown! *Twitter.com/sarahcopywriter*. Retrieved February 21, 2010, from http://twitter.com/sarahcopywriter/statuses/9436865337

O'Carroll, L. (February 15, 2012). Times Digital Subscribers Rise to Just under 120,000. *Guardian Website*. Retrieved March 7, 2012, from http://www.guardian.co.uk/media/2012/feb/15/times-digital-subscribers-rise

O'Loughlin, B. (April 20, 2010). TV Debate: Initial Twitter Analysis Shows Level of Support for Party Leaders and Winners by Topic. *New Political Communication Unit Website*. Retrieved April 20, 2010, from http://newpolcom.rhul.ac.uk/npcu-blog/2010/4/20/tv-debate-initial-twitter-analysis-shows-level-of-support-fo.html

Oakeshott, I. (February 21, 2010). Gordon Brown Forced To Deny Hitting Staff. *Sunday Times Website*. Retrieved February 21, 2010, from http://www.timesonline.co.uk/tol/news/politics/article7034938.ece#cid=OTC-RSS&attr=797084

Oborne, P. (April 22, 2010). Dirty Tricks of the REAL Nasty Party. *Daily Mail Website*. Retrieved April 22, 2010, from http://www.dailymail.co.uk/debate/article-1267912/General-Election-2010-Liberal-Democrats-dirty-tricks-real-nasty-party.html

Operation Leakspin. (2010). Crowdsourcing WikiLeaks Content. *Reddit Website*. Retrieved July 27, 2011, from http://www.reddit.com/r/leakspin

Ostrom, E. (1990). *Governing the Commons: The Evolution of Institutions for Collective Action.* Cambridge: Cambridge University Press.

Owen, D. (2010). Media in the 2008 Election: 21st Century Campaign, Same Old Story. In L. J. Sabato (Ed.), *The Year of Obama: How Barack Obama Won the White House* (pp. 167–186). London: Longman.

Oxford Internet Survey. (2007). *The Internet in Britain: 2007.* Oxford: Oxford Internet Institute.

Oxford Internet Survey. (2009). *The Internet in Britain: 2009.* Oxford: Oxford Internet Institute.

Oxford Internet Survey. (2011). *Next Generation Users: the Internet in Britain, 2011.* Oxford: Oxford Internet Institute.

Pack, M. (April 22, 2010). I liked a YouTube video—Sky News Debate: Nick Clegg opening statement http://youtu.be/5EFnJ_pQ2hI?a. *Twitter.com/markpack*. Retrieved April 22, 2010, from http://twitter.com/markpack/status/12661723684

Packer, G. (2010). The Right to Secrecy. *The New Yorker Website*. Retrieved November 29, 2010, from http://www.newyorker.com/online/blogs/georgepacker/2010/11/the-right-to-secrecy.html

Pappas, A. (2010). Die-Hard "West Wing" Fans Keep Show Going by Assuming Characters' Identities on Twitter. *Daily Caller Website*. Retrieved December 2, 2010, from http://dailycaller.com/2010/11/29/die-hard-'west-wing'-fans-keep-show-going-by-assuming-characters-identities-on-twitter/print/

Parsons, T. (1951). *The Social System.* New York: Free Press.

Patterson, T. E. (1993). *Out of Order.* New York: Knopf.

Patterson, T. E. (1998). Time and News: The Media's Limitations as an Instrument of Democracy. *International Political Science Review*, 19 (1), 55–67.

Pedersen, J. S., & Dobbin, F. (2006). In Search of Identity and Legitimation: Bridging Organizational Culture and Neoinstitutionalism. *American Behavioral Scientist*, 49 (7), 897–907.

Pew Research Center. (November 13, 2008a). High Marks for the Campaign, a High Bar for Obama. *Pew Research Center for the People and the Press Website*. Retrieved December 13, 2011, from http://www.people-press.org/2008/11/13/section-5-the-press-and-campaign-2008/

Pew Research Center. (2008b). Many Say Press Has Been Too Tough on Palin, Positive Ratings for Coverage of Financial Crisis. *Pew Research Center for the People and the Press Website*. Retrieved February 28, 2012, from http://www.people-press.org/2008/10/09/many-say-press-has-been-too-tough-on-palin

Pew Research Center. (March 27, 2008c). Obama and Wright Controversy Dominate News Cycle. *Pew Research Center for the People and the Press Website*. Retrieved December 6, 2011, from http://www.people-press.org/2008/03/27/obama-and-wright-controversy-dominate-news-cycle/

Pew Research Center. (October 11, 2012). One-in-Ten "Dual-Screened" the Presidential Debate. *Pew Research Center for the People and the Press Website*. Retrieved October 12, 2012, from http://www.people-press.org/2012/10/11/one-in-ten-dual-screened-the-presidential-debate

Phillips, K. (July 26, 2007). Clinton–Obama Commander Duel: Part 4. *New York Times Website*. Retrieved December 14, 2011, from http://thecaucus.blogs.nytimes.com/2007/07/26/clinton-obama-commander-duel-part-4/

Pierce, A. (April 19, 2010). Who's to Blame for Cameron's TV Nightmare? *Daily Mail*.

Pitney, N. (September 25, 2008). Palin Talks Russia With Katie Couric (VIDEO). *Huffington Post Website*. Retrieved December 2, 2011, from http://www.huffingtonpost.com/2008/09/25/palin-talks-russia-with-k_n_129318.html

Plasser, F., & Plasser, G. (2002). Global Political Campaigning: A Worldwide Analysis of Campaign Professionals and Their Practices. Westport, CT: Praeger.

Plouffe, D. (2010). *The Audacity To Win: How Obama Won and How We Can Beat the Party of Limbaugh, Beck, and Palin* (Second ed.). London: Penguin.

Political Scrapbook. (March 6, 2010). Macrory Meltdown: Tory Head of Press Proves David Cameron Right With Bizarre Twitter Tirade. *Political Scrapbook Website*. Retrieved May 28, 2012, from http://politicalscrapbook.net/2010/03/macrory-meltdown-tory-head-of-press-proves-david-cameron-right-with-bizarre-twitter-tirade/

Pool, I. d. S. (1983a). *Forecasting the Telephone: A Retrospective Technology Assessment*. Norwood, NJ: Ablex Publishing Corporation.

Pool, I. d. S. (1983b). *Technologies of Freedom*. Cambridge, MA: Harvard University Press.

Popkin, S. L. (2006). Changing Media, Changing Politics. *Perspectives on Politics*, 4 (2), 327–341.

Populus. (2010). Post Debate Poll—April 15, 2010. *Populus Website*. Retrieved April 20, 2010, from http://www.populuslimited.com/the-times-post-debate-poll-april-15-2010-150410.html

Porter, A., Hope, C., & Prince, R. (April 19, 2010). Cameron Thinks Positive to Counter Threat From Clegg. *Daily Telegraph*, p. 1.

Powell, L. (2010). Obama and Obama Girl: YouTube, Viral Videos, and the 2008 Presidential Campaign. In J. A. Hendricks & R. E. Denton Jr (Eds.), *Communicator-in-Chief: How Barack Obama Used New Media Technology to Win the White House* (pp. 83–104). Plymouth, UK: Lexington Books.

Powell, M. (June 4, 2008). Barack Obama: Calm in the Swirl of History. *New York Times Website*. Retrieved December 6, 2011, from http://www.nytimes.com/2008/06/04/us/politics/04obama.html?_r=1&oref=slogin&pagewanted=all

Prior, M. (2007). *Post-Broadcast Democracy: How Media Choice Increases Inequality in Political Involvement and Polarizes Elections*. New York: Cambridge University Press.

Ranerup, A. (2007). Electronic Government as a Combination of Human and Technological Agency: Testing the Principle of Symmetry. *Information Polity: The International Journal of Government and Democracy in the Information Age*, 12 (3), 153–167.

Rasiej, A., & Sifry, M. L. (November 12, 2008). The Web: 2008's Winning Ticket. *Politico.com Website*. Retrieved December 13, 2011, from http://www.politico.com/news/stories/1108/15520.html

Rawnsley, A. (2010a). *The End of the Party: The Rise and Fall of New Labour*. London: Viking.

Rawnsley, A. (February 21, 2010b). RT @lucymanning: National Bullying Helpline tells ITV News they have had several calls from staff at Downing Street complaining about bu … *Twitter.com/*

andrewrawnsley. Retrieved February 21, 2010, from http://twitter.com/andrewrawnsley/status/9435705626

Rawnsley, A. (February 22, 2010c). @TimMontgomerie Sir Gus O'Donnell spoke to the Prime Minister about his behaviour. My source for that could not be better. *Twitter.com/andrewrawnsley*. Retrieved February 22, 2010, from http://twitter.com/andrewrawnsley/statuses/9483015813

Redden, J., & Witshge, T. (2010). A New News Order? Online News Content Examined. In N. Fenton (Ed.), *New Media, Old News: Journalism and Democracy in the Digital Age* (pp. 171–186). London: Sage.

Reese, S. D. (1991). Setting the Media's Agenda: A Power Balance Perspective. *Communication Yearbook*, 14, 309–340.

Richardson, K., Parry, K., & Corner, J. (2012). *Political Culture and Media Genre: Beyond the News*. Basingstoke, UK: Palgrave Macmillan.

Rifkin, J. (1987). *Time Wars: The Primary Conflict in Human History*. New York: Henry Holt.

Risse, T. (2004). Global Governance and Communicative Action. *Government and Opposition*, 39 (2), 288–313.

Rizzo, T. (2008). YouTube: The New Cinema of Attractions. *Scan: Journal of Media Arts Culture*, 5 (1). Retrieved July 10, 2012, from http://scan.net.au/scan/journal/display.php?journal_id=109

Robinson, N. (February 21, 2010a). Brown's Behaviour. *Nick Robinson's Newslog*. Retrieved February 21, 2010, from http://www.bbc.co.uk/blogs/nickrobinson/2010/02/browns_behaviou.html

Robinson, N. (February 21, 2010b). Mandelson Comments Backfire. *Nick Robinson's Newslog*. Retrieved February 21, 2010, from http://www.bbc.co.uk/blogs/nickrobinson/2010/02/mandelson_comme.html

Robinson, N. (February 21, 2010c). No 10 Questions Helpline in Brown "Bullying" Row. *Nick Robinson's Newslog*. Retrieved February 21, 2010, from http://www.bbc.co.uk/blogs/nickrobinson/2010/02/helplines_invol.html

Robinson, N. (April 15, 2010). Queasy Feeling. *Nick Robinson's Newslog*. Retrieved April 15, 2010, from http://www.bbc.co.uk/blogs/nickrobinson/2010/04/queasy_feeling.html

Rogers, P. (April 16, 2010). Finally, the Leaders' Debate. *The Times Election Blog*. Retrieved April 30, 2010, from http://timesonline.typepad.com/election10/2010/04/finally-the-leaders-debate.html

Rosenberg, H., & Feldman, C. S. (2008). *No Time to Think: The Menace of Media Speed and the 24-Hour News Cycle*. New York: Continuum.

Roshco, B. (1975). *Newsmaking*. Chicago: University of Chicago Press.

Rusbridger, A. (January 28, 2011). WikiLeaks: The Guardian's Role in the Biggest Leak in the History of the World. *Guardian Website*. Retrieved June 10, 2011, from http://www.guardian.co.uk/media/2011/jan/28/wikileaks-julian-assange-alan-rusbridger

Rutenberg, J. (September 3, 2008). THE CAUCUS; Fallout for Larry King. *New York Times Website*. Retrieved December 3, 2011, from http://query.nytimes.com/gst/fullpage.html?res=940CE7DF1331F930A3575AC0A96E9C8B63

Sabato, L. J. (2010). The Election of Our Lifetime. In L. J. Sabato (Ed.), *The Year of Obama: How Barack Obama Won the White House* (pp. 31–74). London: Longman.

Said, E. (1994). *Culture and Imperialism*. New York: Knopf.

Saldhana, A. (2003). Review Essay: Actor Network Theory and Critical Sociology. *Critical Sociology*, 29 (3), 419–432.

Sampson, R. J., MacIndoe, H., McAdam, D., & Weffer-Elizondo, S. (2005). Civil Society Reconsidered: The Durable Nature and Community Structure of Collective Civic Action. *American Journal of Sociology*, 111 (3), 673–714.

Sandler, T. (2010). Common-Property Resources: Privatization, Centralization, and Hybrid Arrangements. *Public Choice*, 143 (3–4), 317–324.

Sanger, D. E., Glanz, J., & Becker, J. (November 28, 2010). Around the World, Distress Over Iran. *New York Times Website*. Retrieved June 20, 2011, from http://www.nytimes.com/2010/11/29/world/middleeast/29iran.html?pagewanted=all

SaveOurSovereignty2. (September 11, 2008). Sarah Palin ABC Interview with Charlie Gibson Part 1. *YouTube*. Retrieved December 2, 2011, from http://www.youtube.com/watch?v=3ALsjhDDdaA

Schlesinger, P. (1977). Newsmen and Their Time-Machine. *British Journal of Sociology*, 28 (3), 336–350.

Schlesinger, P. (1978). *Putting "Reality" Together: BBC News*. London: Constable.

Schmidt, S. (2009). Comments on Campaign Organization and Strategy. In K. H. Jamieson (Ed.), *Electing the President 2008: The Insiders' View* (pp. 55–83). Philadelphia: University of Pennsylvania Press.

Scott, D., & Barnett, C. (2009). Something in the Air: Civic Science and Contentious Environmental Politics in Post-Apartheid South Africa. *Geoforum*, 40 (3), 373–382.

Scott, J., & Marshall, G. (2009). Ontology. In J. Scott & G. Marshall (Eds.), *Oxford Dictionary of Sociology*. Online version. Oxford: Oxford University Press. Retrieved November 21, 211, from http://www.oxfordreference.com/view/10.1093/acref/9780199533008.001.0001/acref-9780199533008-e-1610?rskey=dExJRo&result=6&q=Ontology

Seidman, S. A. (2010). Barack Obama's 2008 Campaign for the U.S. Presidency and Visual Design. *Journal of Visual Literacy*, 29 (1), 1–27.

Sellers, P. (2010). *Cycles of Spin: Strategic Communication in the U.S. Congress*. New York: Cambridge University Press.

Shah, S. K. (2006). Motivation, Governance, and the Viability of Hybrid Forms in Open Source Software Development. *Management Science*, 52 (7), 1000–1014.

Shane, S. (January 15, 2011). Cables From American Diplomats Portray U.S. Ambivalence on Tunisia. *New York Times Website*. Retrieved July 18, 2011, from http://www.nytimes.com/2011/01/16/world/africa/16cables.html

Shane, S., & Lehren, A. W. (November 28, 2010). Leaked Cables Offer Raw Look at U.S. Diplomacy. *New York Times Website*. Retrieved July 18, 2011, from http://www.nytimes.com/2010/11/29/world/29cables.html

Shapira, I., & Warrick, J. (December 12, 2010). WikiLeaks' Advocates are Wreaking "Hacktivism." *Washington Post Website*. Retrieved December 12, from http://www.washingtonpost.com/wp-dyn/content/article/2010/12/11/AR2010121103152.html

Shearman, S. (June 23, 2011). MailOnline Closes Gap on NYT. *MediaWeek Website*. Retrieved March 5, 2012, from http://www.mediaweek.co.uk/news/1076525/MailOnline-closes-gap-NYT

Shim, D. (2006). Hybridity and the Rise of Korean Popular Culture in Asia. *Media, Culture and Society*, 28 (1), 25–44.

Shipman, T. (April 22, 2010). Nick Clegg's Nazi Slur on Britain. *Daily Mail Website*. Retrieved April 22, 2010, from http://www.dailymail.co.uk/news/election/article-1267921/GENERAL-ELECTION-2010-Nick-Clegg-Nazi-slur-Britain.html

Shome, R. (2006). Thinking Through the Diaspora: Call Centers, India, and a New Politics of Hybridity. *International Journal of Cultural Studies*, 9 (1), 105–124.

Siebert, F. S., Peterson, T., & Schramm, W. (1956). *Four Theories of the Press: The Authoritarian, Libertarian, Social Responsibility, and Soviet Communist Concepts of What the Press Should Be and Do*. Urbana: University of Illinois Press.

Sifry, M. L. (May 1, 2007). The Battle to Control Obama's MySpace. *TechPresident Website*. Retrieved December 13, 2011, from http://techpresident.com/blog-entry/battle-control-obamas-myspace

Sifry, M. L. (December 31, 2009). The Obama Disconnect: What Happens When Myth Meets Reality. *TechPresident Website*. Retrieved December 23, 2011, from http://techpresident.com/blog-entry/the-obama-disconnect

Singel, R. (February 18, 2009). WikiLeaks Forced to Leak Its Own Secret Info—Update. *Wired Website*. Retrieved June 22, 2011, from http://www.wired.com/threatlevel/2009/02/wikileaks-force/

Sklar, R. (1987). Developmental Democracy. *Comparative Studies in Society and History*, 29 (4), 686–714.

Sky News. (April 12, 2010a). Sky News to Capture Instant Reaction to Leaders' Debates via Text Polling. *Sky News Website.* Retrieved April 16, 2010, from http://www.skypressoffice.co.uk/SkyNews/Resources/showarticle.asp?id=2952

Sky News. (2010b). Sky News, February 22.

Sky News. (2010c). Sunday Live with Adam Bolton, February 21.

Slack, J. (April 21, 2010). How the LibDems Would Release 60,000 Convicts. *Daily Mail Website.* Retrieved April 21, 2010, from http://www.dailymail.co.uk/debate/article-1267658/General-Election-2010-How-Lib-Dems-release-60-000-convicts.html

Slajda, R. (December 1, 2010). How Lieberman Got Amazon to Drop Wikileaks. *Talking Points Memo Website.* Retrieved July 26, 2011, from http://tpmmuckraker.talkingpointsmemo.com/2010/12/how_lieberman_got_amazon_to_drop_wikileaks.php

Smith, D. (December 8, 2010). WikiLeaks Cables: Shell's Grip on Nigerian State Revealed. *Guardian Website.* Retrieved July 18, 2011, from http://www.guardian.co.uk/business/2010/dec/08/wikileaks-cables-shell-nigeria-spying

Smith, R. L. (1972). *The Wired Nation: Cable TV: The Electronic Communications Highway.* New York: Harper & Row.

Snider, M. (October 30, 2008). Late-night Laughs Capture the Online Vote. *ABC News Website.* Retrieved December 9, 2011, from http://abcnews.go.com/Technology/story?id=6145335&page=1#.TuHv-yM9Ww4

Socialbakers. (June 27, 2012). Facebook Statistics by Country. *Socialbakers Website.* Retrieved June 27, 2012, from http://www.socialbakers.com/facebook-statistics/

Sparrow, A. (April 15, 2010). Leaders' Debate Live Blog. *Guardian Website.* Retrieved April 15, 2010, from http://www.guardian.co.uk/politics/blog/2010/apr/15/leaders-debate-live-blog

Spinuzzi, C. (2003). *Tracing Genres Through Organizations: A Sociocultural Approach to Information Design.* Cambridge, MA: MIT Press.

Stacey, K., & Pickard, J. (April 15, 2010). Cameron Warns of "Sluggish" TV Debate. *Financial Times Website.* Retrieved April 29, 2010, from http://www.ft.com/cms/s/0/ed6f0ab4-4860-11df-9a5d-00144feab49a.html

Stanyer, J. (2001). *The Creation of Political News: Television and British Party Political Conferences.* Brighton: Sussex Academic Press.

Star, A., & New York Times Staff (Eds.). (2011). *Open Secrets: WikiLeaks, War, and American Diplomacy* (Kindle ed.). New York: New York Times.

Stelter, B. (March 27, 2008). Finding Political News Online, the Young Pass it On. *New York Times Website.* Retrieved November 24, 2011, from http://www.nytimes.com/2008/03/27/us/politics/27voters.html?_r=2&hp=&adxnnl=1&oref=slogin&adxnnlx=1206666163-YpoMNe/u2DIXJ6Q+JgPlLQ

Sun. (February 21, 2010). Brown Denies Bully Allegations. *Sun Website.* Retrieved February 21, 2010, from http://www.thesun.co.uk/sol/homepage/news/2862173/Brown-denies-bully-allegations.html

Sunday Mirror. (February 21, 2010). PM staff "Called Bully Helpline." *Sunday Mirror Website.* Retrieved February 21, 2010, from http://www.mirror.co.uk/news/latest/2010/02/21/pm-staff-called-bullying-helpline-115875-22059901/

Sunday Telegraph. (February 21, 2010a). Gordon Brown Attacked by Anti-Bullying Chief. *Sunday Telegraph Website.* Retrieved February 21, 2010, from http://www.telegraph.co.uk/news/newstopics/politics/gordon-brown/7286800/Gordon-Brown-attacked-by-anti-bullying-chief.html

Sunday Telegraph. (February 21, 2010b). Gordon Brown Criticised by Anti-Bullying Head. *Sunday Telegraph Website.* Retrieved February 21, 2010, from http://www.telegraph.co.uk/news/newstopics/politics/gordon-brown/7286639/Gordon-Brown-criticised-by-anti-bullying-head.html

Sunday Telegraph. (February 21, 2010c). Gordon Brown Denies "Malicious" Claim He Mistreated Staff. *Sunday Telegraph Website.* Retrieved February 21, 2010, from http://www.telegraph.co.uk/news/newstopics/politics/gordon-brown/7283579/Gordon-Brown-denies-malicious-claim-he-mistreated-staff.html

Sunday Telegraph. (February 21, 2010d). Lord Mandelson Defends Gordon Brown Against Bullying Claims. *Sunday Telegraph Website*. Retrieved February 21, 2010, from http://www.telegraph.co.uk/news/newstopics/politics/gordon-brown/7284679/Lord-Mandelson-defends-Gordon-Brown-against-bullying-claims.html

Surowiecki, J. (2004). *The Wisdom of Crowds*. London: Little, Brown.

Sweney, M. (April 28, 2010). Leaders' Debate: Nearly 700 Complain to OFCOM Over Treatment of Nick Clegg. *Guardian Website*. Retrieved May 13, 2010, from http://www.guardian.co.uk/media/2010/apr/28/leaders-debate-complaints

Sweney, M. (October 5, 2011). U.K. Web Ad Spend Defies Slowdown. *Guardian Website*. Retrieved February 28, 2012, from http://www.guardian.co.uk/media/2011/oct/05/uk-web-ad-spend

Tapper, J. (December 8, 2010). Exclusive: Sarah Palin Under Cyber-Attack from Wikileaks Supporters in "Operation Payback." *ABC News Website*. Retrieved June 20, 2011, from http://blogs.abcnews.com/politicalpunch/2010/12/exclusive-palin-under-cyber-attack-from-wikileaks-supporters-in-operation-payback.html?loc=interstitialskip

Taylor, T. D. (1997). *Global Pop: World Music, World Markets*. London: Routledge.

Teachout, Z. (October 10, 2007). You Don't Have the Power. *TechPresident Website*. Retrieved December 23, 2011, from http://techpresident.com/blog-entry/you-don%E2%80%99t-have-power

The Colbert Report. (July 24, 2008). The Colbert Report. *TV.com Website*. Retrieved December 6, 2011, from http://www.tv.com/shows/the-colbert-report/garrett-reisman-1218292/

The Labour Party. (April 16, 2010). The Leaders' Debate. *Labour Party Website*. Retrieved April 16, 2010, from http://www2.labour.org.uk/the-leaders-debate

Thompson, L., & Cupples, J. (2008). Seen and not Heard? Text Messaging and Digital Sociality. *Social and Cultural Geography*, 9 (1), 95–108.

Times. (April 15, 2010). Leaders' Debate Live Blog. *Times Website*. Retrieved April 15, 2010, from http://www.timesonline.co.uk/tol/news/politics/article7098806.ece

Tindall, A. (2010). just spent an hour listening to the scaremongering of a corrupt, paranoid homophobe—Julian Lewis, New Forest East CON MP/PPC. *Twitter.com/andrewtindall*. Retrieved May 21, 2012, from http://twitter.com/#!/andrewtindall/statuses/12454732789

Toner, M. E. (2010). The Impact of Federal Election Laws on the 2008 Presidential Election. In L. J. Sabato (Ed.), *The Year of Obama: How Barack Obama Won the White House* (pp. 149–165). London: Longman.

Tuchman, G. (1978). *Making News: A Study in the Construction of Reality*. New York: Free Press.

Twapperkeeper. (2010a). Twitter Hashtag Archive for #nickcleggsfault. *Twapperkeeper.com*. Retrieved May 14, 2010, from http://twapperkeeper.com/allnotebooks.php

Twapperkeeper. (2010b). Twitter Hashtag Archives for #ukelection, #ge2010, and #ge10. *Twapperkeeper.com*. Retrieved May 14, 2010, from http://twapperkeeper.com/allnotebooks.php

U.K. Charity Commission. (February 25, 2010). Charity Commission Opens Inquiry into National Bullying Helpline. *Charity Commission Website*. Retrieved February 25, 2010, from http://www.charitycommission.gov.uk/RSS/News/pr_national_bullying.aspx

U.K. Office for National Statistics. (2009). *Internet Access 2008: Households and Individuals*. Cardiff: Office for National Statistics.

U.K. Office of Communications. (2008). *The Communications Market 2008*. London: HMSO.

U.K. Office of Communications. (June 30, 2010). Halt in Decline of Flagship TV News Programmes. *U.K. Office of Communications Website*. Retrieved March 2, 2012, from http://media.ofcom.org.uk/2010/06/30/halt-in-decline-of-flagship-tv-news-programmes/

U.K. Office of Fair Trading. (2008). *Newspaper and Magazine Distribution in the United Kingdom*. London: HMSO.

U.K. Office of Fair Trading. (2009). *Review of the Local and Regional Media Merger Regime: Final Report*. London: HMSO.

U.S. Department of Justice. (July 19, 2011). Sixteen Individuals Arrested in the United States for Alleged Roles in Cyber Attacks. *U.S. Department of Justice Website*. Retrieved July 19, 2011, from http://www.justice.gov/opa/pr/2011/July/11-opa-944.html

United States Army Counterintelligence Center. (2008). WikiLeaks.org—An Online Reference to Foreign Intelligence Services, Insurgents, or Terrorist Groups? *WikiLeaks Website*. Retrieved June 10, 2011, from http://mirror.wikileaks.info/leak/us-intel-wikileaks.pdf

Vaccari, C. (2010). "Technology Is a Commodity": The Internet in the 2008 United States Presidential Election. *Journal of Information Technology and Politics*, 7 (4), 318–339.

Valenzuela, J. S. (1992). Democratic Consolidation in Post-Transitional Settings: Notion, Process, and Facilitating Conditions. In S. Mainwaring, G. O'Donnell & J. S. Valenzuela (Eds.), *Issues in Democratic Consolidation: The New South American Democracies in Comparative Perspective* (pp. 64–66). Notre Dame: University of Notre Dame Press.

Vargas, J. A. (November 20, 2008). Obama Raised Half a Billion Online. *Washington Post Website*. Retrieved December 14, 2011, from http://voices.washingtonpost.com/44/2008/11/obama-raised-half-a-billion-on.html

Wade, P. (2005). Hybridity Theory and Kinship Thinking. *Cultural Studies*, 19 (5), 602–621.

Wadensjö, C. (2008). The Shaping of Gorbachev: On Framing in an Interpreter-Mediated Talk-Show Interview. *Text and Talk*, 28 (1), 119–146.

Waghorne, R. (April 21, 2010). The LibDems are a Party Full of Shadow Lobbyists. *Daily Mail Website*. Retrieved April 21, 2010, from http://www.dailymail.co.uk/debate/article-1267633/GENERAL-ELECTION-2010-The-Lib-Dems-party-shadow-lobbyists.html

Wallace, N. (2009). Comments on the Vice Presidential Campaign. In K. H. Jamieson (Ed.), *Electing the President 2008: The Insiders' View* (pp. 13–33). Philadelphia: University of Pennsylvania Press.

Wallenstein, A. (September 19, 2008). NBC's Websites See Surge in Traffic. *Adweek Website*. Retrieved December 2, 2011, from http://www.adweek.com/news/technology/nbcu-web-sites-see-surge-traffic-109765

Wallsten, K. (2010). "Yes We Can": How Online Viewership, Blog Discussion, Campaign Statements, and Mainstream Media Coverage Produced a Viral Video Phenomenon. *Journal of Information Technology and Politics*, 7 (2–3), 163–181.

Walters, S. (January 31, 2010a). Angry Gordon Brown "Hit Out at Aide and Yanked Secretary From Her Chair." *Mail on Sunday Website*. Retrieved June 15, 2010, from http://www.dailymail.co.uk/news/article-1247357/Angry-Gordon-Brown-hit-aide-yanked-secretary-chair.html

Walters, S. (February 21, 2010b). Gordon Is Not a Bully, Claims Mandelson as PM is Accused of Abusing Downing Street Staff. *Mail on Sunday Website*. Retrieved February 21, 2010, from http://www.dailymail.co.uk/news/article-1252584/Gordon-bully-claims-Mandelson-PM-accused-abusing-Downing-Street-staff.html

Wang, G., & Yeh, E. Y.-Y. (2005). Globalization and Hybridization in Cultural Products: The Cases of Mulan and Crouching Tiger, Hidden Dragon. *International Journal of Cultural Studies*, 8 (2), 175–193.

Warren, M. (1884). On the Etymology of Hybrid (Lat. Hybrida). *American Journal of Philology*, 5 (4), 501–502.

Watson, R., & Coates, S. (April 19, 2010). Rivals Set Their Sights on "Churchill" Clegg. *Times*, pp. 4–5.

Watt, N., & Wintour, P. (April 19, 2010). Conservatives: Tories Not for Turning Despite Lib Dem Surge, Says Cameron. *Guardian*, p. 12.

Wau-Holland-Stiftung. (April 16, 2011). Project 04: Enduring Freedom of Information: Preliminary Transparency Report 2010. *Wau-Holland-Stiftung Website*. Retrieved July 20, 2011, from http://www.wauland.de/files/2010_Transparenzbericht-Projekt04_en.pdf

We Got Rage Against the Machine to Number 1 … (2010). *We Got Rage Against the Machine to #1, We Can Get the Lib Dems into Office Facebook Group*. Retrieved May 7, 2010, from http://www.facebook.com/group.php?gid=113749985304255

Weaver, E. (2009). QCon Presentation. *Evan Weaver's Website*. Retrieved April 30, 2010, from http://blog.evanweaver.com/articles/2009/03/13/qcon-presentation/

Weinberger, D. (2007). *Everything is Miscellaneous: The Power of the New Digital Disorder*. New York: Henry Holt and Company.

Whatmore, S. (2002). *Hybrid Geographies: Natures, Cultures, Spaces*. London: Sage.

Whitlock, C. (April 8, 2011). U.S. Was Told of Yemen Leader's Vulnerability. *Washington Post Website*. Retrieved July 27, 2011, from http://www.washingtonpost.com/world/us-was-told-of-plot-to-overthrow-yemen-leader/2011/04/07/AFBCY7xC_story.html

WikiLeaks. (May 15, 2009a,). Draft: The Most Wanted Leaks of 2009. *WikiLeaks Website*. Retrieved June 24, 2011, from http://mirror.wikileaks.info/wiki/Draft_The_Most_Wanted_Leaks_of_2009

WikiLeaks. (June 2, 2009b). WikiLeaks wins Amnesty International 2009 Media Award. *WikiLeaks Website*. Retrieved July 22, 2011, from http://mirror.wikileaks.info/wiki/WikiLeaks_wins_Amnesty_International_2009_Media_Award

WikiLeaks. (September 1, 2011). Global: Guardian Journalist Negligently Disclosed Cablegate Passwords. *WikiLeaks Website*. Retrieved June 8, 2012, from http://www.wikileaks.org/Guardian-journalist-negligently.html

WikiLeaks. (February 27, 2012). WikiLeaks: the GIFiles. *WikiLeaks Website*. Retrieved February 27, 2012, from http://wikileaks.org/the-gifiles.html

Williams, B. A., & Delli Carpini, M. X. (2011). *After Broadcast News: Media Regimes, Democracy, and the New Information Environment*. Cambridge: Cambridge University Press.

Winnett, R., & Swaine, J. (April 22, 2010). Nick Clegg, the Lib Dem Donors and Payments into His Private Account; Exclusive Donor Cash Mystery. *Daily Telegraph*, p. 1.

Wintour, P. (March 3, 2010). Party Leaders Agree TV Election Debate Rules. *Guardian Website*. Retrieved April 29, 2010, from http://www.guardian.co.uk/tv-and-radio/2010/mar/03/tv-debates-party-leaders-politics

Wood, B. (2004). A World in Retreat: The Reconfiguration of Hybridity in 20th-Century New Zealand Television. *Media, Culture and Society*, 26 (1), 45–62.

Wu, T. (2010). *The Master Switch: The Rise and Fall of Information Empires*. New York: Knopf.

Ye, S., & Wu, F. (2010). Measuring Message Propagation and Social Influence on Twitter.com. *Paper to The Second International Conference on Social Informatics (SocInfo'10)*. Retrieved August 30, 2010, from http://sites.google.com/site/yeshao/mj.pdf

Yelland, D. (April 19, 2010). The Rise of Clegg Could Lock Murdoch and the Media Elite Out of UK Politics. *Guardian*, p. 28.

YouGov. (April 15, 2010). Instant Reactions: The Great Debate. *YouGov Website*. Retrieved April 15, 2010, from http://today.yougov.co.uk/politics/instant-reactions-great-debate

Young, D. G. (2011). Political Entertainment and the Press' Construction of Sarah Feylin. *Popular Communication*, 9 (4), 251–265.

Young, S. (2009). Sky News Australia: The Impact of Local 24-hour News on Political Reporting in Australia. *Journalism Studies*, 10 (3), 401–416.

Young, T. (April 19, 2010). Tonight's Polls: Lib Dem Surge Holds Up. *Daily Telegraph Website*. Retrieved April 19, 2010, from http://blogs.telegraph.co.uk/news/tobyyoung/100035455/tonights-polls-lib-dem-surge-holds-up

YouTube. (2010). Search: UK Election. *YouTube Website*. Retrieved May 4, 2010, from http://www.youtube.com/results?search_query=uk+election&aq=f

Ytreberg, E. (2009). Extended Liveness and Eventfulness in Multi-Platform Reality Formats. *New Media and Society*, 11 (4), 467–485.

Zarb, S. (February 21, 2010). The National Bullying Helpline says "Your call is confidential to us and you will be treated with dignity and respect at all times." hmmmm. *Twitter.com/sachazarb*. Retrieved February 21, 2010, from http://twitter.com/sachazarb/statuses/9437424123

Zaret, D. (2000). *Origins of Democratic Culture: Printing, Petitions, and the Public Sphere in Early-Modern England*. Princeton: Princeton University Press.

Zeleny, J. (July 13, 2008). Political Satire, but Obama Isn't Laughing. *New York Times Website*. Retrieved November 30, 2011, from http://thecaucus.blogs.nytimes.com/2008/07/13/political-satire-but-obama-is-not-laughing/

Index

Printed in the USA/Agawam, MA
September 9, 2013

579785.167